SANTA FE, TAOS & ALBUQUERQUE

1st Edition

Where to Stay and Eat for All Budgets

Must-See Sights and Local Secrets

Ratings You Can Trust

Excerpted from *Fodor's New Mexico*

Fodor's Travel Publications   New York, Toronto, London, Sydney, Auckland

www.fodors.com

FODOR'S SANTA FE, TAOS & ALBUQUERQUE
Editor: Paul Eisenberg

Editorial Production: Eric B. Wechter
Editorial Contributor: Andrew Collins
Maps: David Lindroth, *cartographer*; Robert Blake, Rebecca Baer, *map editors*
Design: Fabrizio La Rocca, *creative director*; Guido Caroti, *art director*; Moon Sun Kim, *cover designer*; Melanie Marin, *senior picture editor*
Production/Manufacturing: Robert B. Shields
Cover Photo: ThinkStock/SuperStock

COPYRIGHT
Copyright © 2007 by Fodor's Travel, a division of Random House, Inc.

Fodor's is a registered trademark of Random House, Inc.

All rights reserved under International and Pan-American Copyright Conventions. Published in the United States by Fodor's Travel, a division of Random House, Inc., and simultaneously in Canada by Random House of Canada Limited, Toronto. Distributed by Random House, Inc., New York.

No maps, illustrations, or other portions of this book may be reproduced in any form without written permission from the publisher.

First Edition

ISBN 978–1–4000–1752–2

ISSN 1095–3876

ABOUT OUR WRITER
Santa Fe resident **Andrew Collins,** a former Fodor's editor, updated the chapters on Santa Fe, Albuquerque, Taos, and Side Trips from the Cities, as well as the Essentials and front sections of the book. Andrew has authored more than a dozen guidebooks, including *Fodor's Gay Guide to the USA.* He also writes a syndicated weekly newspaper travel column and has contributed to *Travel & Leisure, New Mexico Magazine, Sunset,* and dozens of other periodicals.

SPECIAL SALES
This book is available for special discounts for bulk purchases for sales promotions or premiums. Special editions, including personalized covers, excerpts of existing books, and corporate imprints, can be created in large quantities for special needs. For more information, write to Special Markets/Premium Sales, 1745 Broadway, MD 6-2, New York, New York 10019, or e-mail specialmarkets@randomhouse.com.

AN IMPORTANT TIP & AN INVITATION
Although all prices, opening times, and other details in this book are based on information supplied to us at press time, changes occur all the time in the travel world, and Fodor's cannot accept responsibility for facts that become outdated or for inadvertent errors or omissions. So **always confirm information when it matters,** especially if you're making a detour to visit a specific place. Your experiences—positive and negative—matter to us. If we have missed or misstated something, **please write to us.** We follow up on all suggestions. Contact the New Mexico editor at editors@fodors.com or c/o Fodor's at 1745 Broadway, New York, New York 10019.

PRINTED IN THE UNITED STATES OF AMERICA

10 9 8 7 6 5 4 3 2 1

Be a Fodor's Correspondent

Your opinion matters. It matters to us. It matters to your fellow Fodor's travelers, too. And we'd like to hear it. In fact, we *need* to hear it.

When you share your experiences and opinions, you become an active member of the Fodor's community. That means we'll not only use your feedback to make our books better, but we'll publish your names and comments whenever possible. Throughout our guides, look for "Word of Mouth," excerpts of your unvarnished feedback.

Here's how you can help improve Fodor's for all of us.

Tell us when we're right. We rely on local writers to give you an insider's perspective. But our writers and staff editors—who are the best in the business—depend on you. Your positive feedback is a vote to renew our recommendations for the next edition.

Tell us when we're wrong. We're proud that we update most of our guides every year. But we're not perfect. Things change. Hotels cut services. Museums change hours. Charming cafés lose charm. If our writer didn't quite capture the essence of a place, tell us how you'd do it differently. If any of our descriptions are inaccurate or inadequate, we'll incorporate your changes in the next edition and will correct factual errors at fodors.com *immediately.*

Tell us what to include. You probably have had fantastic travel experiences that aren't yet in Fodor's. Why not share them with a community of like-minded travelers? Maybe you chanced upon a beach or bistro or B&B that you don't want to keep to yourself. Tell us why we should include it. And share your discoveries and experiences with everyone directly at fodors.com. Your input may lead us to add a new listing or highlight a place we cover with a "Highly Recommended" star or with our highest rating, "Fodor's Choice."

Give us your opinion instantly at our feedback center at www.fodors.com/feedback. You may also e-mail editors@fodors.com with the subject line "New Mexico Editor." Or send your nominations, comments, and complaints by mail to New Mexico Editor, Fodor's, 1745 Broadway, New York, NY 10019.

You and travelers like you are the heart of the Fodor's community. Make our community richer by sharing your experiences. Be a Fodor's correspondent.

Happy Traveling!

Tim Jarrell, Publisher

CONTENTS

MAPS

CLOSE UPS

ABOUT THIS BOOK

Our Ratings

Sometimes you find terrific travel experiences and sometimes they just find you. But usually the burden is on you to select the right combination of experiences. That's where our ratings come in.

As travelers we've all discovered a place so wonderful that its worthiness is obvious. And sometimes that place is so experiential that superlatives don't do it justice: you just have to be there to know. These sights, properties, and experiences get our highest rating, **Fodor's Choice**, indicated by orange stars throughout this book.

Black stars highlight sights and properties we deem **Highly Recommended**, places that our writers, editors, and readers praise again and again for consistency and excellence.

By default, there's another category: any place we include in this book is by definition worth your time, unless we say otherwise. And we will.

Disagree with any of our choices? Care to nominate a place or suggest that we rate one more highly? Visit our feedback center at www.fodors.com/feedback.

Budget Well

Hotel and restaurant price categories from ¢ to $$$$ are defined in the opening pages of each chapter. For attractions, we always give standard adult admission fees; reductions are usually available for children, students, and senior citizens. Want to pay with plastic? **AE, D, DC, MC, V** following restaurant and hotel listings indicate if American Express, Discover, Diners Club, MasterCard, and Visa are accepted.

Restaurants

Unless we state otherwise, restaurants are open for lunch and dinner daily. We mention dress only when there's a specific requirement and reservations only when they're essential or not accepted—it's always best to book ahead.

Hotels

Hotels have private bath, phone, TV, and air-conditioning and operate on the European Plan (aka EP, meaning without meals), unless we specify that they use the Continental Plan (CP, with a continental breakfast), Breakfast Plan (BP, with a full breakfast), or Modified American Plan (MAP, with breakfast and dinner) or are all-inclusive (including all meals and most activities). We always list facilities but not whether you'll be charged an extra fee to use them, so when pricing accommodations, find out what's included.

Many Listings

- ★ Fodor's Choice
- ★ Highly recommended
- ✉ Physical address
- ✛ Directions
- ⌂ Mailing address
- ☎ Telephone
- 🖷 Fax
- ⊕ On the Web
- ✉ E-mail
- 🖃 Admission fee
- ◷ Open/closed times
- ▶ Start of walk/itinerary
- Ⓜ Metro stations
- 🖃 Credit cards

Hotels & Restaurants

- 🏨 Hotel
- 🛏 Number of rooms
- ♨ Facilities
- ⑪ Meal plans
- ✕ Restaurant
- ⌂ Reservations
- 🏛 Dress code
- ↘ Smoking
- ⚑ BYOB
- ✕🏨 Hotel with restaurant that warrants a visit

Outdoors

- ⛳ Golf
- ⛺ Camping

Other

- ♥ Family-friendly
- 🛈 Contact information
- ⇨ See also
- ✉ Branch address
- ☞ Take note

WHAT'S WHERE

ALBUQUERQUE	With the state's international airport, fast-growing Albuquerque is the gateway to New Mexico and the state's business, finance, education, and industry capital. Its residents—like its architecture, food, and art—reflect a confluence of Native American, Hispanic, and Anglo culture.
SANTA FE	On a 7,000-foot-high plateau at the base of the Sangre de Cristo Mountains, Santa Fe is one of the most visited small cities in the United States, with an abundance of museums, one-of-a-kind cultural events, art galleries, first-rate restaurants, and shops.
TAOS	World-famous museums and galleries, stunning views of the desert and Sangre de Cristo Mountains, and charming, cottonwood-shaded streets lined with adobe buildings are a few of the attractions of this town. Nearby historic Taos Pueblo and Ranchos de Taos are other draws.
SIDE TRIPS FROM THE CITIES	Encompassing the stunning mountains and the remnants of a 2,000-year-old Pueblo civilization, this region includes the many artsy and historic villages surrounding Albuquerque, Santa Fe, and Taos. The area is laced with worthy scenic drives.

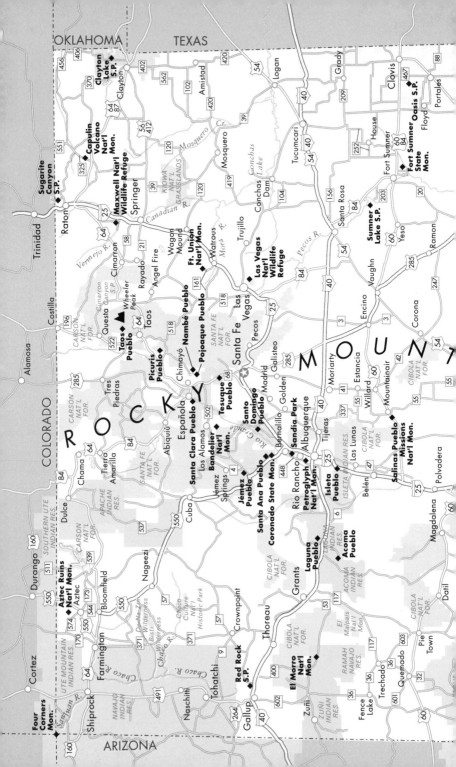

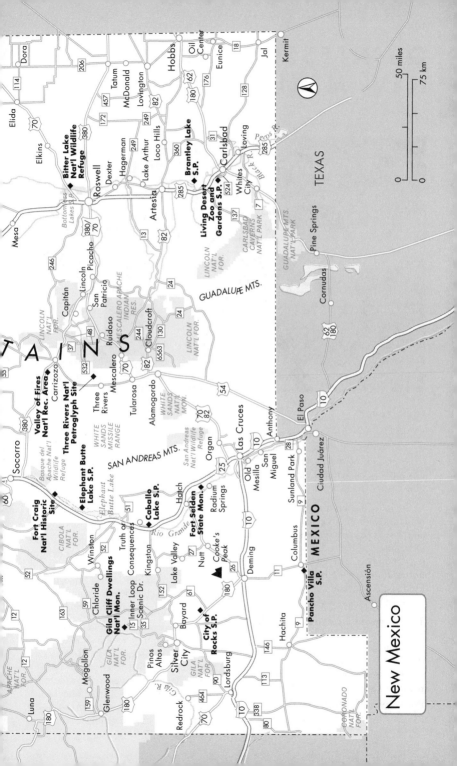

New Mexico

QUINTESSENTIAL NEW MEXICO

Chile Fever

Nothing sets New Mexican food apart from other cuisines so distinctly as the chile pepper, permutations of which locals will heap upon just about any dish, from blue-corn enchiladas to turkey sandwiches.

Chiles have long been a staple of both Hispanic and indigenous cuisine in the region, and they come in two varieties: red or green. Depending on the restaurant, or even the particular batch, green *or* red may be the hotter variety. Servers always ask which kind you'd prefer, and if you can't decide, try them both by answering "Christmas."

The village of Chimayó produces the best red chiles in the state, while the small town of Hatch, down near Las Cruces, harvests the best green chiles. You can often find fresh roasted green chiles at fairs and festivals—or even by the side of the road, especially during fall harvest time.

Ancient Peoples

Nowhere in the United States will you find communities that have been continuously inhabited for a longer period than the oldest pueblos of New Mexico, Acoma and Taos. Acoma has been a living, working community for more than 1,000 years—the cliff-top city here is perhaps the most dramatically situated pueblo in the state, and a must-see attraction, especially since the tribe opened its stunning new cultural center and museum in 2006. Taos Pueblo, which contains the largest collection of multistory pueblo dwellings in the country, also dates back more than a millennium.

But these are just 2 of the state's 19 pueblos, not to mention the Indian Pueblo Cultural Center in Albuquerque, and outstanding museums on Native American arts and culture in Santa Fe. Ancient, now-deserted sites, such as Chaco and Aztec, offer further opportunities to explore and learn about New Mexico's thriving indigenous culture.

If you want to get a sense of New Mexico culture, and indulge in some of its pleasures, start by familiarizing yourself with the rituals of daily life. These are a few highlights—things you can take part in with relative ease.

The Cradle of Creativity

New Mexico draws all kinds of vibrant spirits, both to visit and relocate, but the state is particularly a magnet for artists. Santa Fe, with its dozens of prestigious galleries and art museums, claims the third largest art market in the nation, after New York City and Los Angeles. The much-smaller town of Taos claims a similarly exciting gallery scene, and countless small villages in the northern Rio Grande Valley—from Abiqui (where Georgia O'Keeffe lived) to Madrid—hold studio tours once or twice a year, when local artists open their home studios to the public.

The state's largest city, Albuquerque, is no slouch when it comes to the arts—galleries have popped up all over the city in recent years.

Peak Experiences

With nearly 50 peaks towering higher than 12,000 feet, New Mexico is truly a wonderland for people who love to play in the mountains—it's partly this vertiginous topographical feature that gives the state its unparalleled beauty. The southern spine of the Rocky Mountain range, known as the Sangre de Cristos, runs right down through the center of the state, looming over Taos and Santa Fe. The stunning Sandia Mountains face the city of Albuquerque, and similarly beautiful peaks of the Jémez Mountains overlook Los Alamos.

It's easy to experience the Land of Enchantments high-country. Hiking trails lead to some of the highest points in the state, and several first-rate ski areas have been carved out of New Mexico's mountains, including Taos Ski Valley, Angel Fire, and Ski Santa Fe in the Sangre de Cristos, and Los Alamos's Pajarito Mountain Ski Area in the Jémez range.

WHEN TO GO

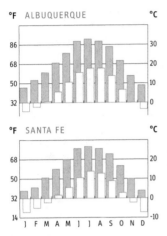

The cool, dry climates of Santa Fe and Taos are a lure in summer, as is the skiing in Taos and Santa Fe in winter. Christmas is a wonderful time to be in New Mexico because of Native American ceremonies as well as the Hispanic religious folk plays, special foods, and musical events. Santa Fe is at its most festive at this time, with incense and piñon smoke sweetening the air and the darkness of winter illuminated by thousands of *farolitos*: these glowing paper-bag lanterns line walkways, doorways, rooftops, and walls. With glowing lights reflected on the snow, Santa Fe is never lovelier.

Most ceremonial dances at the pueblos occur in summer, early fall, and at Christmas and Easter. Other major events—including the Santa Fe Opera, Chamber Music Festival, and Native American and Spanish markets—are geared to the heavy tourist season of July and August. The Santa Fe Fiesta and New Mexico State Fair in Albuquerque are held in September, and the Albuquerque International Balloon Fiesta in October.

Hotel rates are generally highest during the peak summer season but fluctuate less than those in most major resort areas. ■ TIP→ **If you plan to come in summer, be sure to make reservations in advance.** You can avoid the heaviest crowds by coming in spring or fall.

Climate

Albuquerque, Santa Fe, and Taos are quite cool year-round, with nippy winters and moderate summers that are cooled further by oft-occuring afternoon thunderstorms. The region can be delightful in late fall but can surprise you with rare early snowfall. Spring weather is unpredictable; it can be mild and cool with late-season snow, or hot and gusty. In the summer months, Albuquerque can see temperatures climb to around 100°F. Higher elevations are always within a reasonable drive of this area. October is one of the best months to visit: the air is crisp, and colors are brilliant.

🔗 Forecasts **Weather Channel** (⊕ www.weather.com)

Charts indicate average daily maximum and minimum temperatures for areas of the state.

IF YOU LIKE

Historic Sites

There's no state in the Union with a richer historical heritage than New Mexico, which contains not only buildings constructed by Europeans well before the Pilgrims set foot in Massachusetts but also still-inhabited pueblos that date back more than a millennium.

The entire state can feel like one massive archaeological dig, with its mystical Native American ruins and weathered adobe buildings. Stately plazas laid out as fortifications by the Spanish in the 17th century still anchor many communities, including Albuquerque, Santa Fe, and Taos. And side trips from these cities lead to ghost towns and deserted pueblos that have been carefully preserved by historians. Here are some of the top draws for history buffs.

- Established in 1706, Albuquerque's bustling **Old Town** has been a center of commerce and social life ever since. The San Felipe de Neri Catholic Church, erected in 1793, is a tranquil escape from the crowds.

- Santa Fe's **San Miguel Mission** is a simple, earth-hue adobe structure built in about 1625—it's the oldest church still in use in the continental United States.

- A United Nations World Heritage Site, the 1,000-year-old **Taos Pueblo** has the largest collection of multistory pueblo dwellings in the United States.

- The oldest public building in the United States, the Pueblo-style **Palace of the Governors** anchors Santa Fe's historic Plaza and has served as the residence for 100 Spanish, Native American, Mexican, and American governors; it's now the state history museum.

Hiking Adventures

At just about every turn in the Land of Enchantment, whether you're high in the mountains or low in a dramatic river canyon, hiking opportunities abound. Six national forests cover many thousands of acres around New Mexico, as do 34 state parks and a number of other national and state monuments and recreation areas. The ski areas make for great mountaineering during the warmer months, and the state's many Native American ruins are also laced with trails.

Hiking is a year-round activity in New Mexico, as you can virtually always find temperate weather somewhere in the state. Consider the following areas for an engaging ramble.

- About midway between Santa Fe and Albuquerque, **Kasha-Katuwe Tent Rocks National Monument** is so-named because its bizarre rock formations look like tepees rising over a narrow box canyon. The hike here is relatively short and only moderately challenging, offering plenty of bang for the buck.

- It's one of the more strenuous hiking challenges in the state, but the 8-mi trek to New Mexico's highest point, **Wheeler Peak** (elevation 13,161 feet), rewards visitors with stunning views of the Taos Ski Valley.

- From the northeastern fringes of Albuquerque, **La Luz Trail** climbs 9 mi (and an elevation of more than 3,000 feet) to Sandia Crest.

- About an hour's drive north of Taos, **Wild Rivers Recreation Area** affords ramblers a chance to explore the dramatic confluence of the Rio Grande and Red Rivers.

IF YOU LIKE

Burger Joints

In a state with plenty of open ranching land and an appreciation for no-nonsense, home-style eating, it's no surprise that locals debate intensely about where to find the best burger in town.

In New Mexico, the preferred meal is a green-chile cheese burger—a culinary delight that's available just about anyplace that serves hamburgers. Burgers served in tortillas or sopaipillas also earn plenty of kudos, and increasingly, you'll find establishments serving terrific buffalo, lamb, turkey, and even tuna and veggie burgers.

- With about 75 locations throughout the state, the New Mexico chain **Blake's Lotaburger** has become a cult favorite for its juicy Angus beef burgers. Just order at the counter, take a number, and wait for your meal (which is best accompanied by a bag of seasoned fries).

- A friendly and funky little roadhouse about a 15-minute drive south of Santa Fe, **Bobcat Bite** is a much-loved source of outstanding green-chile burgers. Loyalists order them rare.

- Feasting on a burger at the **Mineshaft Tavern** is a big reason to stop in the tiny village of Madrid, as you drive up the fabled Turquoise Trail from Albuquerque to Santa Fe. This rollicking bar serves hefty patties.

- Albuquerque's **Casa de Benavidez** has long captured the fancies of burger aficionados with its delicious burger wrapped inside a fluffy sopaipilla.

Dramatic Photo Ops

New Mexico's spectacular landscapes and crystal-clear atmosphere can help just about any amateur with a decent camera produce professional-quality photos. Many of the common scenes around the state seem tailor-made for photography sessions: terra-cotta-hued adobe buildings against azure blue skies, souped-up low-rider automobiles cruising along wide-open highways, rustic fruit and chile stands by the side of the road.

In summer, dramatic rain clouds contrasted with vermilion sunsets create memorable images. Come fall, shoot the foliage of cottonwood and aspen trees, and in winter, snap the state's snowcapped mountains.

- The **High Road to Taos,** a stunning drive from Santa Fe with a rugged alpine backdrop, encompasses rolling hillsides studded with orchards and tiny picturesque villages.

- More than 1,000 balloons lift off from the **Albuquerque International Balloon Fiesta,** affording shutterbugs countless opportunities for great photos—whether from the ground or the air. And there are year-round opportunities to soar above the city.

- The dizzyingly high **Rio Grande Gorge Bridge,** near Taos, stands 650 feet above the Rio Grande—the reddish rocks dotted with green scrub contrast brilliantly against the blue sky.

- Each July, **Spanish Market** brings hundreds of artisans and their colorful wares to the historic Plaza in Santa Fe. It's a particularly wonderful chance to shoot this city center, but the Plaza is photo-worthy any time of year.

GREAT ITINERARY

ALBUQUERQUE TO TAOS: NEW MEXICO MOUNTAIN HIGH

Day 1: Albuquerque

Start out by strolling through the shops of Old Town Plaza, then visit the New Mexico Museum of Natural History and Science. Also be sure to check out the Albuquerque Museum of Art and History, and also try to make your way over to the Albuquerque Biological Park, which contains the aquarium, zoo, and botanic park. For lunch, try the atmospheric Monica's or the sophisticated St. Clair Winery and Bistro, both near the Old Town center.

Later in the afternoon, you'll need a car to head east a couple of miles along Central to reach the University of New Mexico's main campus and the nearby Nob Hill District. Start with a stroll around the UNM campus with its many historic adobe buildings; if you have time, pop inside either the Maxwell Museum of Anthropology or the University Art Museum. When you're finished here, walk east along Central into Nob Hill and check out the dozens of offbeat shops. If it's summer, meaning that you still have some time before the sun sets, it's worth detouring from Old Town to Far Northeast Heights (a 15-minute drive), where you can take the Sandia Peak Aerial Tramway 2.7 mi up to Sandia Peak for spectacular sunset views of the city. Either way, plan to have dinner back in Nob Hill, perhaps at Graze or Flying Star. If you're still up for more fun, check out one of the neighborhood's lively lounges; head back downtown for a bit of late-night barhopping.

Days 2 & 3: Santa Fe

On Day 2, head to Santa Fe early in the morning by driving up the scenic Turquoise Trail; once you arrive in town, explore the adobe charms of the downtown central Plaza. Visit the Palace of the Governors and browse the wares of the Native American vendors there. At the Museum of Fine Arts you can see works by Southwestern artists, and at the Museum of International Folk Art you can see how different cultures in New Mexico and elsewhere in the world have expressed themselves artistically. Give yourself time to stroll the narrow, adobe-lined streets of this charming downtown, and treat yourself to some fine New Mexican cuisine in the evening, perhaps with a meal at La Choza or Maria's.

On your second day in town, plan to walk a bit. Head east from the Plaza up to Canyon Road's foot, perusing the galleries. Have lunch at one of the restaurants midway uphill, such as Sol or El Farol. From here, you can either continue walking 2 mi up Canyon, and then Upper Canyon, roads to the Randall Davey Audubon Center, or you can take a cab there. If you're up for some exercise, hike the foothills—there are trails within the center's property and also from the free parking area (off Cerro Gordo Road) leading into the Dale Ball Trail Network. You might want to try one of Santa Fe's truly stellar, upscale restaurants your final night in town, either Geronimo on Canyon Road, or the restaurant at the Inn of the Anasazi, a couple of blocks from the Plaza. Later in the evening, enjoy cocktails at the city's swankest lounge, Swig.

Day 4: Abiquiu

From Santa Fe, drive north up U.S. 285/84 through Española, and then take U.S. 84 from Española up to Abiquiu, the fabled community where Georgia O'Keeffe lived and painted for much of the final five decades of her life. On your way up, before you reach Española, make the detour toward Los Alamos and spend the morning visiting Bandelier National Monument. In Abiquiu, plan to tour Georgia O'Keeffe's home (*See* Tip #2, *below*).

Days 5 & 6: Taos

Begin by strolling around Taos Plaza, taking in the galleries and crafts shops. Head south two blocks to visit the Harwood Museum. And then walk north on Paseo del Pueblo to the Taos Art Museum at the Fechin House. In the afternoon, drive out to the Rio Grande Gorge Bridge. Return the way you came to see the Millicent Rogers Museum on your way back to town. In the evening, stop in at the Adobe Bar at the Taos Inn and plan for dinner at Joseph's Table. On the second day, drive out to the Taos Pueblo in the morning and tour the ancient village while the day is fresh. Return to town and go to the Blumenschein Home and Museum, lunching afterward at the Dragonfly Café. After lunch

drive out to La Hacienda de los Martinez for a look at early life in Taos and then to Ranchos de Taos to see the San Francisco de Asís Church.

Day 7: The High Road

On your final day, drive back down toward Albuquerque and Santa Fe via the famed High Road, which twists through a series of tiny, historic villages—including Peñasco, Truchas, and Chimayó. In the latter village, be sure to stop by El Santuario de Chimayó. Have lunch at Léona's Restaurante or Rancho de Chimayó, and do a little shopping at Ortega's Weaving Shop. From here, it's a 30-minute drive to Santa Fe, where you can spend a final night, or a 90-minute drive to Albuquerque.

Alternatives

On Day 4, as you drive up through Abiquiu, if you're more a fan of historic railroads than Georgia O'Keeffe, continue up U.S. 84 to Chama, and ride the famed Cumbres & Toltec Scenic Railroad in the morning, and then cut east on U.S. 64 to reach Taos. After visiting Taos Pueblo on Day 6, consider doing the Enchanted Circle tour rather than returning to town. This 84-mi loop runs through the scenic villages of Questa, Red River, Eagle Nest, and Angel Fire.

Albuquerque

WORD OF MOUTH

"I always take a ride on the Sandia Peak Tramway. Every time is like the first. You get on at the base, you look up and think to yourself well it couldn't be all that bad . . . then you reach the top of the foothill, and the whole world bursts open like a dream!"

—BeachBoi

"Definitely go to a pueblo! Preferably after visiting the Cultural Center in Albuquerque."

—laurieb_nyny

Updated by
Andrew Collins

AT FIRST GLANCE, ALBUQUERQUE APPEARS TO BE A TYPICAL SUN BELT city, stretching out more than 100 square mi with no grand design, architectural or otherwise, to hold it together. The city's growth pattern seems as free-spirited as all those hot-air balloons that take part in the Albuquerque International Balloon Fiesta every October. With a bit of exploration, however, this initial impression of an asphalt maze softens as you get a sense of Albuquerque's distinctive neighborhoods. The charms of Albuquerque may not jump out to greet you, but the blend of Spanish, Mexican, Native American, Anglo, and Asian influences makes this a vibrant multicultural metropolis well worth exploring. In fact, the city's most distinctive components—first-rate museums and performing arts venues; well-preserved Spanish-colonial, Victorian, and art deco architecture; both sophisticated and funky restaurants and B&Bs; and offbeat shops and galleries—measure up to those you'd find in most U.S. cities this size. You just have to persevere beyond the suburban sprawl and strip-mall excess to find all the good stuff.

An unpretentious, practical city with a metro population nearing 700,000, Albuquerque is the center of New Mexico's educational institutions and financial, business, manufacturing, and medical industries. Its people are easygoing, and the state's three primary cultures rub elbows more comfortably here than anywhere else in New Mexico. Many Albuquerqueans have descended from one or more of three groups: Native Americans, some of whom arrived more than 10,000 years ago; 17th-century Spaniards who came on horseback to conquer and convert; or the European and American trappers, fortune seekers, traders, and merchants who made the arduous journey across the Santa Fe Trail. From its humble beginning as a settlement of Spanish families in what is now known as Old Town, Albuquerque grew into a trade and transportation center. It became an important station on the Spaniards' El Camino Real, or the Royal Road, which wound from Mexico City to Santa Fe and was for centuries New Mexico's primary link to the outside world.

Albuquerque was established in 1706 as a farming settlement near a bend in the Rio Grande. Named for Spain's duke of Alburquerque (the first "r" was later dropped), then viceroy of Mexico, it prospered, thanks to its strategic location on a trade route and its proximity to several Native American pueblos, which were a source of commerce and provided protection from raiding nomadic tribes. The nearby mountains and river forest yielded ample wood, and farming excelled right from the start in the fertile Rio Grande Valley. The settlers built a chapel and then a larger structure, San Felipe de Neri Catholic Church, named after a 16th-century Florentine saint. For protection, the first homes were built around a central plaza like those in other Spanish settlements. The fortresslike community could be entered from the four corners only, making it easier to defend. This four-block area, Old Town, is now the city's tourist hub, filled with shops, galleries, and restaurants.

It would have made sense for the town to simply grow outward, expanding from its central hub. But the Rio Grande gradually changed course, moving farther and farther west, and Albuquerque followed. Albuquerque grew up and down the river valley, with long plots extending along the river to the south and north of the Old Town settlement, each one with a short stretch of river frontage for irrigation. In 1880 the railroad came to central New Mexico, its tracks bypassing Old Town by a good 2 mi and causing another population shift. Old Town wasn't exactly abandoned, but New Town sprouted near the depot and grew until it eventually enveloped Old Town. The city experienced huge growth around the turn of the 20th century, as railroad workers flooded the city.

Then came Route 66. Opened in 1926 and nicknamed "The Mother Road" by John Steinbeck, it sparked much of Albuquerque's modern economic development. Surging through town during the 1930s and '40s, the route had as much impact as the railroad and the river combined. The burgeoning city swelled around the asphalt—motels, gas stations, diners, and truck stops formed a sea of neon that celebrated American mobility. During World War II Albuquerque flourished with the growth of a major air base, Kirtland. It and other military-related facilities such as Sandia National Laboratory remain economic linchpins.

Albuquerque's economy continues to diversify. Intel, the world's largest computer-chip maker, has one of its biggest manufacturing centers here, across the river in the fast-growing northern suburb of Rio Rancho. Intel's presence has stimulated population and housing growth and attracted additional high-tech businesses. That the city has a substantial arts scene is apparent the moment you step off a plane at Albuquerque International Sunport and see the works of New Mexican artists throughout the terminal. The city has significant museums and galleries and is a magnet for artists, writers, poets, filmmakers, and musicians.

Many engaging towns, parks, and Indian pueblos are just outside Albuquerque. The pueblo residents continue to preserve their customs in a changing world. Each pueblo has its own customs, history, art, and design. Visitors are generally welcome, particularly on feast days, which occur throughout the year. For information on the communities and pueblos just outside the city, see the Side Trips from the Cities chapter.

EXPLORING ALBUQUERQUE

Colorful Historic Route 66 is Albuquerque's Central Avenue, unifying, as nothing else, the diverse areas of the city—Old Town cradled at the bend of the Rio Grande; the rapidly rejuvenating downtown business, government, and entertainment center to the east; the University of New Mexico farther east, and the Nob Hill strip of restaurants and shops past the university. The railroad tracks and Central Avenue divide the city into quadrants—Southwest, Northwest, Southeast, and Northeast. ⚠ Although it's generally easy to negotiate the city's gridlike geography, many attractions are a considerable distance apart, making a car a necessity (car-rental rates are quite reasonable here, however).

Albuquerque's terrain is diverse. Along the river in the north and south valleys, the elevation hovers at about 4,800 feet. East of the river, the land rises gently to the foothills of the Sandia Mountains, which rise to higher than 6,000 feet; the 10,378-foot summit is a grand spot from which to view the city below. West of the Rio Grande, where much of Albu-

GREAT ITINERARIES

Most visitors to Albuquerque combine a stay here with some explorations of the entire northern Rio Grande Valley. If you're looking for the perfect regional tour, combine either of the short Albuquerque itineraries here with those provided in the Side Trips from the Cities chapter, which covers several great areas within a 60- to 90-minute drive of Albuquerque as well as covering Isleta Pueblo and the towns of Corrales and Bernalillo, just on the outskirts of Albuquerque.

IF YOU HAVE 1 DAY

One of the best places to kick off the day is the Gold Street Caffe, where you can enjoy breakfast in the heart of downtown before checking out the shops and galleries on Gold and Central avenues. From here, it's a short drive or 30-minute walk west along Central to reach Old Town, where you can explore the shops and museums of the neighborhood. Definitely be sure to check out the Albuquerque Museum of Art and History, and also try to make your way over to the Albuquerque Biological Park, which contains the aquarium, zoo, and botanic park. For lunch, try the atmospheric Monica's or the sophisticated St. Clair Winery and Bistro, both near the Old Town center.

Later in the afternoon, you'll need a car to head east a couple of miles along Central to reach the University of New Mexico's main campus and the nearby Nob Hill District. Start with a stroll around the UNM campus with its many historic adobe buildings; if you have time, pop inside either the

Maxwell Museum of Anthropology or the University Art Museum. When you're finished here, walk east along Central into Nob Hill and check out the dozens of offbeat shops. If it's summer, meaning that you still have some time before the sun sets, it's worth detouring from Old Town to Far Northeast Heights (a 15-minute drive), where you can take the Sandia Peak Aerial Tramway 2.7 mi up to Sandia Peak for spectacular sunset views of the city. Either way, plan to have dinner back in Nob Hill, perhaps at Graze or Flying Star. If you're still up for more fun, check out one of the neighborhood's lively lounges or head back downtown for a bit of late-night barhopping.

IF YOU HAVE 3 DAYS

Follow the morning portion of the one-day itinerary above, and then spend the rest of your day exploring Old Town. With the extra time, you can hit the innovative Explora Science Center, the small but fascinating American International Rattlesnake Museum, and the National Hispanic Cultural Center of New Mexico, which is a 10-minute drive away on the southern edge of downtown. At the end of the day, head to one of the trendy, relative new restaurants that have sprung up in the revitalized downtown, such as Slate Street Cafe or Standard Diner.

On your second day, rent a car and drive out to see the more than 25,000 ancient Native American rock drawings at Petroglyph National Monument. From here, follow Coors Boulevard up to Paseo del Norte, heading east to Balloon Fiesta Park, home to the fascinating

1

Anderson-Abruzzo International Balloon Museum. From here, hop on I-25 north for one exit, getting off onto Tramway Road, which leads east into the foothills to Sandia Peak Aerial Tramway. Here, take the tram 2.7 mi up to Sandia Peak for spectacular views of the city. You can grab lunch up here at High Finance Restaurant, and then walk off your meal with a hike along the crest of the mountain. Depending on how much time you spend on the mountain hiking and exploring and also how exhausted you are, you might either head back to your accommodation to rest a while or drive directly back down Tramway to Sandia Resort & Casino to test your luck on the slots and tables. Either way, when it is time for dinner, head to Bien Shur, the superb restaurant on Sandia Resort's rooftop, where you can first sip cocktails in the open-air lounge while admiring the view of the city before sampling some of the best contemporary food around in the adjacent restaurant.

On your final day, spend the morning checking out the museums at the University of New Mexico, and then enjoy a leisurely afternoon exploring Nob Hill, as described in the one-day itinerary above. If you have some extra time, consider driving north of Old Town to Rio Grande Nature Center State Park, in the North Valley, and then perhaps continue north up Rio Grande Boulevard for some wine-touring at Anderson Valley Vineyards and Casa Rondena Winery. It's not far from here to such appealing dinner options as Casa de Benavidez for great New Mexican fare or Cafe Voila for urbane French bistro cuisine.

WORD OF MOUTH

"Because Albuquerque is at 1 mile in elevation and as far north as Memphis the city has four very distinct seasons. Early October temperatures are usually in the mid 70s during the day and mid to upper 40s at night. Layered clothing is best for a trip to Balloon Fiesta Park."

–daveabq

"Old Town is 'Museum Central' for Albuquerque—you have the Albuquerque Museum (art) the National Atomic Museum, the Natural History Museum, and Explora (hands-on children's museum). . . . You might just enjoy visiting the Rio Grande Nature Center—we always enjoy watching the migrating birds, and there are a couple of fairly easy walking trails. It's peaceful and not too busy."

–ElendilPickle

"My favorite neighborhood is Nob Hill, which is near the University of New Mexico. It's located from approximately Central to Garfield and Yale to Carlisle. . . . There are wonderful shops and restaurants [there], mostly located along Central Ave. Also, Nob Hill is in close proximity to downtown, only a few miles away."

–lovetherain

querque's growth is taking place, the terrain rises abruptly in a string of mesas topped by five volcanic cones. The changes in elevation from one part of the city to another result in corresponding changes in temperature, as much as 10°F at any time. It's not uncommon for snow or rain to fall on one part of town but for it to remain dry and sunny in another.

Old Town & Downtown

Albuquerque's social and commercial anchor since the settlement was established in 1706, Old Town and the surrounding blocks contain the wealth of the city's top cultural attractions, including several excellent museums. The action extends from the historic Old Town Plaza for several blocks in all directions—most of the museums are north and east of the Plaza. In this area you'll also find a number of restaurants and scads of shops. Some of these places are touristy and should be overlooked, but the better ones are included in the Where to Eat and Shopping sections of this chapter. It's a rather drab 1¼-mi walk or drive southeast along Central Avenue to reach Albuquerque's up-and-coming downtown, but it's worth making your way here. Although downtown doesn't have many formal attractions, this bustling neighborhood is one of the West's great urban comebacks—it's a diverting place to wander, shop, and nosh for a couple of hours.

What to See

Albuquerque Biological Park. This city's foremost outdoor attraction and nature center, the park comprises the recently restored Tingley Beach as well as three distinct attractions, Albuquerque Aquarium, Rio Grande Botanic Garden, and Rio Grande Zoo. The garden and aquarium are located together (admission gets you into both facilities), although the zoo is a short drive southeast. You can also ride the scenic *Rio Line* vintage narrow-gauge railroad between the zoo and gardens and aquarium complex; rides cost $2 or are free if you purchase a combination ticket to all of the park's facilities.

Two main components of the Albuquerque Biological Park, **Albuquerque Aquarium and Rio Grande Botanic Garden** (⌧ 2601 Central Ave.) are a huge draw with kids but also draw plenty of adult visitors. At the aquarium, a spectacular shark tank with floor-to-ceiling viewing is among the most popular of the marine exhibits here. A video follows the path of a drop of water as it forms in the Rocky Mountains, enters the upper Rio Grande, and finally spills into the Gulf of Mexico. The Spanish-Moorish garden is one of three walled gardens near the entrance of the 20-acre botanic garden. The glass conservatory has two pavilions, including a seasonal butterfly conservatory open late May through late September. The smaller one exhibits desert plants, and the

> **WORD OF MOUTH**
>
> "How about the . . . Biopark? The Indian Pueblo Cultural Center? Explora Science Center; strolling on Central in Nob Hill; Natural History and Science. . . . I've done or been to all and recommend them!"
> —DebitNM

IF YOU LIKE

NIGHTLIFE & THE ARTS

Even more than Santa Fe, Albuquerque claims a bustling, youthful nightlife scene and numerous performing-arts options. Cultural strengths include several first-rate performance venues, a fine symphony, and a handful of excellent theaters. The city also has a nice variety of bars, including a burgeoning club district downtown and some lively collegiate spots in Nob Hill.

SHOPPING

Although visitors to Albuquerque sometimes observe the sprawling shopping-center and strip-mall developments and assume that the Duke City is mostly the domain of chain outlets, you can find some superb, high-quality independent shops in this city, especially in funky Nob Hill and the rejuvenated downtown. Nob Hill, which runs along old Route 66, specializes in offbeat stores carrying vintage clothing, arty home furnishings, and peculiar novelty gifts. Downtown's retail sector is still taking off, as the neighborhood had become rather down-and-out over the years. As with Nob Hill, it's a good bet for unusual stores, from the city's leading chocolatier, Theobroma, to one of the state's favorite Native American trading posts, Skip Maisel. The mother lode for shopaholics, however, is Old Town, which abounds with shops selling Native American and Spanish-colonial arts and crafts, clothing, and the usual array of souvenirs. All three neighborhoods also have an increasing number of art galleries, and the prices here tend to be considerably lower than in Santa Fe.

SPORTS & THE OUTDOORS

You're never far from outdoor diversions in Albuquerque, a city that also follows its professional and college sports teams with great fervor. University of New Mexico's football and men's and women's basketball teams are first-rate and draw huge crowds, as do the Albuquerque Isotopes, the Triple A minor-league baseball team of the Florida Marlins. As for participant sports, there's great biking in several parts of the city as well as the ski area atop Sandia Crest—the parks and recreation department even publishes a highly detailed bike map. Golfing is another favorite pastime, and you'll find excellent municipal courses in town and a highly acclaimed tournament course at the University of New Mexico.

larger houses the Mediterranean collection. Shark Reef Cafe serves breakfast and lunch. Fans of trains enjoy watching the Garden Model Railroad, which runs along a shaded path in two 400-foot loops. In summer there are music concerts given on Thursday at the Botanic Garden. And from late November through late December, the Botanic Garden comes alive each evening from 6 to 9 PM for the River of Lights festival, a walk-through show of holiday lights and decorations.

The 64-acre **Rio Grande Zoo** (⊠ 903 10th St. SW)—an oasis of waterfalls, cottonwood trees, and naturalized animal habitats—is one of the best-managed and most attractive zoos of its kind. More than 250

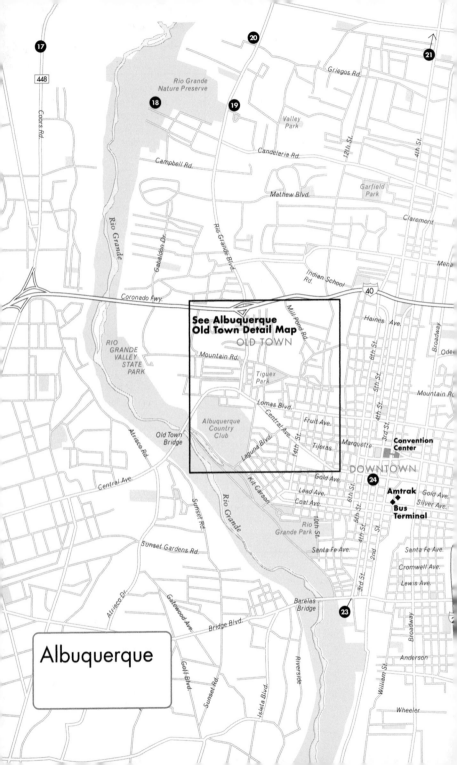

Albuquerque

Old Town

Downtown

See Albuquerque
Old Town Detail Map

OLD TOWN

DOWNTOWN

Convention
Center

Amtrak
Bus
Terminal

Rio Grande
Nature Preserve

Valley
Park

Garfield
Park

RIO
GRANDE
VALLEY
STATE
PARK

Albuquerque
Country
Club

Old Town
Bridge

Barelas
Bridge

Rio Grande

Rio Grande

448

Coors Rd.

Griegos Rd.

Candelaria Rd.

Campbell Rd.

Mathew Blvd.

12th St.

4th St.

Claremont

Mesa

Odel

Indian School
Rd.

40

Coronado Fwy.

Haines Ave.

Broadway

6th St.

5th St.

4th St.

3rd St.

Mountain St.

Mountain Rd.

Tiguex
Park

Lomas Blvd.

Central Ave.

Fruit Ave.

Marquette

Tijeras

14th St.

Laguna Blvd.

Gold Ave.

Lead Ave.

Coal Ave.

Gold Ave.

Silver Ave.

6th St.

5th St.

4th St.

2nd St.

3rd St.

Santa Fe Ave.

Cromwell Ave.

Lewis Ave.

Anderson

Wheeler

Broadway

William St.

Santa Fe Ave.

Rio
Grande Park

Kit Carson

Sunset Rd.

Sunset Gardens Rd.

Central Ave.

Atrisco Rd.

Gabaldon Dr.

Rio Grande Blvd.

Mill Pond Rd.

Rio Grande Blvd.

Atrisco Dr.

Gatewood Ave.

Bridge Blvd.

Golf Blvd.

Sunset Rd.

Isleta Blvd.

Riverside

17

20

21

18

19

23

24

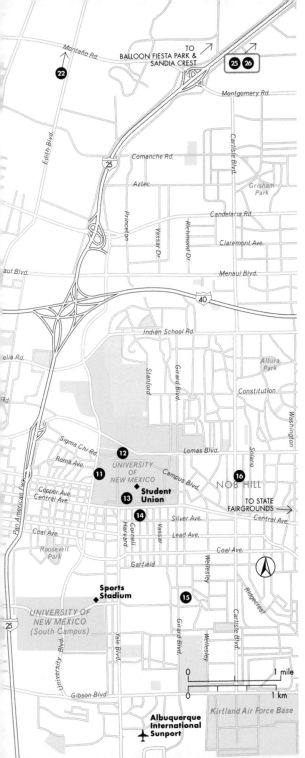

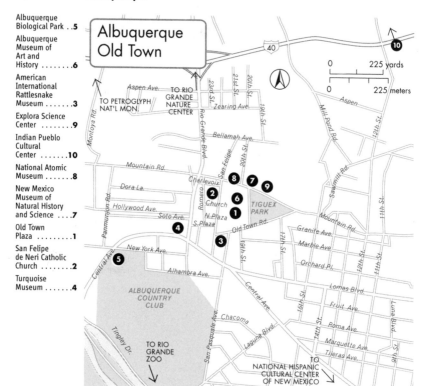

species of wildlife from around the world live here, including giraffes, camels, polar bears, elephants, zebras, and koalas. The Tropical America exhibit offers a bit of contrast for dry Albuquerque, replicating a jungle rain forest and containing toucans, spider monkeys, and brilliant orchids and bromeliads. In keeping with its mission of wildlife care and conservation, the zoo has established captive breeding programs for more than a dozen endangered species. Concerts are performed on the grounds on summer Friday evenings. There's a café on the premises. The *Thunderbird Express* is a ¾-scale train that runs in a nonstop loop around the zoo, and during the 20-minute ride, conductors talk in depth about the zoo and its environments. It's free with combo tickets, or $2 otherwise (buy tickets onboard or at the Africa exhibit).

The newly renovated **Tingley Beach** (⊠ 1800 Tingley Dr. SW, south of Central Ave. and just east of Central Ave. bridge) is a recreational arm of the biological park that consists of three ponds, created in the 1930s by diverting water from the Rio Grande. The former swimming hole (no swimming or boating is permitted on the ponds these days) had been largely abandoned for many years before being renovated in 2004 and 2005; now it includes a snack bar; a train station for the *Rio Line,* which runs between the Aquarium and garden complex and the zoo; and three

A GOOD TOUR

Numbers correspond to the Albuquerque and Albuquerque Old Town maps.

Soak up the air of history in **Old Town Plaza** ▶ ❶, and then cross the street and visit **San Felipe de Neri Catholic Church** ❷. Cutting diagonally across the plaza, head south to the corner of San Felipe Street and Old Town Road to drop in on the **American International Rattlesnake Museum** ❸. Walk south on San Felipe and west on Central Avenue to the corner of Rio Grande Boulevard, where in a strip mall you find the **Turquoise Museum** ❹. Farther west on Central, along a historic section of Route 66 lined with shabby vintage motels, is the **Albuquerque Botanical Park** ❺, which consists of the Albuquerque Aquarium, Botanic Garden, Rio Grande Zoo, and Tingley Beach. Then take a five-minute stroll over to two of the city's cultural institutions, the **Albuquerque Museum of Art and History** ❻ and the **New Mexico Museum of Natural History and Science** ❼. Kids enjoy the **National Atomic Museum** ❽ and the **Explora Science Center** ❾, which are also within walking distance. You need to hop in your car (or take

city Bus 66) to visit the **Indian Pueblo Cultural Center** ❿ downtown and the **New Mexico Holocaust & Intolerance Museum** ㉔, and the **National Hispanic Cultural Center** ㉓.

🕙 TIMING TIPS→ The best time to begin a visit to Old Town is in the morning, before the stores open at 10 and the daily rush of activity begins. In the beaming morning light, the echoes of the past are almost palpable (and you might find parking). Plan to spend an hour and a half at the Old Town sites, an hour in the Albuquerque Museum of Art and History, and two hours in the New Mexico Museum of Natural History and Science. In the afternoon, you can either drive up to the Indian Pueblo Cultural Center or drive downtown, where you can explore this up-and-coming neighborhood, visit the New Mexico Holocaust & Intolerance Museum, or continue driving south to the National Hispanic Cultural Center. It's impractical to see everything in this area in one day, so consider breaking up your tour into two days if you wish to see every attraction.

ponds stocked with trout for fishing (you can buy gear and fishing licenses at a fishing-tackle shop on premises). On the north pond, you can sail your model electric- or wind-powered boats. To the west of the ponds, the cottonwood bosque (wetlands forest) fringes the river, and there are ecological tours of the bosque are given in summer.

✉ *903 10th St. SW, Tingley Park* ☎ *505/764–6200* ⊕ *www.cabq.gov/biopark* 🎟 *Free Tingley Beach and grounds, $7 Albuquerque Aquarium and Rio Grande Botanic Garden (combined ticket), $7 Rio Grande Zoo, $12 combination ticket for all attractions, which includes unlimited rides on trains* 🕙 *Daily 9–5, until 6 on weekends, June–Aug.*

6 Albuquerque Museum of Art and History. This modern structure, which Fodor'sChoice underwent a spectacular 40,000-square-foot expansion in 2004, houses ★ the largest collection of Spanish-colonial artifacts in the nation, along with relics of the city's birth and development. The centerpiece of the colonial exhibit is a pair of life-size models of Spanish conquistadors in original chain mail and armor. Perhaps the one on horseback is Francisco Vásquez de Coronado, who, in search of gold, led a small army into New Mexico in 1540—the turning point in the region's history. Among the museum's attractions are treasure chests filled with pearls and gold coins, religious artifacts, and early maps (some dating from the 15th century and showing California as an island). A multimedia presentation chronicles the development of the city since 1875. The sculpture garden contains 45 works by 20th-century southwestern artists that include Glenna Goodacre, Michael Naranjo, and Luís Jiménez. Free tours of the museum sculpture garden, which contains more than 50 works, are offered mid-April through mid-October, Tuesday–Saturday at 10 AM. Across from the museum, Tiguex Park is a tree-shaded, grassy plot that hosts many events, including arts and crafts fairs and concerts. ⌧ *2000 Mountain Rd. NW, Old Town* ☎ *505/243–7255* ⊕ *www. albuquerquemuseum.com* ⌧ *$4* ⊘ *Tues.–Sun. 9–5.*

⟳ 3 American International Rattlesnake Museum. Included in the largest collection of different species of living rattlers in the world are such rare and unusual specimens as an albino western diamondback. The museum's labels, its engaging staff, and a video supply visitors with the lowdown on these venomous creatures—for instance, that they can't hear their own rattles and that the human death rate from rattlesnake bites is less than 1%. The mission here is to educate the public on the many positive benefits of rattlesnakes, and to contribute to their conservation. ⌧ *202 San Felipe St. NW, Old Town* ☎ *505/242–6569* ⊕ *www.rattlesnakes. com* ⌧ *$3.50* ⊘ *Mon.–Sat. 10–6, Sun. noon–5 (hrs sometimes shorter in winter, call ahead).*

★ ⟳ 9 Explora Science Center. Albuquerque's cultural corridor received another jewel in 2003, when this imaginatively executed science museum opened right across from the New Mexico Museum of Natural History and Science. Explora bills itself as an all-ages attraction, but there's no question that many of the hands-on exhibits—from a high-wire bicycle to kinetic sculpture display—are geared especially to children, with hands-on exhibits about science, technology, and art. There are also a playground and a freestanding staircase that appears to "float" between floors. ⌧ *1701 Mountain Rd. NW, Old Town* ☎ *505/224–8300* ⊕ *www. explora.mus.nm.us* ⌧ *$7* ⊘ *Mon.–Sat. 10–6, Sun. noon–6.*

★ ⟳ 10 Indian Pueblo Cultural Center. The multilevel semicircular design at this museum was inspired by Pueblo Bonito, the prehistoric ruin in Chaco Canyon in northwestern New Mexico. Start by watching the museum's video, which discusses the history of the region's Pueblo culture. Then move to the upper-level alcove, where each of the state's 19 pueblos has a space devoted to its particular arts and crafts. Lower-level exhibits trace the history of the Pueblo people. Youngsters can touch Native American pottery, jewelry, weaving, tools, and dried corn at the Hands-On

Corner and also draw petroglyph designs and design pots. Paintings, sculptures, jewelry, leather crafts, rugs, souvenir items, drums, beaded necklaces, painted bowls, and fetishes are for sale. Ceremonial dances are performed on weekends at 11 and 2, and there are also arts-and-crafts demonstrations each weekend. The Pueblo Harvest Café is a great spot for lunch, where you can try such Native American fare as blue-corn pancakes and Indian tacos. ✉ *2401 12th St. NW, Los Duranes* ☎ *505/843–7270 or 800/766–4405* ⊕ *www.indianpueblo.org* 🎫 *$6* ⊙ *Daily 9–5.*

8 **National Atomic Museum.** Currently in a temporary space in Old Town, this popular museum traces the history of the atomic age and how nuclear science has dramatically influenced the course of modern history. Exhibits include replicas of Little Boy and Fat Man (the bombs dropped on Japan at the end of World War II), and there are children's programs and an exhibit about X-ray technology. As of this writing, the museum has plans to move into a larger space and reopen as the National Museum of Nuclear Science and History, but that move appears to be several years off. ✉ *1905 Mountain Rd. NW, Old Town* ☎ *505/245–2137* ⊕ *www.atomicmuseum.com* 🎫 *$5* ⊙ *Daily 9–5.*

NEED A BREAK?

On the edge of Old Town, toward downtown and near several museums, **Golden Crown Panaderia** (✉ 1103 Mountain Rd. NW, Old Town ☎ 505/243–2424 or 877/382–2924) is an aromatic bakery known for two things: the ability to custom-design and bake unbelievably artful breads that can depict just about any person or place, and hearty green-chile bread (made with tomatoes, cilantro, Parmesan, green chile, and onions). You can also order hot cocoa, cappuccino, bizcochito cookies (the official state cookie), New Mexican wedding cookies topped with powdered sugar, pumpkin-filled empanadas, and plenty of other sweets. There's seating on a small patio. It's closed Sunday and Monday.

23 **National Hispanic Cultural Center of New Mexico.** A showcase for Latino culture and genealogy in Albuquerque's old Barelas neighborhood, this dramatic, contemporary space contains several art galleries and performance venues, a 10,000-volume genealogical research center and library, a restaurant, and a television studio. Exhibits include displays of photography and paintings by local artists as well as by internationally known names. The center mounts performances of flamenco dancing, bilingual theater, and traditional Spanish and New Mexican music. This is the largest Latino cultural center in the country, and with a $10 million programming endowment (Rita Moreno and Edward James Olmos are among the notables on the national board), the center provides top-notch entertainment in its stunning Roy E. Disney Center for Performing Arts and smaller Albuquerque Journal Theatre, and it hosts major traveling art exhibits in its first-rate museum, which also houses an esteemed permanent collection. An architectural showpiece, the center

Fodor's Choice
★

WORD OF MOUTH
"National Hispanic Cultural Center = wonderful exhibits in a lovely building."   –Schildc1

borrows from a variety of Spanish cultures, from Moorish Spain to the American Southwest. One historic feature is a vintage WPA-era school that now contains a research library and an excellent restaurant, La Fonda del Bosque, which serves excellent New Mexican fare. ⊠ *1701 4th St. SW, at Bridge St., Barelas* ☎ *505/246–2261* ⊕ *www.nhccnm.org* ⊠ *$3* ⊙ *Tues.–Sun. 10–5.*

㉔ New Mexico Holocaust & Intolerance Museum. Although it occupies a rather modest storefront in downtown Albuquerque, this moving museum packs plenty of punch with its poignant exhibits that document genocide and persecution against persons throughout history, with special emphasis, of course, placed upon the Holocaust carried out by the Nazis before and during World War II. Exhibits inside touch on child slave labor, the rescue of Bulgarian and Danish Jews, a re-created gate from a concentration camp, the Nuremburg Trials, and many artifacts related to Holocaust survivors and the Nazis. There are also areas that discuss other genocides throughout history, from the Bataan Death March to the extinguishing of indigenous cultures. ⊠ *415 Central Ave. NW, Downtown* ☎ *505/247–0606* ⊕ *www.nmholocaustmuseum.org* ⊠ *Donation suggested* ⊙ *Tues.–Sat. 11–3.*

★ ⟳ ❼ New Mexico Museum of Natural History and Science. The world of wonders at Albuquerque's most popular museum includes the simulated volcano (with a river of bubbling hot lava flowing beneath the see-through glass floor), the frigid Ice Age cave, and the world-class dinosaur exhibit hall. The Evolator—short for Evolution Elevator—a six-minute high-tech ride, uses video, sound, and motion to whisk you through 35 million years of New Mexico's geological history. A film in the Extreme Screen DynaTheater makes viewers feel equally involved. Arrive via the front walkway, and you'll be greeted by life-size bronze sculptures of a 21-foot-long horned pentaceratops and a 30-foot-long carnivorous albertosaur. The LodeStar Science Center features a state-of-the-art planetarium. ⊠ *1801 Mountain Rd. NW, Old Town* ☎ *505/841–2800* ⊕ *www.nmnaturalhistory.org* ⊠ *Museum $6, DynaTheater $6, planetarium $6; combination ticket for any 2 attractions $11, for any 3 attractions $16* ⊙ *Daily 9–5.*

★ ⟳ ❶ Old Town Plaza. Don Francisco Cuervo y Valdés, a provincial governor of New Mexico, laid out this small plaza in 1706. No slouch when it came to political maneuvering, he named the town after the duke of Alburquerque, viceroy of New Spain. He hoped flattery would induce the duke to waive the requirement that a town have 30 families before a charter was issued—there were only 15 families living here in 1706. The duke acquiesced. (Albuquerque is nicknamed "The Duke City," so he's hardly been forgotten.) Today the plaza is an oasis of tranquillity filled with shade trees, wrought-iron benches, a graceful white gazebo, and strips of grass. Roughly 200 shops, restaurants, cafés, galleries, and several cultural sites in *placitas* (small plazas)

> **DID YOU KNOW?**
>
> New Mexico is officially a bilingual state. One out of three families speaks Spanish at home.

A GOOD WALK

The impeccably landscaped grounds of the University of New Mexico surround a central area containing knolls, a duck pond, fountains, waterfalls, and benches. The **Maxwell Museum of Anthropology** ▶ ⑪ is in the Anthropology Building on the western edge of the campus, only a few minutes' walk from the duck pond. From the Maxwell, walk east past Alumni Chapel and turn left. At the duck pond walk north on Yale past University House. You come to a four-way stop at Yale and Las Lomas streets. The **Jonson Gallery** ⑫ is the second building on the northeast corner of this intersection. Walk south past the duck pond, between Zimmerman Library and Ortega Hall. Continue south under a walkway and left, past the Student Union Building, to the **University Art Museum** ⑬, in the Center for the Arts (use the Stanford Drive and Central Avenue entrance). At the corner of Central Avenue and Cornell Drive is the sales and exhibition gallery of the **Tamarind Institute** ⑭. Nine blocks south of Central along Girard Boulevard is the **Ernie Pyle Branch Library** ⑮. Back on Central Avenue, you're a 10-minute walk from UNM campus to the edge of **Nob Hill** ⑯, where you can shop, café-hop, and admire the historic residential and commercial architecture. ⊘ TIMING TIPS→ Seeing the University of New Mexico could take the better part of a day. Spend an hour strolling the grounds, maybe catching some rays by the duck pond. Allot an hour for each subsequent stop. All facilities are open year-round, but some are closed from Saturday to Monday. Save Nob Hill for late afternoon or even the evening, which is when this neighborhood really comes alive.

and lanes surround Old Town Plaza. The scents of green chile, enchiladas, and burritos hang in the air. During fiestas Old Town comes alive with mariachi bands and dancing señoritas. Event schedules and maps, which contain a list of public restrooms, are available at the **Old Town Visitors Center** (✉ 303 Romero St. NW, Old Town ☎ 505/243–3215), across the street from the San Felipe de Neri Catholic Church. The center is open daily, typically 9–4:30 but usually a bit later in summer.

❷ **San Felipe de Neri Catholic Church.** More than two centuries after it first welcomed worshippers, this structure, erected in 1793, is still active. The building, which replaced Albuquerque's first Catholic church, has been enlarged and expanded several times, but its adobe walls and other original features remain. Small gardens front and flank the church; the inside is dark and quiet. Next to it is a small museum that displays relics—vestments, paintings, carvings—dating from the 17th century. ⚠ There's a hidden treasure behind the church: inside the gnarled tree is a statue that some speculate depicts the Virgin Mary. ✉ *2005 Plaza NW, Old Town* ☎ *505/243–4628* ⊘ *Church open to public daily 8 AM–dusk; museum Mon.–Sat. 1–4. Call ahead to confirm hrs.*

GOOD TERM

Adobe: A brick of sun-dried earth and clay, usually stabilized with straw; a structure made of adobe.

❹ **Turquoise Museum.** A novel attraction, this small museum focuses on the beauty, mythology, and physical properties of turquoise, a semiprecious but widely adored gemstone that many people understandably associate with the color of New Mexico's skies. A simulated mine shaft leads to one-of-a-kind showpieces and examples from more than 60 mines on four continents. Displays show how turquoise is formed and highlight its uses by Native Americans in prehistoric times. At the education center you can learn how to distinguish the real McCoy from plastic. ✉ *2107 Central Ave. NW, Old Town* ☎ *505/247–8650* 💲 *$4* ☺ *Weekdays 9:30–5, Sat. 9:30–4.*

NEED A BREAK?

On the east side of town in the historic Huning Highland district, the **Grove Cafe & Market** (✉ 600 Central Ave. SE, Downtown ☎ 505/248–9800) is a good stop as you continue from this area to the University of New Mexico and Nob Hill districts. Opened in spring 2006, this airy, modern establishment offers such breakfast treats as poached eggs with prosciutto and Parmesan, tuna niçoise, and aged-salami sandwiches with olive tapanade, arugula, and imported provolone on sourdough bread. You can dine on the arbored patio. Or come by for a loose-leaf tea or latte with a cupcake.

University of New Mexico & Nob Hill

Established in 1889, the University of New Mexico is the state's leading institution of higher education, with internationally recognized programs in anthropology, biology, Latin American studies, and medicine. Its many outstanding galleries and museums are open to the public free of charge. The university's Pueblo Revival–style architecture is noteworthy, particularly the old wing of Zimmerman Library and the Alumni Chapel, both designed by John Gaw Meem, a Santa Fe–based architect who was one of the chief 20th-century proponents of the Pueblo style.

What to See

❶⑤ **Ernie Pyle Library.** After several visits to New Mexico, Ernie Pyle, a Pulitzer prize–winning news reporter, built a house in 1940 that now contains the smallest branch of the Albuquerque Public Library. On display are photos, handwritten articles by Pyle, and news clippings about his career as a correspondent during World War II and his death from a sniper's bullet on April 18, 1945, on the Pacific island of Ie Shima. ✉ *900 Girard Blvd. SE, University of New Mexico* ☎ *505/256–2065* ⊕ *www.cabq. gov/library* 💲 *Free* ☺ *Tues., Thurs.–Sat. 10–6, Wed. 11–7.*

⑫ **Jonson Gallery.** The home and studio of Raymond Jonson (1891–1982) house the abstract, colorful works on paper of this Transcendentalist painter who focused on mass and form. The gallery mounts a major Jonson retrospective each summer and also exhibits works by other contemporary painters. ✉ *1909 Las Lomas Blvd. NE, University of New Mexico* ☎ *505/277–4967* ⊕ *www.unm.edu/~jonsong* 💲 *Free* ☺ *Tues.–Fri. 9–4.*

⑪ **Maxwell Museum of Anthropology.** Many of the more than 2½ million artifacts at the Maxwell, the first public museum in Albuquerque (estab-

CLOSE UP

Neon & Nostalgia

1

MID-20TH-CENTURY AMERICAN motorists came to know their country firsthand via Route 66. Today, frequent flyers enviously wonder about the romance of the open road. Long before the prosperous age of the two-car family, the 2,400 mi of Route 66 opened in 1926 to link eight states, from Chicago to Los Angeles. It came to be known by the nickname John Steinbeck gave it—"The Mother Road." The nation's outlet for movement and change has become enveloped in nostalgia. Today in New Mexico, from the Texas to the Arizona border, it's still possible to experience vestiges of the old Route 66.

Built in part to aid rural communities and the transportation of agricultural goods, Route 66 evolved into a farmer's escape from the Dust Bowl of the 1930s, and then a tryst for the love affair between Americans and their automobiles. The route's other nickname, "America's Main Street," was due to the fact that the road incorporated towns' main streets, and because of this, communities thrived. Along the highway that ran as vividly through the imagination as through the landscape, many discovered their ability to move on beyond the confines of their own hometown. They found places along the road that appeared to offer a better opportunity to prosper and to reinvent their destiny.

The 1940s and '50s were the heyday of the highway, as Nat King Cole crooned the lyrics to Bobby Troup's song of the road. The road's adventure was overplayed in the '60s television series *Route 66*, and by 1970, nearly all of the two-laner was trumped by four-lane interstate highways. Along Route 66, the possibility of connection with America's people and places

lived beyond every bend in the road. By contrast, the interstate would dampen travel with franchised monotony. Most of the bypassed Route 66 communities dried up and blew away like tumbleweeds. In many of these ghost towns, only a few crumbling buildings and fading signs remain as markers to a vanished age.

By hopping on and off I-40, it's possible to find the quieter, slower two-laner that's held on to its name. The feeling of adventure still flickers in Tucumcari at twilight, when the neon signs of the Buckaroo Motel, the Westerner Drive-In, and the Blue Swallow light up the cobalt sky. In Santa Rosa, at Joseph's Cafe, the Fat Man continues to beckon. In Albuquerque, you can drive down Central Avenue, stopping at the Route 66 Diner or the Route 66 Malt Shop and heading past the El Vado. And in Gallup, dine at Earl's Restaurant or the Eagle Cafe, and book a room at the stars of yesteryear's hotel, El Rancho Hotel. Between Albuquerque and Gallup, this ribbon of road takes you through dusty towns with names like poetry: Budville, Cubero, McCartys, Thoreau. These places also once offered the traveler the filling stations, motor courts, curio shops, and cafés that gave comfort on a long drive, and every road tripper today hopes to happen upon such an undiscovered (but really just forgotten) place.

For information on dining and lodging along Route 66, contact the **National Historic Route 66 Federation** (☎ 909/336-6131 ⊕ www.national66.com) or contact the **New Mexico Office of Tourism** (☎ 800/545-2040 ⊕ www.newmexico.org) and request the free "Route 66 in New Mexico" brochure.

lished in 1932), come from the Southwest. Two permanent exhibitions chronicle 4 million years of human history and the lifeways, art, and cultures of 11,500 years of human settlement in the Southwest. The photographic archives contain more than 250,000 images, including some of the earliest photos of Pueblo and Navajo cultures. The museum shop sells traditional and contemporary southwestern Native American jewelry, rugs, pottery, basketry, and beadwork, along with folk art from around the world. In the children's section are inexpensive books and handmade tribal artifacts. ✉ *University of New Mexico, University Blvd., 1 block north of Grand Ave.* ☎ *505/277-4405* ⊕ *www.unm.edu/ ~maxwell* ✉ *Free* ☯ *Tues.–Fri. 9–4, Sat. 10–4.*

⑯ Nob Hill. The heart of Albuquerque's Route 66 culture and also its hippest, funkiest retail and entertainment district, Nob Hill is the neighborhood just east of UNM, with its commercial spine extending along Central Avenue (old Route 66). Along this stretch you'll find dozens of offbeat shops, arty cafés, and student hangouts, and on the blocks just north and south of Central Avenue, you'll see a number of historic Pueblo Revival homes, most built during the early 20th century. Most of the hipper and more gentrified businesses are along the stretch of Central between UNM and Carlisle Boulevard, but the activity is gradually moving east. Old art deco strip malls and vintage motels along this stretch are slowly being transformed into new restaurants and shops. The neighborhood was developed during the 1930s and '40s, peaked in prosperity and popularity during the 1950s, and then fell into a state of decline from the 1960s through the mid-'80s. It was at this time that a group of local business and property owners formed a neighborhood group and banded together to help turn the neighborhood around, and Nob Hill has been enjoying great cachet and popularity ever since. ✉ *Central Ave., from University of New Mexico campus east to Washington St., Nob Hill.*

⑭ Tamarind Institute. This world-famous institution played a major role in reviving the fine art of lithographic printing, which involves working with plates of traditional stone and modern metal. Tamarind certification is to a printer what a degree from Juilliard is to a musician. A small gallery within the facility exhibits prints and lithographs. Guided tours (reservations essential) are conducted on the first Friday of each month at 1:30. ✉ *108 Cornell Dr. SE, University of New Mexico* ☎ *505/277-3901* ⊕ *www.unm.edu/~tamarind* ✉ *Free* ☯ *By appt., Tues.–Fri. 9–5.*

⑬ University Art Museum. A handsome facility inside the UNM Center for the Arts, the museum holds New Mexico's largest collection of fine art. Works of old masters share wall space with the likes of Picasso and O'Keeffe, and many photographs and prints are on display. Lectures and symposia, gallery talks, and guided tours are regularly scheduled. ✉ *University of New Mexico Center for the Arts, north of Central Ave. entrance opposite Yale Blvd.* ☎ *505/277-4001* ⊕ *unmartmuseum.unm. edu* ✉ *Free* ☯ *Tues. 9–4 and 5–8, Wed.–Fri. 9–4, Sun. 1–4.*

NEED A BREAK? The definitive student hangout but also a great place for anybody to satisfy an appetite into the wee hours, **Frontier Restaurant** (✉ 2400 Central Ave. SE ☎ 505/266-0550) is across from UNM and open 24/7 for inexpensive diner-style American and New Mexican chow. The breakfast burritos in this rambling restaurant are delicious, as are the hefty cinnamon buns.

Elsewhere in Albuquerque

Most of the other attractions in the city lie north of downtown, Old Town, and the University of New Mexico and Nob Hill areas. You can combine some of these attractions into one tour, especially the three wineries (⇨ *see* Great Itineraries for suggestions), but because these attractions lie some distance from one another, it may be most practical to tackle each one on its own.

What to See

㉒ Anderson-Abruzzo International Balloon Museum. Opened in 2005 at Balloon Fiesta Park, the dramatic museum celebrates the city's legacy as the hot-air ballooning capital of the world. This dashing, massive facility is named for Maxie Anderson and Ben Abruzzo, who pioneered ballooning in Albuquerque and were part of a team of three aviators who made the first manned hot-air balloon crossing of the Atlantic Ocean in 1978. You can understand the reason for constructing such a large museum when you examine some of the exhibits inside—these include several actual balloons of important historic note as well as both large- and small-scale replicas of balloons and zeppelins. You'll also see vintage balloon baskets, actual china and flatware used from the ill-fated *Hindenburg* as well as an engaging display on that tragic craft, and dynamic displays that trace the history of the sport, dating back to the first balloon ride, in 1783. Kids can design their own balloons at one particularly creative interactive exhibit. There's a large museum shop offering just about any book or product you could imagine related to hot-air ballooning, and as of this writing, a café was under construction.

★ The museum anchors Albuquerque's Balloon Fiesta Park, home to the legendary **Albuquerque International Balloon Fiesta** (☎ 505/821–1000 or 888/422–7277 ⊕ www.balloonfiesta.com), which began in 1972 and runs for nearly two weeks in early October. Albuquerque's long history of ballooning dates from 1882, when Professor Park A. Van Tassel, a saloon keeper, ascended in a balloon at the Territorial Fair. During the fiesta, which is the largest hot-air-balloon gathering anywhere, you can watch the Special Shapes Rodeo, when hundreds of unusual balloons, including depictions of the old lady who lived in the shoe, the pink pig, and dozens of other fanciful characters from fairy tales and popular culture, soar high above the more than a million spectators. There are night flights, obstacle races, and many other surprising balloon events. Book your hotel far in advance if you plan to attend, and note that hotel rates also rise during the fiesta. ✉ *9201 Balloon Museum Dr. NE, off Alameda Blvd. west of I–25, Northeast Heights* ☎ *505/768–6020* ⊕ *www.balloonmuseum.com* ✎ *$4* ☉ *Tues.–Sun. 9–5.*

⑳ Anderson Valley Vineyards. A low-key winery that was established in 1973 and enjoys a dramatic, pastoral North Valley setting not far from the Rio Grande, Anderson Valley specializes in chardonnay and cabernet sauvignon. The staff in the intimate tasting room is friendly and knowledgeable, and you can sip your wine while relaxing on an enchanting patio with wonderful views of the Sandia Mountains in the distance. In this agrarian, tranquil setting, it's hard to imagine that you're just a little more than 3 mi north of the bustle of Old Town and downtown. ✉ *4920 Rio Grande Blvd. NW, North Valley* ☎ *505/344–7266* ☒ *Free* ⊗ *Tues.–Sun. noon–5.*

> **DID YOU KNOW?**
>
> Franciscan monks first planted their grapevines in New Mexico before moving more successfully to northern California.

★ ⑲ **Casa Rondeña Winery.** Perhaps the most architecturally stunning of New Mexico's wineries, Casa Rondeña strongly resembles a Tuscan villa, with its green-tile roof winery and verdant grounds laced with gardens and fountains. The winery produces a superb cabernet franc, one of the most esteemed vintages in New Mexico. Features that you can see during your visit include a vintage oak fermentation tank and a Great Hall with soaring ceilings, where tastings are conducted. The winery hosts a number of events, including a chamber music festival with wine receptions and dinners. ✉ *733 Chavez Rd., North Valley* ☎ *505/344–5911 or 800/706–1699* ⊕ *www.casarondena.com* ☒ *Free* ⊗ *Wed.–Sat. 10–6, Sun. noon–6.*

㉕ **Gruet Winery.** It's hard to imagine a wine tasting experience with less curb appeal. Gruet Winery sits along an ugly access road paralleling I–25, sandwiched between an RV showroom and a lawn-furniture store. But behind the vaguely castlelike exterior of this otherwise modern industrial building, you're afforded the chance to visit one of the nation's most acclaimed producers of sparkling wines. Gruet had been famous in France since the 1950s for its champagnes. Here in New Mexico, where the Gruet family has been producing wine since 1984, it's earned similar kudos for its six sparkling wines as well as for impressive pinot noirs and chardonnays. Many of the state's top restaurants now carry Gruet vintages. Tastings include the chance to sample five wines and to take home a souvenir glass. ✉ *8400 Pan American Freeway NE, Northeast Heights* ☎ *505/821–0055 or 888/857–9463* ⊕ *www.gruetwinery.com* ☒ *Free; $5 for a 5-wine tasting* ⊗ *Weekdays 10–5, Sat. noon–5; tours Mon.–Sat. at 2.*

⑰ **Petroglyph National Monument.** Beneath the stumps of five extinct volcanoes, this park encompasses more than 25,000 ancient Native American rock drawings inscribed on the 17-mi-long West Mesa escarpment overlooking the Rio Grande Valley. For centuries, Native American hunting parties camped at the base, chipping and scribbling away. Archaeologists believe most of the petroglyphs were carved on the lava formations between the years 1100 and 1600, but some images at the park may date as far as 1000 BC. Walking trails provide access to them. A paved trail at **Boca Negra Canyon** (north of the visitor center on Unser Boulevard, beyond Montaño Road) leads past several dozen petroglyphs. The trail at **Rinconado Canyon** (south of the visitor center on Unser) is unpaved. ✉ *Visitor center, Unser Blvd. NW at Western Trail Rd., West Side* ☎ *505/899–0205* ⊕ *www.nps.gov/petr* ☒ *$1 weekdays, $2 weekends* ⊗ *Daily 8–5.*

1

☺ ❶ **Rio Grande Nature Center State Park.** Along the banks for the Rio Grande, this year-round 170-acre refuge in a portion of the Bosque is the nation's largest cottonwood forest. If bird-watching is your thing, you've come to the right place: this is home to all manner of birds and migratory waterfowl. Constructed half aboveground and half below the edge of a pond, the park's glass-walled library has viewing windows that provide a look at what's going on at both levels, and speakers broadcast the sounds of the birds you're watching into the room. You may see birds, frogs, ducks, and turtles. The park has active programs for adults and children and trails for biking, walking, and jogging. ⚠ **Keep your eye out for what appears to be a game of jacks abandoned by giants: these jetty jacks were built in the 1950s to protect the Rio Grande levees from flood debris.** ✉ *2901 Candelaria Rd. NW, North Valley* ☎ *505/344–7240* ⊕ *www.nmparks. com* 🎫 *$1; grounds free* ☉ *Nature Center daily 10–5, park daily 8–5.*

★ ☺ ❷ **Sandia Peak Aerial Tramway.** Tramway cars climb 2.7 mi up the steep western face of the Sandias, giving you a close-up view of red rocks and tall trees—it's the world's longest aerial tramway. From the observation deck at the 10,378-foot summit you can see Santa Fe to the northeast and Los Alamos to the northwest—all told, you're able to see some 11,000 square miles of spectacular scenery. Cars leave from the base at regular intervals for the 15-minute ride to the top. If you're lucky, you can see birds of prey soaring above or mountain lions roaming the cliff sides. An exhibit room at the top surveys the wildlife and landscape of the mountain, as well as some trails. Narrators point out what you're seeing below, including the barely visible remnants of a 1953 plane crash that killed all 16 passengers onboard.

If you want to tie a meal in to the excursion, there's the upscale **High Finance Restaurant** (☎ 505/243–9742 ⊕ www.highfinancerestaurant. com) on top of the mountain (serving steaks, lobster tail, and good burgers at lunch), and a more casual spot, **Sandiago's** (☎ 505/856–6692 ⊕ www.sandiagos.com), at the tram's base. High Finance affords clear views from every table, making it a favorite destination for a romantic dinner—the food isn't bad, but it's more about the scenic experience here. ⚠ **It's much colder and windier at the summit than at the tram's base, so pack an appropriate jacket, as it would be a shame to spend most of your time at the top huddling inside the visitor center rather than walking around it to drink up the views.** You can also use the tram as a way to reach the Sandia Peak ski and mountain-biking area (⇨ *See* the Sandia Park section *of* the Side Trips from the Cities chapter). ✉ *10 Tramway Loop NE, Far Northeast Heights* ☎ *505/856–7325* ⊕ *www.sandiapeak.com* 🎫 *$15* ☉ *Memorial Day–Labor Day, daily 9–9; Sept.–May, daily 9–8.*

★ ☺ ❷ **Unser Racing Museum.** Albuquerque is home to the illustrious auto-racing family, the Unsers, whose four generations of drivers have dominated the sport since the early 20th century. The most famous of the clan include Bobby Unser Sr. and Al

WORD OF MOUTH
"If you decide to take the Tram in ABQ, go up just before sunset and watch the sun go down from the top! It is really neat."   –DebitNM

Unser Sr., and their assorted children and grandchildren. Exhibits at this state-of-the-art museum, which opened in fall 2005, include a display on Pikes Peak, Colorado, where the Unsers first began racing; a study of the family's legacy at the Indianapolis 500; memorabilia on the family and the industry; a technological look at race cars; and several vintage autos. ⊠ *1776 Montaño Rd. NW, North Valley* ☎ *505/341–1776* ⊕ *www.unserracingmuseum.com* ☐ *$7* ☼ *Daily 10–4.*

WHERE TO EAT

Here's some news that might surprise foodies: when you get right down to it, Albuquerque has nearly as many sophisticated, inspired restaurants as vaunted Santa Fe. The trick is finding them all amid Albuquerque's miles of ubiquitous chain options (most of the better restaurants are on the North Side, along the I–25 corridor) and legions of other less-than-savory dives, but if you look, you'll be rewarded with innovative food, and generally at prices much lower than in Santa Fe or other major Southwestern cities. The Duke City has long been a place for hearty home-style cooking in big portions, and to this day, it's easy to find great steak-and-chops houses, retro diners, and authentic New Mexican restaurants, most of them offering plenty of grub for the price.

Until the early 2000s, it had been a bit more challenging to find truly memorable independent restaurants serving contemporary and creative fare, but the scene has changed a lot since then and continues to evolve. Particularly in Nob Hill, downtown, and Old Town, hip new restaurants have opened, offering swank decor and complex and artful variations on modern Southwest, Mediterranean, Asian, and other globally inspired cuisine. The city has also made tremendous strides with its ethnic cuisine—fine Greek, Japanese, Korean, Persian, Thai, Vietnamese, and South American restaurants continue to open at a rapid rate all over town, making this New Mexico's best destination for ethnic fare.

WHAT IT COSTS				
$$$$	$$$	$$	$	¢
RESTAURANTS over $30	$24–$30	$17–$24	$10–$17	under $10

Prices are per person for a main course at dinner, excluding 8.25% sales tax.

American–Casual

¢–$ ✕ **66 Diner.** Dining at this '50s-style art deco diner is a must for fans of Route 66 nostalgia, and the upbeat decor and friendly service also make it a hit with families. The specialties here are many: chicken-fried steak, burgers, malted milk shakes, enchiladas. Plenty of breakfast treats are available, too. ⊠ *1405 Central Ave. NE, University of New Mexico* ☎ *505/247–1421* ⊕ *www.66diner. com* ☐ *AE, D, MC, V.*

> **DID YOU KNOW?**
>
> The mean altitude of the entire state of New Mexico is more than a mile above sea level.

Barbecue

¢–$$ ✕**Quarters BBQ.** All you've ever dreamed of finding in a barbecue joint awaits you when you walk into this dark den. The Albuquerque institution, going strong since the early '70s, serves tender, smoky, falling-off-the-bone ribs and chicken, brisket, and sausage—it's hard to know where to dive in first. You'll need a fistful of napkins, that's for sure. The sauce is more tangy than sweet, and slow smoking with a secret recipe makes for the winning combination. Top steaks and Alaskan king crab legs are also available. ✉ *801 Yale Blvd. SE, University of New Mexico* ☎ *505/843–7505* ▭ *AE, MC, V* ☺ *Closed Sun.*

Brazilian

$–$$ ✕**Tucanos Brazilian Grill.** There isn't much point in going to Tucanos if you don't love meat. Sure, they serve some vegetables, but the real focus is on *churrascos*, South American–style grilled skewers of beef, chicken, pork, and turkey that parade endlessly out of the open kitchen on the arms of enthusiastic waiters. Carnivority aside, one unexpected treat, if it's available, is the grilled pineapple. The noisy, high-ceiling spot next to the downtown Century 14 Downtown movie theater is a good place to go for drinks, too, and if you're looking for either a stand-alone cooler or a liquid partner for your hearty fare, look no further than a bracing *caipirinha*, the lime-steeped national cocktail of Brazil. ✉ *110 Central Ave. SW, Downtown* ☎ *505/246–9900* ⊕ *www.tucanos.com* ▭ *AE, D, MC, V.*

Cafés

★ ¢–$ ✕**Flying Star.** Flying Star has become a staple and mini-phenom for many Albuquerqueans, and although it's a chain, each outpost offers something a little different. The cavernous downtown branch opened in 2005, and it's become a favorite for its striking setting inside the historic Southern Union Gas Co. building, designed by John Gaw Meem in 1950. The concept works on many levels: it's a newsstand,

> **WORD OF MOUTH**
>
> "A good, varied local diner chain. Venues fit their surroundings; go to the Central one for the university crowd, the Rio Grande for outdoor seating with pets, the two NE Heights for families."
>
> –Xander on Flying Star

late-night coffeehouse (there's free Wi-Fi), a bakery, and a great restaurant serving a mix of creative Asian, American, and New Mexican dishes (plus several types of wine and beer). Great options include Greek pasta with shrimp, green-chile cheeseburgers, Thai-style tofu salad with tangy lime dressing, turkey and Jack cheese melt sandwiches, and *machacado* (a breakfast casserole of turkey sausage, bacon, eggs, black beans, cheddar-jack cheese, potatoes, onions, tomatoes, and red and green chile). Desserts change often, but there's always a tantalizing array of cakes, pies, cookies, and brownies. For a winning pick-me-up, employ some strong hot coffee to wash down a tall slice of the fantastic coconut cream pie.

The Far Northeast Heights branch has the largest and most attractive patio of the bunch, with great views of the Sandia Mountains. It's a good bet if you're hungry after a visit to the Sandia Peak Aerial Tramway, and this branch also has an especially large work area where you can plug in your laptop and enjoy the free Wi-Fi. The Nob Hill locale is the most atmospheric, drawing college students, yuppies, gays and lesbians, artsy types, and all other walks of life. This branch is open the latest, it's set amid the funky shops along Nob Hill's historic Route 66, and it's not far from the airport, making it perfect for a quick pre- or post-flight meal. The North Valley locale is ideal for a break if you're visiting Rio Grande Nature Center State Park or the North Valley wineries, or you've just gone hot-air ballooning. The Uptown branch is close to a pair of shopping malls and has the same great food and vibe of the other branches, but this one has the smallest dining room of the bunch. Opened in August 2006, the West Side outpost is just south of the Corrales border, perfect if you're exploring the antiques shops and wineries of this funky little town or you've just been to either Petroglyphs National Monument or the Balloon Fiesta Park, which is just a couple of miles to the east. ⊠ *723 Silver Ave., Downtown* ☎ *505/244–8099* ⊠ *4501 Juan Tabo Blvd., Far Northeast Heights* ☎ *505/275–8311* ⊠ *3416 Central Ave. SE, Nob Hill* ☎ *505/255–6633* ⊠ *4026 Rio Grande NW, North Valley* ☎ *505/344–6714* ⊠ *8001 Menaul Blvd., Uptown* ☎ *505/293–6911* ⊠ *10700 Corrales Rd., West Side* ☎ *505/938–4717* ⊕ *www.flyingstarcafe.com* ⊟ *AE, D, DC, MC, V.*

★ ¢–$ ✕ **Gold Street Caffe.** A culinary cornerstone of downtown Albuquerque's renaissance, this dapper storefront café with exposed-brick walls and high ceilings serves some of the tastiest breakfast fare in town, plus lunch and dinner entrées. In the morning, go with eggs Eleganza (two poached eggs atop a green-chile brioche with local goat cheese), along with a side of honey–red chile–glazed bacon. Later in the day, consider polenta-dusted tilapia with a sundried-tomato cream sauce, or seared-beef chopped salad with fried rice noodles and chile-lime vinaigrette. You can also just hang out among the hipsters and office workers, sipping a caramel latte and munching on one of the tasty desserts. ⊠ *218 Gold Ave. SW, Downtown* ☎ *505/765–1633* ⊟ *MC, V* ⊗ *No dinner Sun. and Mon.*

Contemporary

$$–$$$$ ✕ **Ambrozia Cafe & Wine Bar.** In a modest but charming bungalow on the edge of Old Town, Ambrozia scores raves in part for its exhaustive wine list, but also for its ambitiously creative food. You might begin with the signature lobster "corn dog"—skewered lobster tails with jalapeño corn batter, served with chipotle ketchup, mustard cream, and avocado rémoulade. Next consider citrus-marinated pork loin grilled over charred tomato and chorizo grits with black bean–corn salsa and a

> **WORD OF MOUTH**
>
> "The hostess seated us in the back room which I felt claustrophobic in, so like the three bears, we ended up in the middle room. Very nice." –Dave on the Ambrozia Cafe

sweet plantain crema. Presentation here is just as artful as the food it-self. The dining room is clean and simple, the perfect backdrop for such colorful food. There's a popular happy hour on weekdays where discounted wines by the glass are served, and Sunday brunch here is terrific. ⊠ *108 Rio Grande Blvd. NW, Old Town* ☎*505/242–6560* ⊕*www.ambroziacafe. com* ▭ *AE, D, DC, MC, V* ⊗ *Closed Mon. No dinner Sun.*

$$–$$$$
Fodor's Choice
★
✕**Bien Shur.** The panoramic city and mountain views are part of the draw at this fine restaurant on the top floor of the stunning seven-story San-dia Casino complex, but Bien Shur is also one of the most sophisticated restaurants in the city. Even if you're not much for gambling, it's worth coming here for chef Salim Khoury's superbly crafted contemporary fare. You might start with beef carpaccio with marinated Vidalia onions and black-truffle oil, before moving on to Chilean seabass poached in olive oil with spinach risotto, or grilled Rocky Mountain elk chops with smoked corn–and–green chile tamales and blackberry jus. ⊠ *Sandia Re-sort & Casino, Tramway Rd. NE just east of I–25, Far Northeast Heights* ☎ *505/796–7500* ⊕ *www.sandiacasino.com* ▭ *AE, D, MC, V* ⊗ *Closed Mon. and Tues. No lunch.*

$–$$$$
✕**Seasons Rotisserie & Grill.** Upbeat yet elegant, this Old Town eatery is an easy place to have a business lunch or a dinner date, and it's con-venient to museums and shops. The kitchen serves innovative grills and pastas, such as wood-roasted duck breast with Gorgonzola–sweet po-tato gratin and grilled prime New York strip steak with garlic-mashed potatoes and black-truffle butter; great starters include seared raw tuna with cucumber-ginger slaw, and pecan-crusted three-cheese chiles rel-lenos with butternut squash coulis. The rooftop patio and bar provides evening cocktails and lighter meals. ⊠ *2031 Mountain Rd. NW, Old Town* ☎ *505/766–5100* ⊕ *www.seasonsonthenet.com* ▭ *AE, D, DC, MC, V* ⊗ *No lunch weekends.*

$$–$$$
Fodor's Choice
★
✕**Artichoke Cafe.** Locals praise the Artichoke for its service and French, contemporary American, and Italian dishes prepared, whenever possi-ble, with organically grown ingredients. Specialties include house-made ravioli stuffed with ricotta and butternut squash with a white wine, sage, and butter sauce; and pan-seared sea scallops wrapped in prosciutto with red potatoes, haricots vert, and wax beans. The appetizers are so tasty you may want to make a meal out of them. The building is about a cen-tury old, in the historic Huning Highland district on the eastern edge of downtown, but the decor is uptown modern. The two-tier dining room spills out into a small courtyard. ⊠ *424 Central Ave. SE, Downtown* ☎ *505/243–0200* ⊕ *www.artichokecafe.com* ▭ *AE, D, DC, MC, V* ⊗ *Closed Sun. No lunch Sat.*

★ **$$–$$$**
✕**Zinc Wine Bar and Bistro.** A snazzy spot in lower Nob Hill, fairly close to UNM, Zinc captures the essence of a San Francisco neighborhood bistro with its high ceilings, hardwood floors, and white tablecloths and dark-wood straight-back café chairs. You can drop in to sample wine from the long list, nosh on tasty contemporary cooking, or listen to live music downstairs in the Blues Cellar. From the kitchen, consider the starter of asparagus-and-artichoke tart with baby greens and spicy dried-fruit tapenade; or the main dish of oven-roasted wild Alaskan halibut with a Parmesan-asparagus risotto cake, braised leek, and fennel, with a

roasted–red pepper vinaigrette. The kitchen uses organic ingredients whenever available. ✉ *3009 Central Ave. NE, Nob Hill* ☎ *505/254–9462* ⊕ *www.zincabq.com* ⊟ *AE, D, MC, V* ☯ *No lunch Sat.*

★ **$–$$** ✕ **Slate Street Cafe.** An airy, high-ceiling dining room with a semi-circular central wine bar and modern lighting, this stylish restaurant sits amid pawn shops and bail bond outposts on a quiet, unprepossessing side street downtown. But once inside, you'll find a thoroughly sophisticated, colorful space serving memorable, modern renditions of classic American fare, such as fried chicken and meat loaf. The starters are especially notable, including Japanese-style fried rock shrimp with orange habañero sauce, and bruschetta topped with honey-cured ham and Brie. Banana-stuffed brioche French toast is a favorite at breakfast and Saturday brunch. More than 30 wines by the glass are served. ✉ *515 Slate St. NW, Downtown* ☎ *505/243–2210* ⊕ *www.slatestreetcafe.com* ⊟ *AE, D, MC, V* ☯ *Closed Sun.*

¢–$ ✕ **Graze.** Local star-chef Jennifer James helms the kitchen at this bright

Fodor'sChoice and informal tapas-inspired restaurant. Here in this airy, high-ceiling

★ dining room you can nosh on small plates of creative and generally healthful ingredients bursting with big flavors. Consider buttermilk-soaked fried calamari with sweet onions, chickpeas, baby tomatoes, and sambal oil; linguini tossed with smoked trout, capers, and preserved lemon; or ancho-barbecue pork spare ribs with corn on the cob—or just nosh on a selection of artisanal cheeses or a few of James's signature deviled eggs. Next door, try a mango margarita in Graze's sexy lounge, Gulp. ✉ *3128 Central Ave. SE, Nob Hill* ☎ *505/268–4729* ⊕ *www.grazejj.com* ⊟ *AE, D, MC, V* ☯ *Closed Sun. and Mon.*

¢–$ ✕ **Standard Diner.** In the historic Huning Highland district just east of downtown, the Standard opened in 2006 inside a 1930s Texaco station with high ceilings, massive plate-glass windows, and rich tile floors—it's at once thoroughly elegant yet totally casual, serving upscale yet affordable takes on traditional diner standbys. The long, interesting menu dabbles in meal-size salads (try the chicken-fried-lobster Caesar salad), burgers (including a terrific one topped with crab cakes and hollandaise sauce), sandwiches, and traditional diner entrées given nouvelle flourishes (Moroccan-style

> **GOOD TERM**
>
> If you want both green or red chile peppers with your meal, ask your server for "Christmas."

pot roast, mac and cheese with smoked salmon and green chiles, flat-iron steak with poblano cream sauce and bell pepper–ginger puree). Kick everything up with a side of wasabi-mashed potatoes, and save room for the twisted tiramisu (espresso-soaked lady fingers, dulce de leche mascarpone, agave-poached pears, and candied pine nuts. ✉ *320 Central Ave. SE, Downtown* ☎ *505/243–1440* ⊟ *AE, D, MC, V.*

Continental

$–$$ ✕ **St. Clair Winery and Bistro.** The state's largest winery, located in the southern New Mexico town of Deming, St. Clair Winery has a charming and affordable restaurant and tasting room in Old Town. It's part of a small shopping center on the west side of the neighborhood, just south of I–40. You enter a shop with a bar for wine tasting and shelves of wines and gourmet goods, which leads into the dark and warmly lighted dining room. There's also a large, attractive patio. At lunch, sample the panini sandwich of New Mexico goat cheese and roasted peppers. Dinner treats include crab-and-artichoke dip, garlic chicken slow-cooked in chardonnay, and pork tenderloin with merlot and raspberry-chipotle sauce. On weekends, St. Clair serves a popular Sunday brunch. ⊠ *901 Rio Grande Blvd., Old Town* ☎ *505/243–9916 or 888/870–9916* ⊕ *www.stclairvineyards.com* ⊟ *AE, D, MC, V.*

French

$–$$$ ✕ **Cafe Voila.** Despite its Northeast Heights setting in a modern shopping center surrounded by sleek, contemporary office parks, Cafe Voila feels thoroughly Parisian in spirit and ambience, thanks in part to the welcoming staff led by owners and hosts Debbie and Christian Tournier. Choose a seat in the romantic, flower- and plant-filled dining room or on the sunny patio. The kitchen prepares everything here from scratch, with specialties that include crepes with leeks and salmon, lobster ravioli in creamy saffron sauce, braised veal shank with red-wine demi-glace, and fresh Dover sole with almond-butter sauce. Top everything off with a slice of cheesecake finished with raspberry coulis. ⊠ *7600 Jefferson St. NE, Northeast Heights* ☎ *505/821–2666* ⊕ *www.cafevoila.com/* ⊟ *AE, MC, V* ⊙ *Closed Sun. No dinner Mon.*

Greek

$–$$ ✕ **Yanni's Mediterranean Grill and Opa Bar.** Yanni's is a casual, airy place serving marinated grilled lamb chops with lemon and oregano, grilled yellowfin sole encrusted with Parmesan cheese, pastitsio (a Greek version of mac and cheese), and spinach, feta, and roasted garlic pizzas. The popular vegetarian plate includes a surprisingly good meatless moussaka, tabouleh, spanako-

> **WORD OF MOUTH**
>
> "Yanni's Mediterranean is somewhat of a local monument. What started out as a small gyro restaurant has blossomed into one of Albuquerque's top eateries."
> –Natalie Peters

pita, and stuffed grape leaves. There's a huge patio off the main dining room, and next door you can sip cocktails and mingle with locals at Opa Bar. ⊠ *3109 Central Ave. NE, Nob Hill* ☎ *505/268–9250* ⊕ *www.yannisandopabar.com* ⊟ *AE, D, MC, V.*

Italian

★ **$–$$$** ✕ **Scalo Northern Italian Grill.** Nob Hill trendsetters have long gathered at this informal art deco eatery to experience well-chosen Italian wines and first-rate pasta, seafood, and grills. Most of the multilevel dining area looks onto the lively bar and an open kitchen. Best bets include roasted wild salmon with warm spinach and bacon salad, and grilled double pork chops with pear-cherry conserves, Gorgonzola-mashed po-

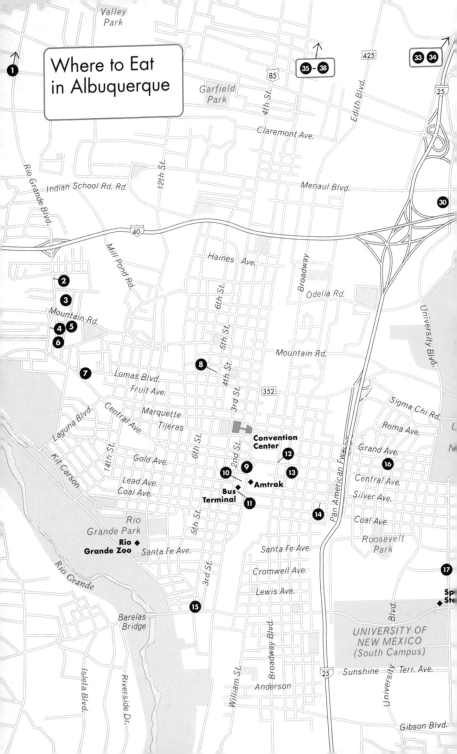

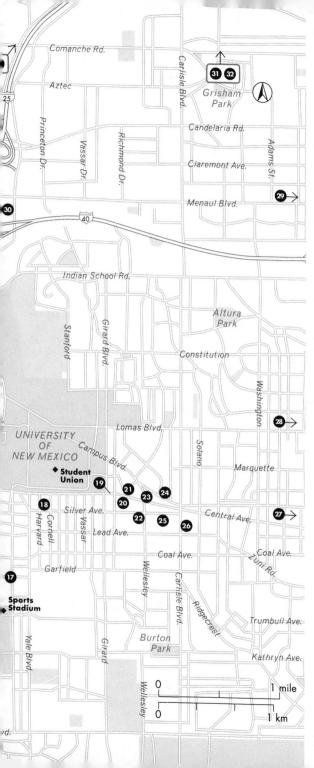

tatoes, and sautéed radicchio. The homemade desserts are mighty fine, among them lemon–goat cheese cheesecake with fresh berry compote. ⊠ *Nob Hill Shopping Center, 3500 Central Ave. SE, Nob Hill* ☎ *505/ 255–8781* ⊟ *AE, DC, MC, V* ⊗ *No lunch Sun.*

Japanese

¢–$ ✕ **Crazy Fish.** A good bet for relatively straightforward sushi and sashimi, Crazy Fish is an attractive, upbeat storefront space with minimal fuss and gimmickry—just clean lines and a black-and-gray color scheme. Friendly young servers whisk out plates of fresh food to a mix of students and yuppies. In addition to sushi, the kitchen prepares such favorites as crispy chicken, and seared-albacore salad with a ginger-soy dressing. Tempura-fried bananas make for a sweet ending. ⊠ *3015 Central Ave. NE, Nob Hill* ☎ *505/232–3474* ⊟ *AE, D, MC, V* ⊗ *Closed Sun. and Mon.*

New Mexican

$–$$ ✕ **Casa de Benavidez.** The fajitas at this sprawling local favorite with a romantic patio are among the best in town, and the chile is faultless; the burger wrapped inside a sopaipilla is another specialty, as are the chimichangas packed with beef. The charming restaurant occupies a late-19th-century Territorial-style house. ⊠ *8032 4th St. NW, North Valley* ☎ *505/898–3311* ⊕ *casadebenavidez.net* ⊟ *AE, D, DC, MC, V* ⊗ *No dinner Sun.*

★ ¢–$$ ✕ **Monica's El Portal.** Locals in the know favor this rambling, assuredly authentic New Mexican restaurant on the west side of Old Town over the more famous, though less reliable, standbys around Old Town Plaza. Monica's has a prosaic dining room plus a cute tiled patio, and the service is friendly and unhurried yet efficient. If you've never had *chicharrones* (fried pork skins), try them here with beans stuffed inside a flaky sopaipilla. Or consider the traditional blue-corn chicken or beef enchiladas, and the savory green-chile stew. This is honest, home-style food, and lunch here may just fill you up for the rest of the day. ⊠ *321 Rio Grande Blvd. NW, Old Town* ☎ *505/247–9625* ⊟ *AE, D, MC, V* ⊗ *Closed Mon. No dinner weekends.*

¢–$ ✕ **El Patio.** A university-area hangout, this sentimental favorite has consistently great food served in the funky patio. Go for the green-chile chicken
Fodor'sChoice enchiladas, the best in town, or any of the heart-healthy and vegetarian selections. But watch out for the fiery green chiles served at harvest-time. Note that liquor isn't served, but beer and wine are—they do make decent-tasting "margaritas" using wine. ⊠ *142 Harvard St. NE, University of New Mexico* ☎ *505/268–4245* ⌫ *Reservations not accepted* ⊟ *MC, V.*

¢–$ ✕ **Los Cuates.** A short drive northeast of Nob Hill and UNM, Los Cuates doesn't get as much attention as some of the city's more touristy New Mexican restaurants, but the food here is purely delicious, prepared with pure vegetable oil rather than lard, which is one reason it's never as greasy as at some competitors. Also, the green chile stew is vegetarian (unless you request meat). All the usual favorites are served here, but top picks include the roast-beef burrito covered with melted cheese, and the tostada *compuesta* (a corn tortilla stuffed with beef, beans, rice, potatoes, carne adovada, and chile con queso). ⊠ *5016–B Lomas Blvd. NE, Nob Hill* ☎ *505/268–0974* ⊕ *www.loscuatesrestaurants.com* 🍴 *Reservations not accepted* ⊟ *AE, D, DC, MC, V.*

¢–$ ✕ **Sadie's.** One of the city's longtime favorites for simple but spicy no-nonsense New Mexican fare, Sadie's occupies a long, fortresslike adobe building. Specialties include carne adovada, spicy beef burritos, and chiles rellenos. The service is always prompt, though sometimes there's a wait for a table. While you're waiting, try one of the excellent margaritas. Sadie's salsa is locally renowned and available by the jar for takeout. ⊠ *6230 4th St. NW, North Valley* ☎ *505/345–5339* ⊕ *www.sadiessalsa.com* ⊟ *AE, D, MC, V.*

★ ¢ ✕ **Barelas Coffee House.** Barelas may look like a set in search of a script, but it's the real deal: diners come from all over the city to sup in this old-fashioned chile parlor in the Hispanic Historic Route 66 neighborhood south of downtown. You may notice looks of quiet contentment on the faces of the many dedicated chile eaters as they dive into their bowls of Barelas's potent red. There's also tasty breakfast fare. The staff treats everybody like an old friend—indeed, many of the regulars who come here have been fans of Barelas for decades. ⊠ *1502 4th St. SW, Barelas* ☎ *505/843–7577* 🍴 *Reservations not accepted* ⊟ *D, MC, V* ☾ *Closed Sun. No dinner.*

¢ ✕ **Duran's Central Pharmacy.** This expanded Old Town lunch counter with a dozen tables and a tiny patio just might serve the best tortillas in town. A favorite of old-timers who know their way around a blue-corn enchilada, Duran's is an informal place whose patrons give their food the total attention it deserves. ⊠ *1815 Central Ave. NW, Old Town* ☎ *505/ 247–4141* ⊟ *No credit cards* ☾ *No dinner.*

Pizza

¢ ✕ **Il Vicino.** The gourmet pizzas at Il Vicino are baked in a European-style wood-fired oven. If a suitable combination of the 25 possible toppings eludes you, try the rustica pie, a buttery cornmeal crust topped with roasted garlic, artichokes, kalamata olives, and capers. The kitchen also turns out excellent Caesar salad, spinach lasagna, and designer

> **WORD OF MOUTH**
>
> "[It has a] wood oven, variety of fine quality toppings and, surprise, good olive oil to accentuate. And good microbrew to boot."
>
> –Andrew Mook on Il Vicino

sandwiches. It's also a great place to sample house-brewed beers, including the Wet Mountain India Pale Ale, which consistently wins awards at the Great American Beer Festival. There's another branch, usually less crowded, in a shopping center not too far from Sandia Peak Aerial Tramway. ⊠ *3403 Central Ave. NE, Nob Hill* ☎ *505/266–7855* ⊠ *11225 Montgomery Blvd., Far Northeast Heights* ☎ *505/271–0882* ⊕ *www.ilvicino.com* 🍴 *Reservations not accepted* ⊟ *MC, V.*

Steak

$$–$$$$ ✕ **Gruet Steakhouse.** The acclaimed Gruet winemaking family operates this chic but casual steak house inside the historic Monte Vista Fire Station, a 1930s WPA-built beauty in the heart of Nob Hill. More than a mere showcase for promoting Gruet's outstanding sparkling wines, pinot noirs, and chardonnays, the steak house presents con-

> **GOOD TERM**
>
> Kiva fireplace: A corner fireplace whose round form resembles that of a kiva, a ceremonial room used by Native Americans of the Southwest.

sistently excellent food (including an addictive side dish, lobster-whipped potatoes). Among the apps, try the panfried Dungeness crab cake with a traditional rémoulade sauce. The flat-iron steak topped with chunky Maytag blue cheese is a favorite main dish, along with the rare ahi tuna Wellington with wild mushroom duxelle and seared foie gras. Finish off with a distinctive rose-water-infused ricotta cheesecake topped with candied oranges and toasted-almond sugar. A kiva fireplace warms the patio in back. The same owners run Gruet Grille, a contemporary bistro in Northeast Heights. ⊠ *3201 Central Ave. NE, Nob Hill* ☎ *505/256–9463* ⊕ *www.gruetsteakhouse.com* ⊟ *AE, D, MC, V* ◷ *No lunch.*

$$–$$$$ ✕ **Rancher's Club.** Hotel restaurants in Albuquerque aren't generally special dining destinations in and of themselves, but this clubby, old-world steak house in the Albuquerque Hilton earns raves among carnivores for its delicious aged steaks and ribs. The dining room is hung with saddles, mounted bison heads, and ranching-related art. If you're looking to impress a date or clients, order the sublime fillet of Kobe beef with cream spinach, lobster-mashed potatoes, and morel-mushroom jus. Other great standbys include elk chops, fillet of ostrich, porterhouse steak, and the Hunter's Grill of antelope, venison, and wild boar sausage. ⊠ *Albuquerque Hilton, 1901 University Blvd. NE, Midtown* ☎ *505/889–8071* ⊟ *AE, D, DC, MC, V* ◷ *No lunch weekends.*

$–$$$ ✕ **Council Room Steakhouse.** Set just off the main lobby of the snazzy Sandia Resort & Casino, the clubby, softly lighted Council Room offers a relaxing alternative to the clattering slot machines of the gaming area, which is safely out of earshot. The kitchen here turns out reasonably priced, classic renditions of old-school steak-house favorites, from the beer-battered megastack of onion rings to a chilled iceberg lettuce wedge topped with beefsteak tomatoes and bacon and slathered in blue cheese dressing. In addition to the usual steak cuts, consider the full rack of smoked baby back ribs, or the Colorado lamb shank braised with tomatoes, raisins, and pine nuts and served with garlic-mashed potatoes. The house margaritas are stellar even by New Mexico standards. Try the green-chile apple pie, a spicy-sweet marriage that works far better than you'd ever expect. ⊠ *Sandia Resort & Casino, Tramway Rd. NE, just east of I–25, Far Northeast Heights* ☎ *505/796–7500* ⊕ *www.sandiacasino. com* ⊟ *AE, D, MC, V* ◷ *No lunch.*

$–$$$ ✕ **High Noon Restaurant and Saloon.** In a former woodworking shop in one of Old Town's late-18th-century adobe buildings, touristy but festive High Noon literally exudes warmth with its kiva fireplaces and is accented further by viga ceilings, brick floors, handmade Southwestern furniture, New Mexican art, and a copper-top bar. The kitchen delivers decent steaks and such traditional New Mexico favorites as beef enchiladas and green-chile stew. Among menu highlights are bison rib eye, twin pork medallions encrusted with pine nuts with a red-chile coulis, and flame-broiled fresh salmon. From Thursday to Sunday there's flamenco guitar. ⊠ *425 San Felipe St. NW, Old Town* ☎ *505/765–1455* ▭ *AE, D, DC, MC, V.*

> **WORD OF MOUTH**
>
> "We were certainly fooled by the outward appearance of this establishment. Once we ventured into [High Noon], it was one of our best dining experiences in ABQ."
> –Ben Gibson

Thai

¢–$ ✕ **Thai Crystal.** In a state that's sorely lacked good Thai restaurants until recently, this beautiful space filled with Thai artwork and decorative pieces has been a welcome addition to the blossoming Gold Street shopping district. The extensive menu includes a mix of typical Thai specialties (pineapple fried rice, chicken satay, beef panang curry) as well as some less predictable items, such as steamed mussels topped with red coconut curry, and pork sautéed with a spicy mint, chile, and onion sauce. ⊠ *109 Gold Ave. SW, Nob Hill* ☎ *505/244–3344* ▭ *AE, MC, V.*

Vietnamese

★ ¢ ✕ **May Cafe.** Few tourists ever make their way to this astoundingly inexpensive and wonderfully authentic Vietnamese restaurant a short drive east of Nob Hill, in an uninspired neighborhood just off old Route 66. Favorites from the extensive menu include rare-beef noodle soup; stir-fried noodles with veggies, fish balls, chicken, barbecue pork, and pork; spicy fish baked in a hot pot; and catfish with lemongrass sauce. You'll also find plenty of vegetarian options, including knock-out spring rolls. Friendly, prompt service and a simple, attractive dining room add to the experience. ⊠ *111 Louisiana Blvd. SE, Nob Hill* ☎ *505/265–4448* ▭ *AE, MC, V* ⊘ *Closed Sun.*

WHERE TO STAY

With few exceptions, Albuquerque's lodging options fall into two categories: modern chain hotels and motels, and distinctive and typically historic inns and B&Bs. Of larger hotels, you won't find many that are independently owned, historic, or especially rife with personality, although Central Avenue—all across the city—is lined with fascinating old motor courts and motels from the 1930s through the '50s, many of them with their original neon signs and quirky roadside architecture. Alas, nearly all of these are run-down and substandard; they should be avoided unless you're extremely adventurous and can't resist the super-low rates (often as little as $18 a night).

If you're seeking charm and history, try one of the many excellent inns and B&Bs (including those in Corrales and Bernalillo, just north of Albuquerque, listed in the Side Trips from the Cities chapter). Although the cookie-cutter chain hotels may appear largely interchangeable, there are several properties that stand out above the rest, and many of these are described below. Two parts of the city with an excellent variety of economic plain-Jane franchise hotels (Hampton Inn, Comfort Inn, Courtyard Marriott, etc.) are the Airport and the north I–25 corridor. As opposed to many other cities, Albuquerque's airport is extremely convenient to attractions and downtown, and the north I–25 corridor also offers easy access to sightseeing and dining as well as the Balloon Fiesta Park. Wherever you end up staying in Albuquerque, you can generally count on finding rates considerably lower than the national average, and much cheaper than in Santa Fe and Taos.

WHAT IT COSTS					
	$$$$	$$$	$$	$	¢
HOTELS	over $260	$190–$260	$130–$190	$70–$130	under $70

Prices are for two people in a standard double room in high season, excluding 12%–13% tax.

Downtown & Old Town

$$–$$$
Fodor'sChoice
★
🏨 **Embassy Suites Hotel Albuquerque.** This swanky new all-suites high-rise with a striking contemporary design sits on a bluff alongside I–40, affording guests fabulous views of the downtown skyline and vast desert mesas to the west, and the verdant Sandia Mountains to the east. Rooms are large, in the Embassy Suites tradition, all with living areas that have pull-out sleeper sofas, refrigerators, dining and work areas, microwaves, and coffeemakers. You'll also find two phones and two TVs in each suite. Included in the rates is a nightly reception with hors d'oeuvres and cocktails, and a full breakfast each morning. With so much living and sleeping space and a great location accessible to downtown, Nob Hill, and the airport, this is a great option if you're staying in town for a while or traveling with a family. ⊠ *1000 Woodward Pl. NE, 87102 Downtown* ☎ *505/245–7100 or 800/EMBASSY* 🖷 *505/247–1083* ⊕ *embassysuites.hilton.com* ⌁ *261 suites* ♨ *Dining room, refrigerators, cable TV, Wi-Fi, meeting rooms, bar, free parking* ☰ *AE, D, MC, V* ⏐◎⏐*BP.*

$$–$$$
🏨 **Hyatt Regency Albuquerque.** Adjacent to the Albuquerque Convention Center, the city's most sumptuous hotel comprises a pair of soaring, desert-color towers that figure prominently in the city's skyline. The gleaming art deco–inspired interior is refined and not overbearing. The contemporary rooms in mauve, burgundy, and tan combine Southwestern style with all the amenities you'd expect of a high-caliber business-oriented hotel, including Wi-Fi and plush bathrobes. McGrath's Bar and Grill serves steaks, chops, chicken, and seafood, and there's also a Starbucks on-site. ⊠ *330 Tijeras Ave. NW, 87102 Old Town* ☎ *505/842–1234 or 800/233–1234* 🖷 *505/766–6710* ⊕ *http://albuquerque.hyatt.com* ⌁ *395 rooms, 14 suites* ♨ *Restaurant, café, cable TV, Wi-Fi, pool, health*

1

club, massage, 2 bars, shops, business services, meeting rooms, parking (fee) ⊟ *AE, D, DC, MC, V.*

★ **$$–$$$** La Posada de Albuquerque. Opened in 1939 by Conrad Hilton (who honeymooned here with Zsa Zsa Gabor), this glamorous 10-story hotel on the National Register of Historic Places captures vintage New Mexico's elegance—the lobby bar is one of the classiest places around for cocktails. The tiled lobby fountain, circular balcony, massive vigas, and Native American murals lend the place an easy Southwestern charm. As of this writing, the hotel was closed and in the midst of a massive refurbishment, which is expected to capture the hotel's original splendor but also infuse it with much-needed modern touches and amenities. The new incarnation of the hotel is expected to reopen in spring 2007. Guests have privileges at a health club across the street. ⊠ *125 2nd St. NW, 87102 Old Town* ☎ *505/242–9090 or 800/777–5732* 🖷 *505/242–8664* ⊕ *www.laposada-abq.com* 🛏 *110 rooms, 4 suites* ⚶ *Restaurant, room service, some microwaves, cable TV, massage, 2 bars, laundry service, meeting rooms, parking (fee)* ⊟ *AE, D, DC, MC, V.*

$–$$ Böttger Mansion of Old Town. Charles Böttger, a German immigrant, built this pink two-story mansion in 1912. The lacy, richly appointed rooms vary greatly in size and decor; some have four-poster beds, slate floors, claw-foot tubs, or pressed-tin ceilings. All have down comforters, fluffy pillows, and terry robes—and a few are said to be haunted by a friendly ghost or two. The Wine Cellar Suite, in the basement, can accommodate up to six guests and has a kitchenette. A grassy courtyard fronted by a patio provides an escape from the Old Town crowds. Breakfast might consist of stuffed French toast or perhaps burritos smothered in green chile, which you can also enjoy in your room. ⊠ *110 San Felipe St. NW, 87104 Old Town* ☎ *505/243–3639 or 800/758–3639* ⊕ *www.bottger.com* 🛏 *7 rooms, 1 2-bedroom suite* ⚶ *Some in-room hot tubs, some kitchenettes, cable TV, in-room VCRs, parking (fee); no smoking* ⊟ *AE, MC, V* ⏏ *BP.*

★ **$–$$** Casas de Suenos. This historic compound of 1930s- and '40s-era adobe casitas is perfect if you're seeking seclusion and quiet yet seek easy proximity to museums, restaurants, and shops—Casas de Suenos is a few blocks south of Old Town Plaza, but on a peaceful residential street fringing the lush grounds of Albuquerque Country Club. The individually decorated units, which open onto a warren of courtyards and gardens, come in a variety of shapes and configurations. Typical features include Saltillo-tile floors, wood-burning kiva-style fireplaces, leather or upholstered armchairs, skylights, and contemporary Southwestern furnishings. Many rooms have large flat-screen TVs with DVD players and CD stereos, and some sleep as many as four adults. The full breakfast is served outside in the garden when the weather permits, and inside a lovely artists' studio at other times. ⊠ *310 Rio Grande Blvd. SW, 87104 Old Town* ☎ *505/247–4560 or 800/665–7002* 🖷 *505/242–2162* ⊕ *www.casasdesuenos.com* 🛏 *21 casitas* ⚶ *Some kitchens, cable TV, some in-room DVD/VCRs, some in-room hot tubs, free parking* ⊟ *AE, MC, V* ⏏ *BP.*

$–$$ Doubletree Hotel. A two-story waterfall splashes down a marble backdrop in the lobby of this 15-story downtown hotel, with attractive, classy

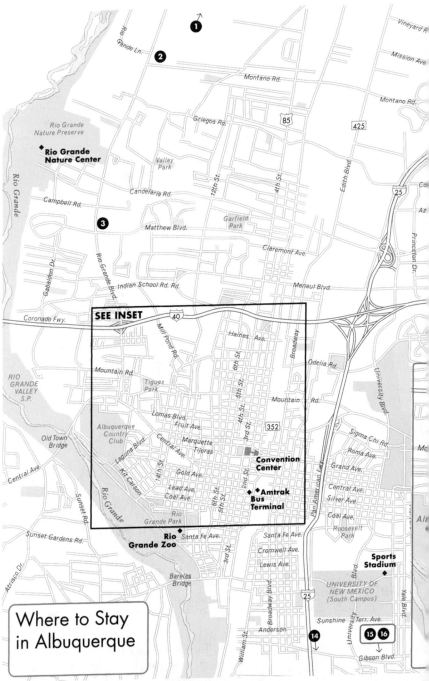

Where to Stay in Albuquerque

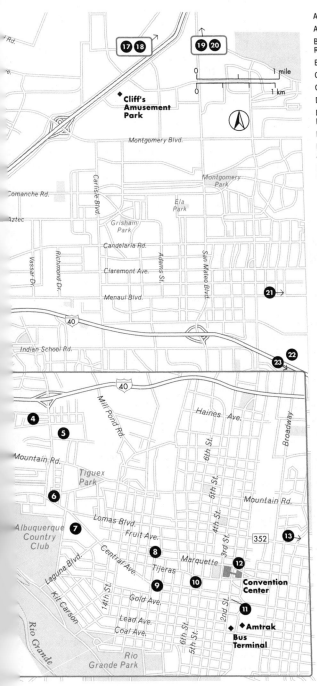

rooms that contain custom-made Southwestern furniture and complementary art. The restaurant at the foot of the waterfall is called, appropriately, La Cascada (The Cascade). Breakfast, a lunch buffet, and dinner, from fresh seafood to Southwestern specialties, are served. ⊠ *201 Marquette Ave. NW, 87102 Old Town* ☎ *505/247–3344 or 800/ 222–8733* 🖷 *505/247–7025* ⤶ *295 rooms* 🖧 *Restaurant, room service, cable TV, pool, bar, laundry service, business services, meeting rooms, parking (fee)* ▤ *AE, D, DC, MC, V.*

$–$$ ⊞ **Hotel Albuquerque at Old Town.** This modern 11-story hotel rises distinctly above Old Town's ancient structures. The large rooms have desert-color appointments, hand-wrought furnishings, and tile bathrooms with Southwest accents but a slightly dated look; every room has a small balcony with no patio furniture but nice views. Cristobal's serves commendable Spanish-style steaks and seafood, and Cafe Plazuela offers more casual American and New Mexican food. A fine flamenco guitarist entertains in the lounge. Treatments and facials are available at Joseph's Salon & Day Spa. ⊠ *800 Rio Grande Blvd. NW, 87104 Old Town* ☎ *505/843–6300 or 877/901–7666* 🖷 *505/842–8426* ⊕ *www.hotelabq. com* ⤶ *165 rooms, 22 suites* 🖧 *2 restaurants, room service, refrigerators, cable TV, pool, gym, spa, hot tub, massage, bar, business services, meeting rooms, free parking* ▤ *AE, D, DC, MC, V.*

$–$$
Fodor'sChoice
★
⊞ **Mauger Estate B&B.** This 1897 Queen Anne mansion was the first home in Albuquerque to have electricity. Oval windows with beveled and "feather-pattern" glass, hardwood floors, high ceilings, a redbrick exterior, and a front veranda are among the noteworthy design elements. Rooms have refrigerators and baskets stocked with munchies, triplesheeted beds with soft feather duvets, irons and boards, and fresh flowers. There's also a two-bedroom, two-bathroom town house next door. Guests have access to a full-service health club a few blocks away. The same owners run the outstanding Hacienda Antigua B&B in a quiet North Valley neighborhood, not far from the city's wineries and the Balloon Fiesta Park. ⊠ *701 Roma Ave. NW, 87102 Old Town* ☎ *505/242–8755 or 800/719–9189* 🖷 *505/842–8835* ⊕ *www.maugerbb.com* ⤶ *8 rooms, 1 2-bedroom town house* 🖧 *Refrigerators, cable TV, free parking, some pets allowed* ▤ *AE, D, DC, MC, V* ⋈ *BP.*

¢–$ ⊞ **Best Western Rio Grande Inn.** Although part of the Best Western chain, this contemporary four-story low-rise just off I–40—a 10-minute walk from Old Town's plaza—has an attractive Southwestern design and furnishings, plus such modern touches as free high-speed Internet. The heavy handcrafted wood furniture, tin sconces, and artwork in the rooms come from local suppliers and artisans. That locals are familiar with the Albuquerque Grill is a good indicator of the restaurant's reputation. It's a good value. ⊠ *1015 Rio Grande Blvd. NW, 87104 Old Town* ☎ *505/ 843–9500 or 800/959–4726* 🖷 *505/843–9238* ⊕ *www.riograndeinn. com* ⤶ *173 rooms* 🖧 *Restaurant, room service, refrigerators, cable TV, Wi-Fi, pool, gym, outdoor hot tub, bar, laundry facilities, business services, meeting rooms, free parking* ▤ *AE, D, DC, MC, V.*

¢–$ ⊞ **Hotel Blue.** Formerly a bland chain hotel, this 1960s four-story hotel received an art deco makeover in the early 2000s and rebranded itself as a trendy boutique property. In reality, it is intimate and the art deco rooms are fairly attractive (with white walls and furniture and simple black accents), but it would be a serious stretch to call this place hip or truly of the boutique genre. Still, although it's not fancy, the rates are terrific considering the central location and great amenities, such as dual-line phones, free local calls, 25-inch TVs, hair dryers, and irons and ironing boards. It overlooks a small park, is a short stroll from downtown's many lively music clubs and restaurants, and is a short drive or 15-minute walk from Old Town. ✉ *717 Central Ave. NW, 87102 Old Town* ☎ *505/924–2400 or 877/878–4868* 🖷 *505/924–2465* ⊕ *www. thehotelblue.com* 🛏 *125 rooms, 10 suites* ⚐ *Restaurant, cable TV with movies, pool, gym, bar, meeting rooms, free parking* 🖃 *AE, D, DC, MC, V* ⊙| *CP.*

Uptown

$–$$ ⛉ **Albuquerque Marriott.** This 17-story upscale uptown property draws a mix of business and leisure travelers; it's close to two shopping malls and not too far from Nob Hill. Kachina dolls, Native American pottery, and other regional artworks decorate the elegant public areas. The rooms are traditional American, with walk-in closets, armoires, and crystal lamps, but have Southwestern touches. Rooms on all but the first few floors enjoy staggering views, either of Sandias to the east or the vast mesas to the west. Ceilo Sandia specializes in steaks and contemporary New Mexican fare. ✉ *2101 Louisiana Blvd. NE, 87110 Uptown* ☎ *505/881–6800 or 800/228–9290* 🖷 *505/888–2982* ⊕ *www.marriott. com* 🛏 *405 rooms, 6 suites* ⚐ *Restaurant, room service, refrigerators, cable TV with movies, some in-room VCRs, indoor-outdoor pool, gym, hot tub, sauna, bar, laundry facilities, laundry service, concierge floor, business services, meeting rooms, free parking* 🖃 *AE, D, DC, MC, V.*

$ ⛉ **Sheraton Albuquerque Uptown.** Within easy distance of the airport and a couple shopping malls, this newly renovated property meets the consistent Sheraton standard with a compact but pleasant lobby with a cozy bar area and a tiny gift shop. Earthy and muted reds, oranges, and sand-shaded colors accent the lobby and functional but ample rooms, whose nicer touches include a second sink outside the bathroom, comfy mattresses, and bathrobes. ✉ *2600 Louisiana Blvd. NE, 87110 Uptown* ☎ *505/881–0000 or 800/252–7772* 🖷 *505/881–3736* ⊕ *www. sheratonuptown.com* 🛏 *294 rooms* ⚐ *Restaurant, room service, refrigerators, cable TV with movies and video games, Wi-Fi, indoor pool, gym, sauna, concierge floor, business services, meeting rooms* 🖃 *AE, D, DC, MC, V.*

⛺ **Albuquerque Central KOA.** At town's edge, off Historic Route 66 in the foothills of the Sandia Mountains, this well-equipped campground has expansive views, a dog run, and wireless Internet, but only a few trees. Reservations are essential in October. ✉ *12400 Skyline NE, Exit 166 off I–40, Uptown* ☎ *505/296–2729 or 800/562–7781* ⊕ *www. koakampgrounds.com* ⚐ *Grills, flush toilets, full hookups, partial hookups (electric and water), dump station, drinking water, guest laundry, showers, fire grates, picnic tables, electricity, public telephone, general store, service station, play area, swimming (pool)* 🛏 *206 sites, 100 with full hookup* 🖃 *$38–$62; cabins $47–$70* 🖃 *AE, D, MC, V.*

North Side

$$-$$$$ 🏨 **Sandia Resort & Casino.** Completed in early 2006 after much antici-
Fodor'sChoice pation, this seven-story casino resort has set the new standard for lux-
★ ury in Albuquerque. Ceramic bath tiles, walk-in showers with separate
tubs, 32-inch plasma TVs, handcrafted wooden furniture, louvered
wooden blinds, and muted, natural color palettes lend elegance to the
spacious rooms, most of which have sweeping views of the Sandia
Mountains or the Rio Grande Valley. The 700-acre grounds, which are
in the Far Northeast Heights, just across I–25 from Balloon Fiesta Park,
ensure privacy and quiet and include a superb golf course and an am-
phitheater that hosts top-of-the-line music and comedy acts. The fabu-
lous Green Reed Spa offers a wide range of treatments, many of them
using local clay and plantlife. One of the city's best restaurants, Bien
Shur, occupies the casino's top floor, and there are three other places to
eat on-site. The casino is open 24 hours. ⊠ *Tramway Rd. NE just east
of I–25, 87122 Old Town* ☎ *505/796–7500 or 800/526–9366* ⊕ *www.
sandiacasino.com* ⇗ *198 rooms, 30 suites* ⚭ *4 restaurants, room serv-
ice, cable TV, Wi-Fi, pool, hot tub, health club, spa, 18-hole golf course,
driving range, amphitheater, 3 bars, casino, laundry service, meeting
rooms, business center, free parking.*

$-$$$ 🏨 **Marriott Pyramid.** This curious ziggurat-shape 10-story building fits
in nicely with the other examples of postmodern architecture that have
sprung up in northern Albuquerque in recent years. It's the most upscale of a slew of reputable chain hotels in the area, and it's an excellent base for exploring the North Valley or even having somewhat easier
access to Santa Fe than the hotels downtown or near the airport. Rooms
have sponge-painted walls and dapper country French decor. They open
onto a soaring atrium lobby. Perks include evening turndown service
and newspapers delivered to the room each morning. ⊠ *5151 San Francisco Rd. NE, 87109 Northeast Heights* ☎ *505/821–3333 or 800/466–
8356* 🖷 *505/828–0230* ⊕ *www.marriott.com* ⇗ *248 rooms, 54 suites*
⚭ *Restaurant, room service, refrigerators, cable TV, Wi-Fi, pool, gym,
hot tub, bar, laundry facilities, laundry service, meeting rooms, free parking* ⊟ *AE, D, DC, MC, V.*

$$ 🏨 **Los Poblanos Inn.** Designed by acclaimed architect John Gaw Meem,
Fodor'sChoice this rambling, historic inn lies outside of Albuquerque's sprawl, on 25
★ acres of organic farm fields, lavender plantings, and gardens on the town's
north side, near the Rio Grande and just across the street from Ander-
son Valley Vineyards—with all the greenery and the quiet pace of life
here, you'd never know you're in the desert, or in the middle of one of
the Southwest's largest cities. You reach the inn via a spectacular tree-
lined lane. Every accommodation has a private entrance and contains
folk paintings, painted viga ceilings, and high-quality linens. Rooms also
contain bath products made on-site, including lavender soap and oils;
all have kiva fireplaces, too. The property also includes the 15,000-square-
foot La Quinta Cultural Center, a conference space available for meet-
ings that contains a dramatic fresco by Peter Hurd. There's also a library
with beautiful artwork. ⊠ *4803 Rio Grande Blvd. NW, 87107 North
Valley* ☎ *505/344–9297 or 866/344–9297* 🖷 *505/342–1302* ⊕ *www.*

lospoblanos.com ⌨ *3 rooms, 4 suites, 2 guest houses* ♿ *Some full kitchens, some refrigerators, cable TV in some rooms, some in-room VCR/ DVDs, Wi-Fi, massage, meeting rooms, free parking* ▤ *AE, MC, V* ⊙ *BP.*

★ **$–$$** ▦ **Cinnamon Morning B&B.** A private, beautifully maintained, pet-friendly compound set back from the road and a 10-minute drive north of Old Town, Cinnamon Morning is just south of Rio Grande Nature Center State Park and a perfect roost if you want to be close to the city's wineries and the launching areas used by most hot-air-ballooning companies. Three rooms are in the main house, a richly furnished adobe home with colorful decorations and a lush garden patio. Additionally, there's a secluded two-bedroom guest house with a bath, full kitchen, private entrance, living room, and fireplace; and a colorfully painted one-bedroom casita with a private patio, Mexican-style furnishings, a viga ceiling, and a living room with a sleeper sofa. The full breakfasts here are filling and delicious, served by a roaring fire in winter or in the courtyard in summer. ✉ *2700 Rio Grande Blvd. NW, 87104 North Valley* ☎ *505/345– 3541 or 800/214–9481* 🖷 *505/342–2283* ⊕ *www.cinnamonmorning. com* ⌨ *3 rooms, 1 casita, 1 guest house* ♿ *Some kitchenettes, cable TV in some rooms, in-room VCRs, Wi-Fi, some pets allowed* ⊙ *BP.*

★ **¢–$** ▦ **Nativo Lodge Hotel.** Although it's priced similarly to a number of generic midrange chain properties on the north side, this five-story property has more character than most, especially in the expansive public areas, bar, and restaurant, which have an attractive Southwestern motif that includes hand-carved panels depicting symbols from Native American lore and river-rock walls. Rooms have wing chairs, work desks, Wi-Fi, and dual-line phones. The hotel is just off I–25, but set back far enough to avoid highway noise; several movie theaters and a bounty of restaurants are nearby. ✉ *6000 Pan American Freeway NE, 87109 Northeast Heights* ☎ *505/798–4300 or 888/628–4861* ⊕ *www.buynewmexico.com* ⌨ *147 rooms, 3 suites* ♿ *Restaurant, room service, refrigerators, cable TV, Wi-Fi, pool, gym, hot tub, sauna, bar, laundry facilities, business services, meeting rooms, free parking* ▤ *AE, D, DC, MC, V.*

¢ ▦ **Inn at Paradise.** Near the first tee of the lush Paradise Hills Golf Club, this pleasant, well-priced B&B resort atop the West Mesa is a golfer's dream: the 6,895 yards of bluegrass fairways and bent-grass greens challenge players of all levels. Works by local artists and craftspeople decorate the large rooms, which are filled with attractive, if functional, contemporary furnishings; the two suites have fireplaces. Many rooms have balconies overlooking the golf course. Golf packages are available. It's an outstanding value and a good bet if you want to be close to Petroglyphs National Monument or Corrales. ✉ *10035 Country Club La. NW, 87114 West Side* ☎ *505/898–6161 or 800/938–6161* 🖷 *505/ 890–1090* ⊕ *www.innatparadise.com* ⌨ *16 rooms, 2 suites, 1 apartment* ♿ *Kitchens, cable TV, 18-hole golf course, hot tub, massage, free parking* ▤ *AE, D, MC, V* ⊙ *CP.*

¢ ▦ **Motel 6.** By far one of the cleanest and most pleasant of the dozens of super-cheap budget motels around town, this three-story no-frills cookie cutter sits along the I–25 access road on the north side, close to the Balloon Fiesta Park and Sandia Casino. There's no view and no ambience, but you can't beat the price, and all rooms are off safe interior hallways.

✉ *8510 Pan American Freeway NE, 87113 Northeast Heights* ☎ *505/ 821–1472 or 800/466–8356* 🖷 *505/821–7344* ⊕ *www.motel6.com* ⇆ *79 rooms* ⚫ *Cable TV, pool, laundry facilities, free parking, some pets allowed* ▭ *AE, D, DC, MC, V.*

Airport

★ **$–$$** 🏨 **Wyndham Albuquerque Hotel.** Only 350 yards from the airport, this 15-story hotel sits up high on a mesa with vast views of the Sandia Mountains to the east and downtown Albuquerque to the northwest. It's handy being so close to the terminal, and the Southwest-accented rooms have large work desks, data ports, and coffeemakers. Rojo Grill ranks among the better hotel restaurants in town. ✉ *2910 Yale Blvd. SE, 87106 Airport* ☎ *505/843–7000 or 800/996–3426* 🖷 *505/843–6307* ⊕ *www. wyndham.com* ⇆ *276 rooms, 2 suites* ⚫ *Restaurant, room service, cable TV, Wi-Fi, 2 tennis courts, pool, gym, lobby lounge, airport shuttle, free parking* ▭ *AE, D, DC, MC, V.*

$ 🏨 **Holiday Inn Select Albuquerque Airport.** Opened just west of the airport in 2006, this upscale, four-story hotel sits high on a bluff, affording nice views of downtown and the western mesa as well as the Sandia Mountains. Some suites have whirlpool tubs. The indoor pool and high-tech fitness room, along with a 24-hour business center, make this a favorite with business travelers. ✉ *1501 Sunport Pl. SE, 87106 Airport* ☎ *505/ 944–2255 or 800/315–2621* ⊕ *www.ichotelsgroup.com* ⇆ *110 rooms, 20 suites* ⚫ *Restaurant, room service, cable TV, Wi-Fi, some in-room hot tubs, indoor pool, gym, lobby lounge, laundry facilities, business center, airport shuttle, free parking* ▭ *AE, D, DC, MC, V.*

¢–$ 🏨 **Hampton Inn Airport.** The best of the mid-price options near the airport, the Hampton Inn can be counted on for clean, updated rooms with plenty of handy perks (free Wi-Fi, a pool, on-the-run breakfast bags to take with you to the airport or wherever you're off to that day). ✉ *2231 Yale Blvd. SE, 87106 Airport* ☎ *505/246–2255 or 800/426–7866* 🖷 *505/246–2255* ⊕ *www.hamptoninn.com* ⇆ *62 rooms, 9 suites* ⚫ *Dining room, cable TV, Wi-Fi, indoor pool, gym, hot tub, lobby lounge, laundry facilities, business services, meeting rooms, airport shuttle, free parking* ▭ *AE, D, DC, MC, V.*

NIGHTLIFE & THE ARTS

For the 411 on arts and nightlife, consult the Sunday editions of the *Albuquerque Journal* (⊕ www.abqjournal.com), the Friday edition of the *Albuquerque Tribune* (⊕ www.abqtrib.com), or the *Weekly Alibi* (⊕ www.alibi.com).

Nightlife

Bars & Lounges

Atomic Cantina (✉ 315 Gold Ave. SW, Downtown ☎ 505/242–2200), a hip downtown lounge popular for its cool juke box and extensive happy hours, draws a mix of students, yuppies, and music fans. Many nights there's live music, from punk to rockabilly to trance.

Carom Club (✉ 301 Central Ave. NW, Downtown ☎ 505/243–6520), opened in 2006 by billiards champ Ramona Biddle, is the city's premier billiards facility, with 21 tables plus a variety of TVs showing sports. This swanky lounge also serves up good food, from tuna tartare to blackened rib-eye steaks.

Graham Central Station (✉ 4770 Montgomery Blvd. NE, Northeast Heights ☎ 505/883–3041), part of a rowdy regional chain of massive nightclubs, consists of four distinct bars under one roof: country-western, rock, dance, and Latin. It's open Wednesday–Saturday.

Kelly's Brew Pub (✉ 3222 Central Ave. SE, Nob Hill ☎ 505/262–2739) occupies a stylish late-1930s former Ford dealer and service station. Drink house-brewed oatmeal stout or Belgian ale on the sprawling pet-friendly patio (you can get a bowl of dog food for $1.95) or inside the large dining room, and fill up on buffalo burgers, chicken wings, and guac and chips if you're feeling peckish.

Launchpad (✉ 422 Central Ave. SE, Downtown ☎ 505/255–8295) has long been a venue for some of the city's best rock and alternative bands.

Martini Grill (✉ 4200 Central Ave. SE, Nob Hill ☎ 505/242–4333) offers live piano in a swank setting; this gay-popular spot is also a respectable restaurant serving burgers, sandwiches, pastas, and salads.

O'Niell's Pub (✉ 4310 Central Ave. SE, Nob Hill ☎ 505/256–0564) moved into a handsome new space in summer 2006, where it continues to serve good Mexican and American comfort food and present jazz, bebop, and other musicians in a cheery neighborhood bar near the University of New Mexico.

O-PM (✉ 211 Gold Ave. SE, Downtown ☎ 505/243–0955) brings in a hip, well-dressed crowd for lounge music, live piano on some nights, and rotating art exhibits. The furnishings are cool and comfy, especially in the upstairs bar.

Pulse (✉ 4100 Central Ave. SE, Nob Hill ☎ 505/255–3334) ranks among the most popular of Albuquerque's handful of gay and lesbian bars, with a busy dance floor and a big patio out back.

Sauce–Liquid Lounge–Raw (✉ 405 Central Ave. SW, Downtown ☎ 505/242–5839) is really three hipster-infested bars in one. Dark and inviting with big, foofy cocktails and some of the top DJs in town, this cool compound is also a smart bet for curing the late-night munchies. At Raw, you can sample sushi and sake.

Casino

Sandia Casino (✉ Tramway Rd. NE at I–25, Far Northeast Heights ☎ 505/796–7500 or 800/526–9366 ⊕ www.sandiacasino.com) is a light, open, airy resort with an enormous gaming area brightened up by soaring ceilings and big windows. In addition to 1,700 slot machines, you'll find craps, blackjack, mini baccarat, and several versions of poker.

Comedy Clubs

Laff's Comedy Club (✉ 6001 San Mateo Blvd. NE, Northeast Heights ☎ 505/296–5653) serves up the live laughs (and dinner) Wednesday–Sunday.

Live Music

In addition to Sandia Casino, listed below, several casinos at Indian pueblos in the metro area book fairly prominent live-music acts.

The 12,000-seat **Journal Pavilion** (⊠ 5601 University Blvd. SE, Mesa del Sol ☎ 505/452–5100 or 505/246–8742 ⊕ www.journalpavilion.com) amphitheater attracts big-name acts such as Green Day, Nine Inch Nails, Stevie Nicks, and the Dave Matthews Band.

Outpost Performance Space (⊠ 210 Yale Blvd. SE, University of New Mexico ☎ 505/268–0044 ⊕ www.outpostspace.org) programs an eclectic slate, from local nuevo-folk to techno, jazz, and traveling East Indian ethnic.

From April through October, the 4,200-seat **Sandia Casino Amphitheater** (⊠ Tramway Rd. NE just east of I–25, Far Northeast Heights ☎ 505/796–7778 ⊕ www.sandiacasino.com) is part of the stunning Sandia Casino Resort & Casino, at the very northern end of the city. It hosts big-name music acts and comedians, such as Bill Cosby, Earth Wind and Fire, and Kenny Rogers.

The Arts

Music

The **New Mexico Symphony Orchestra** (☎ 505/881–8999 or 800/251–6676 ⊕ www.nmso.org) plays pops, Beethoven, and, at Christmas, Handel's *Messiah*. Most performances are at 2,000-seat Popejoy Hall.

Popejoy Hall (⊠ University of New Mexico Arts Center, Central Ave. NE at Stanford Dr. SE ☎ 505/277–4569 or 800/905–3315 ⊕ www.popejoyhall.com) presents concerts, from rock and pop to classical, plus comedy acts, lectures, and national tours of Broadway shows.

Theater

Albuquerque Little Theater (⊠ 224 San Pasquale Ave. SW, Old Town ☎ 505/242–4750 ⊕ www.swcp.com/-alt) is a nonprofit community troupe that's been going strong since 1930. Its staff of professionals teams up with local volunteer talent to produce comedies, dramas, musicals, and mysteries. The company theater, across the street from Old Town, was built in 1936 and designed by John Gaw Meem. It contains an art gallery, a large lobby, and a cocktail lounge.

★ The stunningly restored **KiMo Theater** (⊠ 423 Central Ave. NW, Downtown ☎ 505/768–3522 or 505/768–3544 ⊕ www.cabq.gov/kimo), a 1927 Pueblo Deco movie palace, is one of the best places in town to see anything. Jazz, dance—everything from traveling road shows to local song-and-dance acts—might turn up here. Former Albuquerque resident Vivian Vance of *I Love Lucy* fame once performed on the stage.

La Compania de Teatro de Albuquerque (☎ 505/242–7929), a bilingual theater company based at the KiMo Theater, performs classic and contemporary plays in English and Spanish during April, October, and December. The company also appears at the South Broadway Cultural Center.

Rodey Theater (✉ University of New Mexico Arts Center, Central and Stanford SE ☎ 505/277–4569 or 800/905–3315) stages student and professional plays and dance performances throughout the year, including the acclaimed annual Summerfest Festival of New Plays during July and the June Flamenco Festival.

SPORTS & THE OUTDOORS

Albuquerque is blessed with an exceptional setting for outdoor sports, backed by a favorable, if unpredictable, climate. Usually 10°F warmer than Santa Fe's, Albuquerque's winter days are often mild enough for most outdoor activities. The Sandias tempt you with challenging mountain adventures (⇨ *See* the Sandia Park section *of* the Side Trips from the Cities chapter for details on mountain biking and skiing in the Sandia Mountains above Albuquerque); the Rio Grande and its thick forest, the Bosque, provide settings for additional wilderness pursuits.

Participant Sports

The **City of Albuquerque** (☎ 505/768–5300 ⊕ www.cabq.gov/living. html) maintains a diversified network of cultural and recreational programs. Among the city's assets are more than 20,000 acres of open space, four golf courses, 200 parks, 68 paved tracks for biking and jogging, as well as swimming pools, tennis courts, ball fields, playgrounds, and a shooting range.

Amusement Park

Drive down San Mateo Northeast in summer and you can't help but glimpse a roller coaster smack in the middle of the city. **Cliff's Amusement Park** (✉ 4800 Osuna Rd. NE, off I–25 at San Mateo Blvd. NE, Northeast Heights ☎ 505/881–9373 ⊕ www.cliffsamusementpark. com) is a clean, well-run attraction for everyone from two-year-olds on up. It features a wooden-track roller coaster as well as rides for all ages and state fair–type games of chance. The park also has a large waterplay area. Cliff's is open early April through September, but days and hours vary greatly, so call first.

Ballooning

Albuquerque is blessed with a high altitude, mild climate, and steady but manageable winds, making it an ideal destination for ballooning. A wind pattern famously known as the "Albuquerque Box," created by the city's location against the Sandia Mountains, makes Albuquerque a particularly great place to fly.

If you've never been ballooning, you may have a notion that it's an inherently bumpy experience, where changes in altitude replicate the queasiness-inducing feeling of being in a tiny propeller plane. Rest assured, the experience is far calmer than you'd ever imagine. The balloons are flown by licensed pilots (don't call them operators) who deftly switch propane-fueled flames on and off, climbing and descending to find winds blowing the way they want to go—thus, there's no real "steering" involved, which makes the pilots' control that much more admirable. The norm is for pilots to land balloons wherever the wind dictates—thus creating the need for "chase vehicles" that pick you up and return you to your departure point—but particularly skilled pilots can use conditions created by the "Box" to land precisely where you started. But even without this "door-to-door" service, many visitors rank a balloon ride soaring over the Rio Grande Valley as their most memorable experience while in town.

Fodor'sChoice There are several reliable companies around metro Albuquerque that
★ offer tours. A ride will set you back about $160–$180 per person. One of the best outfitters in town is **Rainbow Ryders** (☎ 505/823–1111 or 800/725–2477 ⊕ www.rainbowryders.com), an official Ride Concession for the Albuquerque International Balloon Fiesta. Part of the fun is helping to inflate and, later on, pack away the balloon. And if you thought it best not to breakfast prior to your flight, a continental breakfast and champagne toast await your return.

Bicycling

Albuquerque has miles of bike lanes and trails crisscrossing and skirting the city as well as great mountain-biking trails at Sandia Peak Ski Area (⊃ *See* the Sandia Park section *of* the Side Trips from Albuquerque, Santa Fe & Taos chapter). The city's public works department produces an elaborately detailed **bike map**, which can be obtained free by calling ☎ 505/768–3550 or downloaded from ⊕ www.cabq.gov/bike.

Bikes can be rented at several locations, including **Albuquerque Bicycle Center** (✉ 3330 Coors Blvd. NW, North Valley ☎ 505/831–5739 ⊕ www.albbicyclecenter.com), which has three locations around town. **Two Wheel Drive** (✉ 1706 Central Ave. SE, Old Town ☎ 505/243–8443) is close to UNM, downtown, and Old Town.

Bird-Watching

The Rio Grande Valley, one of the continent's major flyways, attracts many migratory bird species. Good bird-viewing locales include the **Rio Grande Nature Center State Park** (✉ 2901 Candelaria Rd. NW, North Valley ☎ 505/344–7240 ⊕ www.nmparks.com).

Golf

Most of the better courses in the region—and there are some outstanding ones—are just outside of town (⊃ *See* the North-Central New Mexico chapter for details). The four courses operated by the city of Albuquerque actually hold their own pretty nicely, and the rates are extremely fair. Each course has a clubhouse and pro shop, where clubs and other equipment can be rented. Weekday play is first-come, first-served, but reservations are taken for weekends. Contact the **Golf Management Office** (☎ 505/888–8115 ⊕ www.cabq.gov/golf) for details. Of the four city courses, **Arroyo del Oso** (✉ 7001 Osuna Rd. NE, Northeast Heights ☎ 505/884–7505) earns high marks for its undulating 27-hole layout; greens fees are $26 for 18 holes. The 18-hole **Los Altos Golf Course** (✉ 9717 Copper Ave. NE, Northeast Heights ☎ 505/298–1897), one of the region's most popular facilities, has $26 greens fees. There's also a short, par-3, 9-hole "executive course."

★ **Sandia Golf Club** (✉ Tramway Rd. NE just east of I–25, Far Northeast Heights ☎ 505/798–3990 ⊕ www.sandiagolf.com), opened in 2005 at the swanky Sandia Resort & Casino, offers 18 holes set amid lush hilly fairways, cascading waterfalls, and desert brush. Greens fees are $51–$61. The University of New Mexico has two superb courses. Both are open daily and have full-service pro shops, instruction, and snack bars. Greens fees for out-of-staters run about $60 to $70, with cart. **UNM North** (✉ Tucker Rd. at Yale Blvd., University of New Mexico ☎ 505/277–4146) is a first-class 9-hole, par-36 course on the north side of campus.

★ The 18-hole facility at **UNM South** (✉ 3601 University Blvd., just west of airport off I–25, Southeast Heights ☎ 505/277–4546 ⊕ www.unmgolf.com) has garnered countless awards from major golf magazines and hosted PGA and LPGA qualifying events; there's also a short par-3 9-hole course.

Hiking

In the foothills in Albuquerque's Northeast Heights, you'll find great hiking in **Cibola National Forest**, which can be accessed directly from Tramway Road Northeast, about 4 mi east of I–25 or 2 mi north of Paseo del Norte. Just follow the road into the hillside, and you'll find several parking areas (there's a daily parking fee of $3). This is where you'll find the trailhead for the steep and quiet challenging **La Luz Trail**, which climbs some 9 mi (an elevation of more than 3,000 feet) up to the top of Sandia Crest. You can take the Sandia Peak Aerial Tram to the top and then hike down the trail, or vice versa (keep in mind that it can take up to six hours to hike up the trail, and four to five hours to hike down). Spectacular views of Albuquerque and many miles of desert and mountain beyond that are had from the trail. And you can still enjoy a hike along here without going the whole way—if your energy and time are limited, just hike a mile or two and back. No matter how far you hike, however, pack plenty of water.

Spectator Sports

Baseball

Since 2003, the city has hosted Triple A minor league baseball's **Albuquerque Isotopes** (✉ University Ave. SE at Ave. Cesar Chavez SE, University of New Mexico ☎ 505/924–2255 ⊕ www.albuquerquebaseball.com), the farm club of the Major League Florida Marlins; the season runs April through August.

Basketball

It's hard to beat the excitement of home basketball games of the **University of New Mexico Lobos** (✉ University Ave. at Ave. Cesar Chavez, University of New Mexico ☎ 505/925–5626 ⊕ http://golobos.collegesports.com), when 18,000 rabid fans crowd into the school's arena, "the Pit," from November to March. Both the women's and men's teams enjoy huge success every year.

Football

The competitively ranked **University of New Mexico Lobos** (✉ University Ave. at Ave. Cesar Chavez, University of New Mexico ☎ 505/925–5626) play at 40,000-seat University Stadium in the fall.

SHOPPING

Albuquerque's shopping strengths include a handful of cool retail districts, including Nob Hill, Old Town, and the rapidly gentrifying downtown. These are good neighborhoods for galleries, antiques, and home-furnishing shops, bookstores, and offbeat gift shops. Otherwise, the city is mostly the domain of both strip and indoor malls, mostly filled with ubiquitous chain shops, although you can find some worthy independent shops even in these venues.

Shopping Neighborhoods & Malls

The most impressive of the city's malls, **Cottonwood Mall** (✉ Coors Blvd. NW at Coors Bypass, West Side ☎ 505/899–7467), is anchored by Dillard's, Foley's, Mervyn's, JCPenney, and Sears Roebuck and has about 130 other shops, including Williams-Sonoma, Aveda, Cache, and Abercrombie & Fitch. There are a dozen restaurants and food stalls, plus a 14-screen theater.

Albuquerque's **Downtown** (✉ Central and Gold Aves. from 1st to 10th Sts.) has undergone a stunning revitalization since 2000, and by 2010 the neighborhood should have double—or even triple—the number of shops and restaurants. Local developers have made a point of renting strictly to independent businesses, making an effort to keep downtown from turning into just another collection of chain outlets. In the meantime, stroll along Central and Gold avenues (and neighboring blocks) to admire avant-garde galleries, cool cafés, and curious boutiques.

Funky **Nob Hill** (✉ Central Ave. from Girard Blvd. to Washington St.), just east of University of New Mexico and anchored by old Route 66, pulses with colorful storefronts and kitschy signs. At night, neon-lighted boutiques, galleries, and performing-arts spaces encourage foot traffic. Many of the best shops are clustered inside or on the blocks near Nob Hill Business Center, an art deco structure containing several intriguing businesses and La Montañita Natural Foods Co-op, an excellent spot for a snack.

Old Town (✉ Central Ave. and Rio Grande Blvd.) has the city's largest concentration of one-of-a-kind retail shops, selling clothing, home accessories, and Mexican imports. Also here are a slew of galleries, many exhibiting Native American art.

Art Galleries

Amapola Gallery (✉ 205 Romero St. NW, Old Town ☎ 505/242–4311), west of the plaza near Rio Grande Boulevard, is one of the largest co-op galleries in New Mexico. It has a brick courtyard and an indoor space, both brimming with pottery, paintings, textiles, carvings, baskets, jewelry, and other items.

 Coleman Gallery Contemporary Art (✉ 3812 Central Ave. SE, Nob Hill ☎ 505/232–0224) has emerged as one of Nob Hill's leading art spaces, showing works by a number of the state's top contemporary talents.

DSG (✉ 3011 Monte Vista Blvd. NE, Nob Hill ☎ 505/266–7751 or 800/ 474–7751), owned by John Cacciatore, handles works by leading regional artists, including Frank McCulloch, Carol Hoy, Leo Neufeld, Larry Bell, Angus Macpherson, Jim Bagley, Nancy Kozikowski, and photographer Nathan Small.

Gowen Arts (✉ 303 Romero St. NW, #114, Old Town ☎ 505/268–6828) specializes in Native American artists, including wonderful jewelry and metal sculpture.

Mariposa Gallery (✉ 3500 Central Ave. SE, Nob Hill ☎ 505/268–6828) sells contemporary fine crafts, including jewelry, sculptural glass, works in mixed media and clay, and fiber arts. The changing exhibits focus on upcoming artists.

Sumner & Dene (✉ 517 Central Ave. NW, Downtown ☎ 505/842– 1400), a cool art space in the heart of downtown, sells sleek, retro-cool furnishings; unusual jewelry; and whimsical artwork.

Weems Gallery (✉ 2801–M Eubank Blvd. NE, Northeast Heights ☎ 505/ 293–6133 ✉ 303 Romero St. NW, Old Town ☎ 505/764–0302) has paintings, pottery, sculpture, jewelry, weaving, stained glass, and original-design clothes.

★ **Weyrich Gallery** (✉ 2935–D Louisiana Blvd. NE, Uptown ☎ 505/883– 7410) carries distinctive jewelry, fine art, Japanese tea bowls, woodblocks, hand-color photography, and other largely Asian-inspired pieces.

Specialty Stores

Antiques

FodorsChoice **Classic Century Square Antique Mall** (✉ 4516 Central Ave. SE, Nob Hill
★ ☎ 505/268–8080) is a three-story emporium of collectibles and antiques. The emphasis is on memorabilia from the early 1880s to the 1950s. (When the set designers for the television miniseries *Lonesome Dove* needed props, they came here.) Items for sale include art deco and art nouveau objects, retro-cool '50s designs, Depression-era glass, Native American goods, quilts and linens, vintage clothes, and Western memorabilia.

Cowboys & Indians (✉ 4000 Central Ave. SE, Nob Hill ☎ 505/255–4054) carries Native American and cowboy art and artifacts.

Books

Massive **Page One** (✉ 11018 Montgomery Blvd. NE, Far Northeast Heights ☎ 505/294–2026), arguably the best bookstore in Albuquerque, specializes in technical and professional titles, maps, globes, children's titles, and 150 out-of-state and foreign newspapers. Book signings, poetry readings, and children's events are frequently scheduled.

Gifts, Food & Toys

Beeps (✉ Nob Hill Shopping Center, 3500 Central Ave. SE, Nob Hill ☎ 505/262–1900), a Nob Hill favorite, carries cards, T-shirts, and amusing, if bawdy, novelties.

Candy Lady (✉ Mountain Rd. at Rio Grande Blvd., Old Town ☎ 505/ 224–9837 or 800/214–7731) is known as much for its scandalous adult novelty candies as for its tasty red- and green-chile brittle, plus the usual fudge, chocolates, piñon caramels, and candies. A small room, to the right as you enter, displays the "adult" candy, so you can easily pilot any kids in your party past it.

La Casita de Kaleidoscopes (⊠ Poco A Poco Patio, 326–D San Felipe St. NW, Old Town ☎ 505/247–4242) carries both contemporary and vintage kaleidoscopes of all styles, by more than 80 top artists in the field.

Martha's Body Bueno (⊠ 3901 Central Ave. NE, Nob Hill ☎ 505/255–1122) is a wonderful, offbeat boutique with sensual bath items, lingerie, jewelry, candles, and other romantic gifts.

Satellite Toys and Coffee (⊠ 3513 Central Ave. SE, Nob Hill ☎ 505/256–0345) is filled with wind-up toys and collector's items for grown-ups.

Theobroma Chocolatier (⊠ 319 Central Ave. NW, Downtown ☎ 505/247–0848 ⊠ 12611 Montgomery Blvd. NE, Far Northeast Heights ☎ 505/293–6545) carries beautifully handcrafted, high-quality chocolates, truffles, and candies (most of them made on premises), as well as Taos Cow ice cream.

Home Furnishings

A (⊠ 3500 Central Ave. SE, Nob Hill ☎ 505/266–2222) is a Nob Hill stop for housewares, soaps, candles, body-care products, and jewelry.

A branch of a popular regional chain, **El Paso Import Co.** (⊠ 3500 Central Ave. SE, Nob Hill ☎ 505/265–1160) carries distressed and "peely-paint" antique-looking chests and tables loaded with character. If you love the "shabby chic" look, head to this Nob Hill furniture shop.

Hey Jhonny (⊠ 3418 Central Ave. SE, Nob Hill ☎ 505/256–9244) is an aromatic store full of exquisite candles, soaps, pillows, fountains, and other soothing items for the home; there's also a branch that carries more furniture and larger pieces around the corner, at 118 Tulane Street.

★ **Jackalope** (⊠ 6400 San Meteo Blvd. NE, Northeast Heights ☎ 505/349–0955), the favorite Southwestern furniture and bric-a-brac shop in Bernalillo and Santa Fe, opened an Albuquerque branch in 2006. It's a great source of garden furniture, pottery, folk art, and rugs.

Moderno (⊠ 3312 Stanford Dr. NE, Midtown ☎ 505/254–0447) stocks merchandise for contemporary living: handmade steel beds, chairs, mobiles, and modern, locally produced art, rugs, and jewelry.

Objects of Desire (⊠ 3225 Central Ave. NE, Nob Hill ☎ 505/232–3088) is the place to find that special lamp or table from a whimsical and worldly collection of furnishings that appeal to individualized tastes.

Peacecraft (⊠ 3215 Central Ave. NE, Nob Hill ☎ 505/255–5229) supports fair trade and stocks handmade folk art and crafts from all around the world—wooden boxes from Kenya, clothing from Guatemala, hats from Honduras. The store also employs a number of university students on work-study.

Mexican Imports

La Piñata (✉ No. 2 Patio Market, 206 San Felipe St. NW, Old Town ☎ 505/242–2400) specializes in piñatas and papier-mâché products, plus Native American jewelry and leather goods.

Music

Natural Sound (✉ 3422 Central Ave. SE, Nob Hill ☎ 505/255–8295) is an eclectic record store with a large selection of new and used CDs.

Native American Arts & Crafts

Andrews Pueblo Pottery (✉ 303 Romero St. NW, Suite 116, Old Town ☎ 505/243–0414) carries a terrific selection of Pueblo pottery, fetishes, kachina dolls, and baskets for the beginning and seasoned collector.

Bien Mur Indian Market Center (✉ Tramway Rd. NE east of I–25, Northeast Heights ☎ 505/821–5400 or 800/365–5400) in Sandia Pueblo showcases the best of the best in regional Native American rugs, jewelry, and crafts of all kinds. You can feel very secure about what you purchase at this trading post, and prices are fair for what you get.

★ **Gertrude Zachary** (✉ 1501 Lomas Blvd. NW, Old Town ☎ 505/247–4442 ✉ 3300 Central Ave. SE, Nob Hill ☎ 505/766–4700 ✉ 416 2nd St. SW, Old Town ☎ 505/244–1320) dazzles with its selection of Native American jewelry. This may be your best place to shop for a bargain in a good bracelet or ring. Locals buy here, too. A second branch, at 416 2nd Street, carries antiques.

★ **Nizhoni Moses, Ltd.** (✉ 326 San Felipe St. NW, Old Town ☎ 505/842–1808 or 888/842–1808) stocks Pueblo pottery, including the black earthenware pottery of San Ildefonso, as well as the work of potters from Acoma, Santa Clara, Isleta, and Zía. Rare Zuñi and Navajo jewelry is on display, as are Navajo weavings from 1900 to the present.

Skip Maisel Wholesale Indian Jewelry and Crafts (✉ 510 Central Ave. SW, Old Town ☎ 505/242–6526), in business since 1905, has been at this location since 1929. Even its exterior is a piece of art—check out the murals in the entryway alcove. Inside are quality Native American arts and crafts at wholesale prices.

ALBUQUERQUE ESSENTIALS

AIR TRAVEL

See Air Travel *in* New Mexico Essentials.

BUS TRAVEL

For information on reaching Albuquerque by bus, *see* Bus Travel *in* New Mexico Essentials.

Although the city's public bus service, ABQ Ride, provides good coverage, this is still a city where a car is the easiest and most convenient way to get around. Still, buses are fairly practical for getting between downtown, Nob Hill, Old Town, and the airport. The fare is $1 (bills or coins, exact change only). Bus stops are well marked with the line's sunburst signs. 🚩 **Sun Tran** ☎ 505/243–7433 ⊕ www.cabq.gov/transit/tran.html.

CAR RENTAL
See Car Rental *in* New Mexico Essentials.

CAR TRAVEL
Albuquerque sprawls out in all directions, but getting around town is not difficult, despite growing traffic problems as the city's population steadily increases. Drivers here have a spotty reputation, too, often pushing it through yellow lights and failing to use turn signals. The main highways through the city, north–south I–25 and east–west I–40, converge just northeast of downtown and generally offer the quickest access to outlying neighborhoods and the airport. Rush-hour jams are common in the mornings and late afternoons, but they're still far less severe than in most big U.S. cities.

PARKING   Because it's a driving city, most businesses and hotels have free or inexpensive off-street parking, and it's easy to find metered street parking in many neighborhoods. Problems usually arise only when there's a major event in town, such as a concert near University of New Mexico or a festival downtown or in Old Town, when you may want to arrive on the early side to get a space.

EMERGENCIES
In an emergency, dial 911.

🚑 Hospitals **Presbyterian Hospital** ✉ 1100 Central Ave. SE, Downtown ☎ 505/841-1234. **University Hospital** ✉ 2211 Lomas Blvd. NE, University of New Mexico ☎ 505/272-2111.

SIGHTSEEING TOURS
The Albuquerque Museum of Art and History leads free, hour-long historical walks through Old Town at 11 AM except Monday, from March through November.

🚑 **Albuquerque Museum of Art and History** ☎ 505/243-7255 ⊕ www.cabq.gov/museum.

TAXIS
Taxis are metered in Albuquerque, and service is around-the-clock. Given the considerable distances around town, cabbing it can be expensive; figure about $9 from downtown to Nob Hill, and about $20 from the airport to a North Side hotel.

🚑 **Albuquerque Cab** ☎ 505/883-4888. **Yellow Cab** ☎ 505/247-8888.

TRAIN TRAVEL
In summer 2006 the City of Albuquerque launched the state's first-ever commuter train line, the *New Mexico Rail Runner Express.* As of this writing, service is from Bernalillo south through the city of Albuquerque, continuing south through Los Lunas to the suburb of Belén, covering a distance of about 50 mi. The second and final phase of the project, expected to be completed by late 2008, will extend the service north to Santa Fe. For information on Amtrak service, *see* Train Travel *in* New Mexico Essentials.

🚑 Train Information *New Mexico Rail Runner Express* ☎ 505/245-7245 ⊕ www.nmrailrunner.com.

VISITOR INFORMATION

The Albuquerque CVB operates tourism information kiosks at the airport (on the baggage claim level), downtown at the Albuquerque Convention Center (401 2nd St. NW), and in Old Town on Plaza Don Luis, across from San Felipe de Neri church.

Albuquerque Convention and Visitors Bureau ✉ 20 1st Plaza NW, Suite 601, 87125 ☎ 505/842-9918 or 800/284-2282 ⊕ www.itsatrip.org. **State Information Center** ✉ Indian Pueblo Cultural Center, 2401 12th St. NW, 87107 ☎ 505/843-7270 ⊕ www.newmexico.org.

Santa Fe

WORD OF MOUTH

"Santa Fe is a compact and easy town to walk, so I wouldn't worry about a bus tour. Pick up a tourist map and you should be fine."

—beachbum

"June is very hot in NM, even in Santa Fe. Our heat is DRY and some hate it. Why not come in the spring or fall when it is lovely, not scorching. September is still warm, but nice!"

—scsmom

"Don't miss the peddlers on the streets. Makes for good presents, and the numerous galleries (and restaurants) on Canyon Road are not to be missed."

—maria_so

Updated by
Andrew Collins

WITH ITS CRISP, CLEAR AIR AND BRIGHT, SUNNY WEATHER, Santa Fe couldn't be more welcoming. On a plateau at the base of the Sangre de Cristo Mountains—at an elevation of 7,000 feet—the city is surrounded by remnants of a 2,000-year-old Pueblo civilization and filled with reminders of almost four centuries of Spanish and Mexican rule. The town's placid central Plaza, which dates from the early 17th century, has been the site of bullfights, public floggings, gunfights, battles, political rallies, promenades, and public markets over the years. A one-of-a-kind destination, Santa Fe is fabled for its rows of chic art galleries, superb restaurants, and shops selling Southwestern furnishings and cowboy gear.

La Villa Real de la Santa Fe de San Francisco de Asísi (the Royal City of the Holy Faith of St. Francis of Assisi) was founded in the early 1600s by Don Pedro de Peralta, who planted his banner in the name of Spain. In 1680 the region's Pueblo people rose in revolt, burning homes and churches and killing hundreds of Spaniards. After an extended siege in Santa Fe, the Spanish colonists were driven out of New Mexico. The tide turned 12 years later, when General Don Diego de Vargas returned with a new army from El Paso and recaptured Santa Fe.

To commemorate de Vargas's victory, Las Fiestas de Santa Fe have been held annually since 1712. The nation's oldest community celebration takes place on the weekend after Labor Day, with parades, mariachi bands, pageants, the burning of *Zozóbra*—also known as Old Man Gloom—and nonstop parties. "Fiesta" (as it's referred to locally) is but one of many annual opportunities for revelry—from the arrival of the rodeo and the opening week of the Santa Fe Opera in summer to traditional Pueblo dances at Christmastime.

Following de Vargas's defeat of the Pueblos, the then-grand Camino Real (Royal Road), stretching from Mexico City to Santa Fe, brought an army of conquistadors, clergymen, and settlers to the northernmost reaches of Spain's New World conquests. In 1820 the Santa Fe Trail—a prime artery of U.S. westward expansion—spilled a flood of covered wagons from Missouri onto the Plaza. A booming trade with the United States was born. After Mexico achieved independence from Spain in 1821, its subsequent rule of New Mexico further increased this commerce.

The Santa Fe Trail's heyday ended with the arrival of the Atchison, Topeka & Santa Fe Railway in 1880. The trains, and later the nation's first highways, brought a new type of settler to Santa Fe—artists who fell in love with its cultural diversity, history, and magical color and light. Their presence attracted tourists, who quickly became a primary source of income for the largely poor populace.

Santa Fe is renowned for its arts, tricultural (Native American, Hispanic, and Anglo) heritage, and adobe architecture. The Pueblo people introduced adobe to the Spanish, who in turn developed the adobe brick style of construction. In a relatively dry, treeless region, adobe was a suitable natural building material. Melding into the landscape with their earthen colors and rounded, flowing lines, the pueblos and villages were hard to see from afar and thus somewhat camouflaged from raiding nomadic tribes. The region's distinctive architecture no longer repels visitors, it attracts them.

Among the smallest state capitals in the country, Santa Fe has no major airport (Albuquerque's is the nearest). The city's population, an estimated 65,000, swells to nearly double that figure in summer. In winter the skiers arrive, lured by the challenging slopes of Ski Santa Fe and Taos Ski Valley (⇨ Chapter 4). Geared for tourists, Santa Fe can put a serious dent in your travel budget. Prices are highest June–August. Between September and November and between April and May they're lower, and (except for the major holidays) from December to March they're the lowest.

EXPLORING SANTA FE

Humorist Will Rogers said on his first visit to Santa Fe, "Whoever designed this town did so while riding on a jackass, backwards, and drunk." The maze of narrow streets and alleyways confounds motorists, but with shops and restaurants, a flowered courtyard, or an eye-catching gallery at nearly every turn, they're a delight for pedestrians. The trickle of water called the Santa Fe River runs west, parallel to Alameda Street, from the Sangre de Cristo Mountains to the open prairie southwest of town, where it disappears into a narrow canyon before joining the Rio Grande. But in New Mexico there's a *dicho,* or old saying, "*agua es vida*"—"water is life"—be it ever so humble.

There are five state museums in Santa Fe, and purchasing a Museum of New Mexico pass is the most economical way to visit them all. The four-day pass costs $18 and is sold at all five of the museums, which include the Palace of the Governors, Museum of Fine Arts, Museum of Indian Arts and Culture, Museum of International Folk Art, and Museum of Spanish Colonial Art.

Santa Fe Plaza

Much of the history of Santa Fe, New Mexico, the Southwest, and even the West has some association with Santa Fe's central Plaza, which New Mexico governor Don Pedro de Peralta laid out in 1607. The Plaza, already well established by the time of the Pueblo revolt in 1680, was the site of a bullring and of fiestas and fandangos. Freight wagons unloaded here after completing their arduous journey across the Santa Fe Trail. The American flag was raised over the Plaza in 1846, during the Mexican War, which resulted in Mexico's loss of all its territories in the present southwestern United States. For a time the Plaza was a tree-shaded park with a white picket fence. In the 1890s it was an expanse of lawn where uniformed bands played in an ornate gazebo. Particularly festive times on the Plaza are the weekend after Labor Day, during Las Fiestas de Santa Fe, and at Christmas, when all the trees are filled with lights and rooftops are outlined with *farolitos,* votive candles lit within paper-bag lanterns.

Numbers in the text correspond to numbers in the margin and on the Downtown Santa Fe map.

GREAT ITINERARIES

Unless you're in Santa Fe for just a few days, you're probably going to explore the rest of the northern Rio Grande Valley. For the best tour, combine either of these itineraries with those in the Albuquerque, Taos, and Side Trips chapters; the latter includes several side trips within a 60- to 90-minute drive of Santa Fe.

IF YOU HAVE 1 DAY

Breakfast in Santa Fe is a social tradition, so consider heading to one of the city's best breakfast spots, such as Cloud Cliff Bakery or Bagelmania. Drive to Museum Hill, spending the morning checking out the area's two best art collections, the Museum of International Folk Art and Museum of Spanish Colonial Art. Return to the Plaza for lunch at the Plaza Café or, nearby, Santacafé. Stroll around the Plaza area, taking in the shops and galleries, and if you'd like, drop by the Georgia O'Keeffe Museum or Museum of Fine Arts.

By later afternoon, saunter east from the Plaza along San Francisco Street, admiring St. Francis Cathedral Basilica; bear right to Alameda Street, turn left and continue to Paseo de Peralta, and then quickly turn right and then left onto Canyon Road to stroll into the leafy foothills. You pass dozens of galleries, several of which stay open into early evening. Finish with a meal at one of the restaurants midway up Canyon Road.

IF YOU HAVE 3 DAYS

Follow the one-day itinerary's morning portion, but allow time to visit another museum on Museum Hill, either the Museum of Indian Arts and Culture or Wheelwright Museum of the American Indian.

Spend the afternoon ambling about the Plaza area, saving additional museum explorations for your last day.

On your second day, plan to walk a bit. Head east from the Plaza up to Canyon Road's foot, perusing the galleries. Have lunch at one of the restaurants midway uphill, such as Sol or El Farol. From here, you can either continue walking 2 mi up Canyon, and then Upper Canyon, roads to the Randall Davey Audubon Center, or you can take a cab there. Alternatively, you could drive from the start, first parking near Canyon Road to check out the galleries (there's a pay lot across from El Farol), then parking at the center. Either way, once you're at the center, you can hike the foothills—there are trails within the center's property and also from the free parking area (off Cerro Gordo Road) leading into the Dale Ball Trail Network. There may be late-afternoon summer thunderstorms and lightning, so check the forecast before you go, and bring at least a liter of water per person, even for a short stroll.

On your final day, spend the morning at the O'Keeffe or Fine Arts museums near the Plaza, and at the Palace of the Governors. In the afternoon, head a few blocks southwest of the Plaza, crossing Alameda Street, and stroll through the Guadalupe District, which abounds with funky design and furniture shops and galleries. End your explorations with a margarita on the patio of the festive Cowgirl restaurant, which has live music most nights.

IF YOU LIKE

ART GALLERIES

Santa Fe's tourism office claims that the city has the third-largest art market in the country, trailing only New York City and Los Angeles. Granted, it's a little difficult to quantify this boast, but it seems absolutely plausible: the city has more than 200 esteemed art galleries, and a significant number of them carry museum-quality art, some of it with museum-quality prices. In few cities in the world are so many paintings, sculptures, photographs, and other artworks by so many iconic artists—dead and living—available. Even if you're not out to buy art, it's worth visiting some of Santa Fe's most esteemed galleries just to admire it. As you might expect, it's easy to find Southwest, Spanish-colonial, Native American, and other art related to the area, but Santa Fe long ago broke out from its regional aesthetic and now represents artists of all genres and styles, from early-20th-century impressionism to African ethnography. Tree-shaded and narrow Canyon Road, which meanders gracefully up a hill on the east side of downtown, contains dozens of the city's galleries—it's great fun to stroll along here, ducking in and out of shops, especially on Friday, when many galleries have openings. However, more than a few locals-in-the-know write off Canyon Road as touristy and predictable and claim that the best galleries in Santa Fe lie elsewhere, mostly on the blocks around the Plaza and on Paseo de Peralta's eastern fringes. Just about any street you wander near the Plaza or east of it, you're likely to encounter acclaimed galleries.

NIGHTLIFE & THE ARTS

Santa Fe, especially come summer, is something of an arts powerhouse, its glittery reputation for performing-arts culture led by the presence of the internationally adored Santa Fe Opera. But the city also has a top-flight chamber music festival, world-class flamenco dancing, a fine ballet, respectable local theater, a couple of venues for arty films, and numerous spots to catch lectures and concerts or to partake of workshops. And although much of the activity takes place in summer, you can find performances of one kind or another year-round. As much as folks rave about the city's arts scene, they often complain about Santa Fe's nightlife options. But for a city its size, and one where visitors and locals head to bed early and get up early the next day, it really does hold its own. Several of the better restaurants in town have inviting bars or lounges, often with live music. And, similarly, some of the nightspots serve pretty good food. You won't find much in the way of massive warehouse discos and all-night revelry, but Santa Fe does have an intriguing mix of nightspots.

SHOPPING

Just as Santa Fe's art scene has grown in focus from regional to international, the city's shopping options have also increased dramatically, with the strongest growth occurring in the hip Guadalupe District, a few blocks southwest of the Plaza. Here you can find minimalls, such as the Design Center and Sanbusco Market Center, filled with stylish boutiques.

A GOOD WALK

To get started, drop by the information booth at the Plaza's northwest corner, across the street from the clock, where Palace Street meets Lincoln Street (in front of the bank) to pick up a free map. From there, begin your walk around the Plaza. You can get an overview of the history of Santa Fe and New Mexico at the **Palace of the Governors ❶**, which borders the northern side of the Plaza on Palace Avenue. Outside, under the palace portal, dozens of Native American craftspeople sell their wares. From the palace, cross Lincoln Street to the **Museum of Fine Arts ❷**, where the works of regional masters are on display. As you cross Lincoln, note the construction under way on the street's right side—part of the new wing being added to the Palace of the Governors, slated for completion in 2006. The **Georgia O'Keeffe Museum ❸**, on nearby Johnson Street, exhibits the works of its namesake, New Mexico's best known painter. Just down Johnson

Street, the new **Awakening Museum ❹** exhibits the large-scale installation of one-of-a-kind artist Jean-Claude Gaugy.

From the O'Keeffe Museum, return to the Plaza and cut across to its southeast corner to Old Santa Fe Trail, where you can find the town's oldest hotel, **La Fonda ❺**, a good place to soak up a little of bygone Santa Fe. One block east on Cathedral Place looms the imposing facade of **St. Francis Cathedral Basilica ❻**. Across from the cathedral is the **Institute of American Indian Arts, ❼** with its wonderful museum. A stone's throw from the museum is cool, quiet **Sena Plaza ❽**, accessible through two doorways on Palace Avenue.

⏱ TIMING TIPS➔ **It's possible to zoom through this compact area in about five hours—two hours exploring the Plaza and the Palace of the Governors, two hours seeing the Museum of Fine Arts and the Museum of the Institute of American Indian Arts, and an hour visiting the other sites.**

What to See

❹ **Awakening Museum.** This unusual museum celebrates the groundbreaking artwork of Jean-Claude Gaugy, a French-born artist who began work on a large-scale art installation in West Virginia in 1985—it consisted of Gaugy's vibrant, colorful painting on hundreds of wood panels. In 2002, Gaugy moved to Santa Fe and reinstalled his work inside an 11,000-square-foot downtown building. Additionally, the museum contains a meditation garden and an extensive museum shop. Conceptually, it's one of Santa Fe's most fascinating—if rather difficult to describe—museums. ✉ *125 N. Guadalupe St.* ☎ *505/954–4025* ⊕ *www. theawakeningmuseum.org* 🎟 *$3* ⊙ *June–Sept., daily 10–5:30; Oct.–May, Thurs.–Mon. 10–5.*

★ ❸ **Georgia O'Keeffe Museum.** One of many East Coast artists who visited New Mexico in the first half of the 20th century, O'Keeffe returned to live and paint here, eventually emerging as the demigoddess of Southwestern art. O'Keeffe's innovative view of the landscape is captured in

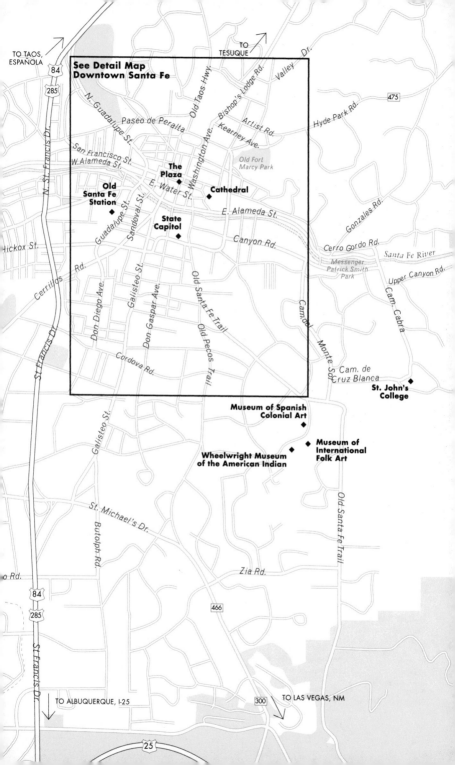

TO TAOS,
ESPAÑOLA

84
285

**See Detail Map
Downtown Santa Fe**

TO
TESUQUE

N. Guadalupe St.

Paseo de Peralta

Old Taos Hwy.

Bishop's Lodge Rd.

Artist Rd.

Valley Dr.

Hyde Park Rd.

475

San Francisco St.
W. Alameda St.

**The
Plaza**

Washington Ave.

Kearney Ave.

Old Fort
Marcy Park

**Old
Santa Fe
Station**

E. Water St.

Cathedral

Gonzales Rd.

Guadalupe St.

Sandoval St.

**State
Capitol**

E. Alameda St.

Canyon Rd.

Cerro Gordo Rd.

Santa Fe River

Hickox St.

Cerrillos Rd.

Don Diego Ave.

Galisteo St.

Don Gaspar Ave.

Old Santa Fe Trail

Old Pecos Trail

Messenger
Patrick Smith
Park

Upper Canyon Rd.

Cam. Cabra

St. Francis Dr.

N. St. Francis Dr.

Cordova Rd.

Cam. del Monte Sol

Cam. de
Cruz Blanca

**St. John's
College**

Galisteo St.

**Museum of Spanish
Colonial Art**

**Museum of
International
Folk Art**

**Wheelwright Museum
of the American Indian**

St. Michael's Dr.

Butolph Rd.

o Rd.

84
285

Zia Rd.

466

Old Santa Fe Trail

St. Francis Dr.

TO ALBUQUERQUE, I-25

300

TO LAS VEGAS, NM

25

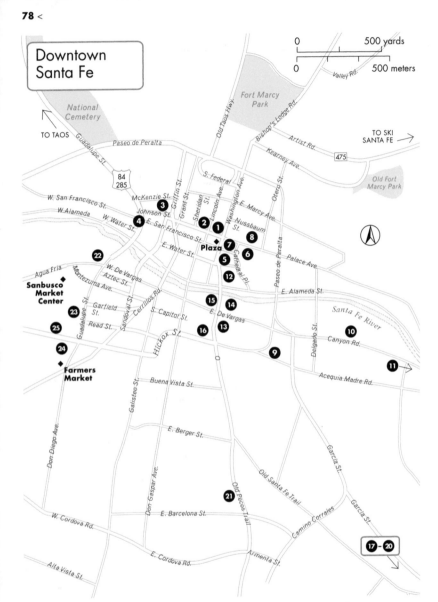

Downtown Santa Fe

From the Plains, inspired by her memory of the Texas plains, and *Jimson Weed,* a study of one of her favorite plants. Special exhibitions with O'Keeffe's modernist peers are on view throughout the year—many of these are exceptional, sometimes even more interesting than the permanent collection. ✉ *217 Johnson St.* ☎ *505/995–1000* ⊕ *www.okeeffemuseum.org* 🎟 *$8, free Fri. 5–8* PM ☾ *Daily Sat.–Thurs. 10–5, Fri. 10–8.*

❼ Institute of American Indian Arts. Containing the largest collection of contemporary Native American art in the United States, this museum's paintings, photography, sculptures, prints, and traditional crafts were created by past and present students and teachers. The institute itself, which moved to the College of Santa Fe campus, was founded as a one-room studio classroom in the early 1930s by Dorothy Dunn, a beloved art teacher who played a critical role in launching the careers of many Native American artists. In the 1960s and 1970s it blossomed into the nation's premier center for Native American arts. Artist Fritz Scholder taught here, as did sculptor Allan Houser. Among their disciples was the painter T. C. Cannon. ✉ *108 Cathedral Pl.* ☎ *505/983–1777* ⊕ *www.iaiancad.org* 🎟 *$4* ☾ *Mon.–Sat. 10–5, Sun. noon–5.*

❺ La Fonda. A *fonda* (inn) has stood on this site, southeast of the Plaza, for centuries. Architect Isaac Hamilton Rapp, who put Santa Fe style on the map, built this area landmark in 1922. Remodeled in 1926 by architect John Gaw Meem, the hotel was sold to the Santa Fe Railway in 1926 and remained a Harvey House hotel until 1968. Because of its proximity to the Plaza and its history as a gathering place for everyone from cowboys to movie stars (Errol Flynn stayed here), it's referred to as "The Inn at the End of the Trail." Major social events still take place here. Have a drink at the fifth-floor Bell Tower Bar (open late spring–early fall), which offers tremendous sunset views. ✉ *E. San Francisco St. at Old Santa Fe Trail* ☎ *505/982–5511.*

NEED A BREAK?

Ecco Gelato (✉ **105 E. Marcy St.** ☎ **505/986–9778**) has a sleek, minimalist café across from the downtown public library with polished-wood floors, large plate-glass windows, and brushed-metal tables. It's known for its creative gelato flavors (strawberry-habañero, saffron-honey, minty–white grape, chocolate-banana) as well as espressos and coffees, pastries, and sandwiches (roast beef–and–blue cheese, dill-tuna with cucumber and sprouts).

★ ❷ Museum of Fine Arts. Designed by Isaac Hamilton Rapp in 1917, the museum contains one of America's finest regional collections. It's also one of Santa Fe's earliest Pueblo Revival structures, inspired by the adobe structures at Acoma Pueblo. Split-cedar *latillas* (branches set in a cross-hatch pattern) and hand-hewn vigas form the ceilings. The 8,000-piece permanent collection, of which only a fraction is exhibited at any given

A GOOD WALK

Begin on Paseo de Peralta at the **Gerald Peters Gallery** ❾, which has an enormous collection. Continue a half block north to Canyon Road. Turn right (east) and follow the road, which unfolds in shadows of undulating adobe walls. Street parking is at a premium, but there's a city-owned pay lot at the corner of Camino del Monte Sol, a few blocks up. Between visits to galleries and shops, take a break at one of the courtyards or fine restaurants. Be sure to stop by the beautiful gardens outside **El Zaguan** ❿. At the intersection of Upper Canyon and Cristo Rey you'll find the massive **Cristo Rey Church** ⓫. Wear good walking shoes and watch out for the irregular sidewalks, which are built of stone and can get icy in winter.

⏱ TIMING TIPS→ A tour of Canyon Road could take a whole day or as little as a few hours. If art is more than a curiosity to you, you may want to view the Gerald Peters Gallery apart from your Canyon Road tour. There's so much to see there that visual overload could hit before you get halfway up the road. Even on a cold day the walk can be a pleasure, with massive, glistening icicles hanging off roofs and a silence shrouding the side streets.

time, emphasizes the work of regional and nationally renowned artists, including the early Modernist Georgia O'Keeffe; realist Robert Henri; the "Cinco Pintores" (five painters) of Santa Fe (including Fremont Elis and Will Shuster); members of the Taos Society of Artists (Ernest L. Blumenschein, Bert G. Philips, Joseph H. Sharp, and E. Irving Couse, among others); and

GOOD TERM

Coyote Fence: A type of wooden fence that surrounds many New Mexico homes; it comprises branches, usually from cedar or aspen trees, arranged vertically and wired tightly together.

the works of noted 20th-century photographers of the Southwest, including Laura Gilpin, Ansel Adams, and Dorothea Lange. Rotating exhibits are staged throughout the year. Many excellent examples of Spanish-colonial–style furniture are on display. An interior *placita* (small plaza) with fountains, WPA murals, and sculpture, and the St. Francis Auditorium are other highlights. Concerts and lectures are often held in the auditorium. ✉ *107 W. Palace Ave.* ☎ *505/476–5072* ⊕ *www.mfasantafe.org* 🎫 *$8, 4-day pass $18 (good at all 5 state museums in Santa Fe), free Fri. 5–8 PM* ⏱ *Tues.–Thurs. and weekends 10–5, Fri. 10–8.*

🌑 ❶ **Palace of the Governors.** A humble-looking one-story adobe on the north
Fodor'sChoice side of the Plaza, the palace is the oldest public building in the United
★ States. Built at the same time as the Plaza, circa 1610 (scholars debate the exact year), it was the seat of four regional governments—those of Spain, Mexico, the Confederacy, and the U.S. territory that preceded New Mexico's statehood, which was achieved in 1912. The building was abandoned in 1680, following the Pueblo Revolt, but resumed its role as government headquarters when Don Diego de Vargas success-

fully returned in 1692. It served as the residence for 100 Spanish, Mexican, and American governors, including Governor Lew Wallace, who wrote his epic *Ben Hur* in its then drafty rooms, all the while complaining of the dust and mud that fell from its earthen ceiling. In 2004, construction began on a brand-new **State History Museum Annex,** behind the palace on Lincoln. It should open in 2008. Simultaneously, the Palace of the Governors is being renovated to its original purpose, as a house-museum. Its rooms will contain period furnishings and exhibits that illustrate the building's many functions over the past four centuries. For significant periods throughout the renovation process, the palace is expected to be closed, so call ahead for the latest details.

> **WORD OF MOUTH**
>
> "[Buy turquoise] from someone you trust or develop your own expertise. Generally speaking, you can expect natural turquoise to have lots of color variation, and it's usually striated. If it looks uniform in color it's probably not natural."
>
> –beach_dweller

Dozens of Native American vendors gather daily under the portal of the Palace of the Governors to display and sell pottery, jewelry, bread, and other goods. With few exceptions, the more than 500 artists and craftspeople registered to sell here are Pueblo or Navajo Indians. The merchandise for sale is required to meet Museum of New Mexico standards: all items are handmade or hand-strung in Native American households; silver jewelry is either sterling (92.5% pure) or coin (90% pure) silver; all metal jewelry bears the maker's mark, which is registered with the museum. Prices tend to reflect the high quality of the merchandise. Don't take photographs without permission.

The palace has been the central headquarters of the Museum of New Mexico since 1913, housing the main section of the **State History Museum,** until it moves into its eventual new home behind the palace, on Lincoln Avenue. Permanent exhibits chronicle 450 years of New Mexico history, using maps, furniture, clothing, housewares, weaponry, and village models. The main rooms contain rotating exhibits, such as "Jewish Pioneers of New Mexico," an exploration of the vital role Jewish immigrants played during the late 19th and early 20th centuries in the state's civic, economic, and cultural development. With advance permission, students and researchers have access to the comprehensive **Fray Angélico Chávez Library** and its rare maps, manuscripts, and photographs (more than 120,000 prints and negatives). The palace is also home to the **Museum of New Mexico Press,** which prints books, pamphlets, and cards on antique presses and hosts bookbinding demonstrations, lectures, and slide shows. There's an outstanding gift shop and bookstore. ⊠ *Palace Ave., north side of Plaza* ☎ *505/476–5100* ⊕ *www.palaceofthegovernors.org* ☜ *$8, 4-day pass $18 (good at all 5 state museums in Santa Fe), free Fri. 5–8* ☉ *Tues.–Thurs. and weekends 10–5, Fri. 10–8.*

★ ❻ **St. Francis Cathedral Basilica.** This magnificent cathedral, a block east of the Plaza, is one of the rare significant departures from the city's ubiquitous Pueblo architecture. Construction was begun in 1869 by Jean Bap-

A GOOD WALK

The **Loretto Chapel** ⑫, facing the Old Santa Fe Trail, behind the La Fonda hotel, is a good place to start your walk. After visiting the chapel, head southeast on Old Santa Fe Trail to the **San Miguel Mission** ⑬. Across from the mission, on De Vargas Street, is the **Oldest House** ⑭. Up and down narrow De Vargas stretches the **Barrio de Analco** ⑮. There are a few galleries worth visiting on De Vargas Street east of Old Santa Fe Trail, and, back across Old Santa Fe Trail on the west side, check out the historic Santa Fe Playhouse. In the early art colony days, literary luminaries like Mary Austin and Witter Bynner would stage shows here. Walk farther away from downtown until you come to the **New Mexico State Capitol** ⑯, which contains some interesting artwork. ⊙ **TIMING TIPS➡** Plan on spending a half hour at each of the churches and the New Mexico State Capitol and an hour exploring the Barrio de Analco. The entire walk can easily be done in about 3½ hours.

tiste Lamy, Santa Fe's first archbishop, working with French architects and Italian stonemasons. The Romanesque style was popular in Lamy's native home in southwest France. The circuit-riding cleric was sent by the Catholic Church to the Southwest to change the religious practices of its native population (to "civilize" them, as one period document puts it) and is buried in the crypt beneath the church's high altar. He was the inspiration behind Willa Cather's novel *Death Comes for the Archbishop* (1927). In 2005 Pope Benedict XVI declared St. Francis the "cradle of Catholicism" in the Southwestern United States, and upgraded the status of the building from mere cathedral to cathedral basilica—it's one of just 36 in the country.

DID YOU KNOW?

Two miniseries based on Larry McMurtry novels, *Lonesome Dove* and *Buffalo Girls*, were shot near Santa Fe.

A small adobe chapel on the northeast side of the cathedral, the remnant of an earlier church, embodies the Hispanic architectural influence so conspicuously absent from the cathedral itself. The chapel's *Nuestra Señora de la Paz* (Our Lady of Peace), popularly known as *La Conquistadora,* the oldest Madonna statue in the United States, accompanied Don Diego de Vargas on his reconquest of Santa Fe in 1692, a feat attributed to the statue's spiritual intervention. Every Friday the faithful adorn the statue with a new dress. Just south of the cathedral, where the parking lot meets Paseo de Peralta, is the **Archdiocese of Santa Fe Museum** (☎ 505/983–3811), a small museum where many of the area's historic, liturgical artifacts are on view. ⊠ *231 Cathedral Pl.* ☎ *505/982–5619* ⊙ *Mon.–Sat. 6–6, Sun. 7–7, except during mass. Mass Mon.–Sat. at 7 and 5:15 PM; Sun. at 8 and 10 AM, noon, and 7 PM. Museum weekdays 8:30–4:30.*

8 Sena Plaza. Two-story buildings enclose this courtyard, which can be entered only through two small doorways on Palace Avenue. Surrounding the oasis of flowering fruit trees, a fountain, and inviting benches are unique, low-profile shops. The quiet courtyard is a good place for repose. The buildings, erected in the 1700s as a single-family residence, had quarters for blacksmiths, bakers, farmers, and all manner of help. ✉ *125 E. Palace Ave.*

Canyon Road

Once a Native American trail and an early-20th-century route for woodcutters and their burros, Canyon Road is now lined with art galleries, shops, and restaurants, earning it the nickname "The Art and Soul of Santa Fe." The narrow road begins at the eastern curve of Paseo de Peralta and stretches for about 2 mi at a moderate incline toward the base of the mountains.

Most establishments are in authentic, old adobe homes with undulating thick walls that appear to have been carved out of the earth. Within many are contemporary and traditional works by artists with internationally renowned names like Fernando Botero to anonymous weavers of ancient Peruvian textiles.

There are few places as festive as Canyon Road on Christmas Eve, when thousands of farolitos illuminate walkways, walls, roofs, and even trees. In May the scent of lilacs wafts over the adobe walls, and in August red hollyhocks enhance the surreal color of the blue sky on a dry summer day.

What to See

11 Cristo Rey Church. Built in 1940 and designed by legendary Santa Fe architect John Gaw Meem to commemorate the 400th anniversary of Francisco Vásquez de Coronado's exploration of the Southwest, this church is the largest Spanish adobe structure in the United States and is considered by many the finest example of Pueblo-style architecture anywhere. The church was constructed in the old-fashioned way by parishioners, who mixed the more than 200,000 mud-and-straw adobe bricks and hauled them into place. The 225-ton stone *reredos* (altar screen) is magnificent. ✉ *Canyon Rd. at Cristo Rey* ☎ *505/983–8528* ☼ *Daily 8–7.*

10 El Zaguan. Headquarters of the **Historic Santa Fe Foundations (HSFF),** this 19th-century Territorial-style house has a small exhibit on Santa Fe architecture and preservation, but the real draw is the small but stunning garden abundant with lavender, roses, and 160-year-old trees. You can relax on a wrought-iron bench and take in the fine views of the hills northeast of town. An HSFF horticulturist often gives free tours and lectures in the garden on Thursday at 1 in summer (call to confirm). ✉ *545 Canyon Rd.* ☎ *505/983–2567* ⊕ *www.historicsantafe.*

Rethinking Santa Fe Style

IN SANTA FE, EVERYTHING FROM THE ANCIENT Palace of the Governors to today's Walgreens is clad in adobe and designed in the Pueblo Revival or Spanish-colonial tradition. Picturesque and charming, this look is not, however, necessarily all that authentic: it dates from the early 20th century, at least as it applies to architecture and urban planning.

Around 1920, less than a decade after New Mexico attained statehood, the city's leaders decided that they could enhance Santa Fe's image, and promote tourism, by instituting urban planning guidelines calling for all new construction in the adobe style. At that time, the Plaza and the blocks around it contained a mix of Italianate, Queen Anne, and other Victorian styles, mixed with Spanish-colonial, and Pueblo Revival buildings.

Some lament that Santa Fe is too uniform, and that the degree to which the city enforces the Santa Fe style verges on the ridiculous. If Santa Fe is going to allow strip malls and tract developments, albeit, thankfully, several miles from the historic district, shouldn't the developers be permitted to design them as they please?

Others argue that Santa Fe, along with much of northern New Mexico's Rio Grande Valley, must rigorously preserve its style, even if it wasn't codified until the 20th century. Aesthetically and architecturally, this part of the country enjoys a singular appearance. The region's buildings may look similar, but they look nothing at all like buildings elsewhere. Besides, an urban design theme developed in the 1920s, based on regional building traditions of the prior few centuries, can legitimately be called historic at this point.

Although city planners began encouraging a unified style from the 1920s onward, officially, Santa Fe adopted its Historic Zoning Ordinance in 1957. Today, the city's Historic Design Review Board checks that all new development fits within these particular guidelines, and that developers conduct a historical study of the surrounding area before embarking on any new construction.

Regardless of how far back you trace Santa Fe style, the look of the city and the Rio Grande Valley's other communities preserves a distinct amalgam of indigenous, Spanish, and Western architectural traditions. We owe the concept of earthen walls and flat roofs to the region's many centuries of Pueblo Indians, although it was the Spaniards who perfected building with adobe bricks. An increase in trade with U.S. states in the 19th century brought a greater variety of materials to the region, leading to an increasing use of timber and metal in building construction. This led to the development of an architectural style unique to the Southwest, Territorial, which combines American Victorian, frontier, Spanish-colonial, and—to a lesser degree—Pueblo Indian design elements.

For a more thorough examination of Santa Fe's design aesthetic and how it has evolved, take a look at Chris Wilson's book, *The Myth of Santa Fe: Creating a Modern Regional Tradition.*

—Andrew Collins

com ✉ *Free* ⊙ *Foundations of-fices weekdays 9–noon and 1:30–5; gardens Mon.–Sat. 9–5.*

❾ **Gerald Peters Gallery.** While under construction, this 32,000-square-foot building was dubbed the "ninth northern pueblo," its scale rivaling that of the eight northern pueblos around Santa Fe. The suavely designed Pueblo-style gallery is Santa Fe's premier showcase for American

and European art from the 19th century to the present. It feels like a museum, but all the works are for sale. Pablo Picasso, Georgia O'Keeffe, Charles M. Russell, Deborah Butterfield, George Rickey, and members of the Taos Society are among the artists represented, along with nationally renowned contemporary ones. ✉ *1011 Paseo de Peralta* ☎ *505/954–5700* ⊕ *www.gpgallery.com* ✉ *Free* ⊙ *Mon.–Sat. 10–5.*

NEED A BREAK?

Locals congregate in the courtyard or on the front portal of **Downtown Subscription** (✉ 376 Garcia St. ☎ 505/983-3085), a block east of Canyon Road. This café-newsstand sells coffees, snacks, and pastries, plus one of the largest assortments of newspapers and magazines in New Mexico. A delightful spot toward the end of gallery row on Canyon Road, right at the intersection with Palace Avenue, the **Teahouse** (✉ 821 Canyon Rd. ☎ 505/992-0972) has both a bright dining area and a tranquil outdoor seating area in a rock garden. In addition to teas from all over the world, you can find extremely well-prepared breakfast and lunch fare.

Lower Old Santa Fe Trail

It was along the Old Santa Fe Trail that wagon trains from Missouri rolled into town in the 1800s, forever changing Santa Fe's destiny. This area off the Plaza is one of Santa Fe's most historic.

What to See

⓯ **Barrio de Analco.** Along the south bank of the Santa Fe River, the barrio—its name means "district on the other side of the water"—is one of America's oldest neighborhoods, settled in the early 1600s by the Tlaxcalan Indians (who were forbidden to live with the Spanish near the Plaza) and in the 1690s by soldiers who had helped recapture New Mexico after the Pueblo Revolt. Plaques on houses on East De Vargas Street will help you locate some of the important structures. Check the performance schedule at the **Santa Fe Playhouse** on De Vargas Street, founded by writer Mary Austin and other Santa Feans in the 1920s.

⓬ **Loretto Chapel.** A delicate Gothic church modeled after Sainte-Chapelle in Paris, Loretto was built in 1873 by the same French architects and Italian stonemasons who built St. Francis Cathedral. The chapel is known for the "Miraculous Staircase" that leads to the choir loft. Legend has it that the chapel was almost complete when it became obvious that there

A GOOD WALK

From the Plaza, head west on San Francisco Street, and then take a left onto Guadalupe Street toward **Santuario de Guadalupe** ㉒, a short way farther on your right. After you visit the Santuario, take your time browsing through the shops and eating lunch in one of the restaurants farther down Guadalupe Street or around the corner at the **Sanbusco Market Center,** a massive warehouse. Check out the innovative shops and the photographic history on the walls near the market's main entrance. Back on Guadalupe, head south past the historic Gross Kelly Warehouse, one of the earliest Santa Fe–style buildings. You pass two huge murals on buildings facing Guadalupe Street depicting the magic realism that flavors so much of New Mexico culture. Note Santa Fe's two train depots—one is

now the site of the touristy Tomasita's Restaurant; the other, set farther back, is the Santa Fe Depot, where the **Santa Fe Southern Railway** ㉓ departs. Continue a short distance south on Guadalupe until you reach **SITE Santa Fe** ㉔ gallery and performance space, set inside a former bottling warehouse. Cater-corner from SITE Santa Fe, **El Museo Cultural de Santa Fe** ㉕ is one of the state's more unusual museums, a combination performance space, classroom, gallery, and event venue that promotes Hispanic culture and education in the City Different.

⏱ TIMING TIPS➡ **A visit to the Santuario de Guadalupe can take 15 minutes to an hour, depending on whether or not there's an art show in progress. If you like shopping, you might spend hours in this neighborhood.**

wasn't room to build a staircase to the choir loft. In answer to the prayers of the cathedral's nuns, a mysterious carpenter arrived on a donkey, built a 20-foot staircase—using only a square, a saw, and a tub of water to season the wood—and then disappeared as quickly as he came. Many of the faithful believed it was St. Joseph himself. The stair-

GOOD TERM

Pueblo Revival: Most homes in this style, modeled after the traditional dwellings of the Southwest Pueblo Indians, are cube or rectangle shaped.

case contains two complete 360-degree turns with no central support; no nails were used in its construction. The chapel closes for services and special events. Adjoining the chapel are a small museum and gift shop. ✉ *211 Old Santa Fe Trail* ☎ *505/982–0092* ⊕ *www.lorettochapel.com* 🎫 *Donation suggested* ⊙ *Mid-Oct.–mid-May, Mon.–Sat. 9–5, Sun. 10:30–5; mid-May–mid-Oct., Mon.–Sat. 9–6, Sun. 10:30–5.*

★ ⑯ **New Mexico State Capitol.** The symbol of the Zía Pueblo, which represents the Circle of Life, was the inspiration for the capitol, also known as the Roundhouse. Doorways at opposing sides of this 1966 structure symbolize the four winds, the four directions, and the four seasons.

A GOOD TOUR

This museum tour begins 2 mi south of the Plaza, an area known as Museum Hill that's best reached by car or via one of the city buses that leave hourly from near the Plaza. Begin at the **Museum of Indian Arts and Culture** ⑰, which is set around **Milner Plaza,** an attractively landscaped courtyard and gardens with outdoor art installations. Many days the Plaza hosts Native American dances, jewelry-making demonstrations, kids' activities, and other interactive events; there's also the Museum Hill Cafe, which is open for lunch (and Sunday brunch) and serves salads, quiche, burgers, sandwiches and wraps, ice cream, and other light fare. To get here from downtown, drive uphill on Old

Santa Fe Trail to Camino Lejo. Across Milner Plaza is the **Museum of International Folk Art (MOIFA)** ⑱. From Milner Plaza, a bike-pedestrian path leads a short way to the **Museum of Spanish Colonial Art** ⑲. Return to Milner Plaza, from which a different bike-pedestrian path leads a short way to the **Wheelwright Museum of the American Indian** ⑳. To reach the **Santa Fe Children's Museum** ㉑ you need to drive back down the hill or ask the bus driver to let you off near it. ⊙ TIMING TIPS→ Set aside a half to full day to see all the museums on the Upper Santa Fe Trail. Kids usually have to be dragged from the Children's Museum, even after an hour or two.

Throughout the building are artworks from the outstanding collection of the Capitol Art Foundation, historical and cultural displays, and hand-crafted furniture—it's a superb and somewhat overlooked array of fine art. The **Governor's Gallery** hosts temporary exhibits. Six acres of imaginatively landscaped gardens shelter outstanding sculptures. ⊠ *Old Santa Fe Trail at Paseo de Peralta* ☎ *505/986–4589* ⊕ *http://legis.state. nm.us/lcs* ⊠ *Free* ⊙ *Weekdays 7–6; tours weekdays by appt.*

⓮ **The Oldest House.** More than 800 years ago, Pueblo people built this structure out of "puddled" adobe (liquid mud poured between upright wooden frames). This house, which contains a gift shop, is said to be the oldest in the United States. ⊠ *215 E. De Vargas St.*

⓭ **San Miguel Mission.** The oldest church still in use in the United States, this
Fodor's Choice   simple earth-hue adobe structure was built in the early 17th century by
★   the Tlaxcalan Indians of Mexico, who came to New Mexico as servants of the Spanish. Badly damaged in the 1680 Pueblo Revolt, the structure was restored and enlarged in 1710. On display in the chapel are priceless statues and paintings and the San José Bell, weighing nearly 800 pounds, which is believed to have been cast in Spain in 1356. In winter the church sometimes closes before its official closing hour. Mass is held on Sunday at 5 PM. Next door in the back of the Territorial-style dormitories of the old St. Michael's High School, a **Visitor Information Center** can help you find your way around northern New Mexico. ⊠ *401 Old Santa Fe Trail* ☎ *505/983–3974* ⊠ *$1* ⊙ *Mission Mon.–Sat. 10–4, Sun. 3–4:30.*

Upper Old Santa Fe Trail & Museum Hill

What to See

★ ⓱ **Museum of Indian Arts and Culture.** An interactive, multimedia exhibition tells the story of Native American history in the Southwest, merging contemporary Native American experience with historical accounts and artifacts. The collection has some of New Mexico's oldest works of art: pottery ves-

sels, fine stone and silver jewelry, intricate textiles, and other arts and crafts created by Pueblo, Navajo, and Apache artisans. You can also see art demonstrations and a video about the life and work of Pueblo potter Maria Martinez. ⊠ *710 Camino Lejo* ☎ *505/476–1250* ⊕ *www. miaclab.org* ⊠ *$8, 4-day pass $18, good at all 5 state museums in Santa Fe* ☉ *Tues.–Sun. 10–5.*

⓲ **Museum of International Folk Art (MOIFA).** At this museum, the premier institution of its kind in the world, you can find amazingly inventive handmade objects—a tin Madonna, a devil made from bread dough, and all kinds of rag dolls. Florence Dibell Bartlett, who founded the museum in 1953, donated its first 4,000 works. In the late 1970s Alexander and Susan Girard, major folk-art collectors, gave the museum 106,000 items. The Hispanic Heritage Wing contains art dating from the Spanish-colonial period (in New Mexico, 1598–1821) to the present. The 5,000-piece exhibit includes religious works—particularly *bultos* (carved wooden statues of saints) and *retablos* (holy images painted on wood or tin). The objects in the Neutrogena Wing are exhibited by theme rather than by date or country of origin—you might, for instance, find a sheer Eskimo parka alongside a Chinese undergarment made of bamboo and cotton webbing. Lloyd's Treasure Chest, the wing's innovative basement section, provides a behind-the-scenes look at more of this collection. You can rummage about storage drawers, peer into microscopes, and, on occasion, speak with conservators and other museum personnel. ⊠ *706 Camino Lejo* ☎ *505/476–1200* ⊕ *www.moifa.org* ⊠ *$8, 4-day pass $18, good at all 5 state museums in Santa Fe* ☉ *Tues.–Sun. 10–5.*

⓳ **Museum of Spanish Colonial Art.** Opened in 2002, this 5,000-square-foot adobe museum occupies a building designed in 1930 by acclaimed architect John Gaw Meem. The Spanish Colonial Art Society formed in Santa Fe in 1925 to preserve traditional Spanish-colonial art and culture. The museum, which sits next to the Museum of New Mexico complex, displays the fruits of the society's labor—one of the most comprehensive collections of Spanish-colonial art in the world. The Hale Matthews Library contains a 1,000-volume collection of books relating to this important period in art history. Objects here, dating from the 16th century to the present, include retablos, elaborate santos, tinwork, straw appliqué, furniture, ceramics, and ironwork. There's also

FodorśChoice
★

a fine collection of works by Hispanic artists of the 20th century. ✉ *750 Camino Lejo* ☎ *505/982–2226* ⊕ *www.spanishcolonial.org/museum. shtml* 🎫 *$6, 4-day pass $18, good at all 5 state museums in Santa Fe* ⊙ *Daily 10–5.*

🅑 ㉑ **Santa Fe Children's Museum.** Stimulating hands-on exhibits, a solar green-house, oversize geometric forms, and a simulated 18-foot mountain-climbing wall all contribute to this underrated museum's popularity with kids. Puppeteers and storytellers perform often. ✉ *1050 Old Pecos Trail* ☎ *505/989–8359* ⊕ *www.santafechildrensmuseum.org* 🎫 *$8* ⊙ *Wed.–Sat. 10–5, Sun. noon–5.*

㉒ **Wheelwright Museum of the American Indian.** A private institution in a building shaped like a traditional octagonal Navajo hogan, the Wheelwright opened in 1937. Founded by Boston scholar Mary Cabot Wheelwright and Navajo medicine man Hastiin Klah, the museum originated as a place to house ceremonial materials. Those items are not on view to the public. What is displayed are 19th- and 20th-century baskets, pottery, sculpture, weavings, metalwork, photography, and paintings, including contemporary works by Native American artists. The Case Trading Post on the lower level is modeled after the trading posts that dotted the southwestern frontier more than 100 years ago. It carries an extensive selection of books and contemporary Native American jewelry, kachina dolls, weaving, and pottery. ✉ *704 Camino Lejo* ☎ *505/982–4636 or 800/607–4636* ⊕ *www.wheelwright.org* 🎫 *Free* ⊙ *Mon.–Sat. 10–5, Sun. 1–5; gallery tours weekdays at 2, Sat. at 1.*

Guadalupe District

The historic warehouse and railyard district of Santa Fe is commonly referred to as the Guadalupe District. After the demise of the train route through town, the low-lying warehouses were converted to artists' studios and antiques shops, and bookstores, specialty shops, and restaurants have sprung up. The restored scenic train line puts the town's old depot to use, and eventually this station will be the Santa Fe terminus of the *Railrunner* commuter train service that's planned from Albuquerque sometime in 2008. Presently, the impressive local farmers' market turns the vacant lot at the corner of Guadalupe and Cerrillos into a colorful outdoor fiesta, but as part of a comprehensive redevelopment plan for the neighborhood, this 13-acre lot is slated to be converted into a beautiful, grassy park in the next couple of years. Additional—tentative—plans for the neighborhood include redeveloping much of the dusty parking areas around the old rail depot, building a multiplex cinema, and expanding the neighborhood's retail and entertainment space.

What to See

㉕ **El Museo Cultural de Santa Fe.** As much an educational and community gathering space as a museum, the Santa Fe Cultural Museum celebrates Santa Fe's—and New Mexico's—rich Hispanic heritage by presenting a wide range of events, from children's theater to musical concerts. The museum also sponsors the Contemporary Hispanic Market on the Plaza each July (held the same time as Spanish Market), and the Contemporary Hispanic Artists Winter Market, held at El Museo Cultural in late November. There's also a gallery that exhibits contemporary art by Hispanic artists. A great resource to visitors are the many classes and workshops, which are open to the public, and touch on everything from guitar and Mexican folkloric dance to children's theater and art. The museum occupies what had been a dilapidated liquor warehouse before El Museo took over the space in the late '90s. ⊠ *1615 Paseo de Peralta* ☎ *505/ 992–0591* ⊕ *www.elmuseocultural.org* ✉ *Free; prices vary for events and shows* ☉ *Tues.–Fri. 1–5, Sat. 10–5; additionally for events and shows.*

㉓ Santa Fe Southern Railway. For a leisurely tour across the Santa Fe plateau and into the vast Galisteo Basin, where panoramic views extend for up to 120 mi, take a nostalgic ride on the antique cars of the Santa Fe Southern Railway. The train once served a spur of the Atchison, Topeka & Santa Fe Railway. Today the train takes visitors on 36-mi round-trip scenic trips to Lamy, a sleepy village with the region's only Amtrak service, offering picnics under the cottonwoods (bring your own or buy one from the caterer that meets the train) at the quaint rail station. Shorter runs travel down to the scenic Galisteo Basin. Aside from day trips, the railway offers special events such as a Friday-night "High Desert High Ball" cash bar with appetizers and a Saturday Night Barbecue Train. Trains depart from the Santa Fe Depot, rebuilt in 1909 after the original was destroyed in a fire. There's talk of eventually opening a regional transportation and rail museum here, as part of the efforts to redevelop this part of the Guadalupe District. ⊠ *410 S. Guadalupe St.* ☎ *505/989–8600 or 888/989–8600* ⊕ *www.sfsr. com* ⚠ *Reservations essential* ✉ *Day-trips from $32, dinner trains from $58* ☉ *Call for schedule.*

㉒ Santuario de Guadalupe. A humble adobe structure built by Franciscan missionaries between 1776 and 1795, this is the oldest shrine in the United States to Our Lady of Guadalupe, Mexico's patron saint. The sanctuary, now a nonprofit cultural center, has adobe walls nearly 3 feet thick. Among the sanctuary's religious art and artifacts is a priceless 16th-century work by Venetian painter Leonardo de Ponte Bassano that depicts Jesus driving the money changers from the Temple. Also of note is a portrait of Our Lady of Guadalupe by the Mexican colonial painter José de Alzíbar. Other highlights are the traditional New Mexican carved and painted altar screen, an authentic 19th-century sacristy, a pictorial-history archive, a library devoted to Archbishop Jean Baptiste Lamy that is furnished with many of his belongings, and a garden with plants from the Holy Land. ⊠ *100 Guadalupe St.* ☎ *505/988–2027* ✉ *Donation suggested* ☉ *May–Oct., Mon.–Sat. 9–4; Nov.–Apr., weekdays 9–4.*

★ ㉔ SITE Santa Fe. The events at this nexus of international contemporary art include lectures, concerts, author readings, performance art, and gallery shows. The facility hosts a biennial exhibition every odd-numbered year. There are always provocative exhibitions here, however, and the immense, open space is ideal for taking in the many larger-than-life installations. ⊠ *1606 Paseo de Peralta* ☎ *505/989–1199* ⊕ *www. sitesantafe.org* ✉ *$10, free Fri.* ☉ *Wed., Thurs., and Sat. 10–5, Fri. 10–7, Sun. noon—5.*

WHERE TO EAT

Eating out is a major pastime in Santa Fe. Several high-profile chefs run restaurants here, but quite a few divey joints also serve highly acclaimed food. People sometimes complain about the steep restaurant prices (often as much as what you pay in New York or San Francisco), and although most of the high-end restaurants are worth it, you can find some great bargains if you look around a bit. Eateries frequented by locals and that serve great cuisine are often outside of downtown and away from the Plaza. Waits for tables are very common during the busy summer season, so it's a good idea to call ahead even when reservations aren't accepted, if only to get a sense of the waiting time.

So-called Santa Fe–style cuisine has so many influences that the term is virtually meaningless. Traditional, old-style Santa Fe restaurants serve New Mexican fare, which combines both Native American and Hispanic traditions and differs markedly from Americanized or even authentic Mexican cooking. Many of the better restaurants in town serve a contemporary regional style of cooking that blends New Mexican ingredients and preparations with those of interior and coastal Mexico, Latin America, the Mediterranean, East Asia, and varied parts of the United States. There are a few respected Italian restaurants in town, and a growing number of commendable Asian eateries, but all in all the city's ethnic culinary diversity is a bit limited.

WHAT IT COSTS				
$$$$	$$$	$$	$	¢
RESTAURANTS over $30	$24–$30	$17–$24	$10–$17	under $10

Prices are per person for a main course at dinner, excluding 8.25% sales tax.

American–Casual

$–$$ ✕ **Railyard Restaurant & Saloon.** Set inside a bustling, handsome warehouse in the railyard at the Guadalupe District, this trendy spot operated by the same talented management that runs 315 Restaurant & Wine Bar serves relatively affordable, well-prepared American favorites that have been given nouvelle twists. Good bets include fried buttermilk-chicken strips with Creole rémoulade dipping sauce, and sesame-and-panko-crusted tuna with a soy-honey sauce, and barbecued baby back ribs. Many patrons choose to sit in the casual bar, where both the full and lighter menus are available, and sip on pomegranate margaritas or well-chosen wines by the glass. You can also dine on the large patio during the warmer months. ⊠ *530 S. Guadalupe St.* ☎ *505/989–3300* ▭ *AE, D, MC, V* ⊗ *No lunch Sun.*

¢–$$ ✕ **The Cowgirl.** A rollicking, popular bar and grill with several rooms overflowing with Old West memorabilia, Cowgirl has reasonably priced and tasty Southwestern, Tex-Mex, barbecue, and southern fare. Highlights include barbecue, buffalo burgers, bourbon-glaze pork chops, and

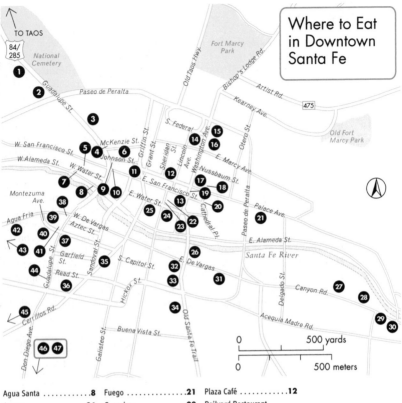

Where to Eat in Downtown Santa Fe

2

salmon tacos with tomatillo salsa. So what's the bad news? Consistently subpar service. Nevertheless, knock back a few drinks and catch one of the nightly music acts—usually rock or blues—and you're likely to leave smiling. Grab a seat on the spacious patio in warm weather. Next door, Cowgirl Pickup has an extensive selection of takeout, including what many consider to be the best breakfast burritos in Santa Fe, plus Taos Cow ice cream. ⊠ *319 S. Guadalupe St.* ☎ *505/982–2565* ⊟ *AE, D, MC, V.*

¢–$ ✕ **Atomic Grill.** Burgers, salads, pizzas, sandwiches, and other light fare are served at this tiny late-night café a block off the Plaza. The food is decent and the service brusque but usually okay. The best attributes are the comfy patio overlooking pedestrian-heavy Water Street, the huge list of imported beers, and the late hours (it's open until 3 most nights)— an extreme rarity in Santa Fe. You'll be glad this place exists when the bars let out and you're famished. ⊠ *103 Water St.* ☎ *505/820–2866* ⊟ *MC, V.*

¢–$ ✕ **Bagelmania.** Tucked down a side street a few blocks northwest of the Plaza, this always-packed breakfast and lunch spot has a nondescript dining room overlooking a big parking lot, but the food is stellar. Breakfast favorites include the Chesapeake Bay Benedict, topped with blue-crab croquettes, and the Lonestar platter (chicken-fried steak, two eggs, and creamy gravy). At lunch, try the roasted rosemary chicken or char-grilled eggplant sandwich. Yes, they have plenty of New York–style bagels and spreads, too, but there's plenty more to choose from here. ⊠ *420 Catron St.* ☎ *505/982–8900* ⊟ *AE, MC, V* ⊗ *No dinner.*

¢–$ ✕ **Bobcat Bite.** This divey grill in a tiny roadhouse a 15-minute drive south of town serves steaks and chops but is famous for one thing: the biggest and juiciest burgers in town. Locals prefer them topped with cheese and green chile. Only early dinners are available, as the place closes by 8 most nights. ⊠ *Old Las Vegas Hwy., 4½ mi south of Old Pecos Trail exit off I–25* ☎ *505/983–5319* ⌂ *Reservations not accepted* ⊟ *No credit cards* ⊗ *Closed Sun.–Tues.*

¢–$ ✕ **San Francisco Street Bar & Grill.** Occupying a sun-filled, second-floor space near the Plaza, this convivial spot offers predictable but inexpensive, well-prepared American fare along with a nice selection of wines, beers, and cocktails. It's a family-friendly, somewhat noisy place with comfy booths and smaller hardwood tables and chairs. Popular starters include fried calamari or pan-seared shrimp salad. The half-pound burger here is superb, along with such reliable standbys as asiago-basil-garlic ravioli and grilled ruby trout with grilled-pineapple salsa. ⊠ *50 E. San Francisco St.* ☎ *505/982–2044* ⊟ *AE, D, MC, V.*

¢–$ ✕ **Sol.** Opened in 2004, this casual spot on Canyon Road offers value and convenience to this gallery-studded thoroughfare with few affordable dining options. Another big plus is the cozy patio overlooking the colorful pedestrian traffic. Sol serves mostly burgers and comfort fare, such as mac and cheese, Belgian waffles, catfish sandwiches, and Caesar salads—and there are also 18 kinds of beer. Although it's open for dinner, the restaurant closes early, at 8. The same chef helms the snazzy and more upscale Canyon Restaurant, across the street. ⊠ *802 Canyon Rd.* ☎ *505/989–1949* ⊟ *AE, D, MC, V.*

¢–$ ✕ **Tesuque Village Market.** A favorite spot for a snack or a full meal before heading to the opera or after shopping at the Tesuque Pueblo Flea Market, this epicurean grocery and people-watching café has a tiny but lovely patio and a less atmospheric indoor seating area. The kitchen serves up tasty American and New Mexican fare—pork chops verde, posole (stew made with lime hominy, pork, chile, and garlic), French toast, Frito pie. Save room for a fresh-baked brownie or cookie. ✉ *NM 590 at Bishop's Lodge Rd., Tesuque, 5 mi north of Santa Fe* ☎ *505/988–8848* ⌣ *Reservations not accepted* ▭ *MC, V.*

¢–$ ✕ **Zia Diner.** This slick diner with a low-key, art deco–style interior serves comfort food prepared with the occasional creative enhancement (consider green chile–piñon meat loaf, for example). Stop in for a full meal (ask about the night's blue-plate special, like Friday's fish Vera Cruz style) or just a classic banana split with homemade hot fudge sauce. Zia's Cobb salad is one of the best in town, and the chicken-fried chicken will fill you up for a good long time. Service is friendly but sometimes slow, and the food is fresh. There's a cheerful patio. Breakfast here is a bargain: try the smoked-salmon breakfast pizza. ✉ *326 S. Guadalupe St.* ☎ *505/988–7008* ⊕ *www.ziadiner.com* ▭ *AE, MC, V.*

Cafés

★ ¢–$ ✕ **Cloud Cliff Bakery.** Breakfast tends to be a big social affair in Santa Fe, and several very good bakeries vie heavily for the morning crowd. Although it's a 10-minute drive south of town, Cloud Cliff Bakery prepares some of the best food, using organic ingredients when possible. For lunch, consider smoked Norwegian salmon with herbed cream cheese, spinach, and tomato, or the black-bean chipotle chili. Breakfast favorites include herb-grilled polenta with mozzarella, green chile sauce, and two eggs any style, and blue corn pancakes with granola. This sleek, modern dining room fills up fast on weekends, so expect a wait. ✉ *1805 2nd St.* ☎ *505/983–6254* ▭ *MC, V* ☺ *No dinner.*

¢–$ ✕ **Mission Cafe.** Tucked down an alley off Old Santa Fe Trail, near the capitol, this sunny, art-filled café inside an 1850s adobe serves some of the tastiest breakfast and lunch fare in town. The food is mostly New Mexican–inspired, including excellent breakfast burritos, as well as delicious pies, strong espresso drinks, and locally produced Tara's Organic Ice Cream, which comes in such unusual flavors as blueberry mint and lemongrass. During the warmer months, dine on the big front patio, shaded with leafy trees. ✉ *237 E. DeVargas St.* ☎ *505/983–3033* ▭ *MC, V* ☺ *No dinner.*

¢–$ ✕ **Whole Body Cafe.** This healthful stop is inside Body Santa Fe, a holistically minded center devoted to bodywork and healing where you'll also find a spa offering a full range of treatments, a yoga studio (with classes open to visitors), a child-care center, and boutique selling a wide range of beauty, health, and lifestyle products, plus jewelry, clothing, music, tarot cards, and all sorts of interesting gifts. The café uses mostly organic ingredients and serves three meals a day, including granola or egg scrambles at breakfast. At lunch try soba noodles with peanuts and a ginger-soy vinaigrette, and at dinner there's a very good lasagna layered with basil-sunflower pesto, portobello mushrooms, spinach, squash, tomatoes, cheese, and marinara sauce. ⊠ *333 Cordova Rd.* ☎ *505/986–0362* ▤ *AE, D, MC, V.*

¢ ╳ **Chocolate Maven.** Although the name of this cheery bakery suggests sweets, and you can definitely get a sugar high here, Chocolate Maven produces impressive savory breakfast and lunch fare. Favorite treats include wild mushroom–and–goat cheese focaccia sandwiches, eggs ménage à trois (one each of eggs Benedict, Florentine, and Madison—the latter consisting of smoked salmon and poached egg), and Caprese salad of fresh mozzarella, basil, and tomatoes. Some of the top desserts include Belgian chocolate fudge brownies, mocha-buttercream torte with chocolate-covered strawberries, and perhaps the best carrot cake in New Mexico. ⊠ *821 W. San Mateo St.* ☎ *505/984–1980* ▤ *AE, D, MC, V* ☽ *No dinner.*

¢ ╳ **Four and Twenty Blackbirds.** Set in a tiny converted 1920s grocery store (it still contains the original deli counter and refrigerator), this café is most famous for its savory and sweet pies, from chicken to gooseberry to coconut cream. But you can drop in at lunchtime to sample such exquisite sandwiches as roast beef with vine-ripened tomatoes and bluecheese cole slaw. There's also a wide selection of kitchen goods, gourmet foods, and fun knickknacks. Parking is at the vintage Texaco station a few doors down. ⊠ *620 Old Santa Fe Trail* ☎ *505/983–7676* ▤ *MC, V* ☽ *No dinner.*

★ ¢ ╳ **Santa Fe Baking Company.** The large, split-level dining room and expansive patio at this long-running café is usually packed with hungry bargain-minded diners and workers and students pecking away on their laptops, taking advantage of the free Wi-Fi. Breakfast is served all day, and you might try the carne adovada burrito or blue corn pancakes. At lunch consider the grilled ham torta with smoked ham, cheddar, and chipotle mayo, or the big chile dog. Lots of juices, coffees, and teas are served, too. On weekend mornings, expect a wait for a table—this place packs 'em in. It closes at 8 PM nightly. ⊠ *504 W. Cordova St.* ☎ *505/988–4292* ▤ *AE, D, MC, V.*

Chinese

¢–$$ ╳ **Chow's.** A pleasing alternative to the many Americanized Chinese restaurants in town, Chow's occupies a modest but cheerful space in a shopping center a few miles south of the Plaza. The kitchen conjures up imaginative Chinese dishes, including a knockout starter of fried wontons stuffed with crab and Parmesan cheese and tossed with an orange-ginger glaze. A worthy entrée is scallops wok-fried with red-chile rings, bok choy, and coconut milk. Green-tea ice cream makes a nice dessert. ⊠ *720 St. Michael's Dr.* ☎ *505/471–7120* ▤ *AE, MC, V* ☽ *Closed Sun.*

Contemporary

$$$–$$$$ ╳ **The Compound.** Three decades ago, this handsome adobe tucked down an alley off Canyon Road epitomized white-glove fine dining. Its fortunes waxed and waned over the years before acclaimed restaurateurs Brett Kemmerer and Mark Kiffin transformed it into one of the state's

culinary darlings. It's still a fancy place, but dress is a cut below formal, and the staff highly attentive but also easygoing. From Chef Kiffin's oft-changing menu consider a starter of calamari grilled with lime, cilantro, and ginger. Memorable entrées include braised New Mexico lamb shank with fire-roasted tomato risotto; and buttermilk roast chicken with creamed fresh spinach and foie gras pan gravy. ⊠ *653 Canyon Rd.* ☎ *505/982–4353* ⊕ *www.compoundrestaurant.com* ⊟ *AE, D, DC, MC, V* ⊗ *No lunch weekends.*

$$$–$$$$ ✕ **Coyote Cafe.** Touristy, bold, and presided over by celebrity chef Mark Miller, this is the restaurant lots of people love to bad-mouth. Say what you will, Coyote Cafe manages to produce consistently original Southwest cooking, and the service is surprisingly pleasant considering the high expectations and sometimes overwhelming crowds. Try pecan-grilled New York sirloin with pasilla chile–fig green mole sauce, or rotisserie pheasant with *huitlacoche* (a wild-mushroom fungus that grows on sweet corn) crepe and truffle-whipped cream. The open dining room can be loud and obnoxiously showy. On the wine list are more than 500 vintages. Inventive, delicious, under-$15 fare is served April through October on the open-air Rooftop Cantina, one of Santa Fe's best bargains. ⊠ *132 W. Water St.* ☎ *505/983–1615* ⊕ *www.coyotecafe.com* ⊟ *AE, D, DC, MC, V* ⊗ *No lunch except at Rooftop Cantina.*

$$$–$$$$ ✕ **Fuego.** An elegant dining room inside La Posada resort, Fuego lacked pizzazz before current chef Rahm Fama took over in 2003. Now it's one of Santa Fe's top restaurants, albeit with sky-high prices. You might start with seared foie gras with apple pie au poivre, before trying free-range *poussin* (young chicken) over a nest of braised leeks and salsify, or roast rack of Colorado elk with parsnip dumplings and a dried-cherry mole. Perhaps the most astounding dish is the artisanal cheese plate—Fuego has one of the largest selections of cheeses west of the Mississippi. The wine list is similarly impressive. Le Menu Découverte allows you to sample a five-course meal of chef's specialties for $95. ⊠ *330 E. Palace Ave.* ☎ *505/954–9676* ⊕ *www.laposadadesantafe.com* ⊟ *AE, D, DC, MC, V* ⊗ *No dinner Mon. and Tues.*

$$$–$$$$ ✕ **Inn of the Anasazi.** Renowned chef Martín Rios has long ranked
Fodor'sChoice among the state's great culinary wizards, and his move in early 2006 to
★ the snazzy Inn of the Anasazi immediately upgraded the hotel's restaurant from merely passable to stellar. The romantic, 90-seat restaurant with hardwood floors, softly indirect lighting, and beam ceilings feels slightly less formal than the other big-ticket dining rooms in town, and Rios's cooking always dazzles. Specialties from the often-changing menu include ahi tuna tartar with artichoke-scallion blinis; pork tenderloin medallions with zinfandel-braised onions, sweet potatoes with piñon nuts, and a red chile–bourbon reduction. The Sunday brunch is terrific. ⊠ *Inn of the Anasazi, 113 Washington Ave.* ☎ *505/988–3030* ⊟ *AE, D, DC, MC, V.*

$$–$$$$ ✕ **Cafe Pasqual's.** This cheerful cubbyhole dishes up Southwestern and
Fodor'sChoice Nuevo Latino specialties for breakfast, lunch, and dinner. Don't be dis-
★ couraged by lines out in front—it's worth the wait. The culinary muse behind it all is Katharine Kagel, who for more than 25 years has been introducing specialties like buttermilk biscuits with sage-bacon gravy,

smoked-trout hash, and poached eggs to diners. Dinner is a more formal affair: char-grilled lamb with pomegranate-molasses glaze, steamed sugar-snap peas, and pan-seared potato cakes is a pleasure; the kicky starter of spicy Vietnamese squid salad with tamarind, garlic, and tomato over arugula is also fantastic. Mexican folk art and colorful tiles and murals by Oaxacan artist Leovigildo Martinez create a festive atmosphere. Try the communal table if you want to be seated in a hurry, although you should still expect a wait. ⊠ *121 Don Gaspar Ave.* ☎ *505/ 983–9340* ⊕ *www.pasquals.com* ⊟ *AE, MC, V.*

$$–$$$$ ✕ **La Casa Sena.** The Southwestern-accented and Continental fare served at La Casa Sena is beautifully presented if not consistently as delicious as it appears. Weather permitting, get a table on the patio surrounded by hollyhocks, flowering shrubs, and centuries-old adobe walls. Typical dishes include the chorizo-stuffed grilled pork tenderloin with roasted sweet-potato puree and peach–prickly pear sauce. There's a knockout lavender crème brûlée on the dessert menu. For a musical meal (evenings only), sit in the restaurant's adjacent, less-pricey Cantina, where the talented staff belt out Broadway show tunes. There's also a wine shop, which sells many of the estimable vintages offered on the restaurant's wine list. ⊠ *Sena Plaza, 125 E. Palace Ave.* ☎ *505/988–9232* ⊕ *www.lacasasena. com* ⊟ *AE, D, DC, MC, V.*

$$–$$$$
Fodor'sChoice
★ ✕ **Geronimo.** Chef Eric DiStefano changes the menu frequently at this superb restaurant in the Borrego House, which dates from 1756. A typical meal might start with seared Hudson Valley foie gras with candied ginger, sugared pecans, brioche French toast, and sundried-cranberry compote. Entrées are artful, like peppered elk tenderloin with applewood-smoked bacon, garlic-mashed potatoes, snap peas, and a brandy-mushroom sauce. The Sunday brunch is also impressive—try the provolone-and-spinach omelet with prosciutto-wrapped halibut and hollandaise sauce. The intimate, white dining rooms have beamed ceilings, wood floors, fireplaces, and cushioned *bancos*. In summer you can dine under the front portal; in winter the bar with fireplace is inviting. ⊠ *724 Canyon Rd.* ☎ *505/982–1500* ⊕ *www.geronimorestaurant. com* ⊟ *AE, MC, V* ⊗ *No lunch Mon.*

★ **$$–$$$** ✕ **Aqua Santa.** One of Santa Fe's longtime favorite chefs, Brian Knox helms the kitchen at this tiny, informal storefront café that happens to serve some of the finest and most inventive food in town. Diners can watch the chef work his wonders in the open kitchen, where he conjures up such sophisticated, yet simple fare as panfried oysters with bitter honey and a balsamic reduction, Tuscan bean soup with white-truffle oil, and braised organic New Mexico lamb with olives and summer squash. Vanilla panna cotta with chocolate sauce and almonds is a representatively delicious dessert. There's an extensive, pricey wine list, too. ⊠ *451 W. Alameda St. (entrance off Water St.)* ☎ *505/982–6297* ⊟ *MC, V* ⊗ *Closed Sun. and Mon. No lunch Tues. or Sat.*

$$–$$$ ✕ **O'Keeffe Cafe.** This swanky but low-key restaurant at the Georgia O'Keeffe Museum turns out some of the most creative fare in town. This is much more than a typical museum café, although the lunches do make a great break following a jaunt through the museum. Dinner is the main event, however, showcasing such tempting and creative fare as sweetbreads with shallots and cherry demi-glace; cashew-encrusted mahimahi over garlic-mashed potatoes with a mango-citrus–butter sauce; and Colorado lamb chops with red chile–honey glaze; and mint-infused couscous. There's an expansive patio in back shaded by leafy trees. ✉ *217 Johnson St.* ☎ *505/946–1065* ⊕ *www.okeeffecafe.com* ▤ *AE, D, MC, V.*

$$–$$$ ✕ **Ristra.** This unprepossessing restaurant in the trendy Guadalupe District presents a first-rate menu of Southwestern-influenced country French cooking. You might start with chorizo-stuffed calamari with watercress and smoked-tomato sauce; roasted rack of lamb with couscous, minted tomatoes, preserved lemon, and Niçoise olives is a tempting main dish. Top off your meal with an almond-butter cake served with warm spiced apples and a mascarpone-caramel sauce. The wines are well selected, and the service is swift and courteous. Navajo blankets hang on stark white walls, and Pueblo pottery adorns the handful of niches. There's also a trendy cocktail bar with its own menu of lighter dishes. ✉ *548 Agua Fria St.* ☎ *505/982–8608* ⊕ *www.ristrarestaurant.com* ▤ *AE, MC, V* ⊗ *No lunch.*

★ **$$–$$$** ✕ **Santacafé.** Minimalist elegance marks the interior of Santacafé, one of Santa Fe's vanguard "food as art" restaurants, two blocks north of the Plaza in the historic Padre Gallegos House. Seasonal ingredients are included in the inventive dishes, which might include Alaskan halibut with English peas, saffron couscous, capers, and preserved lemon. Shiitake-and-cactus spring rolls with ponzu sauce makes a terrific starter, as does the sublime crispy-fried calamari with a snappy lime-chile dipping sauce. The patio is a joy in summer, and the bar makes a snazzy spot to meet friends for drinks just about any time of year. If you're on a tight budget, consider the reasonably priced lunch menu. ✉ *231 Washington Ave.* ☎ *505/984–1788* ⊕ *www.santacafe.com* ▤ *AE, MC, V* ⊗ *No lunch Sun.*

$$–$$$ ✕ **315 Restaurant & Wine Bar.** As if it were on a thoroughfare in Paris rather than on Old Santa Fe Trail, 315 has a Continental, white-tablecloth sophistication, but the offbeat wall art gives it a contemporary feel. Chef-owner Louis Moskow prepares refreshingly uncomplicated fare using organic vegetables and locally raised meats. Seasonal specialties on the ever-evolving menu might include basil-wrapped shrimp with apricot chutney and curry sauce, or grilled boneless lamb loin with crispy polenta, spring vegetables, and green peppercorn sauce. The garden patio opens onto the street scene. There's also a wine bar with an exceptional list of vintages. ✉ *315 Old Santa Fe Trail* ☎ *505/986–9190* ⊕ *www.315santafe.com* ▤ *AE, MC, V* ⊗ *Closed Sun. No lunch Mon.*

$–$$$ ✕ **Amaya.** One of the better hotel restaurants in town, this handsome space inside the Hotel Santa Fe serves first-rate contemporary Southwestern fare. Consider a starter of panko-crusted calamari with jicama slaw, tequila-lime aioli, and balsamic syrup. Among main courses, try venison osso buco with quinoa risotto, root veggies, and a port wine reduction, or oven-roasted game hen with red-chile-honey glaze and apple-sage stuffing. Amaya also presents several Native American–inspired dishes, including a mixed grill platter featuring marinated elk loin, mint-crusted lamb chop, buffalo sausage, and orange-ginger duck. Dine on the shaded patio in warm weather. ✉ *1501 Paseo de Peralta* ☎ *505/982–1200* ⊕ *www.hotelsantafe.co* ▤ *AE, D, DC, MC, V.*

Eclectic

$–$$$ ✕ **Café San Estevan.** This place is perfect when you're seeking a restaurant with very good New Mexican and Continental fare, all of it prepared simply but with ultrafresh, in many cases organic, ingredients and superb presentation. The small and rather noisy dining room is charming nonetheless, with some tables facing a corner fireplace. The poblano chiles rellenos here are superb, stuffed with cheese and onions and served with rice and *calabacitas* (a kind of squash). Also top-notch is the New Mexico organic lamb loin chops with a rosemary demi-glace and sautéed green beans. Chef-owner Estevan Garcia puts on a great show. ⊠ *428 Agua Fria St.* ☎ *505/995–1996* ▤ *AE, D, MC, V* ⊙ *Closed Mon.*

$–$$$ ✕ **Pink Adobe.** Rosalea Murphy opened her restaurant in 1944, and the place still reflects a time when fewer than 20,000 people lived here. The intimate, rambling rooms of this late-17th-century house have fireplaces and artwork and are filled with conversation made over special-occasion meals. The ambience of the restaurant, rather than the mediocre food and spotty service, accounts for its popularity. The steak Dunigan, smothered in green chile sauce and mushrooms, and the savory shrimp Louisianne—fat and deep-fried crispy—are among the Continental, New Mexican, and New Orleans creole dishes served. The apple pie drenched in rum sauce is a favorite. Particularly strong margaritas are mixed in the adjacent Dragon Room bar. ⊠ *406 Old Santa Fe Trail* ☎ *505/983–7712* ⊕ *www.thepinkadobe.com* ▤ *AE, D, DC, MC, V* ⊙ *No lunch weekends.*

★ ¢–$$ ✕ **Plaza Café.** Run with homespun care by the Razatos family since 1947, this café has been a fixture on the Plaza since 1918. The decor—red leather banquettes, black Formica tables, tile floors, a coffered tin ceiling, and a 1940s-style service counter—hasn't changed much in the past half century. The food runs the gamut, from cashew mole enchiladas to New Mexico meat loaf to Mission-style burritos, but the ingredients tend toward Southwestern. You'll rarely taste a better tortilla soup. You can cool it off with an old-fashioned ice cream treat from the soda fountain. All in all, it's a good stop for breakfast, lunch, or dinner. ⊠ *54 Lincoln Ave.* ☎ *505/982–1664* ⌂ *Reservations not accepted* ▤ *AE, D, MC, V.*

¢–$ ✕ **Harry's Roadhouse.** This quirky, always-packed adobe compound
FodorśChoice consists of several inviting rooms, from a diner-style space with counter
★ seating to a cozier nook with a fireplace—there's also an enchanting courtyard out back with juniper trees and flower gardens. The varied menu of contemporary diner favorites, pizzas, New Mexican fare, and bountiful salads is supplemented by a long list of daily specials. Favorites include smoked-chicken quesadillas and grilled-salmon tacos with tomatillo salsa and black beans. Desserts here are a revelation, from the chocolate pudding to the blueberry cobbler. ⊠ *Old Las Vegas Hwy., 1 mi south of Old Pecos Trail exit off I–25* ☎ *505/989–4629* ▤ *AE, D, MC, V.*

¢ ✕ **Green Canteen.** An airy, art-filled restaurant with a handful of outdoor seats, this cheap and cheerful spot near the College of Santa Fe serves creative, organic food. The enormous salad of cherry tomatoes,

Calamata olives, avocado, Gorgonzola, hardboiled eggs, pumpkin seeds, and greens makes a delicious starter. Follow this with an avocado-Brie-mango quesadilla, or a burger topped with green chile and pepper-Jack cheese. There's also a nice selection of wraps, coffees, wines by the glass, and hot teas, but try the locally beloved (and also organic) Santa Fe Cider. It's right beside an independent film cinema in an otherwise nondescript shopping center. ⊠ *1616–A St. Michael's Dr.* ☎ *505/424–6464* ▭ *AE, MC, V* ☉ *Closed Sun.*

Indian

★ ¢–$$ ✕ **India Palace.** Even seasoned veterans of East Indian cuisine have been known to rate this deep-pink, art-filled restaurant among the best in the United States. The kitchen prepares fairly traditional recipes—tandoori chicken, lamb vindaloo, *saag paneer* (spinach with farmer's cheese), shrimp *biryani* (tossed with cashews, raisins, almonds, and saffron rice)—but the presentation is always flawless and the ingredients fresh. Meals are cooked as hot or mild as requested. Try the Indian buffet at lunch. ⊠ *227 Don Gaspar Ave., enter from parking lot on Water St.* ☎ *505/986–5859* ▭ *AE, D, MC, V.*

Italian

$–$$$$ ✕ **Trattoria Nostrani.** This Italian trattoria earns kudos for such stellar fare as steak tartare with shaved asiago, braised baby octopus with soft polenta, and filet mignon with Tuscan vegetable ragu and fried pota-toes. The cozy dining room occupies a late-19th-century Territorial-style house a few blocks from the Plaza. Widespread complaints about the arrogant service seem to be the only drawback. ⊠ *304 Johnson St.* ☎ *505/983–3800* ⊕ *www.trattorianostrani.com* ▭ *AE, DC, MC, V* ☉ *Closed Sun. No lunch.*

★ $–$$ ✕ **Andiamo.** Produce from the farmers' market across the street adds to the seasonal surprises of this intimate northern Italian restaurant set in-side a romantic cottage. Start with the crispy polenta with rosemary and Gorgonzola sauce; move on to the white pizza with roasted garlic, fontina, grilled radicchio, pancetta, and rosemary; and consider such hearty entrées as crispy duck legs with grilled polenta, roasted turnips, and sautéed spinach. ⊠ *322 Garfield St.* ☎ *505/995–9595* ⊕ *www.andiamoonline. com* ▭ *AE, DC, MC, V* ☉ *No lunch.*

$ ✕ **Il Piatto.** Creative pasta dishes like pappardelle with braised duck-ling, caramelized onions, sun-dried tomatoes, and mascarpone-duck au jus, and homemade pumpkin ravioli with pine nuts and brown sage butter grace the menu here. Entrées include grilled salmon with spinach risotto and tomato-caper sauce, and a superb pancetta-wrapped trout with rosemary, wild mushrooms, and polenta. It's a crowded but nev-ertheless enjoyable trattoria with informal ambience, super-low prices, and a snug, urbane bar; the windows are dressed in frilly valances, and a mural of the Italian countryside lines one wall. ⊠ *95 W. Marcy St.* ☎ *505/984–1091* ⊕ *www.ilpiattorestaurant.com* ▭ *AE, MC, V* ☉ *No lunch weekends.*

Japanese

$–$$ ✕ **Izmi Sushi.** Santa Fe's sushi restaurants run the gamut from overpriced to mediocre, an exception being this unassuming strip-mall eatery a 10-minute drive south of the Plaza. Sushi options include surf clam, scallop, eel, toro, and soft-shell crab, but you can also order ginger beef, Korean barbecue, and a wide range of sushi and sashimi "chef's choice" assortments. Don't miss the New Mexico roll, with shrimp tempura, roasted green chile, bell pepper, and crab. ✉ *720 St. Michael's Dr.* ☎ *505/424–1311* ⊕ *www.izmisushi.com* ▤ *AE, D, MC, V* ☉ *Closed Sun. No lunch Sat.*

Latin

$–$$ ✕ **Los Mayas.** Owners Fernando Antillas and Reyes Solano brought the spirit of Latin America with them when they opened this restaurant. They've transformed a nondescript building into a cozy, tile-floored space with a patio. The menu mixes New Mexican, Latin American, and South American recipes. Try the charbroiled skirt steak and cheese rellenos with rice and black beans, or shrimp sautéed with butter and garlic. There's music every night, including flamenco on Saturday. ✉ *409 W. Water St.* ☎ *505/986–9930* ⊕ *www.losmayas.com* ▤ *AE, D, DC, MC, V* ☉ *No lunch.*

¢ ✕ **El Tesoro.** One of the Guadalupe District's better-kept secrets, this small café occupies the high-ceiling foyer of the Sanbusco Center, steps from several boutiques. The tiny kitchen turns out a mix of Central American, New Mexican, and American dishes, all of them using super-fresh ingredients. Grilled tuna tacos with salsa fresca, black beans, and rice; and Salvadorian chicken tamales wrapped in banana leaves are among the tastiest treats. El Tesoro also serves pastries, gelato, lemon bars, hot cocoa, and other snacks, making it a perfect break from shopping. ✉ *Sanbusco Market Center, 500 Montezuma Ave.* ☎ *505/988–3886* ▤ *MC, V* ☉ *No dinner.*

Mexican

¢–$$ ✕ **Bert's la Taqueria.** Salsa fans love this upbeat spot where chips are served with six varieties of the hot stuff. The long-running restaurant moved from a prosaic shopping center off St. Michael's Drive to a charming, historic adobe house in the Guadalupe District in spring 2006, greatly enhancing the dining ambience. Colorful paintings hang on the white-washed walls. The menu mixes the expected Mexican fare—enchiladas, soft tacos—with more unusual regional recipes, such as *chapulines* (grasshoppers—yes, you read that correctly—sautéed with garlic butter). ✉ *416 Agua Fria St.* ☎ *505/474–0791* ▤ *AE, MC, V* ☉ *Closed Sun.*

★ **¢** ✕ **Bumble Bee's Baja Grill.** A bright, new high-ceiling restaurant with closely spaced tables and bumble bee piñatas wafting overhead, Bumble Bee's has quickly delighted locals with its super-fresh Cal-Mex style food, including mahimahi tacos, mammoth burritos with a wide range of fillings, roasted chicken with cilantro-lime rice, and char-grilled trout platters. You order at the counter, grab some snacks from the salsa bar, and wait for your number to come up. There's live jazz on Saturday nights. Beer, wine, and Mexican soft drinks are served. The plastic flatware is a bit off-putting (it breaks easily), but otherwise, this place is a real find. ⊠ *301 Jefferson St.* ☎ *505/820–2862* ⊠ *3701 Cerrillos Rd.* ☎ *505/ 988–3278* ▤ *AE, D, MC, V.*

Middle Eastern

¢–$ ✕ **Cleopatra Cafe.** A quirky, order-at-the-counter Middle Eastern café inside the Design Center home-furnishings mall, Cleopatra serves up ultrafresh Egyptian, Lebanese, and Greek food at bargain prices. You might start with *besara* (fava beans with cilantro, garlic, fried onion, and pita bread). Popular entrées include the falafel plate, with hummus and tabouleh salad, and grilled organic-lamb kebabs with onions, bell peppers, rice, tahini, and Greek salad. Wine, beer, fresh-squeezed lemonade, and Turkish coffee are also offered. ⊠ *418 Cerrillos Rd.* ☎ *505/ 820–7381* ▤ *MC, V* ☯ *Closed Sun.*

New Mexican

$–$$ ✕ **Diego's Cafe.** You have to trek to the north side of downtown to sample some of the most authentic and spicy New Mexican food in Santa Fe. Once inside the cheery, casual dining room, you forget the location, especially when relaxing with one of the potent (even by local standards) margaritas. Best bets here include blue-corn enchiladas, bean-and-chicken-stuffed sopaipilla, posole, and outstanding chile rellenos. Service is typically quick and cheerful. ⊠ *DeVargas Center, 193 Paseo de Peralta* ☎ *505/983–5101* ▤ *MC, V.*

$–$$ ✕ **Gabriel's.** A great option near Pojoaque, perfect before the opera or on your way back to Santa Fe from points north, Gabriel's offers one of the best restaurant settings in the area: a spacious dining room with a Spanish-colonial theme, and a large flower-filled patio with candle-lighted tables. The main event here is the guacamole, prepared with great fanfare table-side. The margaritas are also stellar. Main dishes—steak fajitas, crab enchiladas—are less memorable but still usually quite good, and service is friendly but uneven. ⊠ *U.S. 285/84, just north of Camel Rock Casino, 15 mi north of Santa Fe* ☎ *505/455–7000* ⊕ *www. gabrielsrestaurante.com* ▤ *AE, D, DC, MC, V.*

$–$$ ✕ **Maria's New Mexican Kitchen.** Maria's is proud to serve more than 100 kinds of margaritas. All but a few of the tequilas—many of which are quite rare—are 100% agave. This is also a reliable source of authentic New Mexican fare, including chiles rellenos, blue-corn enchiladas, and green-chile tamales. Strolling guitarists serenade the crowds most nights in this rustic space with a kiva fireplace and wood floors. ⊠ *555 W. Cordova Rd.* ☎ *505/983–7929* ⊕ *www.marias-santafe.com* ▤ *AE, D, DC, MC, V.*

¢–$$ ✕ **The Shed.** The lines at lunch attest to the status of this downtown New Mexican eatery. The rambling adobe dating from 1692 is decorated with folk art, and service is downright neighborly. Even if you're a devoted green chile sauce fan, try the locally grown red chile the place is famous for. Specialties include red-chile enchiladas, green-chile stew with potatoes and pork, posole, and charbroiled Shedburgers. The homemade desserts are fabulous. There's a full bar, too. ⊠ *113½ E. Palace Ave.* ☎ *505/982–9030* ⊟ *AE, DC, MC, V* ☺ *Closed Sun. No dinner Mon.–Wed.*

¢–$ ✕ **Guadalupe Cafe.** Come to this informal café for hefty servings of New Mexican favorites like enchiladas and quesadillas, topped off with sopaipilla and honey, along with some dishes from other cultures, such as falafel and Asian dumplings stuffed with ginger pork. The seasonal raspberry pancakes are one of many breakfast favorites. Service can be brusque and the wait for a table considerable. ⊠ *422 Old Santa Fe Trail* ☎ *505/982–9762* ⌕ *Reservations not accepted* ⊟ *AE, D, DC, MC, V* ☺ *Closed Mon. No dinner Sun.*

¢–$ ✕ **La Choza.** The far-less touristy, harder-to-find, and less expensive sis-
Fodor'sChoice ter to the Shed, La Choza arguably serves even better New Mexican fare.
★ Chicken or pork *carne adovada* burritos, white clam chowder spiced with green chiles, huevos rancheros, and wine margaritas are special-
ties. The dining rooms are dark and cozy, with vigas set across the ceil-
ing and local art on the walls. The staff is friendly and competent. ⊠ *905 Alarid St., near Cerrillos Rd. at St. Francis Dr.* ☎ *505/982–0909* ⊟ *AE, DC, MC, V* ☺ *Closed Sun.*

Pan-Asian

★ $–$$ ✕ **Kasasoba.** Maybe the best all-around Asian restaurant in Santa Fe, this intimate, classy eatery behind the Sanbusco Center has just a handful of tables and specializes in Japanese small plates and noodle dishes. The *zaru soba* (cold buckwheat noodles with nori, wasabi, spring onions, and a dashi-shoyu dipping sauce) with tempura vegetables and shrimp is heavenly, as is sake-steamed striped bass with enoki mushrooms. Uni-crusted sea scallops and a handful of creative maki sushi rolls round out the menu, and there's a short but well-chosen wine list. ⊠ *544 Agua Fria St.* ☎ *505/984–1969* ⊟ *AE, MC, V* ☺ *No lunch.*

$–$$ ✕ **Mu Du Noodles.** This warm and cozy eatery on an unfortunately busy stretch of Cerrillos Road excels both in its friendly and helpful staff and its superb pan-Asian fare. Book ahead on weekends—this place fills up fast. You can count on some great dinner specials each night, too. Sam-
ple sweet-and-sour rockfish with water chestnuts, smoked bacon, and jasmine rice; Vietnamese spring rolls with peanut-hoisin sauce; and stir-
fried tenderloin beef with whole scallions, sweet peppers, bean sprouts, and fat rice noodles. ⊠ *1494 Cerrillos Rd.* ☎ *505/988–1411* ⊕ *www. mudunoodles.com* ⊟ *AE, MC, V* ☺ *Closed Sun. and Mon. No lunch.*

★ ¢–$$ ✕ **Jinja.** Although it's tucked in a shopping center on the north side, a short drive from the Plaza, Jinja is worth the trip for its extremely tasty and creative Asian fare. Specialties include flash-fried calamari with a light mint-lime sauce; Singapore noodles with barbecue pork, chopped peanuts, cilantro, and yellow curry; and Ten Tigers (ten lemongrass-mar-
inated, grilled tiger prawns over fried rice with pineapple salsa and cu-
cumber salad). The sashimi tuna with ginger is another star. The dining room is hip and attractive, and there's a swanky little bar off to one side, perfect for dining alone. A new branch opened in Albuquerque in fall 2006. ⊠ *510 N. Guadalupe St.* ☎ *505/982–4321* ⊟ *AE, D, MC, V.*

Pizza

★ ¢–$$ ✕ **Rooftop Pizzeria.** Santa Fe got its first truly sophisticated pizza parlor in 2006 with the opening of this slick indoor-outdoor restaurant atop the Santa Fe Arcade. The kitchen here scores high marks for its rich and imaginative pizza toppings: consider the one topped with lobster, shrimp, mushrooms, apple-smoked bacon, caramelized leeks, truffle oil, Alfredo sauce, and four cheeses on a blue-corn crust. Antipasti and salads are impressive, too, as there's a wonderful smoked-duck confit–and–peppercorn spread, or the smoked-salmon Caesar salad. There's also an extensive beer and wine list. Although the Santa Fe Arcade's main entrance is on the Plaza, it's easier to access the restaurant from the arcade's Water Street entrance, a few doors up from Don Gaspar Avenue. ⊠ *60 E. San Francisco St.* ☎ *505/984–0008* ▤ *AE, D, MC, V.*

Seafood

¢–$ ✕ **Mariscos la Playa.** Yes, even in landlocked Santa Fe, it's possible to find incredibly fresh and well-prepared seafood served in big portions. This no-frills restaurant surrounded by strip malls is just a short hop south of downtown and serves up absolutely delicious shrimp wrapped in bacon with Mexican cheese. One of the most famous dishes is *caldo vuelve a la vida,* a hearty soup of shrimp, octopus, scallops, clams, crab, and calamari. There's also shrimp soup in a tomato broth, fresh oysters on the half shell, and grilled salmon with pico de gallo. ⊠ *537 W. Cordova St.* ☎ *505/982–2790* ▤ *AE, D, MC, V* ☉ *Closed Tues.*

Southwestern

$–$$ ✕ **Señor Lucky at the Palace.** The owners and chef of Geronimo operate this celebration of cowboy kitsch and Santa Fe chic—the dining room is painted with dramatic cowboy murals and filled with Western Americana. Specialties from the lengthy menu range from the light and simple (Caesar salad with achiote grilled chicken, sweet-corn tortilla soup) to the hearty and complex (two sweet-and-hot-grilled quail with jicama cabbage slaw, grilled red-chile pork chops with cheddar-mashed potatoes). There's also a lavish cocktail menu, great desserts (try the ice cream sandwich version of a peanut-butter-and-jelly sandwich), and extensive wine list. Señor Lucky's is nothing if not original. ⊠ *142 W. Palace Ave.* ☎ *505/982–9891* ⊕ *www.senorluckys.com* ▤ *AE, D, DC, MC, V.*

Spanish

$$–$$$$ ✕ **El Farol.** In this crossover-cuisine town, owner David Salazar sums up his food in one word: "Spanish." Order a classic entrée like paella or make a meal from the nearly 30 different tapas—from tiny fried squid to wild mushrooms. Dining is indoors and out. Touted as the oldest continuously operated restaurant in Santa Fe, El Farol (built in 1835) has a relaxed ambience, a unique blend of the western frontier and contemporary Santa Fe. People push back the chairs and start dancing at around 9:30. The restaurant books outstanding live entertainment,

mostly blues and jazz, and there's usually a festive flamenco performance weekly. ⊠ *808 Canyon Rd.* ☎ *505/983–9912* 🖃 *D, DC, MC, V* ⊗ *No lunch Mon. and Tues.*

★ **$$–$$$** ✕ **El Mesón.** This place is as fun for having drinks and tapas or catching live music (from tango nights to Sephardic music) as for enjoying a full meal. The dignified dining room with an old-world feel has simple

dark-wood tables and chairs, white walls, and a wood-beam ceiling—unpretentious yet elegant. Livelier but still quite handsome is the Chispa bar. Tapas include Serrano ham and fried red potatoes with garlic aioli. Among the more substantial entrées are a stellar paella as well as cannelloni stuffed with veal, smothered with béchamel sauce, and served with manchego cheese au gratin. ⊠ *213 Washington Ave.* ☎ *505/983–6756* 🖃 *AE, MC, V* ⊗ *Closed Sun. and Mon. No lunch.*

Steak

$–$$$$ ✕ **Vanessie.** This classy, lodgelike space with high ceilings and a tremendously popular piano cabaret serves hefty portions of well-prepared chops and seafood. New Zealand rack of lamb, tenderloin of elk, and dry-aged steaks are among the specialties. There's lighter fare—burgers, onion loaf, salads—served in the piano bar, where noted musicians Doug Montgomery and Charles Tichenor perform classical and Broadway favorites well into the evening (no cover). ⊠ *434 W. San Francisco St.* ☎ *505/982–9966* ⊕ *www.vanessiesantafe.com* 🖃 *AE, DC, MC, V* ⊗ *No lunch.*

Thai

¢–$ ✕ **Thai Cafe.** Thai restaurants haven't enjoyed a great deal of success in Santa Fe over the years, but this intimate, warmly lighted space a few blocks from the Plaza has earned consistent praise since it opened in 2005. The aroma of authentic spices fills this art-filled adobe dining room with wide-plank floors, orange walls, and beam ceilings. Here patrons savor such tempting starters as *Tom Ka Gai* (coconut-milk soup with chicken, lemongrass, galangal) and Thai beef salad. Stars among the main dishes include grilled salmon with sweet-and-sour sauce, the seafood mix stir-fried with red curry and pineapple sauce, and stir-fried broccoli with garlic. The kitchen is quite liberal with spices, so ask them to tone down the heat if you're sensitive to such things. ⊠ *329 W. San Francisco St.* ☎ *505/982–3886* 🖃 *AE, DC, MC, V* ⊗ *Closed Mon.*

WHERE TO STAY

In Santa Fe you can ensconce yourself in quintessential Santa Fe style or anonymous hotel-chain decor, depending on how much you want to spend—the city has costlier accommodations than anywhere in the

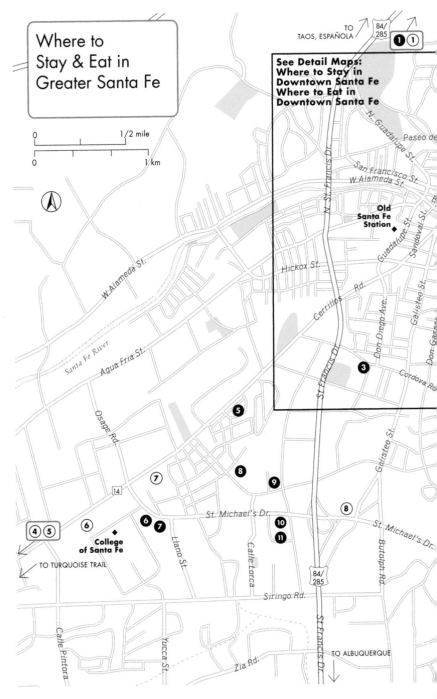

Where to
Stay & Eat in
Greater Santa Fe

0 ——— 1/2 mile

0 ——— 1 km

TO
TAOS, ESPAÑOLA

84/285

1 ①

See Detail Maps:
Where to Stay in
Downtown Santa Fe
Where to Eat in
Downtown Santa Fe

N. Guadalupe St.

Paseo de

San Francisco St.
W. Alameda St.

Old
Santa Fe
Station

Guadalupe St.

Sandoval St.

Galisteo St.

Hickox St.

Cerrillos Rd.

Don Diego Ave.

Don Gaspar

3

Cordova Rd.

W. Alameda St.

Santa Fe River

Agua Fria St.

Osage Rd.

St. Francis Dr.

N. St. Francis Dr.

5

Galisteo St.

8

7

14

9

St. Michael's Dr.

St. Michael's Dr.

4 5

6

College
of Santa Fe

6 7

Llano St.

10

11

Calle Lorca

8

Butolph Rd.

TO TURQUOISE TRAIL

84/285

Siringo Rd.

Calle Pintora

Yucca St.

Zia Rd.

St. Francis Dr.

TO ALBUQUERQUE

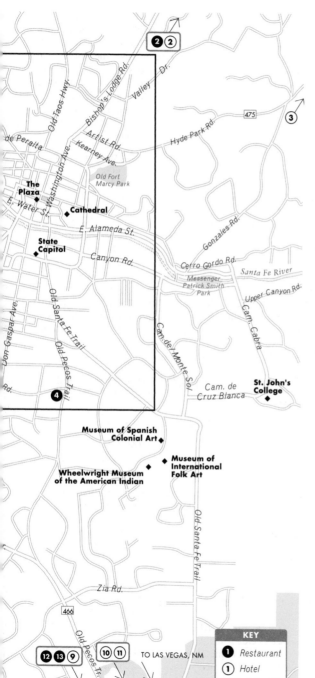

Restaurants ▼
Bert's la Taqueria 6
Bobcat Bite 12
Chocolate Maven 9
Chow's 10
Cloud Cliff Bakery 8
Gabriel's 1
Green Canteen 7
Harry's Roadhouse 13
Izmi Sushi 11
Mu Du Noodles 5
Santa Fe Baking Company 3
Tesuque Village Market 2
Whole Body Cafe 4

Hotels & Campgrounds ▼
Bishop's Lodge Resort & Spa 2
Bobcat Inn 9
Camel Rock Suites 1
El Rey Inn 7
Los Campos RV Resort 4
Rancheros de Santa Fe
Campground 10
Residence Inn 8
Santa Fe Courtyard
by Marriott 5
Santa Fe KOA 11
Silver Saddle Motel 6
Ten Thousand Waves 3

Southwest. Cheaper options are mostly on the southern reaches of Cerrillos (pronounced sah-*ree*-yos) Road, a dreadful, traffic-clogged strip. Quality varies greatly on Cerrillos, but some of the best-managed, most attractive properties are (from most to least expensive) the Holiday Inn, the Courtyard Marriott, and the Motel 6. You pay more the closer you are to the Plaza, but for many visitors it's worth it to be within walking distance of many attractions. Some of the best deals are offered by B&Bs—many of those near the Plaza offer much better values than the big, touristy hotels. Rates drop, often from 30% to 50%, from November to April (excluding Thanksgiving and Christmas).

In addition to the usual array of inns and hotels here, Santa Fe has a wide range of **long- and short-term vacation rentals,** some of them available through the **Management Group** (☎ 866/982–2823 ⊕ www.santaferentals.com). Rates generally range from $100 to $300 per night for double-occupancy units, with better values at some of the two- to four-bedroom properties. Most have fully stocked kitchens. Another route is to rent a furnished condo or casita at one of several compounds geared to travelers seeking longer stays. The best of these is the luxurious **Campanilla Compound** (☎ 505/988–7585 or 800/828–9700 ⊕ www.campanillacompound.com), on a hill just north of downtown; rates run from about $1,400 to $1,800 per week in summer. Another good, similarly priced bet is **Fort Marcy Suites** (☎ 505/988–2800 or 888/600–4990 ⊕ www.fortmarcy.com), on a bluff just northeast of the Plaza with great views. The individually furnished units accommodate two to six guests and come with full kitchens, wood fireplaces, VCRs, and CD stereos—these can be rented nightly or weekly.

WHAT IT COSTS				
$$$$	**$$$**	**$$**	**$**	**¢**
HOTELS over $260	$190–$260	$130–$190	$70–$130	under $70

Prices are for a standard double room in high season, excluding 13.5%–14.5% tax.

Downtown Vicinity

$$$$
FodorsChoice
★

☒ **Inn of the Anasazi.** Unassuming from the outside, this first-rate boutique hotel is one of Santa Fe's finest, with superb architectural detail. The prestigious Rosewood Hotel group took over the property in 2005, carefully upgrading the already sumptuous linens and furnishings. Each room has a beamed viga-and-latilla ceiling, kiva-style gas fireplace, antique Indian rugs, handwoven fabrics, and organic toiletries (including sunblock). Other amenities include full concierge services, twice-daily maid service, exercise bikes upon request, and a library. An especially nice

WORD OF MOUTH

"The rooms (keep in mind that we are very picky) are very nice, upscale, cozy and have very authentic New Mexico charm. The kiva fireplaces are great."

–Dawn, on Inn of the Anasazi

touch in this desert town are the humidifiers in each guest room. A few deluxe rooms have balconies. The staff is thorough, gracious, and highly professional. The restaurant, under the helm of acclaimed chef Martín Rios, is one of the best in New Mexico. ⊠ *113 Washington Ave., 87501* ☎ *505/988–3030 or 800/688–8100* 🖷 *505/988–3277* ⊕ *www. innoftheanasazi.com* ➮ *57 rooms* ⚭ *Restaurant, in-room safes, minibars, cable TV, in-room VCRs, Wi-Fi, bar, library, business services, parking (fee), some pets allowed (fee)* ⊟ *AE, D, DC, MC, V.*

$$$$
Fodor's Choice
★

🖫 **Inn of the Five Graces.** The Garrett hotel group took over what had been a fading property in 2003 and transformed it into a sumptuous hotel with an East-meets-West design that pleases most guests but differs from the usual, ubiquitous Santa Fe style. The suites have Asian and Latin American antiques and art, kilim rugs, jewel-tone throw pillows, and mosaic-tile bathrooms; most have fireplaces, and many have soaking tubs or walk-in steam showers. The personal service really stands out: dream catchers and ghost stories are left on your pillow, refrigerators are stocked, and afternoon margarita and wine-and-cheese spreads, an exquisite breakfast, and even daily walking tours are all available. ⊠ *150 E. DeVargas St., 87501* ☎ *505/992–0957 or 866/992–0957* 🖷 *505/955–0549* ⊕ *www.fivegraces.com* ➮ *22 suites* ⚭ *Some kitchenettes, refrigerators, cable TV, Wi-Fi, massage, free parking, some pets allowed (fee)* ⊟ *AE, MC, V* ⦿ *BP.*

$$$–$$$$

🖫 **Inn at Loretto.** This plush, oft-photographed, ancient pueblo–inspired property attracts a loyal clientele, many of whom swear by the friendly staff and high decorating standards. The lobby opens up to the gardens and pool, and leather couches and high-end architectural details make the hotel a pleasure to relax in. Rooms are among the largest of any downtown property and contain vibrantly upholstered handcrafted furnishings and sumptuous slate-floor bathrooms—many have large balconies overlooking downtown. The restaurant, Baleen, serves estimable, creative Southwestern fare. SpaTerre offers a wide range of Balinese and Thai-style treatments and services. ⊠ *211 Old Santa Fe Trail, 87501* ☎ *505/988–5531 or 800/727–5531* 🖷 *505/984–7988* ⊕ *www. hotelloretto.com* ➮ *134 rooms, 5 suites* ⚭ *Restaurant, cable TV, pool, health club, spa, lounge, shops, business services, meeting rooms, parking (fee)* ⊟ *AE, D, DC, MC, V.*

$$$–$$$$

🖫 **La Fonda.** History and charm are more prevalent in this sole Plaza-front hotel than first-class service and amenities. The pueblo-inspired structure was built in 1922 and enlarged many times. Antiques and Native American art decorate the tiled lobby, and each room has hand-decorated wood furniture, wrought-iron light fixtures, beamed ceilings, and high-speed wireless. Some suites have fireplaces. The 14 rooftop rooms are the most luxurious and include Continental breakfast and private concierge services; there's also an exercise room, garden, and outdoor hot tub there. La Plazuela Restaurant, with its hand-painted glass tiles, serves good and creative

> **WORD OF MOUTH**
>
> "A great historic hotel. We had a basic room for one night and it was fine."
>
> –Sheila on La Fonda

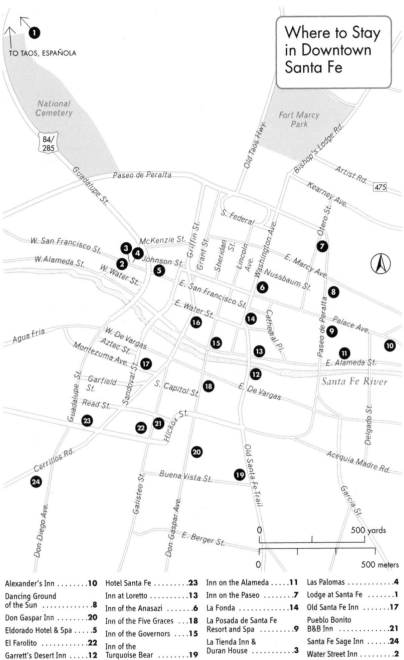

Where to Stay in Downtown Santa Fe

TO TAOS, ESPAÑOLA

National Cemetery

Fort Marcy Park

Southwestern food. Folk and Latin jazz bands rotate nightly in the bar. ⊠ *100 E. San Francisco St., 87501* ☎ *505/982–5511 or 800/523–5002* 🖷 *505/988–2952* ⊕ *www.lafondasantafe.com* ➳ *143 rooms, 24 suites* ☖ *Restaurant, cable TV, Wi-Fi, pool, gym, 3 hot tubs, pool, massage, 2 bars, laundry service, concierge, business services, meeting rooms, parking (fee)* ☰ *AE, D, DC, MC, V.*

$$$–$$$$ 🏨 **La Posada de Santa Fe Resort and Spa.** Rooms here vary, from cozy to high-ceiling to dark and simple, although ongoing renovations and upgrades continue to enhance all rooms, many of which have fireplaces, flat-screen TVs, CD players, leather couches, Spanish-tile bathrooms, and Navajo-inspired rugs. Many accommodations are in an adobe complex surrounding the main building; those in the older casitas, though capturing vintage Santa Fe's artsy charm, lack the newer units' plush feel. The main building contains a handful of high-ceiling Victorian rooms with marble-accent bathrooms. The real stars here are the bar, spa, and common areas, including the Staab House Lounge. The hotel's location, just blocks from the Plaza, is ideal. Fuego restaurant specializes in excellent world-beat contemporary fare. ⊠ *330 E. Palace Ave., 87501* ☎ *505/986–0000 or 866/331–7625* 🖷 *505/982–6850* ⊕ *www. laposadadesantafe.com* ➳ *120 rooms, 39 suites* ☖ *Restaurant, cable TV, Wi-Fi, pool, health club, spa, bar, business services, meeting rooms, parking (fee)* ☰ *AE, D, DC, MC, V.*

$$$– 🏨 **Las Palomas.** It's a pleasant 10-minute walk west of the Plaza to reach this property, which consists of two historic, luxurious compounds, one of them Spanish Pueblo–style adobe, the other done in the Territorial style, with a Victorian ambience. A network of brick paths shaded by mature trees leads past the casitas, connecting them with secluded courtyards and flower gardens. Each casita has a bedroom, full kitchen, living room with pull-out sofa, and fireplace, and each opens onto a terrace or patio. Locally handcrafted wooden and leather sofas, desks, and tables fill these spacious accommodations, along with Native American artwork and sculptures. It's an elegant alternative to the city's upscale full-service hotels, affording guests a bit more privacy and the feel of a private cottage rental. ⊠ *460 W. San Francisco St., 87501* ☎ *505/982–5560 or 877/982–5560* 🖷 *505/982–5562* ⊕ *www. laspalomas.com* ➳ *38 units* ☖ *Kitchens, cable TV, in-room VCRs, Wi-Fi, health club, playground* ⊠ *CP.*

$$–$$$$ 🏨 **Eldorado Hotel & Spa.** Because it's the closest thing Santa Fe has to a convention hotel, the Eldorado sometimes gets a bad rap, but it's actually quite inviting, with individually decorated rooms, a generally helpful staff, and stunning mountain views. Rooms are stylishly furnished with carved Southwestern-style desks and chairs, large upholstered club chairs, and art prints; many have terraces or kiva-style fireplaces. The rooftop pool and gym are great fun, and there's music nightly, from classical Spanish guitar to piano, in the comfortable lobby lounge. A full slate of treatments, from Vichy rain showers to High Mesa salt scrubs, are offered by the hotel's luxe Nidah Spa. The hotel also rents out a number of casitas and suites in a pair of smaller, nearby buildings, the Casa-pueblo Inn and Zona Rosa—these are more intimate and private, and some have full kitchens. ✉ *309 W. San Francisco St., 87501* ☎ *505/988–4455 or 800/955–4455* 🖷 *505/995–4555* ⊕ *www.eldoradohotel.com* 🛏 *201 rooms, 18 suites, 41 apartments, 10 condos* ⚭ *2 restaurants, room service, some kitchens, cable TV with movies, Wi-Fi, pool, health club, hot tub, massage, sauna, spa, bar, lounge, shops, laundry service, concierge, business services, meeting rooms, parking (fee)* ☰ *AE, D, DC, MC, V.*

★ **$$–$$$$** 🏨 **Inn on the Alameda.** Near the Plaza and Canyon Road is one of the Southwest's best small hotels. Alameda means "tree-lined lane," and this one perfectly complements the inn's location by the gurgling Santa Fe River. The adobe architecture and enclosed courtyards strewn with climbing rose vines combine a relaxed New Mexico country atmosphere with the luxury and amenities of a top-notch hotel, from afternoon wine and cheese to free local and toll-free calls to triple-sheeted beds with 300-count Egyptian bedding. Rooms have a Southwestern color scheme, handmade armoires and headboards, and ceramic lamps and tiles—many have patios and kiva fireplaces. The solicitous staff is first-rate. ✉ *303 E. Alameda St., 87501* ☎ *505/984–2121 or 888/984–2121* 🖷 *505/986–8325* ⊕ *www.innonthealameda.com* 🛏 *59 rooms, 10 suites* ⚭ *Some refrigerators, cable TV, gym, hot tubs, massage, bar, library, laundry facilities, concierge, meeting rooms, free parking, some pets allowed (fee)* ☰ *AE, D, DC, MC, V* ¶⊙¶ *CP.*

> **WORD OF MOUTH**
>
> "The third-floor rooms that opened out onto an adjoining balcony were perfect for our group. The staff was unbelievably helpful and friendly."
>
> –Linda on Inn on the Alameda

$$–$$$ 🏨 **Dancing Ground of the Sun.** This attractive compound of 1930s adobe casitas and guest rooms has saltillo-tile floors and handsome, locally made furnishings—aspen-and-willow chairs, Native American drums, and driftwood tables are among the many pieces that recall the region's Native American and Hispanic legacy. The casitas have fully stocked kitchens, and many other units have refrigerators, microwaves, and coffeemakers; many rooms have fireplaces. The inn is on the curve of a busy road that loops around the historic center of town—somewhat noisy, but ideal for access to both the Plaza and Canyon Road. ✉ *711 Paseo de Peralta, 87501* ☎ *505/986–9797 or 888/600–4990* 🖷 *505/986–8082* ⊕ *www.dancingground.com* 🛏 *6 rooms, 5 casitas* ⚭ *Some kitchens, cable TV; no smoking* ☰ *AE, MC, V* ¶⊙¶ *CP.*

$$–$$$ 🏨 **El Farolito.** All the beautiful Southwestern and Mexican furniture in this small, upscale compound is custom-made, and all the art and photography original. Rooms are spacious with fireplaces and separate entrances; some are in their own little buildings. El Farolito has a peaceful downtown location, just steps from the capitol and a few blocks from the Plaza, and rooms are spacious and pleasant. Some have CD players. The same owners run the smaller Four Kachinas inn, which is close by and has one handicapped-accessible room (rare among smaller Santa Fe properties). The continental breakfast here is a real treat, featuring a tempting range of delicious baked goods. ⊠ *514 Galisteo St., 87501* ☎ *505/988–1631 or 888/634–8782* ⊕ *www.farolito.com* ☞ *7 rooms, 1 suite* ☒ *Cable TV, some in-room VCRs; no smoking* ☰ *AE, D, MC, V* ¶ *CP.*

★ $$–$$$ ⬚ **Inn of the Governors.** This rambling hotel by the Santa Fe River received a major makeover in 2004, and is staffed by a polite, enthusiastic bunch. Rooms have a Mexican theme, with bright colors, hand-painted folk art, feather pillows, Southwestern fabrics, and handmade furnishings; deluxe rooms also have balconies and fireplaces. Perks include a complimentary tea and sherry social each afternoon and a quite extensive breakfast buffet along with free Wi-Fi and newspapers. New Mexican dishes and lighter fare like wood-oven pizzas

> **WORD OF MOUTH**
>
> "The location was great. The breakfast buffet was also wonderful. A friendly place."
> –Nancy on Inn of the Governors

are served in the restaurant, Del Charro, which also books first-rate entertainers. ⊠ *101 W. Alameda St., 87501* ☎ *505/982–4333 or 800/234–4534* 🖶 *505/989–9149* ⊕ *www.innofthegovernors.com* ☞ *100 rooms* ☒ *Restaurant, room service, refrigerators, cable TV, Wi-Fi, pool, bar, concierge, business services, meeting rooms, free parking* ☰ *AE, D, DC, MC, V* ¶ *BP.*

$$–$$$ ⬚ **Lodge at Santa Fe.** Rooms at this former Radisson have pleasant Southwestern furnishings and earth-tone fabrics, and higher-end condo units have full kitchens and one or two bedrooms. Renovations in recent years greatly enhanced the hotel's appearance, although service can be hit-or-miss. The hilltop location offers spectacular views east toward the Sangre de Cristo Mountains and south toward the Sandias—but only from certain rooms, so ask when reserving. The Plaza is a five-minute drive, the Santa Fe Opera just a bit farther. Las Mañanitas restaurant serves decent Spanish and Southwestern fare, and the adjacent cabaret is home in summer to flamenco dancer Maria Benitez. Guests have free access to the Santa Fe Spa next door, which has a full health club. ⊠ *750 N. St. Francis Dr., 87501* ☎ *505/992–5800 or 888/563–4373* 🖶 *505/842–9863* ⊕ *www.buynewmexico.com* ☞ *137 rooms, 4 suites, 6 condos* ☒ *Restaurant, room service, cable TV, pool, hot tub, bar, meeting rooms, free parking* ☰ *AE, D, DC, MC, V.*

$$–$$$ ⬚ **Water Street Inn.** The large rooms in this restored adobe 2½ blocks from the Plaza are decorated with reed shutters, antique pine beds, viga-beam ceilings, hand-stenciled artwork, and a blend of cowboy, Hispanic, and Native American art and artifacts. Most have fireplaces, and all have flat-screen TVs with DVD players and CD stereos. Afternoon hors d'oeuvres are served in the living room. A patio deck is available for relaxing. The one negative is that the inn overlooks a parking lot. ⊠ *427 W. Water St., 87501* ☎ *505/984–1193 or 800/ 646–6752* ⊕ *www.waterstreetinn.com* ☞ *8 rooms, 4 suites* ☒ *Cable TV, in-room DVDs, Wi-Fi, outdoor hot tub, free parking* ☰ *AE, DC, MC, V* ¶ *CP.*

$–$$$ ⊡ **Alexander's Inn.** This two-story 1903 Craftsman-style house in the Eastside residential area, a few blocks from the Plaza and Canyon Road, exudes the charm of an old country inn. Rooms are cozy and warm, with American country–style wooden furnishings, family heirlooms, skylights and tall windows, hand-stenciled walls, and dried-flower arrangements. The grounds are dotted with tulips, hyacinths,

and lilac and apricot trees. There's also a pair of two-story cottages with kitchens. The owners also run the seven-room Hacienda Nicholas ($$–$$$), a small adobe house done in Southwestern style and with a more upscale look, and the Madeleine Inn ($–$$$), a lacy Queen Anne house with eight rooms. Guests receive full access to El Gancho Health Club, a 15-minute drive away. ⊠ *529 E. Palace Ave., 87501* ☎ *505/986–1431 or 888/321–5123* ⊕ *www.alexanders-inn.com* ⤳ *5 rooms, 2 with shared bath; 2 cottages* ⌂ *Some kitchens, cable TV, outdoor hot tub, free parking, some pets allowed (fee); no TV in some rooms, no kids under 12 (except in cottage)* ⊟ *D, MC, V* ¹⊙¹ *CP.*

★ **$–$$$** ⊡ **Don Gaspar Inn.** One of the city's best-kept secrets, this exquisitely landscaped and decorated compound is on a pretty residential street a few blocks south of the Plaza. Its three historic houses have three distinct architectural styles: Arts and Crafts, Pueblo Revival, and Territorial. Floral gardens and aspen and cottonwood trees shade the tranquil paths and terraces, and both Southwest and Native American paintings and handmade furnishings enliven the sunny rooms and suites. The Arts and Crafts main house has two fireplaces, two bedrooms, and a fully equipped kitchen. Considering the setting and amenities, it's a great value. ⊠ *623 Don Gaspar Ave., 87505* ☎ *505/986–8664 or 888/986–8664* ⊟ *505/986–0696* ⊕ *www.dongaspar.com* ⤳ *5 rooms, 5 suites, 1 cottage* ⌂ *Cable TV, some in-room hot tubs, some kitchens, refrigerators, free parking; no smoking* ⊟ *AE, MC, V* ¹⊙¹ *CP.*

$–$$$ ⊡ **Hotel St. Francis.** Listed on the National Register of Historic Places, this three-story building, parts of which were constructed in 1923, has walkways lined with turn-of-the-20th-century lampposts and is one block south of the Plaza. The simple, elegant rooms with high ceilings, casement windows, brass-and-iron beds, marble and cherry antiques, and original artworks suggest a refined establishment, but the service can be spotty and many of the rooms (and especially bathrooms) are quite tiny. Afternoon tea, with scones and finger sandwiches, is served daily (not complimentary) in the huge lobby, which rises 50 feet from a floor of blood-red tiles. The hotel bar is among the few places in town where you can grab a bite to eat until midnight. ⊠ *210 Don Gaspar Ave., 87501* ☎ *505/983–5700 or 800/529–5700* ⊟ *505/989–7690* ⊕ *www.hotelstfrancis.com* ⤳ *80 rooms, 2 suites* ⌂ *Restaurant, room service, refrigerators, cable TV, Wi-Fi, bar, gym, laundry service, concierge, business services, meeting rooms, parking (fee)* ⊟ *AE, D, DC, MC, V.*

★ $–$$$ ⊞ **Inn of the Turquoise Bear.** In the 1920s, poet Witter Bynner played host to an eccentric circle of artists and intellectuals, as well as some wild parties in his mid-19th-century Spanish–Pueblo Revival home, which is now a B&B. Rooms are simple but have plush linens. The inn's style preserves the building's historic integrity, and there's plenty of ambience and a ranchlike lobby. You might sleep in the room where D. H. Lawrence slept, or perhaps Robert Oppenheimer's room. The terraced flower gardens provide plenty of places to repose, away from the traffic on Old Santa Fe Trail, which borders the property. This is the quintessential Santa Fe inn. ⊠ *342 E. Buena Vista, 87501* ☎ *505/983–0798 or 800/396–4104* 🖷 *505/988–4225* ⊕ *www.turquoisebear.com* ⟳ *8 rooms, 2 with shared bath; 2 suites* ♻ *Cable TV, in-room VCRs, library, free parking* ▭ *AE, D, MC, V* ⦿⊦ *CP.*

$–$$$ ⊞ **La Tienda Inn and Duran House.** This is an offbeat but charming lodging option that comprises a former neighborhood market and adjacent Territorial-style adobe house (which together make up La Tienda) as well as a second Territorial-style house down the street (Duran House). Rooms throughout are exquisitely furnished with well-chosen country, folk, Southwestern, and Victorian antiques and fine linens and Navajo rugs—the look is refreshingly uncluttered, and some rooms have private patios and kiva fireplaces. The substantial Continental breakfast is served in a flowery garden courtyard in warm weather and in the common room fashioned out of the old market during the cooler months. ⊠ *445–447 W. San Francisco St., 87501* ☎ *505/989–8259 or 800/889–7611* ⊕ *www.latiendabb.com* ⟳ *11 rooms* ♻ *Refrigerators, cable TV, free parking* ▭ *MC, V* ⦿⊦ *CP.*

$$ ⊞ **Hotel Santa Fe.** Picurís Pueblo has controlling interest in this handsome Pueblo-style three-story hotel on the Guadalupe District's edge and a short walk from the Plaza. The light, airy rooms and suites are traditional Southwestern, with locally handmade furniture, wooden blinds, and Pueblo paintings; many have balconies. The hotel gift shop, Santa Fe's only tribally owned store, has lower prices than many nearby retail stores. The 35 rooms and suites in the posh Hacienda wing have corner fireplaces and the use of a London-trained butler. Amaya is one of the better hotel restaurants in town. Informal talks about Native American history and culture are held in the lobby, and Native American dances take place May–October. ⊠ *1501 Paseo de Peralta, 87505* ☎ *505/982–1200 or 800/825–9876* 🖷 *505/984–2211* ⊕ *www.hotelsantafe.com* ⟳ *40 rooms, 91 suites* ♻ *Restaurant, some microwaves, cable TV, pool, outdoor hot tub, massage, bar, laundry service, concierge, meeting rooms, free parking* ▭ *AE, D, DC, MC, V.*

Fodor'sChoice
★

$$ ⊞ **Pueblo Bonito B&B Inn.** Rooms in this 1873 adobe compound have handmade and hand-painted furnishings, Navajo weavings, brick and hardwood floors, sand paintings and pottery, locally carved santos, and Western art. All have kiva fireplaces and private entrances, and many have kitchens. Breakfast is served in the main dining room. Afternoon tea also offers complimentary margaritas. The Plaza is a five-minute walk away. ⊠ *138 W. Manhattan Ave., 87501* ☎ *505/984–8001 or 800/461–4599* 🖷 *505/984–3155* ⊕ *www.pueblobonitoinn.com* ⟳ *13 rooms, 5 suites* ♻ *Dining room, some kitchens, some refrigerators, cable TV, hot tub, laundry facilities, free parking; no smoking* ▭*AE, DC, MC, V* ⦿⊦ *CP.*

$–$$ 🏨 **Garrett's Desert Inn.** This sprawling, U-shape motor court may surround a parking lot and offer relatively little in the way of ambience, but it's well maintained and has an outstanding location a few blocks from the Plaza, smack in the middle of historic Barrio de Analco. The clean, no-frills rooms are done in earthy tones with a smattering of Southwest touches, and there's a pleasant pool and patio as well as an inviting bar that serves cocktails and light food and has a pool table. For the price and location, this is a real find. ✉ *311 Old Santa Fe Trail, 87501* 🕿 *505/982–1851 or 800/888–2145* ⊕ *www.garrettsdesertinn.com* ⇗ *83 rooms* ⌂ *Restaurant, cable TV, pool, billiards, lounge, car rental, meeting rooms, free parking* ⊟ *AE, DC, MC, V* ⦿❘ *CP.*

$–$$ 🏨 **Inn on the Paseo.** This inn is on a busy road, but at least this stretch of Paseo de Peralta is two lanes wide and is in a semi-residential neighborhood a short walk from the Plaza. Rooms are fairly simple but clean and light, some with hardwood floors and all with pleasing Southwestern furnishings and color schemes—some have fireplaces and private patios. The staff is laid-back and friendly. Try to get a room away from the road to avoid traffic noise. The two historic main buildings are joined by a modern lobby with a pitched ceiling, where continental breakfast is served—in warm weather you can dine on the sundeck. ✉ *630 Paseo de Peralta, 87501* 🕿 *505/984–8200 or 800/457–9045* 🖶 *505/989–3979* ⊕ *www.innonthepaseo.com* ⇗ *16 rooms, 2 suites* ⌂ *Cable TV, free parking; no kids under 8, no smoking* ⊟ *MC, V* ⦿❘ *CP.*

★ $–$$ 🏨 **Old Santa Fe Inn.** About four blocks south of the Plaza, in the hip Guadalupe District, this contemporary inn, which opened in 2001 and looks like an attractive, if fairly ordinary, adobe motel, has stunning and spotless rooms with elegant Southwestern furnishings. Tile baths, high-quality linens, and upscale furnishings fill every room, along with two phone lines and CD stereos; many have kiva fireplaces, or balconies and patios. It may not have the staff and all the amenities of a full-service hotel, but the rooms themselves are more inviting than several more-expensive downtown hotels, and the small business center and gym are open 24 hours. Most rooms open onto a gravel parking lot, although chile ristras hanging outside each unit brighten things up. The make-your-own-breakfast-burrito buffet is a nice touch. ✉ *320 Galisteo St., 87501* 🕿 *505/995–0800 or 800/745–9910* 🖶 *505/995–0400* ⊕ *www.oldsantafeinn.com* ⇗ *34 rooms, 9 suites* ⌂ *Some in-room hot tubs, some microwaves, some refrigerators, cable TV, in-room VCRs, Wi-Fi, gym, business services, free parking* ⊟ *AE, D, DC, MC, V* ⦿❘ *CP.*

¢–$ 🏨 **Santa Fe Sage Inn.** On the southern edge of the Guadalupe District, this motel offers affordable low-frills comfort and surprisingly attractive (given the low rates) Southwestern decor within walking distance of the Plaza (six blocks). Special packages are available for three- and four-day stays during peak-season events. Get a room in one of the rear buildings for the most privacy and quiet. There's an informal New Mexico restaurant on premises. ✉ *725 Cerrillos Rd., 87501* 🕿 *505/982–5952 or 866/433–0335* 🖶 *505/984–8879* ⊕ *www.santafesageinn.com* ⇗ *162 rooms* ⌂ *Restaurant, cable TV, Wi-Fi, pool, free parking, some pets allowed* ⊟ *AE, DC, MC, V* ⦿❘ *CP.*

South of Downtown

$$–$$$ 🖼 **Residence Inn.** This compound consists of clusters of three-story adobe town houses with pitched roofs and tall chimneys. Best bets for families or up to four adults traveling together are the one-room suites, which each have a loft bedroom and then a separate sitting area (with a curtain divider) that has a Murphy bed. All units have wood-burning fireplaces. It's right off a major intersection about 3 mi south of the Plaza, but it's set back far enough so that there's no traffic noise. Complimentary full breakfast, evening socials, and grocery-shopping service are provided. Ask for one of the second-floor end units for the best mountain views. ⊠ *1698 Galisteo St., 87505* ☎ *505/988–7300 or 800/331–3131* 🖨 *505/988–3243* ⊕ *www.residenceinn.com* 🛏 *120 suites* ⟂ *Dining room, kitchens, cable TV, Wi-Fi, meeting rooms, free parking* ⊟ *AE, D, DC, MC, V* ⦿ *BP.*

$–$$ 🖼 **El Rey Inn.** The kind of place where Lucy and Ricky might have Fodor'sChoice stayed during one of their cross-country adventures, the El Rey was built ★ in 1930s but has been brought gracefully into the 21st century, its rooms handsomely made over. Rooms are individually decorated and might include antique television armoires, beamed ceilings, upholstered wing chairs and sofas; some have kitchenettes. Bathrooms have been handsomely updated with glass brick and tile. Each unit has a small covered front patio with wrought-iron chairs. Towering shade trees loom over the parking

> **WORD OF MOUTH**
>
> "El Rey is very charming and there's a nice free breakfast. I usually stay there, but you do have to drive down to the plaza area, find a place to park."   –jayne1973

lot, and there's a landscaped courtyard with tables and chairs by the pool. ⊠ *1862 Cerrillos Rd., 87505* ☎ *505/982–1931 or 800/521–1349* 🖨 *505/989–9249* ⊕ *www.elreyinnsantafe.com* 🛏 *79 rooms, 8 suites* ⟂ *Some kitchenettes, cable TV, pool, hot tubs, sauna, exercise equipment, playground, laundry facilities, free parking; no smoking* ⊟ *AE, DC, MC, V* ⦿ *CP.*

$–$$ 🖼 **Santa Fe Courtyard by Marriott.** Of the dozens of chain properties along gritty Cerrillos Road, this is the only bona fide gem, even though it looks like all the others: clad in faux adobe and surrounded by parking lots and strip malls. Don't fret—it's easy to forget about the morose setting once inside this glitzy miniature resort, which comprises several buildings set around a warren of lushly landscaped interior courtyards. Rooms have the usual upscale-chain doodads: mini-refrigerators, coffeemakers, hair dryers, clock radios—there's also high-speed Internet. Aesthetically, the rooms look Southwestern, with chunky carved-wood armoires, desks, and headboards reminiscent of a Spanish-colonial hacienda. ⊠*3347 Cerrillos Rd., 87505* ☎ *505/473–2800 or 800/777–3347* 🖨*505/473–4905* ⊕*www.santafecourtyard.com* 🛏*213 rooms* ⟂ *Restaurant, room service, refrigerators, cable TV, Wi-Fi, pool, gym, hot tub, lounge, shop, laundry facilities, laundry service, business services, free parking* ⊟ *AE, D, DC, MC, V.*

★ $ Bobcat Inn. A delightful, affordable, country hacienda that's a 15-minute drive southeast of the Plaza, this adobe B&B sits amid 10 secluded acres of piñon and ponderosa pine, with grand views of the Sangre de Cristos and the area's high-desert mesas—it's right beside the popular Bobcat Bite restaurant. John and Amy Bobrick run this low-key retreat and prepare expansive full breakfasts as well as high tea on Saturday during the summer high season (these are by reservation only). Arts and Crafts furniture and Southwest pottery fill the common room, in which breakfast is served and guests can relax throughout the day. The unpretentious rooms are brightened by Talvera tiles, folk art, and colorful blankets and rugs; some have kiva fireplaces. The Lodge Room is outfitted with handcrafted Adirondack furniture, and its bathroom has a whirlpool tub. ⊠ *442 Old Las Vegas Hwy., 87505* ☎ *505/988–9239* ⊕ *www.nm-inn.com* ⌐ *5 rooms* ⌂ *Some in-room hot tubs, Wi-Fi, massage, free parking; no room TVs* ⊟ *D, MC, V* ⦿ *BP.*

$ Camel Rock Suites. Although this modern, affordable, all-suites property is operated by the Tesuque Pueblo north of Santa Fe, it's situated about 3 mi south of the Plaza, close to I–25 and behind a small shopping center with an Alberton's grocery store (handy, given the rooms' self-catering facilities). The curb appeal is nil, but it's still more pleasant in this part of town than along traffic-clogged Cerrillos Road, and the reasonable rates and pleasant rooms make this a great bet. Each unit has a separate sitting area, attractive hand-carved wood furniture, fully equipped kitchen, and either two double beds or a queen bed and twin pull-out sofa. An expanded breakfast buffet and organic coffee are included, and you can use the health club and pool at Genoveva Chavez Community Center, which is a 10-minute drive away. ⊠ *3007 St. Francis Dr. (entrance off Zia Rd.), 87505* ☎ *505/989–3600 or 877/989–3600* ⌂ *505/989–1058* ⊕ *www.camelrocksuites.com* ⌐ *120 suites* ⌂ *Kitchens, cable TV, laundry facilities, business services, some pets allowed, free parking* ⊟ *AE, D, MC, V* ⦿ *CP.*

¢   Silver Saddle Motel. Something of an exception to the mostly seedy and sketchy motels along Cerrillos Road, this low-slung adobe property transcends the genre, if barely. Sure, the carpets are a bit faded, the walls thin, the staff less than responsive, and Santa Fe's only strip club is across the street. But there's a kitschy, fun-loving swagger about the place. Most rooms are named for icons of the West (Annie Oakley, Wyatt Earp) and contain related plaques with colorful biographies. Furnishings range from motel drab to quirky Southwest: Talavera-tile bathrooms, serape tapestries, built-in bancos, and equipale chairs. The wildly popular home-furnishings and gift emporium, Jackalope, is next door. ⊠ *2810 Cerrillos Rd., 87505* ☎ *505/471–7663* ⌐ *27 rooms* ⌂ *Some kitchenettes, cable TV, free parking* ⊟ *AE, D, MC, V* ⦿ *CP.*

North of Santa Fe

$$$–$$$$ Bishop's Lodge Resort and Spa. In a bucolic valley at the foot of the Sangre de Cristo Mountains, this 1918 resort is five minutes from the Plaza. Behind the main building is a chapel that was once Archbishop Jean Baptiste Lamy's retreat. Unfortunately, despite the interesting history, the resort has slipped in quality and service in recent years and could

greatly stand an overhaul, especially given the high rates. Outdoor activities include hiking, horseback riding, skeet-shooting, and trapshooting. The two lodge buildings have antique and reproduction Southwestern furnishings—shipping chests, Mexican tinwork, and Native American and Western art; most of the rooms, in the property's other buildings, have less character, though some have fireplaces. The lodge has fitness facilities and is home to the excellent SháNah Spa. The serviceable but overpriced restaurant, specializing in inventive Nuevo Latino fare, serves Sunday brunch. ⊠ *Bishop's Lodge Rd., 2½ mi north of downtown, 87501* ☎ *505/983–6377 or 800/419–0492* ⊕ *www.bishopslodge.com* ⤳ *92 rooms, 19 suites* ♿ *2 restaurants, some refrigerators, cable TV, 2 tennis courts, pool, gym, hot tub, massage, spa, fishing, hiking, horseback riding, bar, children's programs (ages 4–12), business services, meeting rooms, airport shuttle, free parking* ⊟ *AE, D, MC, V.*

$$$–$$$$
Fodor'sChoice
★
🏨 **Ten Thousand Waves.** Devotees appreciate the Zenlike atmosphere of this Japanese-style health spa and small hotel above town. Nine light and airy hillside cottages tumble down a piñon-covered hill below the first-rate spa, which is tremendously popular with day visitors. The sleek, uncluttered accommodations have marble or stone wood-burning fireplaces, CD stereos, fine woodwork, low-slung beds or futons, and courtyards or patios; two come with full kitchens. There's also a cozy, vintage Airstream Bambi trailer available at much lower rates ($99–$109 nightly)—it's a kitschy, fun alternative to the much pricier cottages. The facility has private and communal indoor and outdoor hot tubs and spa treatments. Overnight guests can use the communal tubs for free. The snack bar serves sushi and other healthful treats, and a restaurant is planned, somewhat tentatively, for the next few years, along with additional hotel rooms. ⊠ *3451 Hyde Park Rd., 4 mi northeast of the Plaza* 🖃 *Box 10200, 87501* ☎ *505/982–9304* 🖷 *505/989–5077* ⊕ *www.tenthousandwaves.com* ⤳ *12 cottages, 1 trailer* ♿ *Snack bar, some kitchens, refrigerators, cable TV, some in-room VCRs, some Wi-Fi, outdoor hot tubs, spa, shop, free parking, some pets allowed (fee); no a/c, no TV in some rooms* ⊟ *D, MC, V.*

Camping

🏕 **Los Campos RV Resort.** The only full-service RV park in town lies between a car dealership on one side and open vistas on the other. Poplars and Russian olive trees, a dry riverbed, and mountains rise in the background. ⊠ *3574 Cerrillos Rd.* ☎ *505/473–1949 or 800/852–8160* ♿ *Grills, flush toilets, full hookups, dump station, drinking water, guest laundry, picnic tables, electricity, public telephone, play area, swimming (pool)* ⤳ *95 sites* 🖭 *$30–$37* ⊟ *MC, V.*

★ 🏕 **Rancheros de Santa Fe Campground.** This 22-acre camping park is on a hill in the midst of a piñon forest. Bring your tent or RV, or rent a cabin. You can get LP gas service here. Amenities include free Wi-Fi and cable TV hookups, nightly movies in summer, a hiking trail, a fenced-in dog run, and a recreation room. ⊠ *Old Las Vegas Hwy., Exit 290 from I-25, 10½ mi south of the Plaza* ☎ *505/466–3482 or 800/426–9259* ⊕ *www.rancheros.com* ♿ *Grills, flush toilets, full hookups, dump* station, drinking water, guest laundry, showers, picnic tables, electricity, public telephone, general store, play area, swimming (pool) 🏊 37 tent sites, 95 RV sites, 5 cabins ☜ Tent sites $18–$20, water and electric hookups $24–$27, full hookups $28–$36, cabins $38–$44 ⊟ MC, V ⊙ Mid-Mar.–Oct.

⚠ **Santa Fe KOA.** In the foothills of the Sangre de Cristo Mountains, 20 minutes southeast of Santa Fe, this large campground with tent sites, RV sites, and cabins is covered with piñons, cedars, and junipers. Wi-Fi is available; activities include basketball, ring toss, video games, and free movies. ✉ Old Las Vegas Hwy., Box 95–A, 87505 ☎ 505/466–1419 or 800/562–1514 ⊕ www.koa.com/where/nm/31159.htm ⚲ Flush toilets, partial hookups (electric), drinking water, guest laundry, showers, fire grates, fire pits, picnic tables, electricity, public telephone, general store 🏊 44 RV sites, 26 tent sites, 10 cabins ☜ Tent sites $25, RV sites $32–$38, cabins $42–$45 ⊟ D, MC, V ⊙ Mar.–Oct.

NIGHTLIFE & THE ARTS

Santa Fe ranks among America's most cultured small cities. Gallery openings, poetry readings, plays, and dance concerts take place year-round, not to mention the famed opera and chamber-music festivals. Check the arts and entertainment listings in Santa Fe's daily newspaper, the *New Mexican* (⊕ www.santafenewmexican.com), particularly on Friday, when the arts and entertainment section, "Pasatiempo," is included, or check the weekly *Santa Fe Reporter* (⊕ www.sfreporter.com) for shows and events. Activities peak in the summer.

Nightlife

Culturally endowed though it is, Santa Fe has a pretty mellow nightlife scene, its key strength being live music, which is presented at numerous bars, hotel lounges, and restaurants. Austin-based blues and country groups and other acts wander into town, and members of blockbuster bands have been known to perform unannounced at small clubs while vacationing in the area. But on most nights your best bet might be quiet cocktails beside the flickering embers of a piñon fire or under the stars out on the patio.

Catamount Bar (✉ 125 E. Water St. ☎ 505/988–7222) is popular with the postcollege set; jazz and blues-rock groups play on weekends and some weeknights. The dance floor is small, but there's an enjoyable second-story balcony with seating. This is the best place in town to shoot pool.

★ The **Cowgirl** (✉ 319 S. Guadalupe St. ☎ 505/982–2565) is one of the most popular spots in town for live blues, country, rock, folk, and even comedy, on occasion.

Dragon Room (✉ 406 Old Santa Fe Trail ☎ 505/983–7712), at the Pink Adobe restaurant, has been the place to see and be seen in Santa Fe for decades; flamenco and other light musical fare entertain at the packed bar.

Eldorado Court and Lounge (⊠ 309 W. San Francisco St. ☎ 505/988–4455), in the lobby of the classy Eldorado Hotel, is a gracious lounge where classical guitarists and pianists perform nightly. It has the largest wines-by-the-glass list in town.

★ **El Farol** (⊠ 808 Canyon Rd. ☎ 505/983–9912) restaurant is where locals like to hang out. The roomy, somewhat ramshackle bar area has an old Spanish–Western atmosphere, but you can order some fine Spanish brandies and sherries. On most nights you can listen to live flamenco, country, folk, or blues.

Evangelo's (⊠ 200 W. San Francisco St. ☎ 505/982–9014) is an old-fashioned, smoky street-side bar, with pool tables, 200 types of imported beer, and rock bands on many weekends.

Rodeo Nites (⊠ 2911 Cerrillos Rd. ☎ 505/473–4138) attracts a country-western crowd and lots of singles on the make. It can get a bit rough in the wee hours, so get here on the early side for line dancing and some very hot two-stepping.

Second Street Brewery (⊠ 1814 2nd St. ☎ 505/982–3030), a short drive south of downtown, packs in an eclectic bunch for outstanding microbrewed ales, pretty good pub fare, and live rock and folk. There's an expansive patio, and the staff is friendly.

★ **Swig** (⊠ 135 W. Palace Ave., Level 3 ☎ 505/955–0400), Santa Fe's trendiest upscale lounge, has developed a loyal following for its chichi postmodern decor, rooftop patio, small but swanky disco, and well-dressed crowd. The kitchen serves sublime pan-Asian bar food, including panko-crusted calamari and Szechuan duck breast—a few of these tapas-style dishes make a memorable meal.

Tiny's (⊠ Cerrillos Rd. and St. Francis Dr. ☎ 505/983–9817), a retro-fabulous restaurant serving excellent steaks and New Mexican fare, is a legend in this town with politicos, reporters, and deal-makers. The real draw is the kitsch-filled '50s cocktail lounge.

WilLee's Blues Club (⊠ 401 S. Guadalupe St. ☎ 505/982–0117) presents poundin' blues and some jazz several nights a week in an intimate, often-packed space in the Guadalupe District.

The Arts

The performing arts scene in Santa Fe blossoms in summer. Classical or jazz concerts, Shakespeare on the grounds of St. John's campus, experimental theater at Santa Fe Stages, or flamenco—"too many choices!" is the biggest complaint. The rest of the year is a bit more quiet, but an increasing number of off-season venues have developed in recent years.

The city's most interesting multiuse arts venue, the **Center for Contemporary Arts (CCA)** (⊠ 1050 Old Pecos Trail ☎ 505/982–1338 ⊕ www.ccasantafe.org) presents indie and foreign films, art exhibitions, provocative theater, and countless workshops and lectures.

Concert Venues

A 10-minute drive north of town, **Camel Rock Casino** (✉ U.S. 285/84 ☎ 800/462–2635 ⊕ www.camelrockcasino.com) presents relatively inexpensive pop and rock (Neil Sedaka, Pat Benatar, etc.) concerts.

Santa Fe's vintage downtown movie house was fully restored and converted into the 850-seat **Lensic Performing Arts Center** (✉ 211 W. San Francisco St. ☎ 505/988–1234 ⊕ www.lensic.com) in 2001. The grand 1931 building, with Moorish and Spanish Renaissance influences, hosts the Santa Fe Symphony, theater, classic films, lectures and readings, noted pop and jazz musicians, and many other noteworthy events.

On the campus of the Santa Fe Indian School, the **Paolo Soleri Outdoor Amphitheater** (✉ 1501 Cerrillos Rd. ☎ 505/989–6318) hosts pop, blues, rock, reggae, and jazz concerts spring–fall; past performers have included Bonnie Raitt, Tracy Chapman, and Chris Isaak.

The **St. Francis Auditorium** (✉ Museum of Fine Arts, northwest corner of Plaza) is the scene of cultural events such as theatrical productions and varied musical performances.

Dance

The esteemed **Aspen Santa Fe Ballet** (☎ 505/983–5591 or 505/988–1234 ⊕ www.aspensantafeballet.com) presents several ballet performances throughout the year at the Lensic Performing Arts Center.

Fans of Spanish dance should make every effort to see **Maria Benitez Teatro Flamenco** (✉ Lodge at Santa Fe, 750 N. St. Francis Dr. ☎ 505/955–8562 or 888/435–2636 ⊕ www.mariabenitez.com), who performs from late June through August at the Lodge at Santa Fe. Maria Benitez is one of the world's premier flamenco dancers, and her performances often sell out well in advance.

Film

The intimate **Jean Cocteau** (✉ 418 Montezuma Ave. ☎ 505/988–2711) shows art films and has a pleasant little café.

Music

The acclaimed ★ **Santa Fe Chamber Music Festival** (☎ 505/983–2075 ⊕ www.sfcmf.org) runs mid-July through late August, with performances nearly every night at the St. Francis Auditorium, or, occasionally, the Lensic Performing Arts Center. There are also free youth-oriented concerts given on several summer mornings. You can also attend many rehearsals for free; call for times.

Performances by the **Santa Fe Desert Chorale** (☎ 505/988–2282 or 800/244–4011 ⊕ www.desertchorale.org) take place throughout the summer at a variety of intriguing venues, from the Cathedral Basilica St. Francis to Loretto Chapel. This highly regarded singing group, which was begun in 1982, also performs a series of concerts during the December holiday season.

FodorśChoice ★   **Santa Fe Opera** (☎ 505/986–5900 or 800/280–4654 ⊕ www.santafeopera. org) performs in a strikingly modern structure—a 2,126-seat, indoor-outdoor amphitheater with excellent acoustics and sight lines. Carved

2

into the natural curves of a hillside 7 mi north of the city on U.S. 285/84, the opera overlooks mountains, mesas, and sky. Add some of the most acclaimed singers, directors, conductors, musicians, designers, and composers from Europe and the United States, and you begin to understand the excitement that builds every June. The company, which celebrated its 50th anniversary in 1956, presents five works in repertory each summer—a blend of seasoned classics, neglected masterpieces, and world premieres. Many evenings sell out far in advance, but inexpensive standing-room tickets are often available on the day of the performance. A favorite pre-opera pastime is tailgating in the parking lot before the evening performance—many guests set up elaborate picnics of their own, but you can also preorder picnic meals ($30 per meal) by calling ☎ 505/983–2433 24 hours in advance; pick up your meal up to two hours before the show, at the Angel Food Catering kiosk on the west side of the parking lot. Or you can dine at the Preview Buffet, set up 2½ hours before each performance by the Guilds of the Santa Fe Opera. These meals include a large spread of very good food along with wine, held on the opera grounds. During dessert, a prominent local expert on opera gives a talk about the evening's performance. The Preview Buffet is by reservation only, by calling the opera box office number listed above, and the cost is $48 per person.

Orchestra and chamber concerts are given at St. Francis Auditorium and the Lensic Performing Arts Center by the **Santa Fe Pro Musica** (☎ 505/988–4640 or 800/960–6680 ⊕ www.santafepromusica.com) from September through April. Baroque and other classical compositions are the normal fare; the annual Christmas performance is a highlight.

The **Santa Fe Symphony** (☎ 505/983–1414 or 800/480–1319 ⊕ www.sf-symphony.org) performs seven concerts each season (from October to April) in the Lensic Performing Arts Center.

Theater
The **Greer Garson Theatre Company** (⊠ College of Santa Fe, 1600 St. Michael's Dr. ☎ 505/473–6511 or 800/456–2673 ⊕ www.csf.edu) stages student productions of comedies, dramas, and musicals from October to May.

The oldest extant theater company west of the Mississippi, the **Santa Fe Playhouse** (⊠ 142 E. De Vargas St. ☎ 505/988–4262 ⊕ www.santafeplayhouse.org) occupies a converted 19th-century adobe stable and has been presenting an adventurous mix of avant-garde pieces, classical drama, and musical comedy since 1922. The Fiesta Melodrama—a spoof of the Santa Fe scene—runs late August–mid-September.

Theaterwork (⊠ 1336 Rufina Circle ☎ 505/471–1799 ⊕ www.theaterwork.org) is a well-respected community theater group that performs five plays each season, which runs from September through May.

SPORTS & THE OUTDOORS
The Santa Fe National Forest is right in the city's backyard and includes the Dome Wilderness (5,200 acres in the volcanically formed Jémez Moun-

tains) and the Pecos Wilderness (223,333 acres of high mountains, forests, and meadows at the southern end of the Rocky Mountain chain). The 12,500-foot Sangre de Cristo Mountains (the name translates as "Blood of Christ," for the red glow they radiate at sunset) fringe the city's east side, constant and gentle reminders of the mystery and power of the natural world. To the south and west, sweeping high desert is punctuated by several less formidable mountain ranges. The dramatic shifts in elevation and topography around Santa Fe make for a wealth of outdoor activities. Head to the mountains for fishing, camping, and skiing; to the nearby Rio Grande for kayaking and rafting; and almost anywhere in the area for bird-watching, hiking, and biking.

Participant Sports

For a report on general conditions in the forest, contact the **Santa Fe National Forest Office** (⊠ 1474 Rodeo Rd., 87505 ☎ 505/438–7840 ⊕ www. fs.fed.us/r3/sfe). For a one-stop shop for information about recreation on public lands, which includes national and state parks, contact the **New Mexico Public Lands Information Center** (⊠ 1474 Rodeo Rd., 87505 ☎ 505/438–7542 🖷 505/438–7582 ⊕ www.publiclands.org). It has maps, reference materials, licenses, permits—just about everything you need to plan an adventure in the New Mexican wilderness.

The state-of-the-art **Genoveva Chavez Community Center** (⊠ 3221 Rodeo Rd. ☎ 505/955–4001 ⊕ www.chavezcenter.com) is a reasonably priced (adults $4 per day), top-notch facility with a regulation-size ice rink, an enormous gymnasium, indoor running track, 50-meter pool, leisure pool with waterslide and play structures, aerobics center, state-of-the-art fitness room, two racquetball courts, and a child-care center.

For gear related to just about any outdoors activity you can think of, check out **Sangre de Cristo Mountain Works** (⊠ 328 S. Guadalupe St. ☎ 505/ 984–8221), a well-stocked shop that both sells and rents hiking, climbing, camping, trekking, snowshoeing, and skiing equipment. The staff here can also advise you on the best venues for these activities.

Bicycling
You can pick up a map of bike trips—among them a 30-mi round-trip ride from downtown Santa Fe to Ski Santa Fe at the end of NM 475— from the New Mexico Public Lands Information Center. One excellent place to mountain-bike is the Dale Ball Trail Network, which is accessed from several points, including the road to the ski valley and the east end of Canyon Road.

Bike N' Sport (⊠ 530 W. Cordova Rd. ☎ 505/820–0809) provides rentals and information about guided tours. **Sun Mountain** (⊠ 102 E. Water St. ☎ 505/982–8986) rents mountain bikes and offers a wide range of bike tours. The shop will also deliver to your hotel, any day, year-round.

Bird-Watching
At the end of Upper Canyon Road, at the mouth of the canyon as it wends into the foothills, the 135-acre **Randall Davey Audubon Center** harbors diverse birds and other wildlife. Guided nature walks are given many week-

ends; there are also two major hiking trails that you can tackle on your own. The home and studio of Randall Davey, a prolific early Santa Fe artist, can be toured on Monday afternoons in summer. There's also a nature bookstore. ⊠ *1800 Upper Canyon Rd.* ☎ *505/983–4609* ⊕ *www. audubon.org/chapter/nm/nm/rdac* ⊠ *$2, house tour $5* ⊙ *Weekdays 9–5, weekends 10–4; grounds daily dawn–dusk; house tours Mon. at 2.*

For a knowledgeable insider's perspective, take a tour with **WingsWest Birding** (☎ 800/583–6928 ⊕ http://home.earthlink.net/~wingswestnm/). Guide Bill West leads four- to eight-hour early-morning or sunset tours that venture into some of the region's best bird-watching areas, including Santa Fe Ski Basin, Cochiti Lake, the Jémez Mountains, the Upper Pecos Valley, and Bosque del Apache National Wildlife Refuge.

Fishing

There's excellent fishing spring through fall in the Rio Grande and the mountain streams that feed into it, as well as a short drive away along the Pecos River. **High Desert Angler** (⊠ 451 Cerrillos Rd. ☎ 505/988–7688 or 888/988–7688 ⊕ www.highdesertangler.com) is a superb fly-fishing outfitter and guide service. This is your one-stop shop for equipment rental, fly-fishing tackle, licenses, and advice.

Golf

Marty Sanchez Links de Santa Fe (⊠ 205 Caja del Rio Rd., off NM 599, the Santa Fe Relief Rte. ☎ 505/955–4400 ⊕ www.linksdesantafe.com), an outstanding municipal facility with beautifully groomed 18- and 9-hole courses, sits on high prairie west of Santa Fe with fine mountain views. It has driving and putting ranges, a pro shop, and a snack bar. The greens fees are $31 for the 18-hole course, $22 on the par-3 9-holer.

Hiking

Hiking around Santa Fe can take you into high-altitude alpine country or into lunaresque high desert as you head south and west to lower elevations. For winter hiking, the gentler climates to the south are less likely to be snow packed, while the alpine areas will likely require snowshoes or cross-country skis. In summer, wildflowers bloom in the high country, and the temperature is generally at least 10° cooler than in town. The mountain trails accessible at the base of the Ski Santa Fe area (end of NM 475) stay cool on even the hottest summer days. Weather can change with one gust of wind, so be prepared with extra clothing, rain gear, food, and lots of water. Keep in mind that the sun at 10,000 feet is very powerful, even with a hat and sunscreen. See the Side Trips from the Cities chapter (Chapter 4) for additional hiking areas near Santa Fe.

For information about specific hiking areas, contact the New Mexico Public Lands Information Center. The **Sierra Club** (⊕ www.riogrande. sierraclub.org/santafe/home.html) organizes group hikes of all levels of difficulty; a schedule of hikes is posted on the Web site.

Aspen Vista is a lovely hike along a south-facing mountainside. Take Hyde Park Road (NM 475) 13 mi, and the trail begins before the ski area. After walking a few miles through thick aspen groves you come to panoramic views of Santa Fe. The path is well marked and gently inclines toward Tesuque Peak. The trail becomes shadier with elevation—

snow has been reported on the trail as late as July. In winter, after heavy snows, the trail is great for intermediate-advanced cross-country skiing. The round-trip is 12 mi and sees an elevation gain of 2,000 feet, but it's just 3½ mi to the spectacular overlook. The hillside is covered with golden aspen trees in late September.

A favorite spot for a ramble, with a vast network of trails, is the **Dale Ball Foothills Trail Network**, a network of some 20 mi of paths that winds and wends up through the foothills east of town and can be accessed at a few points, including Hyde Park Road (en route to the ski valley) and the far end of Canyon Road, at Cerro Gordo. There are trail maps and signs at these points, and the trails are very well marked.

★ Spurring off the Dale Ball trail system, the steep but rewarding (and dog-friendly) **Atalaya Trail** runs from the visitor parking lot of St. John's College (off of Camino de Cruz Blanca, on the East Side) up a winding, ponderosa pine–studded trail to the peak of Mt. Atalaya, which affords incredible 270-degree views of Santa Fe. The nearly 6-mi round-trip hike climbs a nearly 2,000 feet (to an elevation of 9,121 feet), so pace yourself. The good news: the return to the parking area is nearly all downhill.

Horseback Riding
New Mexico's rugged countryside has been the setting for many Hollywood westerns. Whether you want to ride the range that Gregory Peck and Kevin Costner rode or just head out feeling tall in the saddle, you can do so year-round. Rates average about $20 an hour. See the Side Trips from the Cities chapter (Chapter 4) for additional horseback listings in Cerrillos, Galisteo, and Ojo Caliente.

Bishop's Lodge (✉ Bishop's Lodge Rd. ☎ 505/983–6377) provides rides and guides year-round. Call for reservations.

Jogging
Because of the city's altitude (7,000–7,500 feet), you may feel heavy-legged and light-headed if you start running shortly after you arrive. Once you become acclimated, though, you can find that this is a great place to run. There's a jogging path along the Santa Fe River, parallel to Alameda, and another at Fort Marcy on Washington Avenue. The winding roads and paths up near the scenic campus of St. John's College are also ideal, although the terrain is quite hilly. Pick up gear and running advice at **Running Hub** (✉ 333 Montezuma Ave., No. 6 ☎ 505/820–2523); the store sponsors informal group runs many days—these are open to anybody.

River Rafting
If you want to watch birds and wildlife along the banks, try the laid-back Huck Finn floats along the Rio Chama or the Rio Grande's

> **WORD OF MOUTH**
>
> "When we go to Santa Fe, my husband usually runs on the trails in and around St. John's College which is up above Santa Fe. I don't know where you live but remember Santa Fe is at 7,000 ft elevation."
> —martym

White Rock Canyon. The season is generally between April and September. Most outfitters have overnight package plans, and all offer half- and full-day trips. Be prepared to get wet, and wear secure water shoes. For a list of outfitters who guide trips on the Rio Grande and the Rio Chama, write the **Bureau of Land Management (BLM), Taos Resource Area Office** (✉ 226 Cruz Alta Rd., Taos 87571 ☎ 505/758–8851 🌐 www.nm.blm.gov), or stop by the BLM visitor center along NM 68 16 mi south of Taos.

Kokopelli Rafting Adventures (✉ 551 W. Cordova Rd. ☎ 505/983–3734 or 800/879–9035 🌐 www.kokopelliraft.com) specializes in trips through the relatively mellow White Rock Canyon as well as white water. **New Wave Rafting** (✉ 1101 Cerrillos St. ☎ 505/984–1444 or 800/984–1444 🌐 www.newwaverafting.com) conducts full-day, half-day, and overnight river trips, with daily departures from Santa Fe. **Santa Fe Rafting Company and Outfitters** (✉ 1000 Cerrillos Rd. ☎ 505/988–4914 or 800/467–7238 🌐 www.santaferafting.com) customizes rafting tours. Tell them what you want—they'll do it.

Skiing

To save time during the busy holiday season you may want to rent skis or snowboards in town the night before hitting the slopes, or early in the morning so you don't waste any time paid for by your pricey lift ticket. **Alpine Sports** (✉ 121 Sandoval St. ☎ 505/983–5155 🌐 www.alpinesports-santafe.com) rents downhill and cross-country skis and snowboards. **Cottam's Ski Rentals** (✉ Hyde Park Rd., 7 mi northeast of downtown, toward Ski Santa Fe ☎ 505/982–0495 or 800/322–8267) rents the works, including snowboards, sleds, and snowshoes.

Ski Santa Fe (✉ End of NM 475, 18 mi northeast of downtown ☎ 505/982–4429, 505/983–9155 conditions 🌐 www.skisantafe.com), open roughly from late November through early April, is a fine, mid-size operation that receives an average of 225 inches of snow a year and plenty of sunshine. It's one of America's highest ski areas—the 12,000-foot summit has a variety of terrain and seems bigger than its 1,700 feet of vertical rise and 660 acres. There are some great powder stashes, tough bump runs, and many wide, gentle cruising runs. The 44 trails are ranked 20% beginner, 40% intermediate, and 40% advanced; there are seven lifts. Snowboarders are welcome, and there's the Norquist Trail for cross-country skiers. Chipmunk Corner provides day care and supervised kids' skiing. The ski school is excellent. Rentals, a good restaurant, a ski shop, and Totemoff Bar and Grill round out the amenities.

Snowshoeing

You can always snowshoe on your own in Santa Fe National Forest, which also has fine cross-country ski trails, by renting poles and shoes at **Alpine Sports** (*see above*), but it's more fun and interesting to take a guided tour. **Outspire Santa Fe** (☎ 505/660–0394 🌐 www.outspire.com) offers guided snowshoe tours in Santa Fe National Forest. No experience is necessary to enjoy this relaxing, wintertime version of hiking.

SHOPPING

Santa Fe has been a trading post for eons. A thousand years ago the great pueblos of the Chacoan civilizations were strategically located between the buffalo-hunting tribes of the Great Plains and the Indians of Mexico. Native Americans in New Mexico traded turquoise and other valuables with Indians from Mexico for metals, shells, parrots, and other exotic items. After the arrival of the Spanish and the West's subsequent development, Santa Fe became the place to exchange silver from Mexico and natural resources from New Mexico for manufactured goods, whiskey, and greenbacks from the United States. With the building of the railroad in 1880, Santa Fe had access to all kinds of manufactured goods as well as those unique to the region via the old trade routes.

The trading legacy remains, but now downtown Santa Fe caters almost exclusively to those looking for handcrafted goods. Sure, T-shirt outlets and major retail clothing shops have moved in, but shopping in Santa Fe consists mostly of one-of-a-kind independent stores. Canyon Road, packed with art galleries, is the perfect place to find unique gifts and collectibles. The downtown district, around the Plaza, has unusual gift shops, clothing, and shoe stores that range from theatrical to conventional, curio shops, and art galleries. The funky, laid-back Guadalupe District, less touristy than the Plaza, is on downtown's southwest perimeter and includes the Sanbusco Market Center and the Design Center.

Farther out on Cerrillos Road, a traffic-jammed strip of shopping centers and chain motels, a new clutch of modern superstores has sprung up alongside Santa Fe's rather ordinary Villa Linda shopping mall. All the usual suspects are out here, around the intersection with Rodeo Road. On Cerrillos out by the I–25 exit, the inevitable **Santa Fe Premium Outlets** (⊠ 8380 Cerrillos Rd., at I–25 ☎ 505/474–4000) contains about 40 shops, including Bass, Coach, Dansk, Eddie Bauer, Jones New York, and Brooks Brothers.

Art Galleries

The following are only a few of the nearly 200 galleries in greater Santa Fe—with the best of representational, nonobjective, Native American, Latin American, cutting-edge, photographic, and soulful works that defy categorization. The Santa Fe Convention and Visitors Bureau (⇨ Visitor Information *in* Santa Fe Essentials, *below*) has a more extensive listing. *The Wingspread Collectors Guide to Santa Fe and Taos* is a good resource and is available in hotels and at some galleries, as well as on the Web at ⊕ www.collectorsguide.com. Check the "Pasatiempo" pullout in the *Santa Fe New Mexican* on Friday for a preview of gallery openings.

Andrew Smith Gallery (⊠ 203 W. San Francisco St. ☎ 505/984–1234) is a significant photo gallery dealing in works by Edward S. Curtis and other 19th-century chroniclers of the American West. Other major figures are Ansel Adams, Edward Weston, O. Winston Link, Henri Cartier-

Bresson, Eliot Porter, Laura Gilpin, Dorothea Lange, Alfred Stieglitz, Annie Liebowitz, and regional artists like Barbara Van Cleve.

Bellas Artes (✉ 653 Canyon Rd. ☎ 505/983–2745), a sophisticated gallery and sculpture garden, has ancient ceramics and represents internationally renowned artists like Judy Pfaff, Phoebe Adams, and Olga de Amaral.

Carole LaRoche (✉ 415 Canyon Rd. ☎ 505/982–1186) displays the owner's striking, archetypal paintings depicting wolves, warriors, and other primeval figures.

Charlotte Jackson Fine Art (✉ 200 W. Marcy St. ☎ 505/989–8688) focuses primarily on monochromatic "radical" painting. Florence Pierce, Joe Barnes, William Metcalf, Anne Cooper, and Joseph Marioni are among the artists producing minimalist works dealing with light and space.

Cline Fine Art (✉ 135 W. Palace Ave. ☎ 505/982–5328) specializes in contemporary paintings and sculpture, especially modernism and regionalism, from Southwestern to European works.

FodorsChoice ★ **Gerald Peters Gallery** (✉ 1011 Paseo de Peralta ☎ 505/954–5700) is Santa Fe's leading gallery of American and European art from the 19th century to the present. It has works by Max Weber, Albert Bierstadt, the Taos Society, the New Mexico Modernists, and Georgia O'Keeffe, as well as contemporary artists.

LewAllen Contemporary (✉ 129 W. Palace Ave. ☎ 505/988–8997) is a leading center for a variety of contemporary arts by both Southwestern and other acclaimed artists, among them Judy Chicago; sculpture, photography, ceramics, basketry, and painting are all shown in this dynamic space.

FodorsChoice ★ **Monroe Gallery** (✉ 112 Don Gaspar Ave. ☎ 505/992–0800) showcases works by the most celebrated black-and-white photographers of the 20th century, from Margaret Bourke-White to Alfred Eisenstaedt.

★ **Nedra Matteucci Galleries** (✉ 1075 Paseo de Peralta ☎ 505/982–4631 ✉ 555 Canyon Rd. ☎ 505/983–2731) exhibits works by California regionalists, members of the early Taos and Santa Fe schools, and masters of American Impressionism and Modernism. Spanish-colonial furniture, Indian antiquities, and a fantastic sculpture garden are other draws of this well-respected establishment.

Niman Fine Arts (✉ 125 Lincoln Ave. ☎ 505/988–5091) focuses on the prolific work of contemporary Native American artists–Hopi painters Arlo Namingha and Michael Namingha.

Peyton Wright (✉ 237 E. Palace Ave. ☎ 505/989–9888), tucked inside a charming cottage, represents some of the most talented emerging and established contemporary artists in the country, as well as antique and even ancient Chinese, pre-Columbian, Russian, and Latin works.

Photo-eye Gallery (✉ 376–A Garcia St. ☎ 505/988–5159) shows contemporary photography that includes the beautiful and sublime; there's also a stellar bookstore.

The Art of Santa Fe

THE ARTISTIC ROOTS OF SANTA FE stretch back to the landscape and the devotion of those who roamed and settled here long before the Santa Fe Trail transplanted goods and people from the East. The intricate designs on Native American pottery and baskets, the embroidery on the ritual dance wear, the color and pattern on Rio Grande weavings, and the delicate paintings and carvings of devotional images called santos all contributed to the value and awareness of beauty that Santa Fe holds as its cultural birthright. The rugged landscape, the ineffable quality of the light, and the community itself continue to draw to Santa Fe a plethora of musicians, writers, and visual artists. The spell of beauty is so powerful here that some people call the town "Fanta Se," but for those who live in Santa Fe the arts are very real (as are economic realities; most artists hold additional jobs—ask your waiter).

With wide-eyed enchantment, visitors often buy paintings in orange, pink, and turquoise that are perfect next to the adobe architecture, blue sky, and red rocks of the New Mexican landscape. When they get home, however, the admired works sometimes end up in a closet simply because it's so hard to integrate the Southwestern look with the tone of the existing furnishings and artwork. Taking the risk is part of the experience. Rather than suffering from buyer's remorse, those who make the aesthetic leap can take the spirit of northern New Mexico home with them. Although it may shake up the home decor, the works are a reminder of a new way of seeing and of all the other values that inspire one to travel in the first place.

Most galleries will send a painting (not posters or prints) out on a trial basis for very interested clients. If looking at art is new to you, ask yourself if your interest is in bringing home a souvenir that says "I was there" or in art that will live in the present and inspire the future, independent of the nostalgia for the "land of enchantment." Santa Fe has plenty of both to offer—use discrimination while you look so you don't burn out on the first block of Canyon Road.

Santa Fe, while holding strong in its regional art identity, emerged in the late 1990s as a more international art scene. Native American and Hispanic arts groups now include the work of contemporary artists who have pressed beyond the bounds of tradition. Bold color and the oft-depicted New Mexico landscape are still evident, but you're just as likely to see mixed-media collages by a Chinese artist currently living in San Francisco. A few Santa Fe outlets, such as the Riva Yares Gallery and evo gallery, are dedicated to representing artists with Latin American roots. "The world is wide here," Georgia O'Keeffe once noted about northern New Mexico. And just as Santa Fe welcomed early Modernist painters who responded to the open landscape and the artistic freedom it engendered, contemporary artists working with edgier media, such as conceptual, performance, and installation art, are finding welcoming venues in Santa Fe, specifically at SITE Santa Fe museum.

Puskin Gallery (✉ 550 Canyon Rd. ☎ 505/982–1990) is yet more evidence that Santa Fe's art scene is about so much more than regional work—here you can peruse works by some of Russia's leading 19th- and 20th-century talents, with an emphasis on impressionism.

Riva Yares Gallery (✉ 123 Grant St. ☎ 505/984–0330) specializes in contemporary artists of Latin American descent. There are sculptures by California artist Manuel Neri, color field paintings by Esteban Vicente, and works by Santa Feans Elias Rivera, Rico Eastman, and others—plus paintings by such international legends as Hans Hofman, Milton Avery, and Helen Frankenthaler.

Santa Fe Art Institute (✉ 1600 St. Michael's Dr. ☎ 505/424–5050), a nonprofit educational art organization that sponsors several artists in residence and presents workshops, exhibitions, and lectures, has a respected gallery whose exhibits change regularly. The institute is set inside a dramatic contemporary building. Past artists in residence have included Richard Diebenkorn, Larry Bell, Moon Zappa, Henriette Wyeth Hurd, and Judy Pfaff.

★ **Shidoni Foundry and Galleries** (✉ Bishop's Lodge Rd., 5 mi north of Santa Fe, Tesuque ☎ 505/988–8001) casts work for accomplished and emerging artists from all over North America. On the grounds of an old chicken ranch, Shidoni has a rambling sculpture garden and a gallery. Self-guided foundry tours are permitted Saturday 9–5 and weekdays noon–1, but the sculpture garden is open daily during daylight hours; you can watch bronze pourings most Saturday afternoons.

Specialty Stores

Antiques & Home Furnishings

Artesanos (✉ 222 Galisteo St. ✉ 1414 Maclovia St. ☎ 505/471–8020) is one of the best Mexican-import shops in the nation, with everything from leather chairs to papier-mâché *calaveras* (skeletons used in Day of the Dead celebrations), and tinware. The location on Maclovia Street specializes in Talavera and other tiles.

At **Asian Adobe** (✉ 530 S. Guadalupe St. ☎ 505/992–6846) browse porcelain lamps, silk scarves, red-lacquer armoires, and similarly stunning Chinese and Southeast Asian artifacts and antiques.

★ **Bosshard Fine Art Furnishings** (✉ 340 S. Guadalupe St. ☎ 505/989–9150) deals in African ethnographica, which complement the vast selection of tapestries, architectural elements, statues, and ceramics from the Southwest as well as Asia.

Casa Nova (✉ 530 S. Guadalupe St. ☎ 505/983–8558) sells functional art from around the world, deftly mixing colors, textures, and cultural icons—old and new—from stylish pewter tableware from South Africa to vintage hand-carved ex-votos (votive offerings) from Brazil.

★ The **Design Center** (✉ 418 Cerrillos Rd.), which occupies an art deco former Chevy dealership in the Guadalupe District, contains some of the most distinctive antique and decorative arts shops in town, plus a couple of small restaurants. Be sure to browse the precious Latin American antiques at **Claiborne Gallery** (☎ 505/982–8019), along with the artful contemporary desks, tables, and chairs created by owner Omer Claiborne. **Gloria List Gallery** (☎ 505/982–5622) specializes in rare 17th- and 18th-century devotional and folk art, chiefly from South America, Italy, Spain, and Mexico. And at **Sparrow & Magpie Antiques** (☎ 505/ 982–1446), look mostly for East Coast and Midwest folk art and textiles, although the shop carries some Southwestern pieces, too.

Design Warehouse (✉ 101 W. Marcy St. ☎ 505/988–1555), a welcome antidote to Santa Fe's preponderance of shops selling Spanish-colonial antiques, stocks super-hip and mod sofas, kitchenware, lamps, and other sleek knickknacks.

Doodlet's (✉ 120 Don Gaspar Ave. ☎ 505/983–3771) has an eclectic collection of stuff: pop-up books, bizarre postcards, tin art, hooked rugs, and stringed lights. Wonderment is in every display case, drawing the eye to the unusual. Note that the store is closed through early 2007 for remodeling.

Foreign Traders (✉ 202 Galisteo St. ☎ 505/983–6441), a Santa Fe institution founded as the Old Mexico Shop in 1927 and still run by the same family, stocks handicrafts, antiques, and accessories from Mexico and other parts of the world.

Jackalope (✉ 2820 Cerrillos Rd. ☎ 505/471–8539), a legendary if somewhat overpriced bazaar, sprawls over 7 acres, incorporating several pottery barns, a furniture store, endless aisles of knickknacks from Latin America and Asia, and a huge greenhouse. There's also an area where craftspeople, artisans, and others sell their wares—sort of a mini–flea market.

Montez Gallery (✉ Sena Plaza Courtyard, 125 E. Palace Ave. ☎ 505/ 982–1828) sells Hispanic works of religious art and decoration, including retablos (holy images painted on wood or tin), bultos (carved wooden statues of saints), furniture, paintings, pottery, weavings, and jewelry.

★ **Nambé Outlets** (✉ 104 W. San Francisco St. ☎ 505/988–3574 ✉ 924 Paseo de Peralta ☎ 505/988–5528) carries the classic metal bowls, vases, and candlesticks made by the acclaimed artisans of the Nambé Pueblo, just north of town; lead crystal, lighting, and porcelain are also sold.

Pachamama (✉ 223 Canyon Rd. ☎ 505/983–4020) carries Latin American folk art, including small tin or silver *milagros,* the stamped metal images used as votive offerings. The shop also carries weavings and Spanish-colonial antiques.

Sequoia (✉ 201 Galisteo St. ☎ 505/982–7000) shows the imaginative, almost surreal, furniture creations of its owner, who was born in India. Curvaceous glass shelves, lamps, and candlesticks mix with paintings and fine linens.

Books

More than a dozen shops in Santa Fe sell used books, and a handful of high-quality shops carry the latest releases from mainstream and small presses.

ALLÁ (✉ 102 W. San Francisco St., upstairs ☎ 505/988–5416) is one of Santa Fe's most delightful small bookstores. It focuses on hard-to-find Spanish-language books and records, including limited-edition handmade books from Central America. It also carries Native American books and music, as well as English translations.

Collected Works Book Store (✉ 208B W. San Francisco St. ☎ 505/988–4226) carries art and travel books, including a generous selection of books on Southwestern art, architecture, and general history, as well as the latest in contemporary literature.

Garcia Street Books (✉ 376 Garcia St. ☎ 505/986–0151) is an outstanding independent shop strong on art, architecture, cookbooks, literature, and regional Southwestern works—it's a block from the Canyon Road galleries.

Nicholas Potter (✉ 211 E. Palace Ave. ☎ 505/983–5434) specializes in used, rare, and out-of-print books. The quixotic shop also stocks used jazz and classical CDs.

Photo-eye Books (✉ 376 Garcia St. ☎ 505/988–5152) stocks new, rare, and out-of-print photography books.

Travel Bug (✉ 839 Paseo de Peralta ☎ 505/992–0418) has a huge array of travel tomes and guidebooks, and USGS and other maps. There's also a cozy coffeehouse with high-speed wireless.

Clothing & Accessories

Women have been known to arrive here in Liz Claiborne and leave in a broomstick skirt and Navajo velvet shirt, but function dictates form in cowboy fashions. A wide-brim hat is essential in open country for protection from heat, rain, and insects, and the pointed toes of cowboy boots slide easily in and out of stirrups, while the high heels help keep feet in the stirrups. Tall tops protect ankles and legs on rides through brush and cactus country and can protect the wearer from a nasty shin bruise from a skittish horse.

Some Western fashion accessories were once purely functional. A colorful bandanna protected an Old West cowboy from sun- and windburn and served as a mask in windstorms, when riding drag behind a herd or, on occasions far rarer than Hollywood would have us believe, when robbing trains. A cowboy's sleeveless vest enhanced his ability to maneuver during roping and riding chores and provided pocket space that his skintight pants—snug to prevent wrinkles in the saddle area—didn't. Belt buckles are probably the most sought-after accessories—gold ones go for as much as $1,000.

Back at the Ranch (✉ 209 E. Marcy St. ☎ 505/989–8110 or 888/962–6687) is an attractive old shop stocked with handmade cowboy boots, from red leather to turquoise snakeskin, along with funky furniture, 1950s blanket coats, jewelry, and buckles. Some things get better with age, especially cowboy boots.

★ **O'Farrell Hats** (⊠ 111 E. San Francisco St. ☎ 505/989–9666) is the domain of America's foremost hatmaker, Kevin O'Farrell. This quirky shop custom-crafts one-of-a-kind beaver-lined cowboy hats that make the ultimate Santa Fe keepsake. This level of quality comes at a cost, but devoted customers—who have included everyone from cattle ranchers to U.S. presidents—swear by O'Farrell's artful creations.

★ **Double Take at the Ranch** (⊠ 321 S. Guadalupe St. ☎ 505/820–7775) ranks among the best consignment stores in the West, carrying elaborately embroidered vintage cowboy shirts, hundreds of pairs of boots, funky old prints, and one-of-a-kind jewelry. The store adjoins Santa Fe Pottery, which carries the works of more than 70 local artists.

Lucchese (⊠ 203 W. Water St. ☎ 505/820–1883) has been crafting some of the West's finest handmade cowboy boots since 1883.

Mirá (⊠ 101 W. Marcy St. ☎ 505/988–3585) clothing for women is slick, eclectic, and funky, combining the adventurous spirit of Mexico with global contemporary fashion. The shop has accessories and collectibles from Latin America, hemp apparel, and knockout vintage-inspired dresses.

Origins (⊠ 135 W. San Francisco St. ☎ 505/988–2323) borrows from many cultures, carrying pricey women's wear like antique kimonos and custom-dyed silk jackets. One-of-a-kind accessories complete the spectacular look that Santa Fe inspires.

Food & Cookery

In the DeVargas shopping center, **Las Cosas Kitchen Shoppe** (⊠ N. Guadalupe St. at Paseo de Peralta ☎ 505/988–3394 or 877/229–7184) carries a fantastic selection of cookery, tableware, and kitchen gadgetry and gifts. The shop is also renowned for its cooking classes, which touch on everything from high-altitude baking to Asian-style grilling.

★ **Todos Santos** (⊠ 125 E. Palace Ave. ☎ 505/982–3855) is a tiny candy shop in an 18th-century courtyard, carrying seen-to-be-believed works of edible art, including chocolate milagros and altar pieces gilded with 23-karat gold or silver leaf. Truffles come in exotic flavors, like rose caramel and lemon verbena.

Jewelry

Karen Melfi Collection (⊠ 225 Canyon Rd. ☎ 505/982–3032) sells high-quality yet moderately priced handmade jewelry and other wearable art.

Primavera (⊠ 209 W. San Francisco St. ☎ 505/995–8552) is highly regarded not only for its imaginative goldsmithing but also for its brightly colored glass–and–wrought-iron lamps, which seem surreally inspired by Louis Tiffany.

Markets

Browse through the vast selection of local produce, meat, flowers, ★ honey, and cheese—much of it organic—at the **Santa Fe Farmers Market** (⊠ Gualadupe St. and Cerrillos Rd. ☎ 505/983–4098 ⊕ www.

santafefarmersmarket.com), which is held Tuesday and Saturday mornings from 7 until noon, late April–early November; in winter, a smaller indoor version is held just on Saturday mornings nearby at El Museo Cultural, in the Railyard on Guadalupe Street. It's a great people-watching event, and there's storytelling for kids as well as a snack bar selling terrific breakfast burritos and other goodies. Additionally, on Thursday afternoons in summer, the market sets up at the Rodeo Fairgrounds on Rodeo Road.

★ **Tesuque Pueblo Flea Market** (⊠ U.S. 285/84, 7 mi north of Santa Fe ☎ 505/995–7767 ⊕ www.tesuquepueblofleamarket.com) was once considered the best flea market in America by its loyal legion of bargain hunters. The Tesuque Pueblo took over the market in the late '90s and raised vendor fees, which increased the presence of predictable, often pricey goods brought in by professional flea-market dealers. In recent years, however, the pueblo has brought in a nice range of vendors, and this market with as many as 500 vendors in peak season is again one of the best shopping events in town. The 12-acre market is next to the Santa Fe Opera and is open Friday–Sunday, mid-March–December.

Native American Arts & Crafts

Frank Howell Gallery (⊠ 103 Washington Ave. ☎ 505/984–1074) stocks lithographs, serigraphs, prints, and posters of the late Frank Howell as well as works by other Native American artists.

Morning Star Gallery (⊠ 513 Canyon Rd. ☎ 505/982–8187) is a veritable museum of Native American art and artifacts. An adobe shaded by a huge cottonwood tree houses antique basketry, pre-1940 Navajo silver jewelry, Northwest Coast Native American carvings, Navajo weavings, and art of the Plains Indians.

Packard's on the Plaza (⊠ 61 Old Santa Fe Trail ☎ 505/983–9241), the oldest Native American arts-and-crafts store on Santa Fe Plaza, sells Zapotec Indian rugs from Mexico and original rug designs by Richard Enzer, old pottery, saddles, kachina dolls, and an excellent selection of coral and turquoise jewelry. Prices are quite high, but so are the standards. There's also an extensive clothing selection.

★ The **Rainbow Man** (⊠ 107 E. Palace Ave. ☎ 505/982–8706), established in 1945, does business in the remains of a building that was damaged during the 1680 Pueblo Revolt. The shop carries early Navajo, Mexican, and Chimayó textiles, along with photographs by Edward S. Curtis, vintage pawn jewelry, Day of the Dead figures, Oaxacan folk animals, and kachinas.

Shush Yaz (⊠ 1048 Paseo de Peralta ☎ 505/992–0441), in the tradition of the great trading posts of Gallup, has been dealing in fine turquoise jewelry, fine baskets, kachina dolls, and pottery—much of it from the early 20th century—for more than 120 years.

Trade Roots Collection (⊠ 411 Paseo de Peralta ☎ 505/982–8168) sells Native American ritual objects, such as fetish jewelry and Hopi rattles. The store is a good source of crafts materials.

SANTA FE ESSENTIALS

AIR TRAVEL

Most visitors to Santa Fe fly into the state's main airport in Albuquerque, about an hour away. There's no air service between Albuquerque and Santa Fe. Great Lakes Aviation flies three or four times daily from Denver to Santa Fe and has code sharing with United and Frontier airlines.

🚩 **Great Lakes Aviation** ☎ 800/554-5111 ⊕ www.greatlakesav.com.

AIRPORTS

Tiny Santa Fe Municipal Airport offers limited services, although there's some talk of expanding the facility and its runways to help lure additional airlines. The airport is 9 mi southwest of downtown.

🚩 **Santa Fe Municipal Airport (SAF)** ✉ Airport Rd. and NM 599 ☎ 505/473-4118.

BUS TRAVEL

Bus service on Texas, New Mexico & Oklahoma Coaches, affiliated with Greyhound Lines, is available to Santa Fe from major cities and towns throughout the region.

The city's bus system, Santa Fe Trails, covers 10 major routes through town and is useful for getting from the Plaza to some of the outlying attractions. Route M is most useful for visitors, as it runs from downtown to the museums on Old Santa Fe Trail south of town, and Route 2 is useful if you're staying at one of the motels out on Cerrillos Road and need to get into town (still a car is a much more practical way to get around). Individual rides cost $1, and a daily pass costs $2. Buses run about every 30 minutes on weekdays, every hour on weekends. Service begins at 6 AM and continues until 11 PM on weekdays, 8–8 on Saturday, and 10–7 (limited routes) on Sunday.

🚩 **Greyhound/Texas, New Mexico & Oklahoma Coaches** ☎ 505/243-4435 or 800/231-2222 ⊕ www.greyhound.com. **Santa Fe Trails** ☎ 505/955-2001 ⊕ www.santafenm.gov/public-works.

CAR RENTAL

Santa Fe is served by several national rental car agencies, including Avis, Budget, and Hertz. Additional agencies with locations in Santa Fe include Advantage, Classy Car Rentals (which specializes in luxury and sports vehicles), Enterprise, Sears, and Thrifty. *See* Car Rental *in* New Mexico Essentials for national rental agency phone numbers.

🚩 **Advantage** ☎ 505/983-9470. **Enterprise** ☎ 505/473-3600. **Sears** ☎ 505/984-8038. **Thrifty** ☎ 505/474-3365 or 800/367-2277.

CAR TRAVEL

South–north–running I–25 actually curves in almost a west–east direction as it cuts just south of Santa Fe, which is 62 mi northeast of Albuquerque. U.S. 285/84 runs north–south through the city. The Turquoise Trail (Chapter 4) is a scenic, two-lane approach to Santa Fe from Albuquerque. The NM 599 bypass, also called the Santa Fe Relief Route, cuts around the city from I–25's Exit 276, southwest of the city, to U.S. 285/

84, north of the city; it's a great shortcut if you're heading from Albuquerque to Española, Abiquiu, Taos, or other points north of Santa Fe.

PARKING Parking in Santa Fe is difficult, but public and private lots can be found throughout the city. Parking meters are well monitored. There are parking garages near the Plaza on San Francisco and Water streets. On weekends, you can park for free in the lots of some of the government buildings near the capitol, which is within walking distance of the Plaza (check signs carefully for specific parking rules).

EMERGENCIES
In an emergency, dial 911.
🔢 Hospital **St. Vincent Hospital** ✉ 455 St. Michael's Dr. ☎ 505/983-3361.
🔢 **24-hour Pharmacy Walgreens** ✉ 1096 St. Francis Dr. ☎ 505/982-4643 ✉ 3298 Cerrillos Rd. ☎ 505/474-3523.

SIGHTSEEING TOURS
GENERAL INTEREST Aboot About has been walking groups through the history, art, and architecture of Santa Fe since the late 1970s. Tours leave daily at 9:30 and 1:30 from the Eldorado Hotel, 9:45 and 1:45 from the Hotel St. Francis, and Saturday and Monday at 9:45 from La Posada Resort. Tours take about two hours. No reservations are required. The company also offers a variety of additional tours on everything from ghosts and legends to Georgia O'Keeffe Country to local culinary rambles. Great Southwest Adventures conducts guided mountain hikes and 7- to 35-passenger van and bus excursions to Bandelier, Abiquiu, Taos, and elsewhere in the region; it also provides a shuttle service to and from downtown hotels and the Santa Fe Opera. Santa Fe Detours conducts bus, river, rail, horseback, and walking tours and organizes rafting and ski packages. This is an excellent choice if you're looking for a general overview of the city and some of the nearby attractions. The walking tours are offered daily at 9:30 and 1:30 from the northeast corner of the Plaza. Custom Tours by Clarice are guided open-air tram excursions that run five times a day from the corner of Lincoln Avenue and West Palace Avenue. These 90-minute tours offer a nice overview of downtown; the company also gives bus and shuttle tours of Bandelier and Taos, and shuttle services from town to the Santa Fe Opera.

Rojo Tours designs specialized trips—to view wildflowers, pueblo ruins and cliff dwellings, galleries and studios, Native American arts and crafts, and private homes—as well as adventure activity tours. Santa Fe Guides is an organization of about 15 respected independent tour guides—their Web site lists each member and his or her specialties.

For an unforgettable bird's-eye view of the region, book a helicopter tour with HeliNM, which offers several different trips, costing from about $75 and up per person—popular destinations include the Turquoise Trail, Tent Rocks and Los Alamos, Pecos Wilderness, and O'Keeffe Country. These tours depart from Santa Fe Municipal Airport, and charters are also available.
🔢 **Aboot About** ☎ 505/988-2774 or 866/614-8404 ⊕ www.abootabout.com. **Custom Tours By Clarice** ☎ 505/438-7116 ⊕ www.santafecustomtours.com. **Great Southwest**

Adventures ☎ 505/455-2700 ⊕ www.swadventures.com. **HeliNM** ☎ 866/995-1058 ⊕ www.helinm.com. **Rojo Tours** ☎ 505/474-8333 ⊕ www.rojotours.com. **Santa Fe Detours** ☎ 505/983-6565 or 800/338-6877 ⊕ www.sfdetours.com. **Santa Fe Guides** ☎ 505/466-4877 ⊕ www.santafeguides.org.

LEARNING EXPERIENCES

Art Adventures in the Southwest takes you into the New Mexico landscape for outdoor art classes with Jane Shoenfeld. All materials are supplied, and all experience levels are welcome. Santa Fe Art Institute is housed in the Visual Arts Center designed by Mexican architect Ricardo Legorreta (a Modernist break from Santa Fe style). The institute (not part of the College of Santa Fe) offers weeklong workshops that have been led by such renowned artists as Phoebe Adams and Richard Diebenkorn. Dormitory quarters are available and studio space is provided. Workshops are offered year-round.

Santa Fe Photographic Workshops offers workshops in photographic processes, including digital imaging, platinum, and travel photography. The workshops have an excellent reputation, and many instructors return year after year. Santa Fe School of Cooking holds night and day classes in regional New Mexican fare.

🖪 **Art Adventures in the Southwest** ☎ 505/986-1108 ⊕ www.skyfields.net. **Santa Fe Art Institute** ✉ 1600 St. Michael's Dr., College of Santa Fe campus ☎ 505/424-5050 ⊕ www.sfai.org. **Santa Fe Photographic Workshops** ☎ 505/983-1400 ⊕ www.sfworkshop.com. **Santa Fe School of Cooking** ☎ 505/983-4511 or 800/982-4688 ⊕ www.santafeschoolofcooking.com.

TAXIS

Capital City Cab Company controls all the cabs in Santa Fe. The taxis aren't metered; you pay a flat fee based on how far you're going, usually $6–$10 within the downtown area. There are no cab stands; you must phone to arrange a ride.

🖪 **Capital City Cab** ☎ 505/438-0000.

BY TRAIN

Amtrak's *Southwest Chief* stops in Lamy, a short drive south of Santa Fe, on its route from Chicago to Los Angeles via Kansas City; other New Mexico stops include Raton, Las Vegas, Albuquerque, and Gallup daily. In summer 2006, the City of Albuquerque launched the state's first-ever commuter train line, the *New Mexico Rail Runner Express.* As of this writing, service is from Bernalillo south through the city of Albuquerque, continuing south through Los Lunas to the suburb of Belén, covering a distance of about 50 mi. The second and final phase of the project, expected to be completed by late 2008, will extend the service north to Santa Fe.

🖪 **Amtrak** ☎ 800/872-7245 ⊕ www.amtrak.com. *New Mexico Rail Runner Express* ☎ 505/245-7245 ⊕ www.nmrailrunner.com.

VISITOR INFORMATION

🖪 **New Mexico Department of Tourism visitor center** ✉ Lamy Bldg., 491 Old Santa Fe Trail, 87503 ☎ 505/827-7400 or 800/733-6396 Ext. 0643 ⊕ www.newmexico.org. **Santa Fe Convention and Visitors Bureau** ✉ 201 W. Marcy St., Box 909, 87501 ☎ 505/955-6200 or 800/777-2489 ⊕ www.santafe.org.

Taos

WORD OF MOUTH

"We both loved Taos—small, but so unassuming. We managed to take in the plaza, Kit Carson Home, Millicent Rogers Museum, Rio Grande Gorge Bridge, Hacienda de los Martínez (hard to find, but worth it!), San Francisco de Asís Church, and, the highlight I think, Taos Pueblo."

–Chele60

"The Taos Pueblo is larger than most, and it does offer some little shops, but it's definitely not a shopping destination. It's more of a place to see how the Indians live/lived."

–JackOneill

Updated by
Andrew Collins

TAOS CASTS A LINGERING SPELL. Set on a rolling mesa at the base of the Sangre de Cristo Mountains, it's a place of piercing light and spectacular views, where the desert palette changes almost hourly as the sun moves across the sky. Adobe buildings—some of them centuries old—lie nestled amid pine trees and scrub, some in the shadow of majestic Taos Mountain. The smell of piñon wood smoke rises from the valley in winter; in spring and summer, it gives way to fragrant sage.

The magic of the area has drawn people here for hundreds of years. The earliest inhabitants were Native Americans of the Taos–Tiwa tribe; their descendants still live and maintain a traditional way of life at Taos Pueblo, a 95,000-acre reserve 3 mi north of what is now the town's commercial center. Spanish settlers, who arrived in the 1500s, brought both farming and Catholicism to the area; their influence can still be seen today at Ranchos de Taos, 4 mi south of town, and at the San Francisco de Asís Church, whose massive adobe walls and *camposanto* (graveyard) are among the most photographed in the country.

In the early 20th century, another population—artists—discovered Taos and began making the pilgrimage here to write, paint, and take photographs. The early adopters of this movement were painters Bert Phillips and Ernest Blumenschein, who were traveling from Denver on a planned painting trip into Mexico in 1898 when they stopped to have a broken wagon wheel repaired in Taos. Enthralled with the earthy beauty of the region, they abandoned their plan to journey farther south, settled, and eventually formed the Taos Society of Artists in 1915. Over the following years, many illustrious artists, including Georgia O'Keeffe, Ansel Adams, and D. H. Lawrence also took up residence in the area, and it is still a mecca for creative types today. The downtown area is now filled with galleries and shops that display the work of local artists, and museums that document Taos's artistic history.

These days, Taos has a variable population of about 6,500 (the 2000 U.S. Census officially places it at 4,700, but there's always an influx during the summer and the winter ski season, and these numbers don't include Arroyo Seco, Taos Ski Valley, and other neighboring villages). Many come here for a break from the urban sprawl of larger U.S. cities; among the escapees are actress Julia Roberts and U.S. Secretary of Defense Donald Rumsfeld.

EXPLORING TAOS

Taos is small and resolutely rustic, and the central area is highly walkable. Sociable Taoseños make the town a welcoming place to explore. You need a car to reach the Rio Grande Gorge and other places of interest beyond Taos proper. Traffic can be heavy in the peak summer and winter seasons (an accident on the main route through town, Paseo del Pueblo, can back up traffic for miles); ask locals about back roads that let you avoid the busy street.

The Museum Association of Taos includes six properties. Among them are the Harwood Museum, Taos Art Museum at the Fechin House, the

GREAT ITINERARIES

IF YOU HAVE 1 DAY

Begin by strolling around **Taos Plaza** ❶, taking in the galleries and Native American crafts shops. Take Ledoux Street south from the west Plaza and go two blocks to visit the **Harwood Museum** ❺. Walk back to the Plaza and cross over to Kit Carson Road, where you can find more shops and galleries as well as the **Kit Carson Home and Museum** ❹. Continue north on Paseo del Pueblo to the **Taos Art Museum at the Fechin House** ❽. In the afternoon, get in the car and head north on Paseo del Pueblo to the traffic light, where you turn left on U.S. 64. to the **Rio Grande Gorge Bridge** ❻. If you're feeling peppy, you can climb down to the river, or just gaze down into the breathtaking chasm from the bridge. Return the way you came, turning right at the light, and drive the short distance to Millicent Rogers Road. Turn right and proceed to the **Millicent Rogers**

Museum ⓬, where you can easily spend the rest of the afternoon. If you're in town for the evening, stop in at the Adobe Bar at the Taos Inn for music and people-watching.

IF YOU HAVE 2 DAYS

Spend the first day doing the one-day tour above. On the second day, drive out to the **Taos Pueblo** ⓫ in the morning and tour the ancient village while the day is fresh. Return to town and go to the **Blumenschein Home and Museum** ❷. Lunch at the nearby Dragonfly Café. After lunch drive out to **La Hacienda de los Martinez** ❾ for a look at early life in Taos and then to **Ranchos de Taos** ❿ to see the beautiful San Francisco de Asís Church. If it's dinnertime, eat at Joseph's Table or the Trading Post Café. If it's still early, drive back to town and browse in the shops on Bent Street and the adjacent John Dunn House Shops.

Millicent Rogers Museum, and buildings in the Kit Carson Historic Museum consortium that include the Blumenschein Home and Museum, the Kit Carson Home and Museum, and La Hacienda de los Martínez. Each of the museums charges $5–$7 for admission, but you can opt for a combination ticket—$20 for all five, valid for one year.

Numbers in the text correspond to numbers in the margin and on the Taos map.

Downtown Taos

More than four centuries after it was laid out, Taos Plaza remains the center of commercial life in Taos. Bent Street, where New Mexico's first American governor lived and died, is an upscale shopping area and gallery enclave.

What to See

 Blumenschein Home and Museum. For an introduction to the history of the Taos art scene, start with Ernest L. Blumenschein's residence, which provides a glimpse into the cosmopolitan lives led by the members of the

Taos Society of Artists, of which Blumenschein was a founding member. One of the rooms in the adobe-style structure dates from 1797. On display are the art, antiques, and other personal possessions of Blumenschein and his wife, Mary Greene Blumenschein, who also painted, as did their daughter Helen. Several of Ernest Blumenschein's vivid oil paintings hang in his former studio, and works by other early Taos artists are also on display. ✉ *222 Ledoux St.* ☎ *505/758–0505* ⊕ *taoshistoricmuseums. com/blumenschein.html* 🏷 *$6, $20 with Museum Association of Taos combination ticket* ⊙ *Apr.–Oct., daily 9–5; Nov.–Mar., daily 10–4.*

☾ ❻ **Firehouse Collection.** More than 100 works by well-known Taos artists like Joseph Sharp, Ernest L. Blumenschein, and Bert Phillips hang in the Taos Volunteer Fire Department building. The exhibition space adjoins the station house, where five fire engines are maintained at the ready and an antique fire engine is on display. ✉ *323 Camino de la Placita* ☎ *505/758–3386* 🏷 *Free* ⊙ *Weekdays 9–4:30.*

☾ ❺ **Governor Bent Museum.** In 1846, when New Mexico became a U.S. possession as a result of the Mexican War, Charles Bent, a trader, trapper, and mountain man, was appointed governor. Less than a year later he was killed in his house by an angry mob protesting New Mexico's annexation by the United States. Governor Bent was married to María Ignacia, the older sister of Josefa Jaramillo, the wife of mountain man Kit Carson. A collection of Native American artifacts, western Americana, and family possessions is squeezed into five small rooms of the adobe building where Bent and his family lived. ✉ *117 Bent St.* ☎ *505/758–2376* 🏷 *$2* ⊙ *Apr.–Oct., daily 9–5; Nov.–Mar., daily 10–4.*

★ ❸ **Harwood Museum.** The Pueblo Revival former home of Burritt Elihu "Burt" Harwood, a dedicated painter who studied in France before moving to Taos in 1916, is adjacent to a museum dedicated to the works of local artists. Traditional Hispanic northern New Mexican artists, early art-colony painters, post–World War II modernists, and contemporary artists such as Larry Bell, Agnes Martin, Ken Price, and Earl Stroh are represented. Mabel Dodge Luhan, a major arts patron, bequeathed many of the 19th- and early-20th-century works in the Harwoods' collection, including *retablos* (painted wood representations of Catholic saints) and *bultos* (three-dimensional carvings of the saints). In the Hispanic Traditions Gallery upstairs are 19th-century tinwork, furniture, and sculpture. Downstairs, among early-20th-century art-colony holdings, look for E. Martin Hennings's *Chamisa in Bloom,* which captures the Taos landscape particularly beautifully. A tour of the ground-floor galleries shows that Taos painters of the era, notably Oscar Berninghaus, Ernest Blumenschein, Victor Higgins, Walter Ufer, Marsden Hartley, and John Marin, were fascinated by the land and the people linked to it. An octagonal gallery exhibits works by Agnes Martin. Martin's seven large canvas panels (each 5 feet square) are

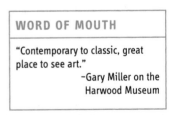

WORD OF MOUTH

"Contemporary to classic, great place to see art."
–Gary Miller on the Harwood Museum

A GOOD WALK

Begin at the gazebo in the middle of **Taos Plaza** ▶ ❶. After exploring the Plaza, head south from its western edge down the small unmarked alley (its name is West Plaza Drive). The first cross street is Camino de la Placita. Across it, West Plaza Drive becomes Ledoux Street. Continue south on Ledoux to the **Blumenschein Home and Museum** ❷ and, a few doors farther south, the **Harwood Museum** ❸. (If you're driving, the parking area for the Harwood Foundation is at Ledoux and Ranchitos Road.)

From the Harwood Foundation, walk back north on Ranchitos Road a few blocks, make a left on Camino de la Placita, and go right onto Don Fernando Road. Follow it east along the north side of the Plaza to Paseo del Pueblo Norte (NM 68), which is the main street of Taos. As you cross NM 68, Don Fernando Road changes to Kit Carson Road. On the north side of Kit Carson Road is the **Kit Carson Home and Museum** ❹. After visiting the home, head back to Paseo del Pueblo Norte and walk north past the Taos Inn to browse through Bent Street's shops, boutiques, and galleries.

In a tiny plaza is the **Governor Bent Museum** ❺, the modest home of the first Anglo governor of the state. Across the street is the John Dunn House. Once the homestead of a colorful and well-respected Taos gambling and transportation entrepreneur, the Dunn House is now a small shopping plaza. At the western end of Bent Street, head north on Camino de la Placita. In about 2½ blocks you'll come to the Taos Volunteer Fire Department building, which doubles as a fire station and the **Firehouse Collection** ❻ exhibition space.

Head east on Civic Plaza and cross Paseo del Pueblo Norte. To the north will be **Kit Carson Park** ❼ and the **Taos Art Museum at the Fechin House** ❽, named for the iconoclastic artist Nicolai Fechin. ⊙ TIMING TIPS➙➙ **The entire walk can be done in a half day, a whole day if you stop to lunch along the way and browse in the shops and galleries. The Taos Art Museum at the Fechin House is closed Monday. Hours vary by season, but visits by appointment are welcomed. Some museums are closed on the weekend, so you may want to do this walk on a Wednesday, Thursday, or Friday. You can tour each of the museums in less than an hour.**

are furnished as they were when the Carson family lived here. The rest of the museum is devoted to gun and mountain-man exhibits, such as rugged leather clothing and Kit's own Spencer carbine rifle with its beaded leather carrying case, and early Taos antiques, artifacts, and manuscripts. ⊠ *Kit Carson Rd.* ☎ *505/758–0505* ✎ *$5, $20 with Museum Association of Taos combination ticket* ⊙ *May–Oct., daily 9–5; Nov.–Apr., daily 10–4.*

NEED A BREAK?

Let the aroma of fresh-ground coffee draw you into the tiny **World Cup** (⊠ 102 Paseo del Pueblo Norte ☎ 505/737-5299), where you can sit at the counter or wander outside to a bench on the porch. Locals engage in political rhetoric here, often slanted toward the left, so be prepared for a rousing debate if you dare to dissent.

🧒 ❼ **Kit Carson Park.** The noted pioneer is buried in the park that bears his name. His grave is marked with a *cerquita* (a spiked wrought-iron rectangular fence), traditionally used to outline and protect burial sites. Also interred here is Mabel Dodge Luhan, the pioneering patron of the early Taos art scene. The 32-acre park has swings and slides for recreational breaks. It's well marked with big stone pillars and a gate. ✉ *211 Paseo del Pueblo Norte* 🕾 *505/758–8234* 🎟 *Free* 🕙 *Late May–early Sept., daily 8–8; early Sept.–late May, daily 8–5.*

❽ **Taos Art Museum at the Fechin House.** The interior of this extraordinary adobe house, built between 1927 and 1933 by Russian émigré artist Nicolai Fechin, is a marvel of carved Russian-style woodwork and furniture that glistens with an almost golden sheen. Fechin constructed it to showcase his daringly colorful paintings. The house has hosted the Taos Art Museum since 2003, with a collection of paintings from more than 50 Taos artists, including founders of the original Taos Society of Artists, among them Joseph Sharp, Ernest Blumenschein, Bert Phillips, E.I. Couse, and Oscar Berninghaus. ✉ *227 Paseo del Pueblo Norte* 🕾 *505/ 758–2690* ⊕ *www.taosartmuseum.org* 🎟 *$8, $20 with Museum Association of Taos combination ticket* 🕙 *Tues.–Sun. 10–5.*

Fodor'sChoice ★

❶ **Taos Plaza.** The first European explorers of the Taos Valley came here with Captain Hernando de Alvarado, a member of Francisco Vásquez de Coronado's expedition of 1540. Basque explorer Don Juan de Oñate arrived in Taos in July 1598 and established a mission and trading arrangements with residents of Taos Pueblo. The settlement developed into two plazas: the Plaza at the heart of the town became a thriving business district for the early colony, and a walled residential plaza was constructed a few hundred yards behind. It remains active today, home to a throng of gift and

> **WORD OF MOUTH**
>
> "Very nice shops, but don't expect the average person to afford much in any of them. If you love window shopping this is the place to go."
> –Jodie on Taos Plaza

coffee shops. The covered gazebo was donated by heiress and longtime Taos resident Mabel Dodge Luhan. On the southeastern corner of Taos Plaza is the **Hotel La Fonda de Taos.** Some infamous erotic paintings by D. H. Lawrence that were naughty in his day but are quite tame by present standards can be viewed ($3 entry fee) in the former barroom beyond the lobby.

NEED A BREAK?

Join the locals at the north or south location of the **Bean** (✉ 900 Paseo del Pueblo Norte 🕾 505/758–7711 ✉ 1033 Paseo del Pueblo Sur 🕾 505/758–5123). The Bean roasts its own coffee, and the south-side location (where you can dine on an outside patio) offers good breakfast and lunch fare. The north location, in an adobe building, displays local artwork and is the most atmospheric of the two.

A GOOD DRIVE

Head south 3 mi on NM 240 (also known as Ranchitos Road) to **La Hacienda de los Martínez** ➤ ⑨. As you pass by the adobe cottages and modest homes dotting the landscape, you get a sense of the area's rural roots. From the hacienda continue south and east another 4 mi to NM 68 and the small farming village of **Ranchos de**

Taos ⑩. Watch for signs for **San Francisco de Asís Church,** which is on the east side of NM 68. The small plaza here contains several galleries worth checking out.

⊙ TIMING TIPS➜ **Set aside about two hours to tour the hacienda, a bit of Ranchos de Taos, and San Francisco de Asís Church.**

3

South of Taos

The first Spanish settlers were farmers who faced raids by non-Pueblo Native Americans like the Comanches. Aspects of this history come alive on this meandering drive south through fields and farmland to a restored hacienda and into a former farming village with its famous, fortresslike church.

What to See

⑨ **La Hacienda de los Martínez.** Spare and fortlike, this adobe structure built between 1804 and 1827 on the bank of the Rio Pueblo served as a community refuge during Comanche and Apache raids. Its thick walls, which have few windows, surround two central courtyards. Don Antonio Severino Martínez was a farmer and trader; the hacienda was the final stop along El Camino Real (the Royal Road), the trade route the Spanish established between Mexico City and New Mexico. The restored period rooms here contain textiles, foods, and crafts of the early 19th century. There's a working blacksmith's shop, usually open to visitors on Saturday, and weavers create beautiful textiles on reconstructed period looms. ⊠ *Ranchitos Rd., NM 240* ☎ *505/758–1000* ⊕ *www. taoshistoricmuseums.com/martinez.html* 🎫 *$6, $20 with Museum Association of Taos combination ticket* ⊙ *Apr.–Oct., daily 9–5; Nov.–Mar., daily 10–4.*

⑩ **Ranchos de Taos.** A few minutes' drive south of the center of Taos, this village still retains some of its rural atmosphere despite the highway traffic passing through. Huddled around its famous adobe church and dusty plaza are cheer-

GOOD TERM

Retablo: Holy image painted on wood or tin.

ful, remodeled shops and galleries standing shoulder to shoulder with crumbling adobe shells. This ranching, farming, and budding small-business community was an early home to Taos Native Americans before being settled by Spaniards in 1716. Although many of the adobe dwellings have seen better days, the shops, modest galleries, taco stands, and two fine restaurants point to an ongoing revival.

★ The massive bulk of **San Francisco de Asís Church** (⊠ NM 68, 500 yards south of NM 518, Ranchos de Taos ☎ 505/758–2754) is an enduring attraction. The Spanish Mission–style church was erected in 1815 as a spiritual and physical refuge from raiding Apaches, Utes, and Comanches. In 1979 the deteriorated church was rebuilt with traditional adobe bricks by community volunteers. Every spring a group gathers to re-mud the facade. The earthy, clean lines of the exterior walls and supporting bulwarks have inspired generations of painters and photographers. The late-afternoon light provides the best exposure of the heavily buttressed rear of the church—though today's image-takers face the challenge of framing the architecturally pure lines through rows of parked cars and a large, white sign put up by church officials; morning light is best for the front. Bells in the twin belfries call Taoseños to services on Sunday and holidays. Monday through Saturday from 9 to 4 you can step inside. In the parish hall nearby (and for a $3 fee) you can view a 15-minute video presentation every half hour that describes the history and restoration of the church and explains the mysterious painting *Shadow of the Cross*, on which each evening the shadow of a cross appears over Christ's shoulder (scientific studies made on the canvas and the paint pigments cannot explain the phenomenon). The fee also allows you to view the painting. ⊠ *Paseo del Pueblo Sur, NM 68, about 4 mi south of Taos Plaza.*

Taos Pueblo to Rio Grande Gorge

What to See

⑫ Millicent Rogers Museum. More than 5,000 pieces of spectacular Native American and Hispanic art, many of them from the private collection of the late Standard Oil heiress Millicent Rogers, are on display here. Among the pieces are baskets, blankets, rugs, kachina dolls, carvings, paintings, rare religious artifacts, and most significantly, jewelry (Rogers, a fashion icon in her day, was one of the first Americans to appreciate the turquoise-and-silver artistry of Native American jewelers). Other important works include the pottery and ceramics of Maria Martinez and other potters from San Ildefonso Pueblo (23 mi north of Santa Fe). Docents conduct guided tours by appointment, and the museum hosts lectures, films, workshops, and demonstrations. ⊠ *1504 Millicent Rogers Rd., from Taos Plaza head north on Paseo del Pueblo Norte and left at sign for CR BA030, also called Millicent Rogers Rd. or Museum Rd.* ☎ *505/758–2462* ⊕ *www.millicentrogers.com* ☑ *$7, $20 with Museum Association of Taos combination ticket* ☉ *Apr.–Sept., daily 10–5; Nov.–Mar., Tues.–Sun. 10–5.*

FodorsChoice
★

> **WORD OF MOUTH**
>
> "Gorgeous building (a former home), exquisite Indian Jewelry as well as blankets and Maria Martinez pottery. You feel like you are visiting someone's home that has REALLY GOOD taste in art of the region. I never miss it when in Taos."
> –Marjorie on the Millicent Rogers Museum

A GOOD DRIVE

Drive 2 mi north on Paseo del Pueblo Norte (NM 68), and keep your eyes peeled for the signs on the right, beyond the post office, directing you to **Taos Pueblo** ⚑ ⓫. To reach the **Millicent Rogers Museum** ⓬ next, return to NM 68 to head north and make a left onto County Road BA030. If you find yourself at the intersection with U.S. 64 and 150, you've gone too far. Continue down the county road to the big adobe wall; the sign for the museum is on the right. This rural road eventually connects back onto Upper Ranchitos Road. After exploring the museum, return to NM 68 north; then make a left on U.S. 64 west to the **Rio Grande Gorge Bridge** ⓭, a stunning marriage of natural wonder and human engineering. Bring along sturdy hiking shoes and plenty of water and snacks for an invigorating walk down into the gorge. But remember, what goes down must come up, and it's an arduous path. TIMING TIPS→ **Plan on spending 1½ hours at the pueblo. Taos can get hot in summer, but if you visit the pueblo in the morning, you'll avoid the heat and the crowds. Winters can be cold and windy, so dress warmly. If your visit coincides with a ceremonial observance, set aside several hours, because the ceremonies, though they are worth the wait, never start on time. Two hours should be enough time to take in the museum and the grandeur of the Rio Grande Gorge Bridge.**

★ ⓭ **Rio Grande Gorge Bridge.** It's a dizzying experience to see the Rio Grande 650 feet underfoot, where it flows at the bottom of an immense, steep rock canyon. In summer the reddish rocks dotted with green scrub contrast brilliantly with the blue sky, where you might see a hawk lazily floating in circles. The bridge is the second-highest expansion bridge in the country. Hold on to your camera and eyeglasses when looking down, and watch out for low-flying planes. The Taos Municipal Airport is close by, and daredevil private pilots have been known to challenge one another to fly under the bridge. Shortly after daybreak, hot-air balloons fly above and even inside the gorge. ✉ *U.S. 64, 12 mi west of town.*

⓫ Fodor'sChoice ★ **Taos Pueblo.** For nearly 1,000 years the mud-and-straw adobe walls of Taos Pueblo have sheltered Tiwa-speaking Native Americans. A United Nations World Heritage Site, this is the largest collection of multistory pueblo dwellings in the United States. The pueblo's main buildings, Hlauuma (north house) and Hlaukwima (south house), are separated by a creek. These structures are believed to be of a similar age, probably built between 1000 and 1450. But the entire site is covered in the UN World Heritage designation. The dwellings have common walls but no connecting doorways—the Tiwas gained access only from the top, via ladders that were retrieved

WORD OF MOUTH

"Taos Pueblo is worth the price of the tour. Our guide grew up in the pueblo and returned to live there after college. She gave many cultural and spiritual insights on the tour." -eileenleft after entering. Small buildings and corrals are scattered about.

The pueblo today appears much as it did when the first Spanish explorers arrived in New Mexico in 1540. The adobe walls glistening with mica caused the conquistadors to believe they had discovered one of the fabled Seven Cities of Gold. The outside surfaces are continuously maintained by replastering with thin layers of mud, and the interior walls are frequently coated with thin washes of white clay. Some walls are several feet thick in places. The roofs of each of the five-story structures are supported by large timbers, or vigas, hauled down from the mountain forests. Pine or aspen *latillas* (smaller pieces of wood) are placed side by side between the vigas; the entire roof is then packed with dirt.

Even after 400 years of Spanish and Anglo presence in Taos, inside the pueblo the traditional Native American way of life has endured. Tribal custom allows no electricity or running water in Hlauuma and Hlaukwima, where varying numbers (usually fewer than 100) of Taos Native Americans live full-time. About 2,000 others live in conventional homes on the pueblo's 95,000 acres. The crystal-clear Rio Pueblo de Taos, originating high above in the mountains at the sacred Blue Lake, is the primary source of water for drinking and irrigating. Bread is still baked in *hornos* (outdoor domed ovens). Artisans of the Taos Pueblo produce and sell (tax-free) traditionally handcrafted wares, such as mica-flecked pottery and silver jewelry. Great hunters, the Taos Native Americans are also known for their work with animal skins and their excellent moccasins, boots, and drums.

Although the population is about 80% Catholic, the people of Taos Pueblo, like most Pueblo Native Americans, also maintain their native religious traditions. At Christmas and other sacred holidays, for instance, immediately after Mass, dancers dressed in seasonal sacred garb proceed down the aisle of St. Jerome Chapel, drums beating and rattles shaking, to begin other religious rites.

The pueblo **Church of San Geronimo,** or St. Jerome, the patron saint of Taos Pueblo, was completed in 1850 to replace the one destroyed by the U.S. Army in 1847 during the Mexican War. With its smooth symmetry, stepped portal, and twin bell towers, the church is a popular subject for photographers and artists (though the taking of photographs inside is discouraged).

The public is invited to certain ceremonial dances held throughout the year: January 1, Turtle Dance; January 6, Buffalo or Deer Dance; May 3, Feast of Santa Cruz Foot Race and Corn Dance; June 13, Feast of San Antonio Corn Dance; June 24, Feast of San Juan Corn Dance; second weekend in July, Taos Pueblo Powwow; July 25 and 26, Feast of Santa Ana and Santiago Corn Dance; September 29 and 30, Feast of San Geronimo Sunset Dance; December 24, Vespers and Bonfire Pro-

Festivals of Tradition

SEVERAL YEARLY FESTIVALS CELEBRATE the Native American and Hispanic roots of Taos. During the last weekend in September, La Hacienda de los Martínez hosts the **Old Taos Trade Fair,** a reenactment of autumn gatherings of the 1820s, when Plains Indians and trappers came to Taos to trade with the Spanish and the Pueblo Indians. The two-day event includes demonstrations of blacksmithing, weaving, and other crafts, a chili cook-off, native foods, music, and dancing.

The **Wool Festival** (⊕ www. taoswoolfestival.org), held in early October in Kit Carson Park, commemorates the long tradition of wool growing and weaving begun

in the 16th century, when Spanish settlers brought the tough little churro sheep to northern New Mexico. Every aspect of the craft "from sheep to shawl" is demonstrated, including shearing, spinning, and weaving. Handmade woolen items are for sale, and you can taste favorite lamb dishes.

During the second weekend of July, the **Taos Pueblo Powwow** (⊕ www.taospueblopowwow.com) attracts Native Americans from many Indian nations. Visitors are welcome to watch the traditional drumming and dancing, shop at the arts-and-crafts market, and partake of fry bread, mutton, green chile sauce, and other local delicacies.

3

---

cession; December 25, Deer Dance or Matachines. While you're at the pueblo, respect the RESTRICTED AREA signs that protect the privacy of residents and native religious sites; do not enter private homes or open any doors not clearly labeled as curio shops; do not photograph tribal members without asking permission; do not enter the cemetery grounds; and do not wade in the Rio Pueblo de Taos, which is considered sacred and is the community's sole source of drinking water.

The small, rather prosaic, and smoke-free Taos Mountain Casino (open daily) is just off Camino del Pueblo after you turn right off Paseo del Pueblo on your way to the main pueblo. ⊠ *Head to right off Paseo del Pueblo Norte just past Best Western Kachina Lodge ☏ 505/758–1028 ⊕ www.taospueblo.com ☒ Tourist fees $10. Guided tours by appt. Still-camera permit $5; note: cameras that may look commercial, such as those with telephoto lenses, might be denied a permit; video-camera permit $5. Commercial photography, sketching, or painting only by prior per-*

DID YOU KNOW?

The privilege of setting up an easel and painting all day at a pueblo will cost you as little as $35 or as much as $150 (at Taos Pueblo).

mission from governor's office (505/758–1028); fees vary; apply at least 10 days in advance ☉ Mon.–Sat., 8–4:30, Sun. 8:30–4:30. Closed for funerals, religious ceremonies, and for 2-month "quiet time" in late win-

ter or early spring, and last part of Aug.; call ahead before visiting at these times.

NEED A BREAK? Look for signs that read FRY BREAD on dwellings in the pueblo: you can enter the kitchen and buy a piece of fresh bread dough that's flattened and deep-fried until puffy and golden brown and then topped with honey or powdered sugar. You also can buy delicious bread that's baked daily in the clay hornos (outdoor adobe ovens) that are scattered throughout the pueblo.

WHERE TO EAT

For a place as remote as Taos, the dining scene is surprisingly varied. You can find the usual coffee shops and Mexican-style eateries but also restaurants serving creatively prepared Continental, Italian, and Southwestern cuisine.

WHAT IT COSTS				
$$$$	**$$$**	**$$**	**$**	**¢**
AT DINNER over $32	$24–$32	$17–$24	$10–$17	under $10

Prices are for a main course, excluding 8.25% sales tax.

Downtown Taos

American

$–$$$ ✕ **Ogelvie's Taos Grill and Bar.** On the second floor of an old two-story adobe building, touristy but festive Ogelvie's is the perfect spot for people-watching from on high, especially from the outdoor patio in summer. You won't find any culinary surprises here, just dependable meat-and-potato dishes. The sure bets are filet mignon with brandy-cream sauce, lamb sirloin with rosemary aioli, and blue-corn enchiladas stuffed with beef or chicken. There's live music many nights. ⊠ *East side of Taos Plaza* ☎ *505/758–8866* ⊕ *www.ogelvies.com* ⊜ *Reservations not accepted* ⊟ *AE, D, DC, MC, V.*

$–$$ ✕ **Bravo!** This restaurant and full bar inside an upscale grocery, beer, and wine shop, is a great stop for gourmet picnic fixings or an on-site meal on the outdoor patio. You can feast on anything from a turkey sandwich to lobster-and-shrimp ravioli to well-prepared pizzas. The beer and wine selection is formidable. ⊠ *1353–A Paseo del Pueblo Sur* ☎ *505/758–8100* ⊕ *www.bravotaos.com* ⊜ *Reservations not accepted* ⊟ *AE, MC, V* ☉ *Closed Sun.*

¢–$ ✕ **Eske's Brew Pub.** This casual dining and quaffing pub is favored by off-duty ski patrollers and river guides. The menu mostly covers hearty sandwiches (try the grilled

> **WORD OF MOUTH**
>
> "This had to be one of our best experiences of our trip to Taos. We ate breakfast there and had wonderful café mochas. The food was hot, fresh, and service was done with a smile."
>
> –Jodie on Bent Street Café

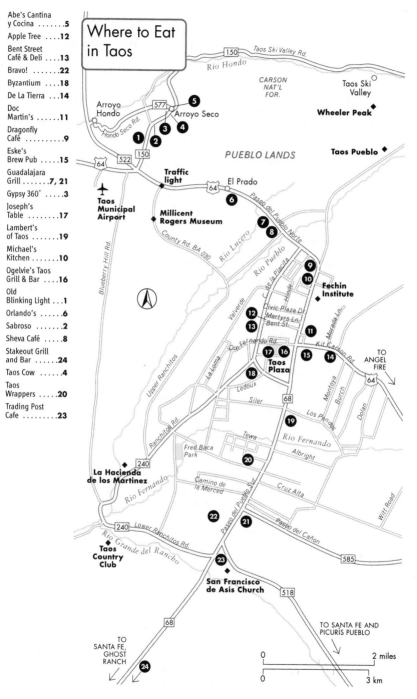

Where to Eat in Taos

Taos Ski Valley Rd.

Rio Hondo

CARSON
NAT'L
FOR.

Taos Ski
Valley

Wheeler Peak ◆

Arroyo
Hondo

577

Arroyo Seco

Hondo Seco Rd.

⑤

③ ④

① ②

522

150

64

PUEBLO LANDS

Taos Pueblo ◆

**Traffic
light**

El Prado

64

Paseo del Pueblo Norte

⑥

✈
**Taos
Municipal
Airport**

**Millicent
Rogers Museum** ◆

County Rd. BA 030

Rio Lucero

⑦

⑧

Rio Pueblo

de la Placita

Hinde

⑨

⑩

**Fechin
Institute** ◆

Valverde

Civic Plaza Dr.

Martyrs Ln.

Bent St.

⑫

⑬

⑪

Morada Ln.

Blueberry Hill Rd.

Don Fernando Rd.

Kit Carson Rd.

⑰ ⑯

⑮

⑭

**TO
ANGEL
FIRE**

64

La Loma

**Taos
Plaza**

⑱

Ledoux

Montoya

Burch

Dolan

Upper Ranchitos Rd.

Siler

68

Tewa

⑲

Los Pandos

Rio Fernando

Albright

Ranchitos Rd.

Fred Baca
Park

⑳

Cruz Alta

Witt Road

240

**La Hacienda
de los Martinez** ◆

Rio Fernando

Camino de
la Merced

Paseo del Pueblo Sur

㉒

㉑

Paseo del Cañon

585

240

Lower Ranchitos Rd.

Rio Grande del Rancho

**Taos
Country
Club** ◆

㉓

◆

**San Francisco
de Asis Church**

518

68

**TO
SANTA FE,
GHOST
RANCH**

㉔

**TO SANTA FE AND
PICURIS PUEBLO**

0   2 miles

0   3 km

bratwurst and sauerkraut sandwich), soups, and salads. The micro-brewery downstairs produces everything from nutty, dark stout to light ales, but you shouldn't leave without sampling the house specialty—Taos green-chile beer. There's live music on weekends, and in good weather you can relax on the patio. ⊠ *106 Des Georges La.* ☎ *505/758–1517* ⊕ *www.eskesbrewpub.com* ▤ *MC, V.*

¢–$ ✕ **Michael's Kitchen.** This casual, homey restaurant serves up a bit of everything—you can order a hamburger while your friend who can't get enough chile sauce can order up vegetarian cheese enchiladas garnished with lettuce and tomatoes. Brunch is popular with the locals (dig into a plate of strawberry-banana-pecan pancakes), and amusing asides to the waitstaff over the intercom contribute to the energetic buzz. Breakfast, lunch, and dinner are served daily, but you must order dinner by 8:30 PM. ⊠ *304 Paseo del Pueblo Norte* ☎ *505/758–4178* ⊕ *www.michaelskitchen.com* ⌔ *Reservations not accepted* ▤ *AE, D, MC, V.*

Cafés

★ ¢–$ ✕ **Bent Street Cafe & Deli.** Try for a seat on the cheery, covered outdoor patio next to giant sunflowers. You can enjoy a breakfast croissant sandwich, smoked turkey for lunch, or a fancier organic New York steak for dinner. Great food can be topped off with a chocolate nut brownie and washed down with beer, wine, and gourmet coffees. There's something on the menu for all budget ranges, even a peanut butter and jam sandwich. Cheerful service is rendered in an old-fashioned country kitchen atmosphere, complete with frilly curtains. Breakfast is served until 11 AM. ⊠ *120 Bent St.* ☎ *505/758–5787* ▤ *MC, V* ☉ *Closed Sun.*

¢–$ ✕ **Dragonfly Café.** This charming breakfast and lunch café bakes its own bread and serves large and tasty omelets (the best one is packed with house-cured gravlax, cream cheese, red onion, and tomato), Swedish pancakes, udon noodle bowls, Vietnamese chicken salad, and panini sandwiches. You can sit out front on a shaded outdoor patio with a fountain when it's warm and watch the tourists go by. Dragonfly also does a brisk mail-order business with its red chile–infused truffles, delicious granola, and many other tasty products. ⊠ *402 Paseo del Pueblo Norte* ☎ *505/737–5859* ⊕ *www.dragonflytaos.com* ▤ *MC, V* ☉ *No dinner.*

¢ ✕ **Taos Wrappers.** A loyal clientele visits this place for take-out lunch, or to eat in a cozy space with tiny tables. Pesto chicken, roasted veggies, and curried tuna are among the healthful ingredients inside flavored tortilla wraps. There are soups, salads, and desserts, too. Breakfast is available on weekends. ⊠ *616 Paseo del Pueblo Sur* ☎ *505/751–9727* ▤ *No credit cards* ☉ *No dinner.*

Contemporary

$$–$$$$ ✕ **Joseph's Table.** Locally renowned chef Joseph Wrede has moved
Fodor'sChoice around the area a bit in recent years, but has settled into what he does
★ best—overseeing his own swank yet friendly restaurant in the La Fonda Hotel on the Taos Plaza. Amid artful surroundings of giant flowers handpainted on walls, you can sample some of the most innovative and masterfully prepared cuisine in the state. You might start with lobster tamales served with roasted-corn puree and trout caviar, before moving on to pistachio-crusted halibut with tarragon butter, strawberries,

and fresh spinach. But the masterpiece here is pepper-crusted elk tenderloin with foie gras and truffle demi-glace. Lighter fare, including addictive duck-fat fries, are available at the bar, and there's an astounding wine list. ⊠ *108–A S. Taos Plaza, La Fonda Hotel* ☎ *505/751–4512* ⊕ *www.josephstable.com* ⊟ *AE, D, DC, MC, V.*

★ $$–$$$ ✕ **Byzantium.** Off a grassy courtyard near the Blumenschein and Harwood museums, this traditional-looking adobe restaurant offers an eclectic menu. Asian, European, and Middle Eastern influences can be tasted in dishes like seafood cakes, duck curry, and vegetable potpie. Service is friendly, and the vibe is low-key—this is a spot relatively few tourists find out about. ⊠ *Ledoux St. and La Placita* ☎ *505/751–0805* ⊟ *AE, MC, V* ☉ *Closed Tues. and Wed. No lunch.*

★ $$–$$$ ✕ **De La Tierra.** A dashing, dramatic, high-ceiling restaurant inside the fancifully plush El Monte Sagrado resort, this chic spot presents daring globally influenced cuisine. Top starters include smoked trout with horseradish-cognac cream, and blue-corn calamari with grilled-pineapple salsa and chipotle-lime vinaigrette. Among the mains, you can't go wrong with the molasses-marinated quail with a parsnip cake and dried-blueberry sauce, or pan-roasted lamb with asiago, grilled asparagus, and sage bread pudding. Tequila-lime pie with white-chocolate–ancho chile crust and prickly pear syrup makes for a happy ending. It's dressy by Taos standards, but you'll still fit in wearing smartly casual threads. ⊠ *317 Kit Carson Rd., El Monte Sagrado Resort* ☎ *505737–9855* ⊕ *www.elmontesagrado.com* ⊟ *AE, D, DC, MC, V.*

$$–$$$ ✕ **Doc Martin's.** The restaurant of the Historic Taos Inn takes its name from the building's original owner, a local physician who saw patients in the rooms that are now the dining areas. The creative menu includes Dungeness crab salad with asparagus, jicama, and avocado-lime vinaigrette, blue-crusted boneless trout with pumpkin-mole, and organic fillet of beef with heirloom tomatoes, blue cheese, and roasted-tomato demi-glace. There's an extensive wine list, and the adjoining Adobe Bar serves up some of the best margaritas in town. In winter ask for a table near the cozy kiva fireplace. ⊠ *Historic Taos Inn, 125 Paseo del Pueblo Norte* ☎ *505/758–1977* ⊕ *www.taosinn.com* ⊟ *AE, D, MC, V.*

★ $–$$$ ✕ **Trading Post Cafe.** Colorful paintings of Southwest scenes, a covered, fenced-in patio, impeccable service and an imaginative menu have made the Trading Post a favorite spot in Ranchos. The beef carpaccio appetizer and signature chicken-noodle soup are both exceptional, and the oven-roasted half duck and New Zealand lamb chops with tomato-mint sauce both make superb main dishes. Flan or homemade raspberry sorbet makes a fine finish. To park, turn east onto NM 518 (Talpa Road) just north of the restaurant, and then walk back along Talpa Road to get to the entrance. ⊠ *4179 Paseo del Pueblo Sur, NM 68, Ranchos de*

Taos ☎ *505/758–5089* ▭ *AE, D, DC, MC, V* ☉ *Closed Mon. No lunch Sun.*

Continental

$$–$$$$ ✕ **Lambert's of Taos.** In what was once an elegant family home, this lace-curtained restaurant looks over lushly cultivated grounds 2½ blocks south of the Plaza. The signature dishes here include Dungeness crab cakes with Thai curry, pepper-crusted lamb with a red-wine demi-glace, and fillet of beef over a potato cake with grilled spinach and horseradish cream. The lengthy wine list includes some of California's finest vintages. ✉ *309 Paseo del Pueblo Sur* ☎ *505/758–1009* ▭ *AE, D, DC, MC, V* ☉ *No lunch.*

Eclectic

★ **$–$$$** ✕ **Apple Tree.** Named for the large tree in its umbrella-shaded courtyard, this terrific lunch and dinner spot is in a historic adobe just a block from the Plaza. Among the well-crafted dishes are barbecued duck fajitas, Baja fish tacos, chipotle-shrimp over corn cakes, and mango-chicken enchiladas. The restaurant has an outstanding wine list. Sunday brunch is great fun here—dig into a plate of Papas Tapadas (two eggs any style over

> ### WORD OF MOUTH
>
> "The menu is a delightful mix of old favorites with a new twist—e.g., the duck fajitas. My wife raved over their baked brie. The ambiance was casual, relaxed, but as you would expect on a Saturday night, busy."
>
> —Steve on Apple Tree

seasoned homefries, with red or green chile, and topped with white cheddar. Expect a bit of a wait if you don't have a reservation. ✉ *123 Bent St.* ☎ *505/758–1900* ⊕ *www.appletreerestaurant.com* ▭ *AE, D, DC, MC, V.*

Mexican

¢–$ ✕ **Guadalajara Grill.** Tasty regional Mexican cuisine, served quickly from these open, spotless kitchens, is popular enough with local patrons that there's a location on both the north and south ends of town. It's ultracasual here (you select your own beer from a cooler, and order from the counter). You can hear Spanish banter from the kitchen while you watch your chicken tacos or green-chile cheese enchiladas being prepared. ✉ *822 Paseo del Pueblo Norte* ☎ *505/737–0816* ✉ *1384 Paseo del Pueblo Sur* ☎ *505/751–0063* ▭ *MC, V.*

Middle Eastern

¢–$ ✕ **Sheva Café.** The Israeli owners here have created an authentic menu that includes delectable falafel, eggplant salad, and stuffed grape leaves served with homemade pita bread. You can dine on organic lamb kebobs served with Israeli salad, or sample one of many vegetarian-friendly (and often kosher) items such as zucchini paté and eggplant-lemon salad. Middle Eastern music and art set the scene, along with works of local artists. An outdoor patio is a lovely place to linger over coffee or one of the many organic desserts prepared by the restaurant's bakery, Magic Flavors. Breakfast is available until 11 daily. ✉ *Overland Ranch, 1405 Paseo del Pueblo Norte* ☎ *505/737–9290* ▭ *D, MC, V.*

New Mexican

★ ¢ ✕ **Orlando's.** This family-run local favorite may be packed during peak hours, while guests wait patiently to devour favorites such as *carne adovada* (red chile–marinated pork), blue-corn enchiladas, and scrumptious shrimp burritos. You can eat in the cozy dining room, outside on the front patio, or call ahead for takeout if you'd rather avoid the crowds. ⊠ *114 Don Juan Valdez La., off Paseo del Pueblo Norte* ☎ *505/751–1450* ▤ *No credit cards* ☾ *Closed Sun.*

Steak

$$–$$$$ ✕ **Stakeout Grill and Bar.** On Outlaw Hill in the foothills of the Sangre
Fodor'sChoice   de Cristo Mountains, this old adobe homestead has 100-mi-long views
★   and sunsets that dazzle. The outdoor patio encircled by a piñon forest has kiva fireplaces to warm you during cooler months. The decadent fare is well-prepared, fully living up to the view it accompanies—try filet mignon, buffalo rib eye with jalapeño sauce, duck with apple-raisin chutney, or—if you're truly up for a challenge—the grilled 32-ounce cowboy steak with chipotle barbecue sauce. Don't miss the tasty desserts, such as Kentucky bourbon pecan pie and crème brûlée with toasted coconut. ⊠ *Stakeout Dr., 8½ mi south of Taos Plaza, east of NM 68, look for cowboy sign* ☎ *505/751–3815* ▤ *AE, D, DC, MC, V* ☾ *No lunch.*

Arroyo Seco & Vicinity

Cafés

¢–$ ✕ **Gypsy 360°.** Set back from the main road in the tiny village of Arroyo Seco, cheap and cheerful Gypsy 360° is a favorite spot for a filling lunch or breakfast, especially on warm days, when you can dine on the patio. The menu borrows from all around the world, with everything from hearty curries to bountiful salads to Japanese sushi rolls, plus some of the juiciest burgers in the area. Organic coffees are served as well as beer and wine. There's a popular brunch on Sunday. ⊠ *480 NM 150* ☎ *505/776–3166* ▤ *MC, V* ☾ *Closed Mon. No dinner.*

¢   ✕ **Abe's Cantina y Cocina.** Family-owned and -operated since the 1940s, Abe's is both store and restaurant. You can have your breakfast burrito, rolled tacos, or homemade tamales at one of the small tables crowded next to the canned goods, or take it on a picnic. ⊠ *489 NM 150, Taos Ski Valley Rd., Arroyo Seco* ☎ *505/776–8643* ▤ *AE, D, MC, V* ☾ *Closed Sun.*

★ ¢   ✕ **Taos Cow.** Locals, travelers headed up to Taos Ski Valley, and visitors to funky Arroyo Seco rejoiced when the famed Taos Cow ice-cream company opened this cozy storefront café in 2005. This isn't merely a place to sample amazing homemade ice cream (including such innovative flavors as piñon-caramel, lavender, and Chocolate Rio Grande, which consists of chocolate ice cream packed with cinnamon-chocolate chunks). You can also nosh on French toast, omelets, turkey-and-Brie sandwiches, black bean–and–brown rice bowls, organic teas and coffees, natural sodas, homemade granola, and more. The friendly but zoned-out staff and burning incense lend a hippie-dippie vibe to the place. ⊠ *485 NM 150* ☎ *505/776–5640* ⊕ *www.taoscow.com* ▤ *MC, V* ☾ *No dinner.*

CLOSE UP

Hostess of Taos

MABEL DODGE LUHAN, a progressive-minded socialite from Buffalo, New York, arrived on the scene in 1917, fell in love with Taos, and stayed. In the high-desert landscape and in the Taos Pueblo culture she found a purpose and unity that she firmly believed ought to be extended to American society at large. When she walked away from her "old, mythical life," aiding her as soul mate and spiritual mainstay was a statuesque Taos Pueblo man, Antonio Luhan, who became her fourth, and last, husband. In the house they built together next to Pueblo land, they hosted many of the era's great artists, writers, philosophers, psychologists, anthropologists, and social reformers. Mabel's friends and acquaintances included Martha Graham, Aldous Huxley, and Carl Jung. Mabel wrote to D. H. Lawrence many times and even tried to send him psychic messages until finally he, too, came to Taos and was profoundly affected by what he found. Although he stayed less than two years all together, some of his finest writing, including *The Plumed Serpent* and several novelettes, essays, and poems, grew out of his experiences in Taos and Mexico. Mabel herself penned several books; *Edge of Taos Desert: An Escape to Reality* (1937) is a part of her autobiography that vividly describes her life in Taos. She and her beloved Tony died within months of each other in 1970. Their house is now a conference center and B&B.

Contemporary

★ $-$$$ ✕ **Sabroso.** Reasonably priced, innovative cuisine and outstanding wines are served in this 150-year-old adobe hacienda, where you can also relax in lounge chairs near the bar, or on a delightful patio surrounded by plum trees. The Mediterranean-influenced contemporary menu changes regularly, but an evening's entrée might be wood-grilled shrimp skewers with clam-broth, risotto cakes, and ratatouille, or New York strip steak with gnocchi and Gorgonzola cream. There's live jazz and cabaret in the piano bar several nights a week. Order from the simpler bar menu if you're seeking something light—the antipasto plate and white-truffle-oil fries are both delicious. ⊠ *470 NM 150, Taos Ski Valley Rd.* ☎ *505/ 776-3333* ⊕ *www.sabrosotaos.com* 🖃 *AE, MC, V* ☼ *Closed Mon. No lunch.*

New Mexican

$-$$$ ✕ **Old Blinking Light.** Just past the landmark "old blinking light" (now a regular stoplight at Mile Marker 1), this rambling adobe is known for its steaks, ribs, and enormous (and potent) margaritas. There's also a long list of tasty apps, such as posole stew and chipotle-shrimp quesadillas. Several huge burgers are available, plus first-rate chicken mole. In summer you can sit out in the walled garden and take in the spectacular mountain view. There's a wineshop on the premises. ⊠ *Taos Ski Valley Rd., between El Prado and Arroyo Seco* ☎ *505/776-8787* ⊕ *www. oldblinkinglight.com* 🖃 *AE, MC, V* ☼ *No lunch.*

WHERE TO STAY

The hotels and motels along NM 68 (Paseo del Pueblo Sur and Norte) suit every need and budget; with a few exceptions, rates vary little between big-name chains and smaller establishments. Make advance reservations and expect higher rates during the ski season (usually from late December to early April) and in the summer. Skiers have many choices for overnighting, from accommodations in the town of Taos to spots snuggled up right beside the slopes, although several of the hotels up at Taos Ski Valley have been converted to condos in recent years, eroding the supply of overnight accommodations. Arroyo Seco is a good alternative if you can't find a room right up in the Ski Valley.

The best deals in town are the bed-and-breakfasts. Mostly family-owned, they provide personal service, delicious breakfasts, and many extras that hotels charge for. The B&Bs are often in old adobes that have been refurbished with style and flair. Many have "casitas," private cabins or lodges separate from the main building.

WHAT IT COSTS					
	$$$$	**$$$**	**$$**	**$**	**¢**
FOR 2 PEOPLE	over $260	$190–$260	$130–$190	$70–$130	under $70

Prices are for a standard double room in high season, excluding 10%–12% tax.

Downtown Taos

$$$$
Fodor'sChoice
★
El Monte Sagrado. Pricey but classy (although the resort has lowered its rates a bit in recent years), El Monte Sagrado is an eco-sensitive New Age haven offering all manner of amenities, from alternative therapies like milk-and-honey body wraps to cooking and wine classes. A short drive away, the property has an expansive ranch property that's available for you to explore on horseback or on foot. Suites and casitas are accented with exotic themes, ranging from Native American designs to foreign flourishes from faraway lands including Japan or Tibet. A popular outdoor area dubbed the Sacred Circle is a patch of grassy land encircled by cottonwoods. The on-site restaurant, De la Tierra, serves daring cuisine. ⊠ *317 Kit Carson Rd., 87571* ☎ *505/758–3502 or 800/828–8267* 🖨 *505/737–2980* ⊕ *www.elmontesagrado.com* ⇆ *18 suites, 18 casitas* ⚘ *2 restaurants, picnic area, room service, some in-room hot tubs, some kitchenettes, minibars, some refrigerators, cable TV, in-room VCRs, Wi-Fi, indoor pool, pond, fitness classes, gym, outdoor hot tubs, Japanese baths, massage, sauna, spa, steam room, bicycles, mountain bikes, archery, billiards, hiking, horseback riding, cross-country skiing, ski storage, snowmobiling, bar, library, piano, recreation room, shop, babysitting, children's programs (ages 4–12), dry cleaning, laundry service, concierge, business services, meeting rooms, some pets allowed (fee)* ⊟ *AE, D, DC, MC, V.*

★ **$$$–$$$$**
Casa de las Chimeneas. Tile hearths, French doors, and traditional viga ceilings grace the "House of Chimneys" B&B, 2½ blocks from the Plaza

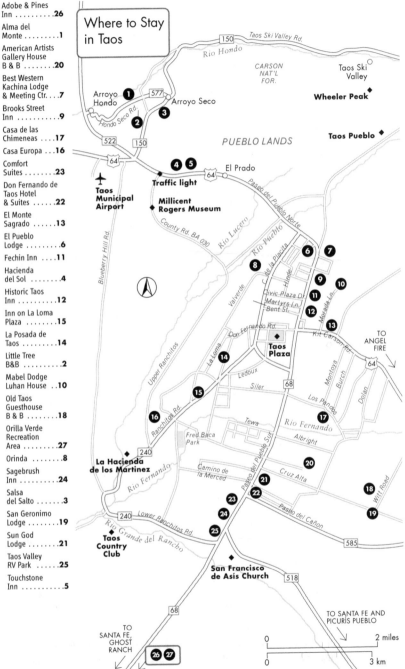

Adobe & Pines Inn **26**

Alma del Monte **1**

American Artists Gallery House B & B **20**

Best Western Kachina Lodge & Meeting Ctr. ...**7**

Brooks Street Inn **9**

Casa de las Chimeneas **17**

Casa Europa ...**16**

Comfort Suites **23**

Don Fernando de Taos Hotel & Suites **22**

El Monte Sagrado **13**

El Pueblo Lodge **6**

Fechin Inn **11**

Hacienda del Sol **4**

Historic Taos Inn **12**

Inn on La Loma Plaza **15**

La Posada de Taos **14**

Little Tree B&B **2**

Mabel Dodge Luhan House ..**10**

Old Taos Guesthouse B & B **18**

Orilla Verde Recreation Area **27**

Orinda **8**

Sagebrush Inn **24**

Salsa del Salto **3**

San Geronimo Lodge **19**

Sun God Lodge **21**

Taos Valley RV Park **25**

Touchstone Inn **5**

Where to Stay in Taos

and secluded behind thick walls. Each room in the 1912 structure has a private entrance, a fireplace, handmade New Mexican furniture, bathrooms with Talvera tiles, and a bar stocked with complimentary beverages. All rooms overlook the gardens, and facilities include a small but excellent spa offering a wide range of treatments. Two-course breakfasts are included, as are full evening meals. ⊠ *405 Cordoba Rd., Box 5303, 87571* ☎ *505/758–4777 or 877/758–4777* 🖷 *505/758–3976* ⊕*www.visittaos.com* ➘ *6 rooms, 2 suites* ⟡ *Picnic area, minibars, some microwaves, some refrigerators, some in-room hot tubs, cable TV, in-room VCRs, gym, outdoor hot tub, sauna, spa, laundry facilities, laundry service, no-smoking rooms; no kids* ⊟ *AE, D, DC, MC, V* ⟋⟍ *MAP.*

★ **$$–$$$$**   🏠 **Hacienda del Sol.** Art patron Mabel Dodge Luhan bought this house in the 1920s and lived here with her husband, Tony Luhan, while building their main house. It was also their private retreat and guesthouse for visiting notables; Frank Waters wrote *People of the Valley* here—other guests have included Willa Cather and D. H. Lawrence. Most of the rooms contain kiva fireplaces, Southwestern handcrafted furniture, and original artwork, and all have CD players. Certain adjoining rooms can be combined into suites. Breakfast is a gourmet affair that might include banana pancakes or stuffed French toast. Perhaps above all else, the "backyards" of the rooms and the secluded outdoor hot tub have a view of Taos Mountain so idyllic it can evoke tears of joy from even the most cynical of travelers. ⊠ *109 Mabel Dodge La., Box 177, 87571* ☎ *505/758–0287 or 866/333–4459* 🖷 *505/758–5895* ⊕ *www.taoshaciendadelsol.com* ➘ *11 rooms* ⟡ *Some refrigerators, some in-room hot tubs, hot tub; no room TVs* ⊟ *AE, D, MC, V* ⟋⟍ *BP.*

★ **$$–$$$$**   🏠 **Inn on La Loma Plaza.** The walls surrounding this Pueblo Revival building date from the early 1800s; the inn itself is listed on the National Register of Historic Places. The rooms have kiva fireplaces, CD stereos, coffeemakers, and Mexican-tile bathrooms, and many have private patios or decks. The living room has a well-stocked library with books on Taos and art. Owners Jerry and Peggy Davis provide helpful advice about the area and serve a generous breakfast, afternoon snacks, and evening coffee. Guests have privileges at the nearby health club (but the inn has its own hot tub). ⊠ *315 Ranchitos Rd., Box 4159, 87571* ☎ *505/758–1717 or 800/530–3040* 🖷 *505/751–0155* ⊕ *www.vacationtaos.com* ➘ *5 rooms, 2 studios* ⟡ *Some kitchenettes, cable TV, in-room VCRs, Wi-Fi, outdoor hot tub, library* ⊟ *AE, D, MC, V* ⟋⟍ *BP.*

★ **$$–$$$**   🏠 **Touchstone Inn.** D. H. Lawrence visited this house in 1929; accordingly, the inn's owner, Taos artist Bren Price, has named many of the antiques-filled rooms after famous Taos literary figures. The grounds overlook part of the Taos Pueblo lands, and this makes for a quiet stay within a mile of Taos Plaza. Some rooms have fireplaces. The enormous Royale Suite has a second-story private deck and large bathroom with Jacuzzi, walk-in shower, and skylight. Early-morning coffee is available in the living room, and breakfasts with inventive vegetarian presentations (such as blueberry pancakes with lemon sauce) are served in the glassed-in patio. The adjacent Riverbend Spa offers a wide range of beauty and skin treatments. ⊠ *110 Mabel Dodge La., Box 1885, 87571* ☎*505/758–0192 or 800/758–0192* 🖷 *505/758–3498* ⊕ *www.touchstoneinn.*

com 🖥 *6 rooms, 3 suites* ⚬ *Cable TV, in-room VCRs, hot tub, spa* ⊟ *MC, V* ⍩ *BP.*

★ $–$$$ 🖪 **American Artists Gallery House Bed & Breakfast.** Each of the immaculate adobe-style rooms and suites here is called a "gallery," and owners LeAn and Charles Clamurro have taken care to decorate them with local arts and crafts. Some have Jacuzzis and all have kiva fireplaces; one family-friendly suite has a full kitchen; and all have private entrances, wood-burning fireplaces, and front porches where you can admire the view of Taos Mountain. Sumptuous hot breakfasts—along with conversation and suggestions about local attractions—are served up at a community table in the main house each morning, where you can often see the resident peacock, George, preening outside the windows. ⊠ *132 Frontier La., Box 584, 87571* ☎ *505/758–4446 or 800/532–2041* 🖷 *505/758–0497* ⊕ *www.taosbedandbreakfast.com* 🖥 *7 rooms, 3 suites* ⚬ *Fans, some in-room hot tubs, some kitchens, some microwaves, some refrigerators, some cable TV, some in-room VCRs, Wi-Fi, outdoor hot tub, some pets allowed (fee)* ⊟ *AE, D, DC, MC, V* ⍩ *BP.*

★ $–$$$ 🖪 **Historic Taos Inn.** Mere steps from Taos Plaza, the inn is listed on the National Register of Historic Places. Spanish-colonial-style architecture including decorative alcoves in rooms provides an authentic feel to this atmospheric property that consists of four buildings, including the upscale Helen's House, which was added in 2006 and contains eight posh rooms. Many units have thick adobe walls, viga ceilings, and other elements typical of vintage Taos architecture. In summer there's dining alfresco on the patio. The lobby, which also serves as seating for the Adobe Bar, is built around an old town well from which a fountain bubbles forth. Many shops and eateries are within walking distance of the inn, and the restaurant, Doc Martin's, is popular with locals. ⊠ *125 Paseo del Pueblo Norte, 87571* ☎ *505/758–2233 or 888/518–8267* 🖷 *505/ 758–5776* ⊕ *www.taosinn.com* 🖥 *41 rooms, 3 suites* ⚬ *Restaurant, cable TV, bar* ⊟ *AE, DC, MC, V.*

★ $$ 🖪 **Fechin Inn.** Artistically savvy guests from other parts of the world journey here just to soak up the atmosphere of grounds once owned by internationally renowned artist Nicolai Fechin (Fechin's home, now converted to the Taos Art Museum, is in front of the inn). You're also likely to spot artists earnestly participating in various workshops the inn sponsors. Many guests are immediately awed by the intricacy of hand-carved woodwork throughout the Fechin, which was created by 52 wood-carvers during a three-year span. Rooms have modern Southwestern furnishings, and suites have separate living rooms with fireplaces. The Fechin is the perfect combination of warmth and gracious sophistication; you can fit in here whether you prefer to wear evening dress or cowboy boots to dinner. It's on a 6-acre tree-shaded plot on the north side of downtown, an easy

> **WORD OF MOUTH**
>
> "My husband and I stayed at the Fechin Inn for five nights. Our suite was nicely decorated and comfortable. It had a fireplace and huge balcony. We had a slight problem during our stay and the staff went out of their way to accommodate us."
>
> –Heide on Fechin Inn

walk from dining and shopping. ⊠ *227 Paseo del Pueblo Norte, 87571* ☎ *505/751–1000 or 800/811–2933* ⊟ *505/751–7338* ⊕ *www.fechininn. com* ⤳ *70 rooms, 14 suites* ⚒ *Dining room, cable TV, in-room VCRs, gym, hot tub, massage, ski storage, lounge, dry cleaning, laundry facilities, laundry service, concierge, meeting rooms, some pets allowed (fee)* ⊟ *AE, D, DC, MC, V* ⦿ *CP.*

$$ 🏨 **La Posada de Taos.** A couple of blocks from Taos Plaza, this family-friendly inn has beam ceilings, a decorative arched doorway, and the intimacy of a private hacienda. Five guest rooms are in the main house; the sixth is a separate cottage with a king-size bed in a separate bedroom, sitting room, and fireplace. The rooms all have mountain or courtyard garden views, and some open onto private patios; almost all have kiva-style fireplaces. Breakfasts are hearty; if you're lucky, they might include baked apple French toast. ⊠ *309 Juanita La., Box 1118, 87571* ☎ *505/758–8164 or 800/645–4803* ⊟ *505/751–4694* ⊕ *www. laposadadetaos.com* ⤳ *5 rooms, 1 cottage* ⚒ *Some in-room hot tubs, cable TV, in-room VCRs; no phones in some rooms* ⊟ *AE, MC, V* ⦿ *BP.*

$–$$ 🏨 **Adobe & Pines Inn.** Native American and Mexican artifacts decorate the main house of this B&B, which has expansive mountain views. Part of the main building dates from 1830. The rooms and suites contain Mexican-tile baths, kiva fireplaces, and fluffy goose-down pillows and comforters, plus such modern touches as flat-screen TVs, DVD players, Wi-Fi, and CD players. Separate casitas and suites are more spacious and offer plenty of seclusion, with private entrances and courtyard access. The owners serve gourmet breakfasts in a sunny glass-enclosed patio. ⊠ *NM 68 and Llano Quemado* ⌖ *Box 837, Ranchos de Taos 87557* ☎ *505/751–0947 or 800/723–8267* ⊟ *505/758–8423* ⊕ *www. adobepines.com* ⤳ *4 rooms, 2 suites, 2 casitas* ⚒ *Some in-room hot tubs, cable TV, in-room DVDs, Wi-Fi, sauna, steam room, some pets allowed (fee)* ⊟ *MC, V* ⦿ *BP.*

$–$$ 🏨 **Best Western Kachina Lodge & Meeting Center.** Just north of Taos Plaza, this two-story Pueblo-style adobe carries the theme of the kachina (a figure representing a masked ancestral spirit) throughout. Guest rooms sustain the Native American motif, with handmade and hand-painted furnishings and colorful bedspreads. From Memorial Day to Labor Day a troupe from Taos Pueblo performs nightly ritual dances outside by firelight. Rates include a wine-and-cheese welcome reception in the early evening. ⊠ *413 Paseo del Pueblo Norte, Box NN, 87571* ☎ *505/ 758–2275 or 800/522–4462* ⊟ *505/758–9207* ⊕ *www.kachinalodge. com* ⤳ *113 rooms, 5 suites* ⚒ *Restaurant, coffee shop, cable TV, in-room VCRs, Wi-Fi, pool, hot tub, bar, shop, laundry facilities, meeting rooms* ⊟ *AE, D, DC, MC, V* ⦿ *BP.*

$–$$ 🏨 **Brooks Street Inn.** An elaborately carved corbel arch, the handiwork of Japanese carpenter Yaichikido, spans the entrance to a shaded, walled garden. Fluffy pillows, fresh flowers, CD stereos, and paintings by local artists are among the grace notes in the rooms; some have fireplaces. Blue-corn pancakes with pineapple salsa, stuffed French toast with an apricot glaze, and other home-baked delights are served at breakfast. ⊠ *119 Brooks St., Box 4954, 87571* ☎ *505/758–1489 or 800/758–1489* ⊕ *www.brooksstreetinn.com* ⤳ *6 rooms* ⚒ *Refrigerators, cable TV, in-room VCRs* ⊟ *AE, MC, V* ⦿ *BP.*

$–$$ ▦ **Casa Europa.** This 17th-century estate on 6 acres, with views of pastures and mountains, is furnished with European antiques and Southwestern pieces. The two main guest areas are light and airy, with comfortable chairs to relax in while the fireplace crackles. Breakfasts are elaborate, and complimentary homemade afternoon baked treats are served, except during ski season, when they're replaced by evening hors d'oeuvres. ⊠ *840 Upper Ranchitos Rd.* ⌖ *HC 68, Box 3F, 87571* ☎ *888/758–9798* ⊜ *505/758–9798* ⊕ *www.casaeuropanm.com* ⤺ *5 rooms, 2 suites* ⌂ *Some in-room hot tubs, some cable TVs, some in-room VCRs, outdoor hot tub, sauna, 2 lounges, some pets allowed (fee); no kids under 14* ⊟ *AE, D, MC, V* ⦸ *BP.*

$–$$ ▦ **Comfort Suites.** Mexican hand-crafted furniture gives these basic but large units (technically they're not full suites but rather rooms with large sitting areas) a sense of Southwestern style. You can enjoy lounging in front of the kiva fireplace in the lobby area, surrounded by *nichos*—enclaves where statues are placed. The property adjoins the popular Sagebrush Inn and is run by the same owners, and guests have access to the Sagebrush facilities. It's one of the better chain options in town. ⊠ *1500 Paseo del Pueblo Sur, Box 1268, 87571* ☎ *505/751–1555 or 888/751–1555* ⊕ *www.taoshotels.com/comfortsuites* ⤺ *60 rooms* ⌂ *Refrigerators, cable TV, pool, hot tub* ⊟ *AE, D, DC, MC, V* ⦸ *CP.*

$–$$ ▦ **Sagebrush Inn.** Georgia O'Keeffe once lived and painted in one of the third-story rooms here, and this adobe-style inn, built in 1929, has retained much of its charm since then. It's not as upscale—or expensive—as many other lodging options in Taos, but it has a comfortable shaded patio with large trees, a good restaurant, and a substantial art collection including antique Navajo rugs, rare pottery, and paintings by Southwestern masters such as R. C. Gorman. Many of the guest rooms have kiva-style fireplaces; some have balconies looking out to the Sangre de Cristo Mountains. There's country-western music nightly. ⊠ *1508 Paseo del Pueblo Sur, Box 557, 87571* ☎ *505/758–2254 or 800/428–3626* ⊜ *505/758–5077* ⊕ *www.sagebrushinn.com* ⤺ *68 rooms, 32 suites* ⌂ *2 restaurants, cable TV, pool, hot tubs, bar, lounge, meeting rooms* ⊟ *AE, D, DC, MC, V* ⦸ *BP.*

$–$$ ▦ **San Geronimo Lodge.** Built in 1925, this lodge sits on 2½ acres that front majestic Taos Mountain and adjoin the Carson National Forest. A balcony library, attractive grounds, many rooms with fireplaces, two rooms designed for people with disabilities, and a room for guests with a pet are among the draws. Hanging Navajo-style rugs, Talvera-tile bathrooms, and beam ceilings lend an authentic Southwestern feel to the rooms. The hotel staff can arrange ski packages. ⊠ *1101 Witt Rd., 87571* ☎ *505/751–3776 or 800/894–4119* ⊜ *505/751–1493* ⊕ *www.sangeronimolodge.com* ⤺ *16 rooms* ⌂ *Cable TV, some in-room VCRs, pool, outdoor hot tub, massage, some pets allowed (fee)* ⊟ *AE, D, MC, V* ⦸ *BP.*

$ ▦ **Don Fernando de Taos Hotel.** The accommodations at this Pueblo-style hotel are grouped around central courtyards and connected by walkways. Appointed with hand-carved New Mexican furnishings, some rooms have fireplaces. A glassed-in atrium with sliding side doors and roof panels surrounds the pool. There's a free shuttle to take guests to the town center. ⊠ *1005 Paseo del Pueblo Sur, 87571* ☎ *505/758–4444 or 800/*

759–2736 🖨 505/758–0055 ⊕ www.donfernandodetaos.com 🛏 110 rooms, 14 suites ♢ Restaurant, some refrigerators, cable TV, indoor-outdoor pool, hot tub, bar, lounge, dry-cleaning, meeting rooms ☰ AE, D, DC, MC, V.

$ 🏠 **Mabel Dodge Luhan House.** This National Historic Landmark was once home to the heiress who drew literati—including D. H. Lawrence and Willa Cather—to Taos. The main house, which has kept its simple, rustic feel, has nine guest rooms; there are eight more in a modern building, as well as a two-bedroom cottage. You can sleep in Mabel's own hand-carved bed; you can also stay in the O'Keeffe Room, which has twin beds, Southwest furnishings, and its own courtyard entrance, or the Ansel Adams Room with its bright white walls and view of nearby Taos Pueblo land. The inn is frequently used for artistic, cultural, and educational workshops. ✉ 240 Morada La., Box 558, 87571 ☎ 505/751–9686 or 800/846–2235 🖨 505/737–0365 ⊕ www.mabeldodgeluhan. com 🛏 16 rooms, 2 with shared bath; 1 suite, 1 guest house ♢ Meeting rooms; no room phones, no room TVs ☰ AE, MC, V ❚⊙❚ BP.

$ 🏠 **Old Taos Guesthouse B&B.** Once a ramshackle adobe hacienda, this homey B&B on 7½ acres has been completely and lovingly outfitted with the owners' hand-carved doors and furniture, Western artifacts, and antiques. Some rooms have the smallest bathrooms you'll ever encounter but have private entrances, and some have fireplaces. There are 80-mi views from the outdoor hot tub, and it's a five-minute drive to town. The owners welcome families. Breakfasts are healthy and hearty. ✉ 1028 Witt Rd., Box 6552, 87571 ☎ 505/758–5448, or 800/758–5448 ⊕ www. oldtaos.com 🛏 7 rooms, 2 suites ♢ Some kitchens, some cable TV, some in-room VCRs, Wi-Fi, outdoor hot tub, some pets allowed (fee); no phones in some rooms ☰ D, MC, V ❚⊙❚ BP.

$ 🏠 **Orinda.** Built in 1947, this adobe estate has spectacular views and country privacy. The rustic rooms have separate entrances, kiva-style fireplaces, traditional viga ceilings, and Mexican-tile baths. Some of the rooms can be combined with a shared living area into a large suite. One has a Jacuzzi. The hearty breakfast is served family-style in the soaring two-story sun atrium amid a gallery of artworks, all for sale. ✉ 461 Valverde, Box 4451, 87571 ☎ 505/758–8581 or 800/847–1837 🖨 505/751–4895 ⊕ www.orindabb.com 🛏 5 rooms ♢ Refrigerators, some in-room hot tubs, cable TV, some in-room VCRs, some pets allowed (fee); no a/c in some rooms, no smoking ☰ AE, MC, V ❚⊙❚ BP.

¢–$ 🏠 **El Pueblo Lodge.** This low-to-the-ground, pueblo-style adobe a few blocks north of Taos Plaza has traditional Southwestern furnishings including colorful blankets spread across wooden floors, along with solid viga crossbeams in the ceilings. Fireplaces in some rooms add to a homey feel. A number of more expensive but well-equipped condominiums also are available as rentals. ✉ 412 Paseo del Pueblo Norte, Box 92, 87571 ☎ 505/758–

> **WORD OF MOUTH**
>
> "The most quiet and comfortable place to stay . . . within walking distance of the plaza and little shops along the way. . . . Service is excellent."
>
> –Fidel on El Pueblo Lodge

8700 or 800/433–9612 🖷 505/758–7321 ⊕ *www.elpueblolodge.com* 🛏 *61 rooms* ↻ *Some kitchenettes, refrigerators, cable TV, pool, hot tub, laundry facilities, some pets allowed (fee)* ▤ *AE, D, MC, V* ⦿ *CP.*

¢ 🖾 **Sun God Lodge.** Though inexpensive, this motel has old-fashioned adobe charm with basic amenities; some rooms have kitchenettes and fireplaces. Right on the main highway, the Sun God is convenient to restaurants and historic sites. ✉ *919 Paseo del Pueblo Sur, 87571* 🕿 *505/758–3162 or 800/821–2437* 🖷 *505/758–1716* ⊕ *www.sungodlodge.com* 🛏 *45 rooms, 11 suites* ↻ *Some kitchenettes, cable TV, some in-room VCRs, outdoor hot tub, laundry facilities, some pets* ▤ *AE, D, MC, V* ⦿ *CP.*

★ ⚠ **Orilla Verde Recreation Area.** You can hike, fish, and picnic among trees and sagebrush at this beautiful area along the banks of the Rio Grande, 10 mi south of Ranchos de Taos, off NM 68 at NM 570. The area has four developed campgrounds with running water, flush toilets, and showers costing $1 for four minutes. Three primitive campgrounds have vault toilets only. To pay the camping fee, leave cash in an envelope provided, drop it in a tube, and the rangers will collect it (or a volunteer sometimes is on hand to collect payments). ☝ *Bureau of Land Management, 226 Cruz Alta Rd., Taos 87571* 🕿 *505/758–4060* ↻ *Flush toilets, drinking water, fire grates, picnic tables* 🛏 *9 RV sites with hookups, 70 developed sites (tent and RV)* 🖃 *$15 (RV with electric and water hookups), $7 (developed campsites), $5 (primitive campsites), $3 (day use)* ▤ *No credit cards.*

⚠ **Taos Valley RV Park.** The sites are grassy, with a few shade trees, in this park 2½ mi from Taos Plaza near the junction of NM 68 and NM 518. A recreation room has video games, TV, and a pool table. Some RV supplies are for sale. There are horseshoes, billiards, and a kitchen area. ✉ *120 Estes Rd., off Paseo del Pueblo Sur, behind Rio Grande Ace Hardware* ☝ *Box 7204, Taos 87571* 🕿 *505/758–2524 or 800/999–7571* ⊕ *www.newmex.com/rv* ↻ *Flush toilets, full hookups, drinking water, showers, picnic tables, electricity, public telephone, general store, play area* 🛏 *60 RV sites, 4 tent sites* 🖃 *RV sites $31–$38, tent sites $22* ▤ *D, MC, V.*

Arroyo Seco

★ $$$ 🖾 **Alma del Monte.** Mountain views abound from the rooms and courtyard of this B&B on the high plain between Taos and the ski valley. The 4-acre property is private; the only neighbors you have are friendly horses from adjoining farms. Some rooms have private outside entryways and fenced gardens, where you can languish in seclusion. Heated saltillo-tile floors, kiva fireplaces, whirlpool baths, Bose stereos, Victorian antiques, generous breakfasts (which feature such creative fare as hazelnut-lemon–cream cheese French toast), and afternoon wine with hors d'oeuvres make it

> **WORD OF MOUTH**
>
> "The inn has 360-degree views of the mountains and the furnishings are superb and immaculate. Each of the 5 rooms has great views and are quiet and private. The owners offer a wealth of information on area restaurants and attractions."
> –Gail on Alma del Monte

CLOSE UP

The Taos Hum

INVESTIGATIONS INTO WHAT CAUSES A MYSTERIOUS low frequency sound dubbed the "Taos Hum" are ongoing, although the topic was more popular during a worldwide news media frenzy in the 1990s. Taos isn't the only place where the mysterious "hum" has been heard, but it's probably the best known locale for the phenomenon. (The Taos Hum, for example, now has been officially documented in Encyclopaedia Britannica.)

Scientists visited Taos during the 1990s in unsuccessful good faith efforts to trace the sound, which surveys indicated were heard by about 2% of the town's population. Described as a frequency similar to the low, throbbing engine of a diesel truck, the Taos Hum has reportedly created disturbances among its few hearers from mildly irritating to profoundly disturbing. In the extreme, hearers say they experience constant problems including interrupted sleep and physical effects such as dizziness and nosebleeds.

Speculation about the Taos Hum abounds. Conspiracy theorists believe the sound originates from ominous secret government testing,

possibly emanating from the federal defense establishment of Los Alamos National Laboratory 55 mi southwest of Taos. The theory correlates with reports of some hearers that the sound began suddenly, as though something had been switched on.

Some investigators say the hearers may have extraordinary sensitivity to low frequency sound waves, which could originate from all manner of human devices (cell phones, for one) creating constant sources of electromagnetic energy. Still other theorists postulate that low frequency sound waves may originate in the Earth's lower atmosphere. One intriguing theory says that the "hum" could be explained by vibrations deep within the Earth, as a sort of precursor to earthquakes (although earthquakes are extremely rare in New Mexico).

Although many believe there's something to the mysterious Taos Hum, less kindly skeptics have dismissed the phenomenon as New Age nonsense linked to mass hysteria. But while you're here, you may as well give it a try (no one need know what you're up to). Find yourself a peaceful spot. Sit quietly. And listen.

3

a hard place to leave, even for skiing. ⊠ *372 Hondo Seco Rd., Box 1434, Taos 87571* ☎ *505/776–2721 or 800/273–7203* 🖷 *505/776–8888* ⊕ *www.almaspirit.com* ➸ *5 rooms* ⚒ *Picnic area, in-room hot tubs, outdoor hot tub, massage, laundry service, kennel; no room TVs, no kids under 15* ⊟ *AE, MC, V* ¶⊚¶ *BP.*

★ **$–$$** 🏠 **Little Tree B&B.** In an authentic adobe house in the open country between Taos and the ski valley, Little Tree's rooms are built around a garden courtyard and have magnificent views of Taos Mountain and the high desert that spans for nearly 100 mi to the west. Some have kiva fireplaces and Jacuzzis, and all are decorated in true Southwestern style. ⊠ *226 County Rd. B143, Arroyo Hondo* ⌂ *Box 509, 87571* ☏ *505/ 776–8467 or 800/334–8467* ⊕ *www.littletreebandb.com* ⟿ *4 rooms* ⌂ *Some cable TV, some in-rooms VCRs, some in-room hot tubs; no TV in some rooms* ⊟ *MC, V* ⎟◯⎟ *BP.*

$–$$ ⊡ **Salsa del Salto.** Rooms at this handsome compound set back from the road to the Ski Valley, just a short drive up from the funky village of Arroyo Seco, are either in the sunny, contemporary main inn building or in separate units with private entrances and a bit more seclusion. The master suite affords panoramic views of the mountains and has a huge bathroom. The Lobo and Kachina rooms are a great value, not as large as some but with romantic glass-brick showers, high beam ceilings, Saltillo-tile floors with radiant heating. Friendly and helpful owners Pam and Jim Maisey worked for Marriott hotels for 25 years, and it shows. Breakfast is a substantial affair, where you might enjoy a shrimp, mushroom, and provolone omelet or salmon eggs Benedict, and there's always a hearty soup or snack presented in the afternoon. ⊠ *543 NM 150, Box 1468, El Prado 87529* ☏ *505/776–2422 or 800/530– 3097* 🖷 *505/776–5734* ⊕ *www.bandbtaos.com* ⟿ *10 rooms* ⌂ *Some cable TV, some in-room DVDs, some in-room hot tubs, Wi-Fi, pool, hot tub* ⊟ *AE, MC, V* ⎟◯⎟ *BP.*

NIGHTLIFE & THE ARTS

Evening entertainment is modest in Taos. Some motels and hotels present solo musicians or small combos in their bars and lounges. Everything from down-home blues bands to Texas two-step dancing blossoms on Saturday and Sunday nights in winter. In summer things heat up during the week as well. For information about what's going on around town pick up *Taos Magazine.* The weekly *Taos News,* published on Thursday, carries arts and entertainment information in the "Tempo" section. The arts scene is much more lively, with festivals every season for nearly every taste.

Nightlife

FodorśChoice ★ The **Adobe Bar** (⊠ Taos Inn, 125 Paseo del Pueblo Norte ☏ 505/758– 2233), a local meet-and-greet spot known as "Taos's living room," books talented acts, from solo guitarists to small folk groups and, two or three nights a week, jazz musicians.

★ **Alley Cantina** (⊠ 121 Teresina La. ☏ 505/758–2121) has jazz, folk, and blues—as well as shuffleboard and board games for those not moved to dance. It's housed in the oldest structure in downtown Taos.

Caffe Tazza (⊠ 122 Kit Carson Rd. ☏ 505/758–8706) presents free evening performances throughout the week—folk singing, jazz, belly dancing, blues, poetry, and fiction readings.

Fernando's Hideaway (⊠ Don Fernando de Taos Hotel & Suites, 1005 Paseo del Pueblo Sur ☏ 505/758–4444) occasionally presents live entertainment—jazz, blues, hip-hop, R&B, salsa, and country music. Complimentary happy-hour snacks are laid out on weekday evenings, 5–7.

The **Kachina Lodge Cabaret** (✉ 413 Paseo del Pueblo Norte ☎ 505/758–2275) usually brings in an area radio DJ to liven up various forms of music and dancing.

The **Sagebrush Inn** (✉ 1508 Paseo del Pueblo Sur ☎ 505/758–2254) hosts musicians and dancing in its lobby lounge. There's usually no cover charge for country-western dancing.

The piano bar at **Sabroso** (✉ CR 150, Arroyo Seco ☎ 505/776–3333) often presents jazz and old standards.

The Arts

Long a beacon for visual artists, Taos is also becoming a magnet for touring musicians, especially in summer, when performers and audiences are drawn to the heady high desert atmosphere. Festivals celebrate the visual arts, music, poetry, and film.

The **Taos Center for the Arts** (✉ 133 Paseo del Pueblo Norte ☎ 505/758–2052 ⊕ www.taoscenterforthearts.org), which encompasses the Taos Community Auditorium, presents films, plays, concerts, dance shows, and the like.

The **Taos Fall Arts Festival** (☎ 505/758–3873 or 800/732–8267 ⊕ www.taosfallarts.com), from late September to early October, is the area's major arts gathering, when buyers are in town and many other events, such as a Taos Pueblo feast, take place.

The **Taos Spring Arts Celebration** (☎ 505/758–3873 or 800/732–8267 ⊕ www.taoschamber.org), held throughout Taos in May, is a showcase for the visual, performing, and literary arts of the community and allows you to rub elbows with the many artists who call Taos home. The Mother's Day Arts and Crafts weekend during the festival always draws an especially large crowd.

Music

From mid-June to early August the Taos School of Music fills the evenings with the sounds of chamber music at the **Taos School of Music Program and Festival** (☎ 505/776–2388 ⊕ www.taosschoolofmusic.com). Running strong since 1963, this is America's oldest chamber music summer program and possibly the largest assembly of top string quartets in the country. Concerts are presented a couple of times a week from mid-June to August, at the Taos Community Auditorium and at Taos Ski Valley. Tickets cost $10–$20. The events at Taos Ski Valley are free.

Solar energy was pioneered in this land of sunshine, and each year in late June the flag of sustainability is raised at the three-day **Taos Solar Music Festival** (⊕ www.solarmusicfest.com). Top-name acts appear, and booths promote alternative energy, permaculture, and other ecofriendly technologies.

SPORTS & THE OUTDOORS

Whether you plan to cycle around town, jog along Paseo del Pueblo Norte, or play a few rounds of golf, keep in mind that the altitude in Taos is higher than 7,000 feet. It's best to keep physical exertion to a minimum until your body becomes acclimated to the altitude—a full day to a few days, depending on your constitution.

Ballooning
Hot-air ballooning has become nearly as popular in Taos as in Albuquerque, with a handful of outfitters offering rides, most starting at about $200 per person. **Paradise Balloons** (☎ 505/751–6098 ⊕ www. taosballooning.com) will thrill you with a "splash and dash" in the Rio Grande River as part of a silent journey through the 600-foot canyon walls of Rio Grande Gorge. **Pueblo Balloon Company** (☎ 505/751–9877 ⊕ www.puebloballoon.com) conducts balloon rides over and into the Rio Grande Gorge.

Bicycling
Taos-area roads are steep and hilly, and none have marked bicycle lanes, so be careful while cycling. The West Rim Trail offers a fairly flat but view-studded 9-mi ride that follows the Rio Grande canyon's west rim from the Rio Grande Gorge Bridge to near the Taos Junction Bridge.

Gearing Up Bicycle Shop (✉ 129 Paseo del Pueblo Sur ☎ 505/751–0365) is a full-service bike shop that also has information about tours and guides. **Native Sons Adventures** (✉ 1033–A Paseo del Pueblo Sur ☎ 505/758–9342 or 800/753–7559) offers guided tours on its mountain bikes.

Fishing
Carson National Forest has some of the best trout fishing in New Mexico. Its streams and lakes are home to rainbow, brown, and native Rio Grande cutthroat trout.

In midtown Taos, **Cottam's Ski & Outdoor** (✉ 207–A Paseo del Pueblo Sur ☎ 505/758–2822 or 800/322–8267 ⊕ www.cottamsoutdoor.com) provides equipment rentals and half- and full-day fly-fishing tours. Shuttles are available to area trails that lead to fishing waters. Free fly-fishing clinics from **Los Rios Anglers** (✉ 126 W. Plaza Dr. ☎ 505/758–

> **DID YOU KNOW?**
>
> Anyone over the age of 12 who wishes to fish must buy a New Mexico fishing license. Many sporting goods stores in the state sell them.

2798 or 800/748–1707 ⊕ www.losrios.com) are offered weekly between May and August. **Solitary Angler** (✉ 204–B Paseo del Pueblo Norte ☎ 505/758–5653 or 866/502–1700 ⊕ www.thesolitaryangler.com) guides fly-fishing expeditions that search out uncrowded habitats. Well-known area fishing guide Taylor Streit of **Taos Fly Shop & Streit Fly Fishing** (✉ 308–B Paseo del Pueblo Sur ☎ 505/751–1312 ⊕ www.taosflyshop. com) takes individuals or small groups out for fishing and lessons.

Golf

The greens fees at the 18-hole, PGA-rated, par-72 championship course at **Taos Country Club** (✉ NM 570, Ranchos de Taos ☎ 505/758–7300) are $65–$78.

Health Clubs & Fitness Centers

The **Northside Health & Fitness Center** (✉ 1307 Paseo del Pueblo Norte ☎ 505/751–1242) is a spotlessly clean facility with indoor and outdoor pools, a hot tub, tennis courts, and aerobics classes. Nonmembers pay $10 per day. The center provides paid child care with a certified Montessori teacher. The **Taos Youth and Family Center** (✉ 407 Paseo del Cañon E ☎ 505/758–4160) has an outdoor Olympic-size ice arena, where rollerblading, volleyball, and basketball take place in summer. There's also a large swimming pool. Admission is $3 per day.

Llama Trekking

As one of the most offbeat outdoor recreational activities in the Taos area, llama trekking is offered by **Wild Earth Llama Adventures** (☎ 505/586–0174 or 800/758–5262 ⊕ www.llamaadventures.com) in a variety of packages, from one-day tours to excursions lasting several days in wilderness areas of the nearby Sangre de Cristo Mountains. Llamas, relatives of the camel, are used as pack animals on trips that begin at $89 for a day hike. Gourmet lunches eaten on the trail are part of the package, along with overnight camping and meals for longer trips.

River Rafting

The Taos Box, at the bottom of the steep-walled canyon far below the Rio Grande Gorge Bridge, is the granddaddy of thrilling white water in New Mexico and is best attempted by experts only—or on a guided trip—but the river also offers more placid sections such as through the Orilla Verde Recreation Area. Spring runoff is the busy season, from mid-April through June, but rafting companies conduct tours March to November. Shorter two-hour options usually cover the fairly tame section of the river. The **Bureau of Land Management, Taos Resource Area Office** (✉ 226 Cruz Alta ☎ 505/758–8851) has a list of registered river guides and information about running the river on your own.

Big River Raft Trips (☎ 505/758–9711 or 800/748–3760 ⊕ www.bigriverrafts.com) offers dinner float trips and rapids runs. **Far Flung Adventures** (☎ 505/758–2628 or 800/359–2627 ⊕ www.farflung.com) operates half-day, full-day, and overnight rafting trips along the Rio Grande and the Rio Chama. **Los Rios River Runners** (☎ 505/776–8854 or 800/544–1181 ⊕ www.losriosriverrunners.com) will take you to your choice of spots—the Rio Chama, the Lower Gorge, or the Taos Box. **Native Sons Adventures** (✉ 1033A Paseo del Pueblo Sur ☎ 505/758–9342 or 800/753–7559 ⊕ www.nativesonsadventures.com) offers several trip options on the Rio Grande.

SHOPPING

Retail options in Taos Plaza consist mostly of T-shirt emporiums and souvenir shops that are easily bypassed, though a few stores, like Blue Rain Gallery, carry quality Native American artifacts and jewelry. The more upscale galleries and boutiques are two short blocks north on Bent Street, including the John Dunn House Shops. Kit Carson Road, also known as U.S. 64, has a mix of the old and the new. There's metered municipal parking downtown, though the traffic can be daunting. Some shops worth checking out are in St. Francis Plaza in Ranchos de Taos, 4 mi south of the Plaza near the San Francisco de Asís Church. Just north of Taos off NM 522 you can find Overland Ranch (including Overland Sheepskin Co.), which has gorgeous sheepskin and leather clothing, along with other shops, galleries, restaurants, and an outdoor path winding through displays of wind sculptures.

Art Galleries

For at least a century, artists have been drawn to Taos's natural grandeur. The result is a vigorous art community with some 80 galleries, a lively market, and an estimated 1,000 residents producing art full- or part-time. Many artists explore themes of the western landscape, Native Americans, and adobe architecture; others create abstract forms and mixed-media works that may or may not reflect the Southwest. Some local artists grew up in Taos, but many—Anglo, Hispanic, and Native Americans—are adopted Taoseños.

Blue Rain Gallery (⊠ 117 S. Plaza ☎ 505/751–0066) carries some of the finest examples of Pueblo pottery and Hopi kachina dolls to be found anywhere, ranging in price from several hundred to several thousand dollars. The owner, Leroy Garcia, takes time to explain the materials and traditions. The gallery also sells Native American–made jewelry and art.

Clay and Fiber Gallery (⊠ 201 Paseo del Pueblo Sur ☎ 505/758–8093) has exhibited first-rate ceramics, glass, pottery, and hand-painted silks and weavings by local artists for the past quarter century.

Envision Gallery (⊠ Overland Ranch Complex, NM 522 north of Taos ☎ 505/751–1344) has contemporary art and an outdoor exhibit of wind sculptures.

Farnsworth Gallery Taos (⊠ 1129 Paseo del Pueblo Norte ☎ 505/758–0776). Best known for his finely detailed paintings of horses, the work of artist John Farnsworth also includes colorful local landscapes, large-scale still-lifes, and scenes of Native American kiva dancers.

Fenix Gallery (⊠ 208–A Ranchitos Rd. ☎ 505/758–9120) is a showcase for contemporary art, exhibiting paintings, sculpture, ceramics, and lithography by established Taos artists.

Gallery Elena (⊠ 111 Morada La. ☎ 505/758–9094) shows the symbolic and impressionistic works of Veloy, Dan, and Michael Vigil.

Inger Jirby Gallery (✉ 207 Ledoux St. ☏ 505/758–7333) displays Jirby's whimsically colored landscape paintings.

★ **J.D. Challenger Gallery** (✉ 221 Paseo del Pueblo Norte ☏ 505/751–6773 or 800/511–6773) is the home base of personable painter J. D. Challenger, who has become famous for his dramatically rendered portraits of Native Americans from tribes throughout North America.

Las Comadres (✉ 228–A Paseo del Pueblo Norte ☏ 505/737–5323) is a women's cooperative gallery showing arts and crafts.

Lumina Fine Art & Sculpture Gardens (✉ 11 NM 230 ☏ 505/776–0123 or 877/558–6462) exhibits paintings by worldwide artists and has 3 acres of sculpture gardens, including works of Japanese stone carvers.

Michael McCormick Gallery (✉ 106–C Paseo del Pueblo Norte ☏ 505/758–1372 or 800/279–0879) is home to the sensual, stylized female portraits of Miguel Martinez and the architectural paintings of Margaret Nes. The gallery also has an extensive collection of Rembrandt etchings.

Mission Gallery (✉ 138 E. Kit Carson Rd. ☏ 505/758–2861) carries the works of early Taos artists, early New Mexico Modernists, and important contemporary artists. The gallery is in the former home of painter Joseph H. Sharp.

> **DID YOU KNOW?**
>
> For more than a century, clear mountain light, sweeping landscapes, and a soft desert palette have drawn artists to Taos.

Navajo Gallery (✉ 210 Ledoux St. ☏ 505/758–3250) shows the works of the internationally renowned Navajo painter and sculptor R. C. Gorman, who died in 2005 and who was known for his ethereal imagery—especially his portraits of Native American women.

Nichols Taos Fine Art Gallery (✉ 403 Paseo del Pueblo Norte ☏ 505/758–2475) has exhibits of oils, watercolors, pastels, charcoal, and pencils from artists representing many prestigious national art organizations. The gallery cooperates with the nearby Fechin Inn to provide art programs and workshops.

Parks Gallery (✉ 127–A Bent St. ☏ 505/751–0343) specializes in contemporary paintings, sculptures, and prints. Mixed-media artist Melissa Zink shows here, as well as painter Jim Wagner.

R. B. Ravens Gallery (✉ 4146 NM 68, Ranchos de Taos ☏ 505/758–7322 or 866/758–7322) exhibits paintings by the founding artists of Taos, pre-1930s weavings, and ceramics.

Robert L. Parsons Fine Art (✉ 131 Bent St. ☏ 505/751–0159 or 800/613–5091) shows Southwest paintings, antiques, and authentic antique Navajo blankets.

Six Directions (✉ 129B N. Plaza ☏ 505/758–5844) has paintings, alabaster and bronze sculpture, Native American artifacts, silver jewelry, and pottery. Bill Rabbit and Robert Redbird are among the artists represented here.

Spirit Runner Gallery (✉ 303 Paseo del Pueblo Norte ☎ 505/758–1132) exhibits colorful acrylic and gold-leaf paintings by Taos native Ouray Meyers.

Studio de Colores Gallery (✉ 115 Quesnel, El Prado near Taos ☎ 505/751–3502 or 888/751–3502) is home to the work of two artists, Ann Huston and Ed Sandoval, who are married to one another but have extremely distinctive styles. Sandoval is known for his trademark *Viejito* (Old Man) images and swirling, vibrantly colored landscapes; Huston specializes in soft-hue still lifes and scenes whose stillness evokes the work of Edward Hopper.

Specialty Stores

Books

Brodsky Bookshop (✉ 226–A Paseo del Pueblo Norte ☎ 505/758–9468) has new and used books—contemporary literature, Southwestern classics, children's titles—piled here and there, but amiable proprietor Rick Smith will help you find what you need.

G. Robinson Old Prints and Maps (✉ John Dunn House, 124–D Bent St. ☎ 505/758–2278) stocks rare books, maps, and prints from the 16th to 19th century.

Moby Dickens (✉ John Dunn House, 124–A Bent St. ☎ 505/758–3050), great for browsing, is a bookstore for all ages. It carries many books on the Southwest as well as a large stock of general-interest books.

Mystery Ink (✉ 121 Camino de la Placita ☎ 505/751–1092) specializes in high-quality used books—mainly mysteries, but also contemporary books, science fiction, and children's books. The shop also carries some foreign-language literature.

Sustaining Cultures (✉ 114 Doña Luz ☎ 505/751–0959) stocks spiritual and new-age books and tapes and offers tarot readings.

Clothing

Aventura (✉ Overland Ranch, 4 mi north of Taos ☎ 505/758–2144), which opened in 2005, produces stylish (and super-warm) contemporary blanket "wraps" as well as other winter-oriented outdoor wear.

Overland Sheepskin Company (✉ NM 522, Overland Ranch, 4 mi north of Taos ☎ 505/758–8820 or 888/754–8352) carries high-quality sheepskin coats, hats, mittens, and slippers, many with Taos beadwork.

Collectibles & Gifts

Horse Feathers (✉ 109–B Kit Carson Rd. ☎ 505/758–7457) is a fun collection of cowboy antiques and

---

DID YOU KNOW?

In New Mexico shops, it's acceptable to ask for a certificate of authenticity, written verification of a piece's origin, or a receipt that lists the materials that make up an item.

vintage western wear—boots, hats, buckles, jewelry, and all manner of paraphernalia.

Twining Weavers & Contemporary Crafts (✉ 129 Kit Carson Rd. ☎ 505/758–9000) sells stunning textiles, blankets, table runners, throws, and the like, using colorful fabrics from Guatemala, as well as a wide range of decorative crafts.

Home Furnishings

Abydos (✉ 7036 SR 518, Talpa ☎ 505/758–0483 or 888/900–0863) sells fine handmade New Mexican–style furniture.

Alhambra (✉ 124 Paseo del Pueblo Sur ☎ 505/758–4161) carries a lovely collection of antiques, Oriental rugs and textiles, and South Asian artifacts.

Casa Cristal Pottery (✉ 1306 Paseo del Pueblo Norte ☎ 505/758–1530), 2½ mi north of the Taos Plaza, has a huge stock of stoneware, serapes, clay pots, Native American ironwood carvings, fountains, sweaters, ponchos, clay fireplaces, Mexican blankets, tiles, piñatas, and blue glassware from Guadalajara.

★ **Country Furnishings of Taos** (✉ 534 Paseo del Pueblo Norte ☎ 505/758–4633) sells folk art from northern New Mexico, handmade furniture, metalwork lamps and beds, and colorful accessories.

La Unica Cosa (✉ 117 Paseo del Pueblo Norte ☎ 505/758–3065) has a striking collection of Zapotec Indian rugs and hangings.

Lo Fino (✉ 201 Paseo del Pueblo Sur ☎ 505/758–0298) carries the works—hand-carved beds, tables, chairs, *trasteros* (free-standing cupboards), and benches—of the 10 top Southwestern furniture and lighting designers, as well as some Native American alabaster sculpture, basketry, and pottery.

Los Ancestros (✉ 66 St. Francis Plaza, Ranchos de Taos ☎ 505/737–5053) stocks Spanish-colonial reproductions and accessories.

Taos Blue (✉ 101–A Bent St. ☎ 505/758–3561) carries jewelry, pottery, and contemporary works by Native Americans (masks, rattles, sculpture), as well as Hispanic *santos* (bultos and retablos).

The **Taos Company** (✉ 124–K Bent St. ☎ 800/548–1141) sells magnificent Spanish-style furniture, chandeliers, rugs, and textiles; Mexican *equipal* (wood and leather) chairs; and other accessories.

Taos Tin Works (✉ 1204–D Paseo del Pueblo Norte ☎ 505/758–9724) sells handcrafted tinwork such as wall sconces, mirrors, lamps, and table ornaments by Marion Moore.

Weaving Southwest (✉ 216–B Paseo del Pueblo Norte ☎ 505/758–0433) represents 25 tapestry artists who make beautiful rugs, blankets, and pillows. The store also sells supplies for weavers, including hand-dyed yarn.

Native American Arts & Crafts

Buffalo Dancer (✉ 103–A E. Plaza ☎ 505/758–8718) buys, sells, and trades Native American arts and crafts, including pottery, belts, kachina dolls, hides, and silver-coin jewelry.

El Rincón Trading Post (⊠ 114 E. Kit Carson Rd. ☎ 505/758–9188) is housed in a large, dark, cluttered century-old adobe. Native American items of all kinds are bought and sold here: drums, feathered headdresses, Navajo rugs, beads, bowls, baskets, shields, beaded moccasins, jewelry, arrows, and spearheads. The packed back room contains Native American, Hispanic, and Anglo Wild West artifacts.

> **DID YOU KNOW?**
>
> Your best guarantee of authenticity, particularly involving Navajo blankets, is to purchase directly from a reputable reservation outlet.

Taos Drums (⊠ NM 68, 5 mi south of Plaza ☎ 505/758–9844 or 800/424–3786) is the factory outlet for the Taos Drum Factory. The store, 5 mi south of Taos Plaza (look for the large tepee), stocks handmade Pueblo log drums, leather lamp shades, and wrought-iron and Southwestern furniture.

Taos General Store (⊠ 223–C Paseo del Pueblo Sur ☎ 505/758–9051) stocks a large selection of furniture and decorative items from around the world, as well as American Indian pots, rugs, and jewelry.

Sporting Goods

Cottam's Ski & Outdoor (⊠ 207–A Paseo del Pueblo Sur ☎ 505/758–2822) carries hiking and backpacking gear, snowboarding and skateboarding equipment, maps, fishing licenses and supplies, and ski equipment, along with related clothing and accessories.

Los Rios Anglers (⊠ 226–C Paseo del Pueblo Norte ☎ 505/758–2798 or 800/748–1707) is a fly-fisherman's haven for fly rods, flies, clothing, books, instruction, and guide service to local streams.

Mudd 'n' Flood Mountain Shop (⊠ 134 Bent St. ☎ 505/751–9100) has gear and clothing for rock climbers, backpackers, campers, and backcountry skiers.

Taos Mountain Outfitters (⊠ 114 S. Plaza ☎ 505/758–9292) has supplies for kayakers, skiers, climbers, and backpackers, as well as maps, books, and handy advice.

TAOS SKI VALLEY

⑭ *NM 150, 22 mi northeast of Taos.*

A trip to Taos Ski Valley begins at the traffic light where you turn right onto NM 150 (Taos Ski Valley Road) from U.S. 64. Along the way, the hamlet of Arroyo Seco, some 5 mi up NM 150 from the traffic light, is worth a stop for lunch (try Gypsy 360° café) and a look at crafts and antiques shops. Beyond Arroyo Seco the road crosses a high plain, then plunges into the Rio Hondo Canyon to follow the cascading brook upstream through the forest to Taos Ski Valley, where NM 150 ends. (It does not continue to Red River, as some disappointed motorists discover.)

Skiers from around the world return to the slopes and hospitality of the Village of Taos Ski Valley every year. This world-class area is known for

3

its alpine village atmosphere, perhaps the finest ski school in the country, and the variety of its 72 runs—it's also slowly but surely becoming more of a year-round destination, as the valley attracts outdoors enthusiasts with spectacular, and often challenging, hiking in summer and fall. Many of the few hotels at the ski valley have been converted to ski-in ski-out condos since the early 2000s, further evidence that the once funky ski area is becoming more of a Colorado-style full-scale resort town. Some of the best trails in Carson National Forest begin at the Village of Taos Ski Valley and go though dense woodland up to alpine tundra. There aren't many summer visitors, so you can have the trails up to Bull-of-the-Woods, Gold Hill, Williams Lake, Italianos, and Wheeler Peak nearly all to yourself. Easy nature hikes are organized by the Bavarian hotel, guided by Shar Sharghi, a botanist and horticulturist. Special events like barn dances and wine tastings occur throughout the nonskiing seasons.

WHERE TO STAY & EAT

$–$$ ✕ **Rhoda's Restaurant.** Rhoda Blake founded Taos Ski Valley with her husband, Ernie. Her slope-side restaurant serves pasta, burgers, and sandwiches for lunch. Dinner fare is a bit more substantive, such as veal medallions with pancetta and seafood chile rellenos with ancho-chile sauce. There's also a kids' menu. ⊠ *Resort Center, on the slope* ☎ *505/776–2005* ▭ *AE, MC, V.*

¢–$$ ✕ **Tim's Stray Dog Cantina.** This wildly popular spot occupies a chalet-style building in the heart of the Taos ski area, and it's a favorite spot not only for breakfast, lunch, and dinner but for après-ski cocktails. Favorites include rainbow trout with lemon butter, chile rellenos, green-chile burgers (both beef and veggie), and—at breakfast—blueberry blue-corn pancakes. ⊠ *105 Sutton Pl.* ☎ *505/776–2894* ▭ *MC, V.*

★ **$$$$** ✕🖫 **The Bavarian.** This luxurious, secluded re-creation of a Bavarian lodge has the only mid-mountain accommodations in the Taos Ski Valley. The King Ludwig suite has a dining room, kitchen, marble bathroom, and two bedrooms with canopied beds. Three suites have whirlpool tubs, and there's a three-bedroom, three-bath apartment. The restaurant ($$–$$$$) serves contemporary Bavarian-inspired cuisine, such as baked artichokes and Gruyère, and braised pork loin with garlic-mashed potatoes and red cabbage. Summer activities include hiking, touring with the resident botanist, horseback riding, rafting, and fishing. Seven-night ski packages are offered. ⊠ *Twining Rd. off NM 150* 🕮 *Box 653, Taos Ski Valley 87525* ☎ *505/776–8020* 🖷 *505/776–5301* ⊕ *www.thebavarian.net* ⇆ *4 suites* ⊝ *Restaurant, kitchenettes, cable TV, in-room VCRs, fishing, hiking, horseback riding* ▭ *AE, MC, V* ☉ *Closed May and early Nov.* ⏹ *BP.*

$$$$ ✕🖫 **Inn at Snakedance.** This modern resort hotel is right on the slopes. The inn has a handsome library where guests can enjoy an après-ski coffee or after-dinner drink next to a fieldstone fireplace. Some rooms have fireplaces. In summer the hotel offers weeklong vacation packages, including a cooking school and fitness adventure

DID YOU KNOW?

Compared with other notable ski areas, New Mexico is more susceptible to extended periods of dry weather that can create meltdowns.

courses. Hondo Restaurant ($$–$$$; no dinner Sunday–Thursday in summer), a frequent winner of the *Wine Spectator* Award of Excellence, turns out esteemed contemporary American cooking, such as curry-crusted lamb chops with blackberry coulis and wild-rice pilaf. ⊠ *Off Taos Ski Valley Rd.* ⓓ *NM 150; Box 89, Village of Taos Ski Valley 87525* ☎ *505/776–2277 or 800/322–9815* 🖷 *505/776–1410* ⊕ *www. innsnakedance.com* ⇝ *60 rooms, 1 condo* ⚐ *Restaurant, minibars, refrigerators, cable TV, exercise equipment, hot tub, massage, sauna, library; no smoking* ⊟ *AE, DC, MC, V* ⊗ *Closed mid-Apr.–Memorial Day* ⦿ *BP.*

$$–$$$ 🏨 **Thunderbird Lodge and Chalet.** This two-story wood-frame inn is only 150 yards from the main lifts, on the sunny side of Taos Ski Valley. A large conference room has board games and a library. There are supervised children's activities during holiday seasons. Lodge rooms are cozy and functional; the six rooms in the adjacent chalet are a bit larger and have king-size beds. Sumptuous breakfast buffets and family-style dinners, which are included in the rates, are served in the pine-panel dining room. Ski-week packages are available. ⊠ *3 Thunderbird Rd., off Taos Ski Valley Rd.* ⓓ *NM 150; Box 87, Village of Taos Ski Valley 87525* ☎ *505/776–2280 or 800/776–2279* 🖷 *505/776–2238* ⊕ *www. thunderbird-taos.com* ⇝ *30 rooms* ⚐ *Restaurant, cable TV, hot tub, massage, sauna, bar, library, recreation room, meeting room* ⊟ *AE, MC, V* ⦿ *MAP.*

★ $–$$ 🏨 **Austing Haus.** Owner Paul Austing constructed much of this handsome, glass-sheathed building, 1½ mi from Taos Ski Valley, along with many of its furnishings. The breakfast room has large picture windows, stained-glass paneling, and an impressive fireplace. Aromas of fresh-baked goods, such as Paul's apple strudel, come from the kitchen. Guest rooms are pretty and quiet with harmonious, peaceful colors; some have four-poster beds and fireplaces. In winter the inn offers weeklong ski packages. ⊠ *NM 150* ⓓ *Box 8, Village of Taos Ski Valley 87525* ☎ *505/776–2649 or 800/748–2932*

> **DID YOU KNOW?**
>
> Major ski resorts have snow machines, but you should check conditions first to avoid disappointment.

🖷 *505/776–8751* ⊕ *www.austinghaus.net* ⇝ *22 rooms, 3 chalets* ⚐ *Dining room, cable TV, hot tub, meeting rooms* ⊟ *AE, DC, MC, V* ⦿ *CP.*

NIGHTLIFE & THE ARTS **Thunderbird Lodge** (⊠ 3 Thunderbird Rd. ☎ 505/776–2280) in the Taos Ski Valley has free jazz nights and country-and-western swing dancing. The Taos School of Music gives free weekly summer concerts and recitals from mid-June to early August at the **Hotel Saint Bernard** (☎ 505/776–2251), at the mountain base (near the lifts) of Taos Ski Valley.

SPORTS & THE OUTDOORS **Wheeler Peak** is a designated wilderness area of Carson National Forest, where travel is restricted to hiking or horseback riding. Part of the Sangre de Cristo Mountains, this 13,161-foot peak is New Mexico's highest. The 8-mi trail to the top begins at the Village of Taos Ski Valley. Only experienced hikers should tackle this strenuous trail. Dress warmly even in summer, take plenty of water and food, and pay attention to *all* warnings and instructions distributed by the forest rangers. Quite a few shorter and less taxing trails also depart from the ski valley and points nearby; trailheads are usually marked with signs. ✉ *Twining Campground, next to ski area parking lot* ☎ *505/758–6200.*

Fodor'sChoice
★
With 72 runs—more than half of them for experts—and an average of more than 320 inches of annual snowfall, **Taos Ski Valley** ranks among the country's most respected—and challenging—resorts. The slopes tend to be tough here (the ridge chutes, Al's Run, Inferno), but 25% (e. g., Honeysuckle) are for intermediate skiers, and 24% (e.g., Bambi, Porcupine) for beginners. It's one of the nation's handful of resorts that still, controversially, bans snowboarding. Taos Ski Valley is justly famous for its outstanding ski schools, one of the best in the country—if you're new to the sport, this is a terrific resort to give it a try. ✉ *Village of Taos Ski Valley* ☎ *505/776–2291* ⊕ *www.skitaos.org* ⌫ *Lift tickets $61* ☉ *Late Nov.–early Apr.*

SHOPPING **Andean Softwear** (✉ 118 Sutton Pl. ☎ 505/776–2508) carries exotic clothing, textiles, and jewelry. Note the deliciously soft alpaca sweaters from Peru. You can bring your ski boots up to the pros at the **Boot Doctor** (✉ 103 Sutton Pl. ☎ 505/776–2489)—if anyone can make 'em fit, they can; if not, they'll find a pair that does. A demo program lets you try skis out. Ski clothing and accessories fill out the store in winter, and in summer you can get hiking clothing, sandals, and clogs.

TAOS ESSENTIALS

AIRPORTS & TRANSFERS

Albuquerque International Sunport is the nearest (130 mi) major airport to Taos. Taos Municipal Airport is 12 mi west of the city but ceased offering commercial service in 2005 and is just open to charters and private planes.

Faust's Transportation offers shuttle service between Albuquerque's airport and Taos, as well as to Taos Ski Valley, Angel Fire, and Red River. The cost is $40 to $50 per person, and the ride takes 2¾–3 hours.
🚖 **Faust's Transportation** ☎ 505/758–3410 or 888/830–3410 ⊕ www.newmexiconet. com/trans/faust/faust.html.

BUS TRAVEL

Texas, New Mexico & Oklahoma Coaches, a subsidiary of Greyhound Lines, runs buses twice a day from Albuquerque to Taos.
🚖 **Texas, New Mexico & Oklahoma Coaches** ☎ 800/231–2222 ⊕ www.greyhound. com.

CAR RENTAL

Cottam Walker rents cars by the day, week, and month.
🚖 **Cottam Walker Ford** ✉ 1320 Paseo del Pueblo Sur ☎ 505/751–3200 ⊕ www. forddetaos.com.

CAR TRAVEL

The main route from Santa Fe to Taos is NM 68, also known as the Low Road, which winds between the Rio Grande and red-rock cliffs before rising to a spectacular view of the plain and river gorge. You can also take the wooded High Road to Taos (⇨ Side Trips from Santa Fe *in* Chapter 4). From points north of Taos, take NM 522; from points east or west, take U.S. 64.

PARKING Major hotels have ample parking. Metered parking areas are all over town; in peak seasons—summer and winter—traffic and parking can be a headache. There's a metered parking lot between Taos Plaza and Bent Street and a free lot on Kit Carson, two blocks east of Paseo del Pueblo.

EMERGENCIES
In an emergency, dial 911.

🖪 Hospital **Holy Cross Hospital** ✉ 1397 Weimer Rd. ☎ 505/758-8883 ⊕ www.taoshospital.org.

LODGING
Taos has a handful of useful reservation and vacation-rental services.

🖪 **Taos Central Reservations** ☎ 505/758-9767 or 800/821-2437 ⊕ www.taoscentralreservations.com. **Taos Lodging** ☎ 505/751-1771 or 800/954-8267 ⊕ www.taoslodging.com.

TAXIS
Taxi service in Taos is sparse, but Faust's Transportation, based in nearby El Prado, has a fleet of radio-dispatched cabs.

🖪 **Faust's Transportation** ☎ 505/758-3410 or 505/758-7359.

TOURS
ORIENTATION TOUR Historic Taos Trolley Tours conducts daily narrated tours of Taos, including stops at the San Francisco de Asís Church, Taos Pueblo, Millicent Rogers Museum, and La Hacienda de los Martínez. Separate history and culture tours also are available. Tours run from May to October and cost $33 each, which covers entry fees to all sights.

SPECIAL-INTEREST TOURS Native Sons Adventures organizes biking, backpacking, rafting, snowmobiling, and horseback and wagon expeditions. Taos Indian Horse Ranch conducts two-hour trail rides, as well as old-fashioned horse-drawn sleigh rides through the Taos Pueblo backcountry—winter weather permitting—complete with brass bells, a Native American storyteller, toasted marshmallows, and green-chile roasts. Tours are by reservation only; no alcohol is permitted. The ranch closes for 42 to 48 days each year to observe the Taos Pueblo Sweats Ceremony; call the Taos Pueblo Governor's Office for the exact dates.

🖪 **Historic Taos Trolley Tours** ☎ 505/751-0366 or 800/753-7559 ⊕ www.taostrolleytours.com. **Native Sons Adventures** ✉ 1033A Paseo del Pueblo Sur, Taos ☎ 505/758-9342 or 800/753-7559. **Taos Indian Horse Ranch** ✉ 1 Miller Rd., Taos Pueblo ☎ 800/659-3210. **Taos Pueblo Governor's Office** ☎ 505/758-9593.

VISITOR INFORMATION
🖪 **Taos Chamber of Commerce** ✉ 1139 Paseo del Pueblo Sur ⌂ Drawer I, Taos 87571 ☎ 505/758-3873 or 800/732-8267 ⊕ www.taosguide.com. **Taos Ski Valley Chamber of Commerce** ☎ 505/776-1413 or 800/517-9816 ⊕ www.taosskivalley.com.

Side Trips from the Cities

WORD OF MOUTH

"One of my favorite things to do near ABQ is the Jémez Mountain Trail. You can spend anywhere from 3–4 hours to a whole day driving this 200-mile (or so) loop. The scenery is constantly changing and there are plenty of worthwhile stops along the way. Bandelier is one of them, but I would recommend at least a half a day for that alone."

–travel_addict

"We really got a kick out of the Tinkertown Museum. What was most fun for us was finding the things that seemed most out of place."

–moldyhotelsaregross

By Andrew Collins

IF YOU'RE PLANNING A TRIP to any of north-central New Mexico's three most important destinations—Albuquerque, Santa Fe, or Taos—it's worth spending an extra day or even just a half day to explore the surrounding area. It's by venturing out of town that you really come to appreciate and understand northern Rio Grande Valley's exceptionally diverse and visually stunning scenery, from dramatic river gorges with sheer basalt walls to the evergreen- and aspen-coated slopes of the highest mountain range in New Mexico, the Sangre de Cristos. Within an hour's drive of Albuquerque, Santa Fe, or Taos are nearly a dozen Indian pueblos, the countryside that inspired Georgia O'Keeffe's artwork, some of the West's finest ski resorts, an emerging crop of prestigious wineries, several insular villages famous for both contemporary and traditional arts and crafts, two villages famous for their curative hot springs, and some of the best hiking, rafting, fly-fishing, and biking terrain you'll ever lay eyes on.

There are at least three road routes to get from Albuquerque to Santa Fe, and then three more from Santa Fe up to Taos. And they all have their charms, even the seemingly mundane trek up I–25 from Albuquerque to Santa Fe. Traveling among the region's three key towns, and opting when time allows for the most scenic and circuitous routing, is one way to experience north-central New Mexico's most alluring off-the-beaten-path scenery. Another is simply to plan a few day trips from Albuquerque, Santa Fe, or Taos, or even to consider spending the night in one of the out-of-the-way communities described in this chapter—the region offers a wealth of lodging options, from funky to five-star elegant, and prices out in the country tend to be considerably lower than in Santa Fe and Taos.

However you go about experiencing the region's smaller communities and less-traveled byways, venture out into the hinterlands as often as you can. You haven't really been to north-central New Mexico until you've explored the cave dwellings at Bandelier National Monument, driven over the dramatic mountain passes of the Enchanted Circle and High Road to Taos, or checked out the acclaimed galleries and funky shops of Madrid and Chimayó. As the old travel cliché goes, in New Mexico, getting there is half the fun.

Exploring North-Central New Mexico

You need a car to embark on any of the side trips described in this chapter, and you should generally allow yourself an extra hour or two to complete most of these journeys. Distances aren't as vast in north-central New Mexico as in the rest of the state: the Turquoise Trail extends only about 70 mi from Albuquerque to Santa Fe and can be managed, if you hustle, in roughly 90 minutes, but to truly appreciate the scenery and attractions along the way, you should really allow anywhere from three to six hours. Same goes for driving the High Road to Taos, the Enchanted Circle, Jémez Country, and Abiquiu. Roads in this part of the state can be windy and even a bit treacherous, espe-

GREAT ITINERARIES

As you tour north-central New Mexico, it's best to mix your explorations of the destinations in this chapter with stops in the region's three main bases: Albuquerque, Santa Fe, and Taos.

IF YOU HAVE 3 DAYS

With just three days, you can make the three most popular driving tours in this chapter with relative ease. Begin your travels in Albuquerque, and drive up the Turquoise Trail on Day 1. Plan to make the side trip up NM 536 to Sandia Crest, and also to take some time admiring the galleries and shops in **Madrid** ❼. There are a handful of overnight accommodations along this route, but you can also just spend your first night in Santa Fe. Make Day 2 your most ambitious one for driving. Start off in Santa Fe and take the Low Road up to Taos, perhaps stopping at Embudo Station for lunch along the way. Once you reach Taos, continue north of town and embark on the Enchanted Circle tour, which loops around the majestic mountains north of town. You can spend the night in **Angel Fire** ❸❺, along the Enchanted Circle, or back in Taos. On Day 3, you can return to Santa Fe (continuing on back down to Albuquerque if need be), by taking the High Road from Taos, passing through the charming villages of **Truchas** ❸❶ and **Chimayó** ❷❾.

IF YOU HAVE 5 DAYS

With an extra two days, you can complete all of the tours described above while allowing some time to make several additional side trips. For Day 1, repeat the itinerary described above, ending your day either at the north end of Turquoise

Trail or in Santa Fe. The following day, drive north from Santa Fe, and at **Española** ❷❷, hang a left and continue north along U.S. 84 into the heart of Georgia O'Keeffe Country. You can spend the night in **Abiquiu** ❷❸; at Rancho de San Juan, just north of Española; or at **Ojo Caliente** ❷❼. Whatever you decide, plan to head north up U.S. 285 on the morning of Day 3, turning east on U.S. 64 (in Tres Piedras), which takes you into Taos. Alternatively, if you're more a fan of historic railroads than you are of Georgia O'Keeffe, plan to spend your second day up in **Chama** ❷❺, and ride the famed Cumbres & Toltec Scenic Railroad in the morning, and then cut east on U.S. 64 to reach Taos. From here, embark on the Enchanted Circle tour, spending the night either in **Angel Fire** ❸❺ or back in Taos. Make the drive back down toward Santa Fe along the High Road on Day 4; however, after you reach **Pojoaque** ❶❸ (where you might stop and spend a couple of hours), make the turn (just north of Pojoaque) onto NM 502 and follow this road up into **Los Alamos** ❶❼, where you can tour some of the museums or check out **Bandelier National Monument** ❶❽. Spend your fourth night here in Los Alamos. The following day, continue west from Los Alamos along NM 4, passing through the Jémez Valley and stopping in **Jémez Springs** ❷⓿. This leads you to U.S. 550, onto which a left turn leads south and into the northern Albuquerque suburbs of **Bernalillo** ❹ and **Corrales** ❸, where more exploring, restaurants, and lodging options await you.

4

cially in snowy winter weather, so take your time and avoid racing around on roads unfamiliar to you.

That being said, virtually every attraction and community covered here can be visited as part of a day trip from Albuquerque, Santa Fe, and/or Taos. If you have only two or three hours, stick with manageable and nearby jaunts. From Albuquerque, head to Isleta Pueblo or the North Valley. From Santa Fe, visit some of the towns just south of town or some of the pueblos to the north—you can even visit Los Alamos or Bandelier in a half day if you're quick. From Taos, it's possible to cover part of the Enchanted Circle, and to drive up to the ski valley, in just two or three hours.

Keep in mind that many of the recreation areas, museums, campgrounds, and even restaurants and lodgings covered in this chapter keep seasonal or limited hours. As it can take a bit of driving to reach some of these places, it's *always* best to phone ahead to avoid disappointment. And if you're unfamiliar with the area, always ask about driving times and current weather conditions. A little planning goes a long way when exploring some of the region's more remote towns and villages.

About the Restaurants

Somehow, just about any meal tastes a little better when it follows a long, windy road trip through magnificent scenery. North-central New Mexico has no shortage of tantalizing "road food"—simple and honest New Mexican fare, diner snacks, juicy burgers, and the like. But in these parts you can also find one of the Southwest's most acclaimed restaurants, Rancho de San Juan, along with several other fine eateries. A number of the restaurants in these parts are informal and operate with seasonal or less than regular hours, so it's always best to call first. Most of them serve dinner on the early side, too, so don't expect to find a restaurant open after 9 PM—or even 8 PM on weeknights. Casual attire is always the norm around here.

About the Hotels

There are several good reasons to consider spending a night in one of the towns covered in this chapter, rather than in Albuquerque, Santa Fe, and Taos. First, distinctive B&Bs and inns are the norm when you get out into the countryside—these properties tend to be more personal than big chain hotels, which predominate in Albuquerque and to a lesser extent in Santa Fe and Taos. Also, you pay higher prices for the same amenities in Santa Fe and Taos, if not Albuquerque, which has quite low hotel rates. If you prefer the sounds of coyotes howling and a pitch-black sky illuminated only by bright stars, you're more likely to appreciate one of the off-the-beaten-path lodgings described in this chapter than a place right in the heart of busy and bustling Albuquerque, Santa Fe, or even Taos. What you may lose in convenience to shopping, dining, and nightlife, you often gain in proximity to great outdoorsy attractions, such as ski resorts and hiking trails.

IF YOU LIKE

ART GALLERIES

Where do artists and arts patrons open galleries when they can't afford the exorbitant rents of Santa Fe and Taos, but they prefer a more scenic setting than Albuquerque? Quite a few of them have chosen to set up galleries in the many alluring, small, and inexpensive villages of north-central New Mexico. The region's arts hub, Madrid–along the Turquoise Trail– continues to grow in eminence, with new galleries opening on a regular basis. Other communities with a strong arts presence include Corrales, Jémez Springs, Abiquiu (the site of Georgia O'Keeffe's artists' studio), Chimayó, and Truchas. Finally, most of the Indian Pueblos in this region have galleries and shops selling pottery, jewelry, crafts, and other fine artworks made by pueblo members.

HIKING

You see them from the historic plazas and bustling downtowns of Albuquerque, Santa Fe, and Taos: towering, often snowcapped, mountains. Travel the side roads and rural highways of north-central New Mexico, and you reach the trailheads leading to amazing hikes through the state's rugged, 12,000- to 13,000-foot mountain peaks. If you're looking for a lot of bang for your buck, hike the ridge along Sandia Crest, reached via the Turquoise Trail, or make the relatively easy but spectacular jaunt through Kasha-Katuwe Tent Rocks National Monument, south of Santa Fe. Wild Rivers Recreation Area, along the Enchanted Circle tour, can also be managed easily as a day hike. You can find more substantial hiking throughout this area, but especially in Kit Carson National Forest, which surrounds Taos–some of the best hikes depart from Taos Ski Valley.

SKIING

Even more than explaining to outsiders that, yes, New Mexico is actually a U.S. state and not a foreign country (seriously, it happens more than you might imagine), New Mexicans tire of insisting that their state has huge mountains, cold winters, and tons of snow–in other words, it's one of the West's prime venues for both downhill and cross-country skiing. The most famous facility in the region, often cited among the greatest ski challenges in the country in polls and ski magazines, is Taos Ski Valley, a 30-minute drive from downtown Taos. But nearby Angel Fire is another first-rate ski resort. Other fine options include Red River (which also offers exceptional cross-country skiing) and Pajarito Mountain.

	$$$$	**$$$**	**$$**	**$**	**¢**
WHAT IT COSTS					
RESTAURANTS	over $30	$24–$30	$17–$24	$10–$17	under $10
HOTELS	over $260	$190–$260	$130–$190	$70–$130	under $70

Restaurant prices are per person for a main course at dinner, excluding the 8.25% sales tax. Hotel prices are for two people in a standard double room in high season, excluding 11%–14% tax.

SIDE TRIPS FROM ALBUQUERQUE

It takes only a few minutes of driving in either direction to leave urban Albuquerque behind and experience some of New Mexico's natural and small-town beauty. Rivers, valleys, canyons, and peaks are just outside the city's limits, and amid them are many villages worth a stop. If you're headed up to Santa Fe, definitely consider traveling there by way of the rambling and tortuous Turquoise Trail, a charming alternative to speedy I–25.

South of Albuquerque

When Francisco Vásquez de Coronado arrived in what is now New Mexico in 1540, he found a dozen or so villages along the Rio Grande in the ancient province of Tiguex, between what is now Bernalillo to the north of Albuquerque and Isleta to the south. Of those, only Sandia and Isleta survive today. The Salinas Pueblo Missions ruins, about 65 mi southeast of Albuquerque, remain a striking example of the Spanish penchant for building churches on sites inhabited by native people.

Isleta Pueblo

❶ *13 mi south of Albuquerque, via I–25 (Exit 213) and NM 47.*

Of the pueblos in New Mexico when the Spanish first arrived, Isleta Pueblo is one of two Tiwa-speaking communities left in the middle of the Rio Grande Valley. It was also one of a handful of pueblos that didn't participate in the Pueblo Revolt of 1680, during which Isleta was abandoned. Some of the residents fled New Mexico with the Spanish to El Paso, where their descendants live to this day on a reservation called Ysleta del Sur. Other members went to live with the Hopi of Arizona but eventually returned and rebuilt the pueblo.

Facing the quiet plaza is Isleta's church, **St. Augustine**, built in 1629. One of the oldest churches in New Mexico, it has thick adobe walls, a viga-crossed ceiling, and an austere interior. Legend has it that the ground beneath the floor has the odd propensity to push church and community figures buried under the floor back up out of the ground; bodies have been reburied several times, only to emerge again.

Polychrome pottery with red and black designs on a white background is a specialty here. The pueblo celebrates its feast days on August 28 and September 4, both in honor of St. Augustine. The tribal government maintains picnicking and camping facilities, several fishing ponds, and a renowned 18-hole golf course. It also runs the **Isleta Casino and Resort** (✉ 11000 Broadway SE ☎ 505/724–3800 or 877/747–5382 ⊕ www.isletacasinoresort.com), which ranks among the state's most popular gaming facilities. It's a large and handsome space with 1,600 slots and myriad gaming tables; the concert hall hosts a mix of oldies, pop stars, and country-western acts—past acts have included Tom Jones, Vince Gill, and Tony Bennett, but competition from improved casino resorts elsewhere in the region has pulled away many of the big-name acts that used to favor Isleta. There's also boxing held throughout the year. Currently there's no hotel at Isleta, but the tribe is planning

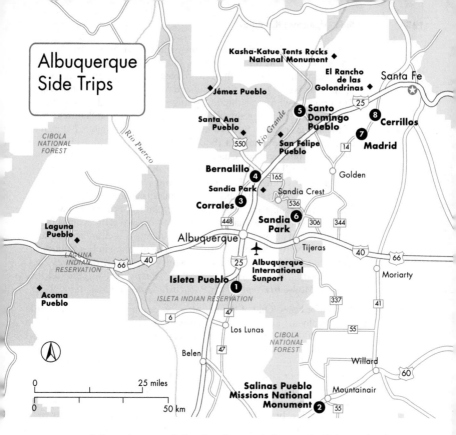

Albuquerque
Side Trips

a full-service, upscale hotel and expanded resort facilities so that it can better compete with other high-profile Native American resorts that have opened around the state in recent years, including Sandia, Santa Ana, and Pojoaque.

Although Isleta is wonderfully picturesque—beehive ovens stand beside adobe homes bedecked with crimson chiles—camera use is restricted here. Only the church may be photographed. ⊠ *Tribal Rd. 40* ☎ *505/869–3111* ⊕ *www.isletapueblo.com* ✉ *Free.*

SPORTS &
THE OUTDOORS

One of the most esteemed facilities in the state, **Isleta Eagle Golf Course** (⊠ 4001 NM 47 ☎ 505/869–0950 or 888/293–9146 ⊕ www.isletaeagle. com) consists of three 9-hole layouts set around three lakes; greens fees are $40–$55 for 18 holes.

Salinas Pueblo Missions National Monument

2 *58 mi (to Punta Agua/Quarai) from Albuquerque, east on I–40 (to Tijeras Exit), south on NM 337 and NM 55; 23 mi from Punta Agua to Abó, south on NM 55, west (at Mountainair) on U.S. 60, and north on NM 513; 34 mi from Punta Agua to Gran Quivira, south on NM 55.*

Salinas Pueblo Missions National Monument is made up of three sites—**Quarai, Abó, and Gran Quivira**—each with the ruins of a 17th-century

Spanish-colonial Franciscan missionary church and an associated pueblo. The sites represent the convergence of two Native American peoples, the Anasazi and the Mogollon, who lived here for centuries before the Spanish arrived. Quarai, the nearest to Albuquerque, was a flourishing Tiwa pueblo whose inhabitants' pottery, weaving, and basket-making techniques were quite refined. On the fringe of the Great Plains, all three of the Salinas pueblos were vulnerable to raids by nomadic Plains Indians. Quarai was abandoned about 50 years after its mission church, **San Purísima Concepción de Cuarac,** was built in 1630. The church's sandstone walls still rise 40 feet out of the earth. At Abó are the remains of the three-story church of San Gregorio and a large unexcavated pueblo. (The masonry style at Abó bore some similarity to that at Chaco Canyon, which has led some archaeologists to speculate that the pueblo was built by people who left the Chaco Canyon area.) A video about Salinas Pueblo can be viewed at Gran Quivira, which contains two churches and some excavated Native American structures. The monument headquarters is in the town of Mountainair. ⊠ *N. Ripley Ave. at W. Broadway (U.S. 60), Mountainair* ☎ *505/847–2585* ⊕ *www.nps.gov/sapu* ⊠ *Free* ☉ *Late May–early Sept., daily 9–6; early Sept.–late May, daily 9–5.*

WHERE TO STAY   ⊡ **Shaffer Hotel.** One of the nation's few remaining structures built in
$ the Pueblo–art deco style, the Shaffer was restored and reopened as a hotel in 2005 after many years of neglect. The 1923 building, in the heart of historic—if modest—downtown Mountainair, offers a wide range of accommodations. The simple "cowboy rooms" share a community bathroom, but all others have private baths, some with original claw-foot tubs. All are done with 1920s and '30s deco antiques and tile bathrooms. Some suites have two bedrooms, and the Wedding Suite has a romantic glass-brick double shower. A festively decorated restaurant serves decent, country-style American and New Mexican fare. Also on-site is Pop's Curio Shop, which carries a quirky mix of jewelry, decorative arts, gifts, and musical instruments. ⊠ *103 W. Main St., Mountainair 87036* ☎ *505/847–2888 or 888/595–2888* 🖷 *505/847–0299* ⊕ *www. shafferhotel.com* ⇴ *11 rooms, 9 with bath; 8 suites* ⚂ *Restaurant, cable TV, Wi-Fi, shop, meeting room* 🗖 *AE, D, MC, V.*

North Valley & Beyond

The land north of Albuquerque is a little bit cooler, a little bit greener, and a lot more pastoral than the city. Drive slowly through Bernalillo and Corrales, and you're bound to see lots of horses, cows, and llamas.

Corrales
❸ *2 mi north of Albuquerque. Take Paseo Del Norte (NM 423) or Alameda Blvd. (NM 528) west from I–25 and head north on Corrales Rd. (NM 448).*

Serene Corrales is an ancient agricultural community now inhabited by artists, craftspeople, and the affluent—plus a few descendants of the old families. Small galleries, shops, and places to eat dot the town, and in fall, roadside fruit and vegetable stands open. Bordered by Albuquerque and Rio Rancho, Corrales makes a pleasant escape to winding dirt roads, fields of corn, and apple orchards. On summer weekends visit the Corrales Farmers' Market; in October, the village holds a Harvest Festival. The village's main drag, NM 448, is one of New Mexico's official scenic byways, lined with grand estates and haciendas and shaded by cottonwoods. Just off the byway, you can break for a stroll through Corrales Bosque Preserve, a shaded sanctuary abutting the Rio Grande that's a favorite spot for bird-watching—some 180 species pass through here throughout the year.

WHERE TO STAY & EAT

$–$$$ ✕ **Casa Vieja.** Set in a rambling early-18th-century compound along the Corrales Scenic Byway and helmed by charismatic chef and local TV personality Jim White, this supposedly haunted hacienda has inspired a devoted following. The menu mixes classic American and New Mexican fare and includes both lighter options and rather rich and lavish entrées. Top picks include crab cakes with mild poblano-chile crème, shrimp sautéed in tequila and lime juice, filet mignon au poivre, and carne adovada burritos. Desserts are made on the premises and include an obscenely rich cinnamon-bun bread pudding with caramel sauce. ⊠ *4541 Corrales Rd.* ☎ *505/898–7489* ⊕ *www.chefwhite.com* ▤ *AE, D, DC, MC, V.*

¢–$ ✕ **Village Pizza.** A Chicago native with a knack for baking runs this ordinarily named joint that serves extraordinarily good pizza. Crusts come in different styles (including Chicago-style deep dish), and a wide range of toppings are offered, including such gourmet fixings as artichoke hearts and smoked oysters. The Corrales calzone is packed with mozzarella and ricotta and slathered with pesto sauce. Locals love the all-you-can-eat buffets (available daily for lunch, Monday and Tuesday for dinner). In back is a rambling courtyard with a couple of big leafy trees and lots of seating. You get a 10% discount if you ride in on horseback. ⊠ *4266 Corrales Rd.* ☎ *505/898–0045* ▤ *AE, D, MC, V.*

★ $ ▦ **Chocolate Turtle B&B.** Hosts Nancy and Dallas Renner run this light-filled four-room hideaway in a quiet neighborhood in West Corrales. It's a short drive from the massive Intel plant in the nearby suburb of Rio Rancho and 20 minutes from downtown Albuquerque, but the setting is as peaceful as can be, this Territorial-style home's large windows and neatly landscaped grounds affording sweeping views of the Sandia Mountains. Fresh flowers and chocolates brighten the rooms, which range from a cozy room with single beds to three more substantial doubles, the most desirable with its own private terrace. All contain well-chosen Southwestern art and furnishings. ⊠ *1098 W. Meadowlark La., Corrales 87048* ☎ *505/898–1800 or 877/298–1800* ⊕ *www. chocolateturtlebb.com* ➟ *4 rooms* ⸖ *Wi-Fi, business services; no room phones, no room TVs* ▤ *AE, D, DC, MC, V* ⺊◯ *BP.*

Bernalillo

➍ *17 mi north of Albuquerque via I–25, 8 mi north of Corrales via NM 448 to NM 528.*

Once a rather tranquil Hispanic village, Bernalillo is today one of New Mexico's fastest-growing towns—it's increasingly absorbing the suburban growth northward from Albuquerque. The town holds a Wine Festival each Labor Day weekend, but the most memorable annual event is the Fiesta of San Lorenzo, which has honored the town's patron saint for nearly 400 years. On August 10, San Lorenzo Day, the entire town takes to the streets to participate in the traditional masked *matachine* dance. Matachines, of Moorish origin, were brought to this hemisphere by the Spanish. In New Mexico various versions are danced to haunting fiddle music, in both Native American pueblos and old Spanish villages at different holidays. Though interpretations of the matachines are inexact, one general theme is that of conquest. One dancer, wearing a devil's mask and wielding a whip, presides over the others. A young girl, dressed in white, is also present.

The town's leading attraction, **Coronado State Monument,** is named in honor of Francisco Vásquez de Coronado, the leader of the first organized Spanish expedition into the Southwest, from 1540 to 1542. The prehistoric **Kuaua Pueblo,** on a bluff overlooking the Rio Grande, is believed to have been the headquarters of Coronado and his army, who were caught unprepared by severe winter weather during their search for the legendary Seven Cities of Gold. A worthy stop, the monument has a museum in a restored kiva, with copies of magnificent frescoes done in black, yellow, red, blue, green, and white. The frescoes depict fertility rites, rain dances, and hunting rituals. The original artworks are preserved in the small visitor center. Adjacent to the monument is **Coronado State Park,** which has campsites and picnic grounds, both open year-round. In autumn the views at the monument and park are especially breathtaking, with the trees turning russet and gold. There's also overnight camping at the adjacent Coronado Campground (505/980–8256). ⊠ *485 Kuaua Rd., off NM 44/U.S. 550* ☎ *505/867–5351* ⊕ *www.nmstatemonuments.org* ⬚ *$3* ⊙ *Wed.–Mon. 8:30–5.*

WHERE TO   ✕ **Prairie Star.** Albuquerque residents often make the drive to this 1920s
STAY & EAT   Pueblo Revival hacienda, renowned for the sunset views from its patio.
★ **$$–$$$$**   The menu combines contemporary American, Southwestern, and classical cuisine, including duck-confit crepes with red-chile-infused blueberries, lemon chèvre, mint, and pistachios, and dry-aged prime New York steak with black truffle potatoes, cheesy collard greens, and roasted garlic–tomato confit. The culinary quality has become consistently outstanding over the years, and the setting is gorgeous. Prairie Star is on the Santa Ana reservation, right beside the Santa Ana Golf Club. ⊠ *288 Prairie Star Rd., Santa Ana Pueblo* ☎ *505/867–3327* ⊕ *www. santaanagolf.com* ▭ *AE, D, DC, MC, V* ⊙ *Closed Mon. No lunch.*

¢–$$ ✕ **Range Cafe & Bakery.** Banana pancakes, giant cinnamon rolls, Asian
Fodor'sChoice   spinach salad, grilled portobello burgers, homemade meat loaf with gar-
★   lic mashed potatoes, steak-and-enchilada platters, and the signature dessert, Death by Lemon, are among the highlights at this quirky spot known for down-home fare with creative touches. All the above, plus a full complement of rich, decadent Taos Cow ice cream, is served in a refurbished mercantile building with a dead-center view of the Sandia Mountains. You can order breakfast fare until 3 PM. There are also two newer branches in Albuquerque, but the original has the best ambience. ⊠ *925 Camino del Pueblo* ☎ *505/867–1700* ⊕ *www.rangecafe.com* ⬚ *Reservations not accepted* ▭ *AE, D, MC, V.*

$$–$$$$ ✕▥ **Hyatt Regency Tamaya.** This spectacular large-scale resort, on 500
Fodor's Choice acres on the Santa Ana Pueblo, includes a top-rated golf course, state-
★ of-the-art spa, and cultural museum and learning center. Most rooms,
swathed in natural stone, wood, and adobe and filled with pueblo-in-
spired textiles and pottery, overlook the Sandia Mountains or cotton-
wood groves; many have balconies or patios. Cultural events include
bread-baking demonstrations (in traditional adobe ovens), storytelling,
and live tribal dance and music performances. Other amenities include
waterslides over two of the outdoor pools, atmospheric bars, guided na-
ture walks, and hot-air ballooning nearby. The Hyatt's outstanding
Corn Maiden restaurant (☉ Closed Sun. and Mon. No lunch) serves out-
standing contemporary fare that mixes New Mexican, Asian, regional
American influences and ingredients. Try buffalo topped with foie gras
and a truffle demi-glace, or crispy-skin duck served with an apple–green
chile pancake and orange-whiskey sauce. The Santa Ana Star Casino is
a free shuttle ride away. And if you're looking for an exceptional horse-
back ride, arrange one with the Tamaya stables. As you drink in eye-
fuls of the spectacular pueblo backcountry and weave among trees and
plantings, you'll wonder why you ever settled for the dull nose-to-butt
riding experiences of yesteryear. If you're too suave to wear the helmet
or gloves offered, by all means do not forego a heavy layer of sunscreen,
especially on your face, ears, and neck. ⊠ *1300 Tuyuna Trail, Santa Ana
Pueblo, 87525* ☎ *505/867–1234 or 800/633–7313* 🖷 *505/771–6180*
⊕ *www.tamaya.hyatt.com* ➲ *331 rooms, 19 suites* ⌂ *3 restaurants,
room service, refrigerators, cable TV with movies, driving range, 18-
hole golf course, 2 tennis courts, 3 pools, health club, spa, basketball,
horseback riding, 3 bars, children's programs (ages 2–14), concierge,
business services, meeting rooms* ⊟ *AE, D, DC, MC, V.*

⚠ **Albuquerque North Bernalillo KOA.** Cottonwoods, pines, evergreens,
and willows shade this park, where morning brings a free pancake
breakfast and in summer free outdoor movies are screened. You can play
badminton, basketball, croquet, horseshoes, and video games. ⊠ *55 S.
Hill Rd., 87004* ☎ *505/867–5227 or 800/562–3616* ⊕ *www.koa.com*
⌂ *Grills, snack bar, laundry facilities, flush toilets, full hookups, show-
ers, picnic tables, swimming (pool)* ➲ *57 RV sites, 36 tent sites, 6 cab-
ins* ⌸ *$21–$51; cabins $37–$56* ⊟ *D, MC, V.*

SHOPPING **Jackalope** (⊠ 834 NM 44/U.S. 550 ☎ 505/867–9813) has acres of im-
ported pottery, crafts, table linens, jewelry, clothing, glass, tinwork,
and furniture from Mexico as well as India, Eastern Europe, and China.
This is a good place to hunt for gifts and a great place to spend an hour
(at least) browsing.

Santo Domingo Pueblo

❺ *40 mi northeast of Albuquerque via I–25; exit on NM 22 and drive 4½
mi west.*

Santo Domingo Pueblo craftspeople sell outstanding *heishi* (shell) jew-
elry and pottery, along with other traditional arts and crafts, year-
round, but the pueblo's three-day Labor Day Arts and Crafts Fair brings
out artists and visitors in full force. The colorful, dramatic Corn Dance,

held in honor of St. Dominic, the pueblo's patron saint, on August 4, attracts more than 2,000 dancers, clowns, singers, and drummers. Painter Georgia O'Keeffe supposedly said the Corn Dance was one of the great events in her life. Still and video cameras, tape recorders, and sketching materials are prohibited. It's quite easy to visit the pueblo as part of a trip to Tent Rocks, covered in the South of Santa Fe section. ⊠ *Off NM 22, 4½ mi west of I–25* ☎ *505/465–2214* 🗺 *Donations encouraged* ☉ *Daily dawn–dusk.*

The Turquoise Trail

FodorsChoice
★

Etched out in the early 1970s and still well traveled is the scenic Turquoise Trail, which follows an old route between Albuquerque and Santa Fe that's dotted with ghost towns now being restored by writers, artists, and other urban refugees. This 70 mi of piñon-studded mountain back road is a gentle roller coaster of panoramic views of the Ortiz, Jémez, and Sangre de Cristo mountains. It's believed that 2,000 years ago Native Americans mined turquoise in these hills. The Spanish took up turquoise mining in the 16th century, and the practice continued into the early 20th century, with Tiffany & Co. removing a fair share of the semiprecious stone. In addition, gold, silver, tin, lead, and coal have been mined here. There's plenty of opportunity for picture-taking and picnicking along the way. The pace is slow, the talk is about the weather, and Albuquerque might as well be on another planet. The entire loop of this trip takes a day, the drive up the Sandia Crest a half day.

Sandia Park

❻ *7 mi north of Tijeras. From Tijeras, take I–40 east and exit north on the Turquoise Trail (NM 14); proceed 6 mi and turn left onto NM 536.*

Ⓒ At the **Sandia Ranger Station** you can pick up pamphlets and maps, and—if there are enough kids in the audience—witness a fire-prevention program with a Smokey the Bear motif. From here you can also embark on a short self-guided tour to the nearby **fire lookout tower** and **Tijeras Pueblo ruins;** the ranger station has maps and can provide details on how to do this. Here you can also pick up information on trails in Cibola National Forest, which encompasses the Sandia Mountains. ⊠ *11776 NM 337, south of I–40* ☎ *505/281–3304* ⊕ *www.fs.fed.us/r3/cibola/districts/ sandia.shtml* 🗺 *Free, $3 for parking in Cibola National Forest* ☉ *Weekdays 8–5, weekends 8:30–5.*

Ⓒ
FodorsChoice
★

It may take months for this odyssey of a place to completely sink in: quirky and utterly fascinating, **Tinkertown Museum** contains a world of miniature carved-wood characters. The museum's late founder, Ross Ward, spent more than 40 years carving and collecting the hundreds of figures that populate this cheerfully bizarre museum, including an animated miniature Western village, a Boot Hill cemetery, and a 1940s circus exhibit. Ragtime piano music, a 40-foot sailboat, and a life-size general store are other highlights. The walls surrounding this 22-room museum have been fashioned out of more than 50,000 glass bottles pressed into cement. This homage to folk art, found art, and eccentric kitsch tends to strike a chord with people of all ages. As you might expect, the gift shop offers plenty of fun oddities. ⊠ *121 Sandia Crest Rd., take Cedar Crest* *exit off I–40 east and follow signs to Sandia Crest turnoff* ☎ *505/281–5233* ⊕ *www.tinkertown.com* 💰 *$3* ⊙ *Apr.–Oct., daily 9–6.*

In Cedar Crest, just off NM 14 a couple of miles south of Sandia Park, the modest but nicely laid-out **Museum of Archaeology & Material Culture** chronicles archaeological finds and contains artifacts dating from the Ice Age to the Battle of Wounded Knee. Exhibits shed light on prehistoric man, buffalo hunting, a history of turquoise mining in north-central New Mexico, and the 1930s excavations of a cave about 15 mi away that offered evidence of some of the earliest human life in North America. ⊠ *22 Calvary Rd.* ☎ *505/281–4745* ⊕ *www.museummarch.org* 💰 *$3* ⊙ *May–Oct., daily noon–7.*

For awesome views of Albuquerque and half of New Mexico, take NM 536 up the back side of the Sandia Mountains through Cibola National ★ Forest to **Sandia Crest.** At the 10,378-foot summit, explore the foot trails along the rim (particularly in summer) and take in the breathtaking views of Albuquerque down below, and of the so-called Steel Forest—the nearby cluster of radio and television towers. Always bring an extra layer of clothing, even in summer—the temperature at the crest can be anywhere from 15 to 25 degrees cooler than down in Albuquerque. If you're in need of refreshments or are searching for some inexpensive souvenirs, visit the **Sandia Crest House Gift Shop and Restaurant** (☎ 505/243–0605), on the rim of the crest.

As you continue north up NM 14 from Sandia Park, after about 12 mi you pass through the sleepy village of **Golden,** the site of the first gold rush (in 1825) west of the Mississippi. It has a rock shop and a mercantile store. The rustic adobe church and graveyard are popular with photographers. Be aware that locals are very protective of this area and aren't known to warm up to strangers.

WHERE TO STAY 🏠 **Elaine's, A Bed and Breakfast.** This antique-filled three-story log-and-
★ **$–$$** stone home is set in the evergreen folds of the Sandia Mountain foothills. Four acres of wooded grounds beckon outside the back door. The top two floors have rooms with balconies and big picture windows that bring the lush mountain views indoors. The third-floor room also has cathedral ceilings and a brass bed; some rooms have fireplaces, and one has its own outside entrance. Breakfast, served in a plant-filled room or outside on a patio with a fountain, often includes fresh fruit, pancakes, or waffles with sausage. ⊠ *Snowline Estate, 72 Snowline Rd.* ⤴ *Box 444, Cedar Crest 87008* ☎ *505/281–2467 or 800/821–3092* ⊕ *www. elainesbnb.com* 🛏 *5 rooms* ⚫ *Some in-room hot tubs, outdoor hot tub; no room phones, no room TVs, no smoking* ⊟ *AE, D, DC, MC, V* ⨂ *BP.*

⚠ **Turquoise Trail Campground and RV Park.** Pine and cedar trees dot this 14-acre park in the Sandias, which has hiking trails with access to the Cibola National Forest. Adjacent to the premises is the Museum of Archaeology & Material Culture. Campsite rates are calculated per person; you will need reservations in October. ⊠ *22 Calvary Rd., 5 mi north of I–40 Exit 175 in Cedar Crest* ☎ *505/281–2005* 📧 *debswe@earthlink.com* ⚫ *Grills, laundry facilities, flush toilets, full hookups, partial hookups (electric and water), dump station, drinking water, showers,* *fire grates, fire pits, picnic tables, electricity, public telephone, general store, play area 🏕 57 sites, 45 with hookups 💲 $15–$25; cabins $29–$58.*

The 18-hole **Paa-Ko Ridge Golf Course** (✉ Sandia Park, 1 Club House Dr. ☎ 505/281–6000 or 866/898–5987 ⊕ www.paakoridge.com) has been voted "The Best Place to Play Golf in New Mexico" by *Golf Digest*. Golfers enjoy vistas of the mesas and the Sandia Mountains from any of five tee placements on each hole. Greens fees are $60–$75. The course is just off NM 14, 3½ mi north of the turnoff for Sandia Crest (NM 536).

Although less extensive and challenging than the ski areas farther north in the Sangre de Cristos, **Sandia Peak** (✉ NM 536 ☎ 505/242–9052, 505/857–8977 snow conditions ⊕ www.sandiapeak.com) is extremely popular with locals from Albuquerque and offers a nice range of novice, intermediate, and expert downhill trails; there's also a ski school. Snowboarding is welcome on all trails, and there's cross-country terrain as well, whenever snow is available. Snowfall can be sporadic, so call ahead to check for cross-country; Sandia has snow-making capacity for about 30 of its 200 acres of downhill skiing. The season runs from mid-December to mid-March, and lift tickets cost $43. Keep in mind that you can also access the ski area year-round via the Sandia Peak Aerial Tramway (*see* Chapter 1, Albuquerque), which is faster from Albuquerque than driving all the way around. In summer, the ski area converts into a fantastic mountain-biking and hiking terrain. The ski area offers a number of packages with bike and helmet rentals and lift tickets. Other summer activities at Sandia Peak include sand-pit volleyball, horseshoes, and picnicking.

Madrid

❼ *37 mi northeast of Albuquerque, 12 mi northeast of Golden on NM 14.*

Totally abandoned when its coal mine closed in the 1950s, Madrid has gradually been rebuilt and is now—to the dismay of some longtime locals—on the verge of trendiness. The entire town was offered for sale for $250,000 back then, but there were no takers. Finally, in the early 1970s, a few artists fleeing big cities settled in and began restoration. Weathered houses and old company stores have been repaired and turned into boutiques and galleries, some of them selling high-quality furniture, paintings, and crafts. Big events here include Old Timers Days on July 4 weekend, and the Christmas open house, held weekends in December, when galleries and studios are open and the famous Madrid Christmas lights twinkle brightly.

NEED A BREAK?

Aged hippies, youthful hipsters, and everyone in between congregate at Java Junction (✉ 2855 NM 14 ☎ 505/438–2772) for lattes, chai, sandwiches, pastries, and other toothsome treats. Upstairs there's a pleasantly decorated room for rent that can sleep up to three guests.

🐾 Madrid's **Old Coal Mine Museum** is a remnant of a once-flourishing industry. Children can explore the old tunnel, climb aboard a 1900 steam train, and poke through antique buildings full of marvelous relics. Museum tickets are available at the Mine Shaft Tavern out front. On weekends at 3 PM from late May to mid-October you can cheer the heroes and hiss the villains of the old-fashioned melodramas performed at the **Engine House Theater.** The theater, inside a converted roundhouse machine shop, has a full-size steam train that comes chugging onto the stage. ✉ *2814 NM 14* ☎ *505/438–3780* ⊕ *www.oldcoalminemuseum.com* 🎟 *Museum $4, melodrama $10* 🕐 *Late May–mid-Oct., weekdays 9:30–5, weekends 9:30–6; mid-Oct.–late May, daily 10–4.*

WHERE TO EAT ✕ **Mineshaft Tavern.** A rollicking old bar and restaurant adjacent to the
★ ¢–$ Old Coal Mine Museum, this boisterous place was a miners' commissary back in the day. Today it serves what many people consider to be the best green-chile cheeseburger in New Mexico, along with ice-cold beer and a selection of other pub favorites and comfort foods. ✉ *2846 NM 14* ☎ *505/473–0743* 🍴 *D, MC, V* 🕐 *No dinner Mon., Tues., and Thurs.*

SHOPPING The town of Madrid has only one street, so the three-dozen-or-so shops and galleries are easy to find.

You can watch live glassblowing demonstrations at **Al Leedom Studio** (☎ 505/473–2054); his vibrant vases and bowls are sold alongside the beautiful handcrafted jewelry of wife Barbara Leedom. The Leedoms' friendly cat and dancing dog are also big crowd pleasers. In a pale-blue cottage in the center of town, the **Ghost Town Trading Post** (☎ 505/471–7605) is a great bet for fine Western jewelry fashioned out of local gemstones (not just turquoise but opal, amber, and onyx). **Johnsen & Swan** (☎ 505/473–1963) stocks fine leather belts, bags, and wallets; beadwork; custom-made chaps; and Western-inspired jewelry and gifts. **Johnsons of Madrid** (☎ 505/471–1054) ranks among the most prestigious galleries in town, showing painting, photography, sculpture, and textiles created by some of the region's leading artists. You could spend hours browsing the fine rugs and furnishings at **Seppanen & Daughters Fine Textiles** (☎ 505/424–7470), which stocks custom textiles from Oaxaca, Navajo weavings, Tibetan carpets, and fine Arts and Crafts tables, sofas, and chairs.

Cerrillos
8 *3 mi northeast of Madrid on NM 14.*

Cerrillos was a boomtown in the 1880s—its mines brimmed with gold, silver, and turquoise, and eight newspapers, four hotels, and 21 taverns flourished. When the mines went dry the town went bust. Since then, Cerrillos has served as the backdrop for feature-film and television westerns, among them *Young Guns* and *Lonesome Dove*. Today, it might easily be mistaken for a ghost town, which it's been well on the way to becoming for decades. Time has left its streets dry, dusty, and almost deserted, although the occasional passing Amtrak or freight train roaring through town serves as a reminder of what century you're in.

Casa Grande (✉ 17 Waldo ☎ 505/438–3008), a 21-room adobe (several rooms of which are part of a shop), has a small museum ($2) with a display of early mining exhibits. There's also a petting zoo ($2) and a scenic overlook. Casa Grande is open daily 8 AM–sunset.

Pack rats and browsers alike ought not to miss the **What-Not Shop** (⌂ 15B 1st St. ☎ 505/471–2744), a venerable secondhand–antiques shop of a half-century's standing packed floor to ceiling with Native American pottery, cut glass, rocks, political buttons, old postcards, clocks, and who knows what else.

WHERE TO
STAY & EAT
¢–$
Fodor'sChoice
★

✕ **San Marcos Cafe.** In Lone Butte, north of Cerrillos, this restaurant is known for its creative fare and nontraditional setting—an actual feed store, with roosters, turkeys, and peacocks running about outside. In one of the two bric-a-brac–filled dining rooms, sample rich cinnamon rolls and such delectables as burritos stuffed with roast beef and potatoes and topped with green chile, and the classic eggs San Marcos, tortillas stuffed with scrambled eggs and topped with guacamole, pinto beans, melted Jack cheese, and red chile. Hot apple pie à la mode with rum sauce is a favorite. Expect a wait on weekends unless you make a reservation. ⌂ *3877 NM 14* ☎ *505/471–9298* ▤ *MC, V* ⊘ *No dinner.*

$$

▥ **High Feather Ranch.** A grand adobe homestead opened as a B&B in 2001, plush High Feather Ranch anchors 65 wide-open acres with breathtaking views of the Ortiz, Jémez, and Sangre de Cristo mountains. It feels completely removed from civilization but is, in fact, within an hour's drive of both Santa Fe and Albuquerque. Although newly built, the sprawling inn contains reclaimed 19th-century timber, antique gates, and fine vintage furnishings. Rooms have high ceilings and plenty of windows, and you're never far from a portal or patio; one room has an outdoor shower in a private courtyard. Rates include an impressive full breakfast. ⌂ *29 High Feather Ranch, off CR 55, 87010* ☎ *505/424–1333 or 800/757–4410* ⊕ *www.highfeatherranch-bnb.com* ⇌ *2 rooms, 1 suite* ₷ *Some in-room hot tubs, massage, hiking, horseback riding, some pets allowed; no room phones, no room TVs, no smoking* ▤ *AE, D, MC, V* ⎪◎⎪ *BP.*

SPORTS &
THE OUTDOORS
★

Rides with **Broken Saddle Riding Co.** (⌂ Off NM 14, Cerrillos ☎ 505/424–7774 ⊕ www.brokensaddle.com) take you around the old turquoise and silver mines the Cerrillos area is noted for. On a Tennessee Walker or a Missouri Fox Trotter you can explore the Cerrillos hills and canyons, 23 mi southeast of Santa Fe. This is not the usual nose-to-tail trail ride.

SIDE TRIPS FROM SANTA FE

You can hardly grasp the profundity of New Mexico's ancient past or its immense landscape without journeying into the hinterland. Each of the excursions below can be accomplished in a day or less, but in the cases of Abiquiu and Los Alamos it's worth considering an overnight. The High Road to Taos is a very full day, so start early or plan to spend the night near or in Taos, or along the way in Chimayó.

South of Santa Fe

The most prominent side trip south of the city is along the fabled Turquoise Trail, an excellent—if leisurely—alternative route to Albuquerque that's far more interesting than I–25; it's covered earlier in this chapter under the Side Trips from Albuquerque section. Although the drive down I–25 offers some fantastic views of the Jémez and Sandia mountains, the most interesting sites south of town require hopping off the interstate. From here you can uncover the region's history at El Rancho de las Golondrinas and enjoy one of New Mexico's most dramatic day hikes at Tent Rocks canyon. Conversely, if you leave Santa Fe via I–25 north and then cut down in a southerly direction along U.S. 285 and NM 41, you come to tiny Galisteo, an engaging little hamlet steeped in Spanish-colonial history.

Pecos National Historic Park

★ ❾ *25 mi east of Santa Fe on I–25.*

Pecos was the last major encampment that travelers on the Santa Fe Trail reached before Santa Fe. Today the little village is mostly a starting point for exploring the Pecos National Historic Park, the centerpiece of which is the **ruins of Pecos,** once a major Pueblo village with more than 1,100 rooms. Twenty-five hundred people are thought to have lived in this structure, as high as five stories in places. Pecos, in a fertile valley between the Great Plains and the Rio Grande Valley, was a trading center centuries before the Spanish conquistadors visited in about 1540. The Spanish later returned to build two missions.

The Pueblo was abandoned in 1838, and its 17 surviving occupants moved to the Jémez Pueblo. Anglo travelers on the Santa Fe Trail observed the mission ruins with a great sense of fascination (and relief—for they knew it meant their journey was nearly over). A couple of miles from the ruins, **Andrew Kozlowski's Ranch** served as a stage depot, where a fresh spring quenched the thirsts of horses and weary passengers. The ranch now houses the park's law-enforcement corps and is not open to the public. You can view the mission ruins and the excavated pueblo on a ¼-mi self-guided tour in about two hours.

The pivotal Civil War battle of Glorieta Pass took place on an outlying parcel of parkland in late March 1862; a victory over Confederate forces firmly established the Union army's control over the New Mexico Territory. The Union troops maintained headquarters at Kozlowski's Ranch during the battle. Check out the park visitor center for information about guided park tours (in summer only) and to see exhibits on the region's checkered history. ✉ *NM 63, off I–25 at Exit 307, Pecos* ☎ *505/757–6414* ⊕ *www.nps.gov/peco* ☜ *$3* ☉ *Late May–early Sept., daily 8–6; early Sept.–late May, daily 8–5.*

Galisteo

❿ *25 mi south of Santa Fe via I–25 north to U.S. 285 to NM 41 south.*

South of Santa Fe lie the immense open spaces of the sublime Galisteo Basin and the quintessential New Mexican village of Galisteo—a harmonious blend of multigenerational New Mexicans and recent migrants who protect and treasure the bucolic solitude of their home. The drive from Santa Fe takes about 30 minutes and offers a panoramic view of the surreal, sculpted landscape of the Galisteo Basin, which is an austere contrast to the alpine country of the Sangre de Cristos. It's a good place to go for a leisurely lunch or a sunset drive to dinner, maybe with

horseback riding. Galisteo is probably most famous for **Vista Clara Ranch** (⊠ NM 41 ☎ 505/466–4772 or 888/663–9772 ⊕ www.vistaclara. com), an ultraposh spa resort known for its holistic approach and incredibly fancy digs. The 140-acre resort closed in 2004 and is, as of this writing, undergoing a complete refurbishment and transformation into a residential condo resort. It's expected to reopen again in mid-2007, with rates beginning at $250 per person, per night.

Founded as a Spanish outpost in 1614 and built largely with rocks from nearby Pueblo ruins, Galisteo has many artists and equestrians (trail rides and rentals are available at local stables). Cottonwoods shade the low-lying pueblo-style architecture, a premier example of vernacular use of adobe and stone. The small church is open only for Sunday services.

WHERE TO STAY & EAT
★ $–$$$

✕⌺ **The Galisteo Inn.** This rambling old adobe hacienda has been transformed into an idyllic inn. Worn pine floors and massive wood beams rich in patina and vistas and patios from which to enjoy them add to the privacy and romance of this upscale refuge, which also has two cozy, economical rooms that share a bath. Many rooms, including one of the inexpensive ones, have fireplaces, and all are decorated with tasteful, understated antiques and hand-crafted newer pieces. The acclaimed La Mancha Restaurant ($–$$$; no dinner Sunday and Monday, reservations essential) serves superb contemporary, Latin-infused cuisine and is well worth a visit whether or not you're staying at the inn. The often-changing menu might feature pistachio-crusted Dungeness crab cakes with pineapple-caper tartar sauce, and an unusual "mac-and-cheese" with orzo pasta, black truffles, oyster mushrooms, goat cheese, and white-truffle essence. There's also a wonderful Sunday brunch as well as a lighter tapas menu. ⊠ *9 La Vega St.* ⌖ *HC 75, Box 4, Galisteo 87540* ☎ *505/ 466–8200 or 866/404–8200* 🖶 *505/466–4008* ⊕ *www.galisteoinn. com* ↪ *11 rooms, 9 with bath; 1 suite* ⌂ *Restaurant, cable TV, Wi-Fi, pool, hot tub, massage, sauna, horseback riding; no kids under 10, no smoking* ⊟ *D, MC, V* ⊠ *BP.*

SPORTS & THE OUTDOORS

Galarosa Stable (⊠ NM 41, Galisteo ☎ 505/466–4654 or 505/670–2467 ⊕ www.galarosastables.com) provides rentals by the half- or full day south of Santa Fe in the panoramic Galisteo Basin.

El Rancho de las Golondrinas
★ ⑪ *15 mi south of Santa Fe off I–25's Exit 276 in La Cienega.*

The "Williamsburg of the Southwest," El Rancho de las Golondrinas ("the ranch of the swallows") is a reconstruction of a small agricultural village with buildings from the 17th to 19th century. Travelers on the El Camino Real would stop at the ranch before making the final leg of the journey north, a half-day ride from Santa Fe in horse-and-wagon time. By car, the ranch is only a 25-minute drive from the Plaza. From I–25, the village is tucked away from view, frozen in time. Owned and operated by the Paloheimo family, direct descendants of those who owned the ranch when it functioned as a *paraje,* or stopping place, the grounds maintain an authentic character without compromising history for commercial gain. Even the gift shop carries items that reflect ranch life and the cultural exchange that took place there.

Self-guided tours survey Spanish-colonial lifestyles in New Mexico from 1660 to 1890: you can view a molasses mill, threshing grounds, and wheelwright and blacksmith shops, as well as a mountain village and a *morada* (meeting place) of the order of Penitentes (a religious fraternity known for its reenactment during Holy Week of the tortures suffered by Christ). Farm animals roam through the barnyards on the 200-acre complex. Wool from the sheep is spun into yarn and woven into traditional Rio Grande–style blankets, and the corn grown is used to feed the animals. During the spring and harvest festivals, on the first weekends of June and October, respectively, the village comes alive with Spanish-American folk music, dancing, and food and crafts demonstrations. ⊠ *334 Los Pinos Rd.* ☏ *505/471–2261* ⊕ *www.golondrinas. org* ≋ *$5* ⊙ *June–Sept., Wed.–Sun. 10–4; some additional weekends for special events.*

WHERE TO
STAY & EAT
$–$$ ✕🅷 **Sunrise Springs Inn.** Down the road from Las Golondrinas, this minire-sort offers guests holistic-based rest and rejuvenation. The sleek, mini-malist accommodations are either in private casitas, with kitchenettes and fireplaces, or in a standard room; four rooms and two suites are located near the Samadhi Spa, which specializes in Far Eastern body work. Other amenities at this lush retreat with ponds and gardens are a Japanese-style teahouse and the Sages Art Center, which holds a raku-pottery studio and offers classes in raku, yoga, and tai chi. You can enjoy fine, globally inspired cuisine at the Blue Heron restaurant ($$–$$$); try the duck confit hot pot with noodles and ginger broth, or house-smoked tofu with sesame-sautéed greens, coconut sweet potatoes, and fresh garden vegetables. ⊠ *242 Los Pinos Rd., Santa Fe 87507* ☏ *505/471–3600 or 800/955–0028* 🖷 *505/471–7365* ⊕ *www.sunrisesprings.com* ➘ *38 rooms, 20 casitas, 2 suites* ⚘ *Restaurant, some kitchenettes, some refrigerators, cable TV, some in-room DVDs, hot tubs, spa, bar, meeting rooms; no TV in some rooms* ⊟ *AE, D, MC, V.*

Kasha-Katuwe Tent Rocks National Monument

⓬ *40 mi south of Santa Fe via I–25, Exit 264.*

Fodor'sChoice
★

This is a terrific hiking getaway, especially if you have time for only one hike. The sandstone rock formations look like stacked tents in a stark, water- and wind-eroded box canyon. Located 45 minutes south of Santa Fe, near Cochiti Pueblo, Tent Rocks offers excellent hiking year-round, although it can get hot in summer, when you should bring extra water. The drive to this magical landscape is equally awesome, as the road heads west toward Cochiti Dam and through the cottonwood groves around the pueblo. It's a good hike for kids. The round-trip hiking distance is only 2 mi, about 1½ hours, but it's the kind of place where you'll want to hang out for a while. Take a camera. There are no facilities here, just a small parking area with a posted trail map and a self-pay admission box; you can get gas and pick up picnic supplies and bottled water at Cochiti Lake Convenience Store. ⊠ *I–25 south to Cochiti Exit 264; follow NM 16 for 8 mi, turning right onto NM 22; continue approximately 3½ more mi past Cochiti Pueblo entrance; turn right onto BIA 92, which after 2 mi becomes Forest Service Rd. 266, a rough road of jarring, washboarded gravel that leads 5 mi to well-marked parking area*

☎ 505/761–8700 ⊕ www.nm.blm.gov ✉ $5 per vehicle ☸ Apr.–Oct., daily 7–7; Nov.–Mar., daily 8–5.

SPORTS &
THE OUTDOORS
The 18-hole, par-72 **Pueblo de Cochiti Golf Course** (✉ 5200 Cochiti Hwy., Cochiti Lake ☎ 505/465–2239 ⊕ www.pueblodecochiti.org/golfcourse. html), set against a backdrop of steep canyons and red-rock mesas, is a 45-minute drive southwest of Santa Fe. Cochiti was designed by Robert Trent Jones Jr. and offers one of the most challenging and visually stunning golfing experiences in the state. Greens fees are $45–$55.

Pueblos near Santa Fe

A pleasant side trip is to visit several of the state's 19 pueblos, including San Ildefonso, one of the state's most picturesque, and Santa Clara, whose lands harbor a dramatic set of ancient cliff dwellings. Between the two reservations sits the ominous landmark called Black Mesa, which you can see from NM 30 or NM 502. The solitary butte has inspired many painters, including Georgia O'Keeffe. Plan on spending one to three hours at each pueblo, and leave the day open if you're there for a feast day, when dances are set to an organic rather than mechanical clock. Pueblo grounds and hiking areas do not permit pets.

Pojoaque Pueblo

13 *17 mi north of Santa Fe on U.S. 285/84.*

There's not much to see in the pueblo's plaza area, but the state visitor center and adjoining **Poeh Cultural Center and Museum** on U.S. 285/84 are worth a visit. The latter is an impressive complex of traditional adobe buildings, including the three-story Sun Tower; the facility comprises a museum, a cultural center, and artists' studios. The museum holds some 8,000 photographs, including many by esteemed early-20th-century photographer Edward S. Curtis, as well as hundreds of works of both traditional and contemporary pottery, jewelry, textiles, and sculpture. There are frequent demonstrations by artists, exhibitions, and, on Saturday from May through September, traditional ceremonial dances. By the early 20th century the pueblo was virtually uninhabited, but the survivors eventually began to restore it. Pojoaque's feast day is celebrated with dancing on December 12. The visitor center is one of the friendliest and best stocked in northern New Mexico, with free maps and literature on hiking, fishing, and the area's history. The crafts shop in the visitor center is one of the most extensive among the state's pueblos; it carries weaving, pottery, jewelry, and other crafts by both Pojoaque and other indigenous New Mexicans.

The pueblo also operates the adjacent **Cities of Gold Casino Resort** (☎ 505/455–3313 or 800/455–3313 ⊕ www.citiesofgold.com), which comprises a 40,000-square-foot casino with the only poker room in northern New Mexico, sports bar and simulcast, Towa Golf Resort, and several shops and restaurants. Additionally, beside Towa Golf Resort, is a 79-room Homewood Suites hotel, which opened in 2005. And as of this writing, construction was underway on a new upscale resort accommodation to be operated by Hilton, called the Buffalo Thunder Resort. This property—which will be similar in scope to the Hyatt Tamaya and

Pueblo Etiquette

WHEN VISITING PUEBLOS AND RESERVATIONS, you're expected to follow a certain etiquette. Each pueblo has its own regulations for the use of still and video cameras and video and tape recorders, as well as for sketching and painting. Some pueblos, such as Santo Domingo, prohibit photography altogether. Others, such as Santa Clara, prohibit photography at certain times; for example, during ritual dances. Still others allow photography but require a permit, which usually costs from $10 to $20, depending on whether you use a still or video camera. The privilege of setting up an easel and painting all day will cost you as little as $35 or as much as $150 (at Taos Pueblo). Associated fees for using images also can vary widely, depending on what kind of reproduction rights you might require. Be sure to **ask permission before photographing anyone in the pueblos**; it's also customary to give the subject a dollar or two for agreeing to be photographed. Native American law prevails on the pueblos, and violations of photography regulations could result in confiscation of cameras.

Specific restrictions for the various pueblos are noted in the individual descriptions. Other rules are described below.

• Possessing or using drugs and/or alcohol on Native American land is forbidden.

• Ritual dances often have serious religious significance and should be respected as such. Silence is mandatory—that means no questions about ceremonies or dances while they're being performed. Don't walk across the dance plaza during a performance, and don't applaud afterward.

• Kivas and ceremonial rooms are restricted to pueblo members only.

• Cemeteries are sacred. They're off-limits to all visitors and should never be photographed.

• Unless pueblo dwellings are clearly marked as shops, don't wander or peek inside. Remember, these are private homes.

• Many of the pueblo buildings are hundreds of years old. Don't try to scale adobe walls or climb on top of buildings, or you may come tumbling down.

• Don't litter. Nature is sacred on the pueblos, and defacing land can be a serious offense.

• Don't bring your pet or feed stray dogs.

• Even off reservation sites, state and federal laws prohibit picking up artifacts such as arrowheads or pottery from public lands.

Sandia resorts near Albuquerque, adjoins the casino and will comprise 400 upscale rooms, an expanded casino, a 35,000-square-foot convention center, and a high-caliber performing arts center. The project is expected to be completed in 2008. Sketching, cameras, and video cameras are prohibited, except during Saturday Native American dances. ⊠ 78 *Cities of Gold Rd., off U.S. 285/84, 17 mi north of Santa Fe* ☎ *505/455–*

3334 ⊕ www.poehmuseum.com ⌨ Donation suggested ⊙ Apr.–Dec., Mon.–Sat. 9–5, Sun. 10–4; Jan.–Mar., Mon.–Sat. 9–5:30, Sun. 10–4.

WHERE TO STAY
$–$$$

🏨 **Homewood Suites Santa Fe–North.** Opened in 2005 on the Pojoaque Pueblo, right by the Cities of Gold Casino and nearly adjacent to Towa Golf Resort, this all-suites extended-stay property is a good bet even if you're not planning to spend much time at Pojoaque—it's a practical base for exploring Los Alamos, the High Road to Taos, Española, and even Taos, and it's just a 20-minute drive north of Santa Fe. All of the brightly furnished units in this immaculately kept three-story adobe hotel have full kitchens, large work areas, and great views of the golf course and surrounding mountains. Rates include full breakfast and an evening snack and cocktail receptions Monday through Thursday nights. The top rooms have fireplaces, and some have two bedrooms. ⊠ *18 Buffalo Trail, Santa Fe 87506* ☎ *505/455–9100 or 800/225–5466* 🖷 *505/455–9111* ⊕ *www.santafenorth.homewoodsuites.com* 🛏 *79 suites* ♿ *Kitchens, cable TV, in-room VCRs, Wi-Fi, gym, pool, 18-hole golf course, putting green, driving range, laundry facilities, business services, meeting rooms, some pets allowed* ☰ *AE, D, MC, V* ⦿⧘ *BP.*

SPORTS &
THE OUTDOORS

The **Towa Golf Resort** (⊠ Cities of Gold Casino Resort, 17746 U.S. 285/84, Pojoaque ☎ 505/455–9000 or 877/465–3489 ⊕ www.towagolf.com) was designed by pro legend Hale Irwin and sits in the foothills of the Sangre de Cristos, with stunning views of the Santa Fe ski basin and the Jémez Mountains over Los Alamos. The challenging 18-hole course opened in 2001; another 9 holes were added in 2003, and plans call for the unveiling of yet another 9 holes down the road, once the new hotel and resort is completed. Greens fees are $64.

Nambé Pueblo

⑭ *4 mi east of Pojoaque on NM 503, 20 mi north of Santa Fe.*

Nambé Pueblo has no visitor center, so the best time to visit is during the October 4 feast day of St. Francis celebration or the very popular July 4 celebration. If you want to explore the landscape surrounding the pueblo, take the drive past the pueblo until you come to **Nambé Falls and Nambé Lake Recreation Area** (☎ 505/455–2304). There's a shady picnic area and a large fishing lake that's open March–November (the cost is $10 for fishing, and $20 for boating—no gas motors are permitted). The waterfalls are about a 15-minute hike in from the parking and picnic area along a rocky, clearly marked path. The water pours over a rock precipice—a loud and dramatic sight given the river's modest size. Overnight RV ($35) and tent ($25) camping are also offered. ⊠ *Nambé Pueblo Rd. off NM 503* ☎ *505/455–4444* ⊕ *www.nambefalls.com* ⌨ *$8 per car.*

San Ildefonso Pueblo

⑮ *23 mi north of Santa Fe via U.S. 285/84 to NM 502 west.*

Maria Martinez, one of the most renowned Pueblo potters, lived here. She first created her exquisite "black on black" pottery in 1919 and in doing so sparked a major revival of all Pueblo arts and crafts. She died in 1980, and the 26,000-acre San Ildefonso Pueblo remains a major center for pottery and other arts and crafts. Many artists sell from their homes, and there are trading posts, a visitor center, and a museum where some of Martinez's work can be seen on weekdays. San Ildefonso is also one of the more visually appealing pueblos, with a well-defined plaza core and a spectacular setting beneath the Pajarito Plateau and Black Mesa. The pueblo's feast day is January 23, when unforgettable buffalo, deer, and Comanche dances are performed from dawn to dusk. Cameras are not permitted at any of the ceremonial dances but may be used at other times with a permit. ⊠ *NM 502* ☏ *505/455–3549* 🎫 *$5 per vehicle, still-camera permit $10, video recorder permit $20, sketching permit $15* ⊙ *Daily 8–5; museum weekdays 8–4:30.*

Santa Clara Pueblo

 27 mi northwest of Santa Fe, 10 mi north of San Ildefonso Pueblo via NM 30.

Santa Clara Pueblo, southwest of Española, is the home of a historic treasure—the awesome **Puyé Cliff Dwellings,** believed to have been built in the 13th to 14th centuries. They can be seen by driving 9 mi up a gravel road through a canyon, south of the village off NM 502. The pueblo also contains four ponds, miles of stream fishing, and picnicking and camping facilities. You can tour the cliff dwellings, topped by the ruins of a 740-room pueblo, on your own or with a guide. Permits for the use of trails, camping, and picnic areas, as well as for fishing in trout ponds, are available at the sites; recreation areas are open April–October, dawn–dusk.

The village's shops sell burnished red pottery, engraved blackware, paintings, and other arts and crafts. All pottery is made via the coil method, not with a pottery wheel. Santa Clara is known for its carved pieces, and Avanyu, a water serpent that guards the waters, is the pueblo's symbol. Other typical works include engagement baskets, wedding vessels, and seed pots. The pueblo's feast day of St. Claire is celebrated on August 12. ⊠ *Off NM 502 on NM 30, Española* ☏ *505/753–7326* 🎫 *Pueblo free, cliff dwellings $5, video and still-camera permits $15* ⊙ *Daily 8–4:30.*

Jémez Country

In the Jémez region, the 1,000-year-old Anasazi ruins at Bandelier National Monument present a vivid contrast to Los Alamos National Laboratory, birthplace of the atomic bomb. You can easily take in part of Jémez Country in a day trip from Santa Fe.

On this tour you can see terrific views of the Rio Grande Valley, the Sangre de Cristos, the Galisteo Basin, and, in the distance, the Sandias. There are places to eat and shop for essentials in Los Alamos and a few roadside eateries along NM 4 in La Cueva and Jémez Springs. There are also numerous turnouts along NM 4, several that have paths leading down to the many excellent fishing spots along the Jémez River.

The 48,000-acre Cerro Grande fire of May 2000 burned much of the pine forest in the lower Jémez Mountains, as well as more than 250 homes in Los Alamos. Parts of the drive are still scarred with charcoaled remains, but most of the vegetation has returned, and many homes have been rebuilt in the residential areas.

Los Alamos

⑰ *35 mi from Santa Fe via U.S. 285/84 north to NM 502 west.*

Look at old books on New Mexico and you rarely find a mention of Los Alamos, now a busy town of 19,000 that has the highest per capita income in the state. Like so many other Southwestern communities, Los Alamos was created expressly as a company town; only here the workers weren't mining iron, manning freight trains, or hauling lumber—they were busy toiling at America's foremost nuclear research facility, Los Alamos National Laboratory (LANL). The facility still employs some 8,000 full-time workers, most who live in town but many others who live in the Española Valley and even northern Santa Fe. The lab has experienced some tough times in recent years, from the infamous Wen Ho Lee espionage case in the late '90s to a slew of alleged security breaches in 2003 and 2004. The controversies have shed some doubt on the future of LANL; at the very least, it's possible that the University of California, which has managed the lab on behalf of the U.S. Department of Energy, may cease its operations of LANL.

A few miles from ancient cave dwellings, scientists led by J. Robert Oppenheimer built Fat Man and Little Boy, the atom bombs that in August 1945 decimated Hiroshima and Nagasaki, respectively. LANL was created in 1943 under the auspices of the intensely covert Manhattan Project, whose express purpose it was to expedite an Allied victory during World War II. Indeed, Japan surrendered—but a full-blown Cold War between Russia and the United States ensued for another four and a half decades.

Despite the negative publicity of recent years, LANL works hard today to promote its broader platforms, including "enhancing global nuclear security" but also finding new ways to detect radiation, fighting pollution and environmental risks associated with nuclear energy, and furthering studies of the solar system, biology, and computer sciences. Similarly, the town of Los Alamos strives to be more well rounded, better understood, and tourist-friendly.

The **Bradbury Science Museum** is Los Alamos National Laboratory's public showcase, and its exhibits offer a balanced and provocative examination of such topics as atomic weapons and nuclear power. You can experiment with lasers; witness research in solar, geothermal, fission, and fusion energy; learn about DNA fingerprinting; and view exhibits about World War II's Project Y (the Manhattan Project, whose participants developed the atomic bomb). ⊠ *Los Alamos National Laboratory, 15th St. and Central Ave.* ☎ *505/667–4444* ⊕ *www.lanl. gov/museum* 🖾 *Free* ⊙ *Tues.–Fri. 9–5, Sat.–Mon. 1–5.*

New Mexican architect John Gaw Meem designed **Fuller Lodge,** a short drive up Central Avenue from the Bradbury Science Museum. The massive log building was erected in 1928 as a dining and recreation hall for a small private boys' school. In 1942 the federal government purchased the school and made it the base of operations for the Manhattan Project. Part of the lodge contains an art center that shows the works of northern New Mexican artists; there's a picturesque rose garden on the grounds. ⊠ *2132 Central Ave.* ☎ *505/662–9331* ⊕ *www.artfulnm. org* 🖭 *Free* ☉ *Mon.–Sat. 10–4.*

NEED A BREAK? Join the ranks of locals, Los Alamos National Laboratory employees, and tourists who line up each morning at **Chili Works** (⊠ 1743 Trinity Dr. ☎ 505/662–7591) to sample one of the state's best breakfast burritos. This inexpensive, simple take-out spot is also worth a stop to grab lunch before heading off for a hike at Bandelier.

The **Los Alamos Historical Museum,** in a log building beside Fuller Lodge, displays exhibits on the once-volatile geological history of the volcanic Jémez Mountains, the 700-year history of human life in this area, and more on—you guessed it—the Manhattan Project. It's rather jarring to observe ancient Anasazi potsherds and arrowheads in one display and photos of an obliterated Nagasaki in the next. ⊠ *1921 Juniper St.* ☎ *505/662–4493* ⊕ *www.losalamoshistory.org* 🖭 *Free* ☉ *Mon.–Sat. 9:30–4:30, Sun. 1–4.*

WHERE TO STAY & EAT

$–$$ ✕ **Blue Window Bistro.** Despite its relative wealth, Los Alamos has never cultivated much of a dining scene, which makes this cheerful and elegant restaurant all the more appreciated by foodies. The kitchen turns out a mix of New Mexican, American, and Continental dishes, from a first-rate Cobb salad to steak topped with Jack cheese and green chile to double-cut pork chops with mashed potatoes, applewood-smoked bacon, and red-onion marmalade. In addition to the softly lighted dining room with terra-cotta walls, there are several tables on a patio overlooking a lush garden. ⊠ *813 Central Ave.* ☎ *505/662–6305* ⊟ *AE, D, DC, MC, V* ☉ *Closed Mon.*

$ ✕🖬 **Quality Inn Los Alamos.** Rooms in this one-story hotel, which became part of the Quality Inn chain following a significant renovation in 2005, have modern Southwestern decor, large work desks, attractive white-tile bathrooms, and sweeping canyon views. A full hot breakfast buffet is included. The hotel's Trinity Beverage Company ($–$$$) serves commendable American fare with contemporary accents, such as pistachio-crusted salmon with pineapple beurre blanc, and seared duck breast with chipotle sauce. There's live music many nights, and a nice selection of microbrew beers. ⊠ *2201 Trinity Dr., 87544* ☎ *505/662–7211 or 877/424–6423* 🖷 *505/661–7714* ⊕ *www.qualityinnlosalamos.com* ⇗ *115 rooms* △ *Restaurant, BBQs, some kitchenettes, refrigerators, cable TV, Wi-Fi, pool, bar, business services, meeting rooms, some pets allowed* ⊟ *AE, D, DC, MC, V* ❤️ *CP.*

$ 🖬 **Best Western Hilltop House Hotel.** Minutes from the Los Alamos National Laboratory, this well-kept three-story hotel hosts both vacationers and scientists. Rooms are done with contemporary, functional furniture and have microwaves, refrigerators, and coffeemakers; deluxe ones have kitchenettes. The very good Blue Window Bistro is next door. ⊠ *400 Trinity Dr., Box 250, 87544* ☎ *505/662–2441 or 800/462–0936*

☎ 505/662–5913 ⊕ www.bestwesternlosalamos.com ⟿ 87 rooms, 13 suites ⚇ Restaurant, room service, some kitchenettes, refrigerators, cable TV, Wi-Fi, indoor pool, gym, hot tub, sauna, lounge, laundry facilities, meeting rooms, some pets allowed ⊟ AE, D, DC, MC, V ¶◯| CP.

SPORTS &
THE OUTDOORS

Tsankawi Trail (pronounced sank-ah-*wee*) will take you through the Pajarito Plateau's ancient rock trails, near Bandelier National Monument. The Pueblo people created the trails in the 1400s as they made their way from their mesa-top homes to the fields and springs in the canyon below. In the 1½ mi loop you can see petroglyphs and south-facing cave dwellings. Wear good shoes for the rocky path and a climb on a 12-foot ladder that shoots between a crevasse in the rock and the highest point of the mesa. This is an ideal walk if you don't have time to explore Bandelier National Monument in depth. It's on the way to Los Alamos, about a 35-minute drive from Santa Fe. ⊠ *From NM 502, take turnoff for White Rock, NM 4; continue west for about 10 mi to sign for Tsankawi on left; trail is clearly marked* ☎ *505/672–3861.*

Pajarito Mountain Ski Area (⊠ 397 Camp May Rd., off NM 501, just west of downtown Los Alamos ☎ 505/662–5725 ⊕ www.skipajarito. com), a small, low-key area near Los Alamos, has some excellent long runs and a good selection of wide-open, intermediate mogul runs, plus a terrain park; the base elevation is 9,200 feet, and there's a vertical rise drop of 1,410 feet. There's no artificial snowmaking, so the slopes are barely open during dry winters and the season runs according to conditions (usually about mid-December through April). But there's never a wait for the five lifts. In summer there's mountain biking on Pajarito's trails.

Bandelier National Monument

⑱ *10 mi south of Los Alamos via NM 501 south to NM 4 east; 40 mi north of Santa Fe via U.S. 285/84 north to NM 502 west to NM 4 west.*

Seven centuries before the Declaration of Independence was signed, compact city-states existed in the Southwest. Remnants of one of the most impressive of them can be seen at **Frijoles Canyon** in Bandelier National Monument. At the canyon's base, beside a gurgling stream, are the remains of cave dwellings, ancient ceremonial kivas, and other stone structures that stretch out for more than a mile beneath the sheer walls of the canyon's tree-fringed rim. For hundreds of years the Anasazi people, relatives of today's Rio Grande Pueblo Indians, thrived on wild game, corn, and beans. Suddenly, for reasons still undetermined, the settlements were abandoned.

Wander through the site on a paved, self-guided trail. If you can climb steep wooden ladders and squeeze through narrow doorways, you can explore some of the cave dwellings and cell-like rooms.

Bandelier National Monument, named after author and ethnologist Adolph Bandelier (his novel *The Delight Makers* is set in Frijoles Canyon), contains 23,000 acres of backcountry wilderness, waterfalls, and wildlife. Sixty miles of trails traverse the park. A small museum in the visitor center focuses on the area's prehistoric and contemporary Native American cultures, with displays of artifacts from 1200 to modern times as well as displays on the forest fires that have devastated parts of the park in recent years. ☎ 505/672–0343 ⊕ *www.nps.gov/band* ⊠ *$10 per vehicle, good for 7 days* ☉ *Late May–early Sept., daily 8–6; early Sept.–Oct. and Apr.–late May, daily 8–5:30; Nov.–Mar., daily 8–4:30.*

Valles Caldera National Preserve

⑲ *15 mi southwest of Los Alamos via NM 4.*

A high-forest drive brings you to the awe-inspiring Valles Grande, which at 14 mi in diameter is one of the world's largest calderas and which became Valles Caldera National Preserve in summer 2000. You can't imagine the volcanic crater's immensity until you spot what look like specks of dust on the lush meadow floor and realize they're cows. Since 2003, the Valles Caldera Trust has managed this 89,000-acre multiuse preserve with the aim to "protect and preserve the scientific, scenic, geologic, watershed, fish, wildlife, historic, cultural, and recreational values of the Preserve, and to provide for multiple use and sustained yield of renewable resources within the Preserve."

The preserve is open to visitors for hiking, cross-country skiing, horseback riding, horse-drawn carriage rides, van wildlife photography tours, mountain-bike tours, bird-watching, and fly-fishing. Most of the activities require reservations and a fee, although there are two free, relatively short hikes signposted from the parking area along NM 4, and no reservations are needed for these. Other self-guided hikes are about 7 mi and cost $10; there's also a guided hike that's 7 mi and costs $15. Shuttle buses take you from the parking area to the trailheads and pick you up again later in the day. Horseback riding is self-guided and costs $20. Fly fishing costs $25, for which you (and up to three friends) are entitled to cast a line into your own designated 1-mi stretch of San Antonio Creek; only 10 fishing permits are issued each day. The season runs late May through late October, and these permits are awarded on a lottery system (lottery tickets cost $5 each). Contact the preserve or visit the Web site for information on other kinds of tours and events. Elk hunting is also offered each fall, again on a lottery basis. ⊠ *NM 4* ☎ *505/ 661–3333 or 866/382–5537* ⊕ *www.vallescaldera.gov.*

Jémez Springs

⑳ *20 mi west of Valles Caldera on NM 4.*

The funky mountain village of Jémez Springs draws outdoorsy types for hiking, cross-country skiing, and camping in the nearby U.S. Forest Service areas. The town's biggest tourist draws are Jémez State Monument and Soda Dam, but many people come here for relaxation at the town's bathhouse.

The geological wonder known as **Soda Dam** was created over thousands of years by travertine deposits—minerals that precipitate out of geothermal springs. With its strange mushroom-shape exterior and caves split by a roaring waterfall, it's no wonder the spot was considered sacred by Native Americans. In summer it's popular for swimming. ⊠ *NM 4, 1 mi north of Jémez State Monument.*

Jémez State Monument contains impressive Spanish and Native American ruins set throughout a 7-acre site and toured via an easy ⅓ mi loop trail. About 700 years ago ancestors of the people of Jémez Pueblo built several villages in and around the narrow mountain valley. One of the villages was Guisewa, or "Place of the Boiling Waters." The Spanish colonists built a mission church beside it, San José de los Jémez, which was abandoned by around 1640. ⊠ *NM 4, Jémez Springs* ☎ *505/829–3530* ⊕ *www.nmstatemonuments.org* ⊠ *$3* ⊙ *Wed.–Mon. 8:30–5.*

The original structure at the **Jémez Spring Bath House** was erected in the 1870s near a mineral hot spring. Many other buildings were added over the years, and the complex was completely renovated into an intimate Victorian-style hideaway in the mid-1990s. It's a funky, low-key spot that's far less formal and fancy than the several spa resorts near Santa Fe. You can soak in a mineral bath for $10 (30 minutes) or $15 (60 minutes). Massages cost between $40 (30 minutes) and $95 (90 minutes). An acupuncturist is available with advance notice. Beauty treatments include facials, manicures, and pedicures. The Jémez Package ($100) includes a half-hour bath, an herbal blanket wrap, and a one-hour massage. You can stroll down a short path behind the house to see where the steaming-hot springs feed into the Jémez River. ⊠ *NM 4* ☎ *505/829–3303 or 866/204–8303* ⊕ *www.jemezspringsbathhouse.com* ⊙ *July–early Sept., daily 10–8; early Sept.–June, daily 10–7:30.*

WHERE TO
STAY & EAT
★ ¢
✕⊞ **Laughing Lizard Inn and Cafe.** Consisting of a simple four-room motel-style inn and a cute adobe-and-stone café with a corrugated-metal roof, the Laughing Lizard makes for a warm and cheerful diversion—it's right in the center of the village. Rooms are cozy and simple with white linens, dressers, books, and porches that look out over the rugged mesa beyond the river valley. Healthful, eclectic fare—apple-walnut sandwiches, sweet potato–and–spinach salads, raspberry-chipotle-chicken burritos, veggie pizzas, herbal teas, offbeat beers, homemade desserts—is served in the homey café (limited hours off-season; call first), which has a saltillo-tile screened porch and an open-air wooden deck. ⊠ *NM 4, 87025* ☎ *505/829–3108* ⊕ *www.thelaughinglizard.com* ➾ *4 rooms* ♭ *Café, cable TV, some pets allowed* ☰ *D, MC, V.*

$
⊞ **Cañon del Rio.** On 6 acres along the Jémez River beneath towering mesas, this light-filled, contemporary adobe inn (formerly called the Riverdancer) has rooms with cove ceilings, tile floors, and Native American arts and crafts. All have French doors and open onto a courtyard with a natural-spring fountain. Wellness packages include massage, acupuncture, and aromatherapy. ⊠ *16445 NM 4, 87025* ☎ *505/829–4377* ⊕ *www.canondelrio.com* ➾ *6 rooms, 1 suite* ♭ *Some kitchens, Wi-Fi, hot tub, massage, hiking; no room TVs* ⍩ *CP* ☰ *AE, D, MC, V.*

Jémez Pueblo

㉑ *12 mi south of Jémez Springs via NM 4; 85 mi west of Santa Fe via U.S. 285/84 and NM 4; 50 mi north of Albuquerque via I–25, U.S. 550, and NM 4.*

As you continue southwest along NM 4, the terrain changes from a wooded river valley with high mesas on either side to an open red-rock valley, the home of the Jémez Pueblo, which is set along the Jémez River. After the pueblo at Pecos was abandoned in 1838, Jémez was the state's only pueblo with residents who spoke Towa (different from Tiwa and Tewa). The Jémez Reservation encompasses 89,000 acres, with two lakes, Holy Ghost Springs and Dragonfly Lake (off NM 4), open for fishing by permit only, April to October on weekends and holidays. The only part of the pueblo open to the public is the **Walatowa Visitor Center,** a fancy Pueblo Revival building that contains a small museum, an extensive pottery and crafts shop, and rotating art and photography exhibits; there's a short nature walk outside. The pueblo is sometimes open to the public for special events, demonstrations, and ceremonial dances—call for details. On weekends April–mid-October (10–6) when weather permits, arts and crafts and traditional foods are sold across the street at the **Jémez Red Rocks Open-Air Market.** The pueblo is noted for its polychrome pottery. The Walatowa gas and convenience store, on NM 4 next to the visitor center, is one of the few such establishments between Los Alamos and Bernalillo. Photographing, sketching, and video recording are prohibited. ⊠ *7413 NM 4* ☎ *505/834–7235* ⊕ *www.jemezpueblo.org* ⌨ *Free* ⊙ *Daily 8–5.*

Georgia O'Keeffe Country

It's a 20-minute drive north of Santa Fe to reach the Española Valley, which leads to the striking mesas, cliffs, and valleys that so inspired the artist Georgia O'Keeffe—she lived in this area for the final 50 years of her life. You first come to the small, workaday city of Española, a major crossroads from which roads lead to Taos, Chama, and Abiquiu. The other notable community in this area is tiny Ojo Caliente, famous for its hot-springs spa retreat.

Española
㉒ *20 mi north of Santa Fe via U.S. 285/84.*

This small but growing city midway along the Low Road from Santa Fe to Taos is a little rough around the edges—it was founded in the 1880s as a stop on the Denver & Rio Grande Railroad, and it lacks the colonial charm of either Santa Fe or Taos. Española is rather busy today and has many cheap burger joints, New Mexican–food restaurants, and a few chain motels, but few reasons to stick around for more than a quick meal. One of the city's modern trademarks are lowriders, which you'll see cruising the streets. They're mostly classic cars that have been retrofitted with lowered chassis and hydraulics that often allow the cars to bump and grind; the cars are often painted with spectacular murals, from religious art to scenes of the region's landscape.

All of the main arteries converge in the heart of town in a confusing, unpleasant maze of drab shopping centers, so watch the signs on the town's south side. Traffic moves slowly, especially on weekend nights when cruisers bring car culture alive.

The region is known for its longstanding weaving traditions, and one place you can learn about this heritage is the **Española Valley Fiber Arts Center** (⊠ 325 Paseo de Oñate ☎ 505/747–3577 ⊕ www.evfac.org

Free ⊙ Mon. 9–8, Tues.–Sat. 9–5), a nonprofit facility set inside an adobe building in the city's historic section. Here you can watch local weavers working with traditional materials and looms and admire (and purchase) their works in a small gallery. There are also classes offered on spinning, weaving, and knitting, which are open to the public and range from one day to several weeks. Emphasis here is placed on the styles of weaving that have been practiced here in the northern Rio Grande Valley since the Spaniards brought sheep and treadle looms here in the late 16th century. The center also celebrates the ancient traditions of New Mexico's Navajo and Pueblo weavers.

Set along NM 68 2 mi north of town, en route to Taos, **Ohkay Casino Resort** (⊠ NM 68 ☎ 505/747–1668 or 877/829–2865 ⊕ www.ohkay. com) comprises a casino with 700 slots, numerous blackjack tables, a 101-room hotel, two restaurants, a lounge with live music and comedy, a gift shop with Pendleton blankets and Native American jewelry, and a sporting clays shooting club.

WHERE TO
STAY & EAT
★ ¢–$$

✕ **El Paragua Restaurant.** With a dark, intimate atmosphere of wood and stone, this historic place started out as a lemonade-cum-taco stand in the late 1950s but is now known for some of the state's most authentic New Mexican and regional Mexican cuisine. Steaks and fish are grilled over a mesquite-wood fire; other specialties include chorizo enchiladas, panfried breaded trout amadine, and menudo. ⊠ 603 Santa Cruz Rd., NM 76 just east of NM 68 ☎ 505/753–3211 or 800/929–8226 ⊕ www. elparagua.com 🗏 AE, DC, MC, V.

$$$$
Fodor'sChoice
★

✕🔲 **Rancho de San Juan.** This secluded 225-acre Relaix & Châteaux compound hugs Black Mesa's base. Many of the inn's rooms are self-contained suites, some set around a courtyard and others amid the wilderness. All rooms have Southwestern furnishings, Frette robes, Aveda bath products, and CD stereos; nearly all have kiva fireplaces. The top units have such cushy touches as two bedrooms, 12-foot ceilings, Mexican marble showers, kitchens, Jacuzzis, and private patios. A spectacular four-course, prix-fixe, contemporary-cuisine dinner is available (by reservation only) in the restaurant Tuesday through Saturday. Past fare has included Texas quail stuffed with corn bread, green chiles, and linguica sausage, and Alaskan halibut with tomatillo-lime salsa, caramelized butternut squash, and creamed spinach. You can hike up to a sandstone shrine on a bluff above the property. In-suite spa and massage services are available. ⊠ U.S. 285, 3½ mi north of U.S. 84 ⌖ Box 4140, Española 87533 ☎ 505/753–6818 ⊕ www.ranchodesanjuan.com 🛏 9 rooms, 6 suites ◊ Restaurant, some in-room hot tubs, some kitchens, massage, hiking; no a/c in some rooms, no room TVs, no kids under 8, no smoking 🗏 AE, D, DC, MC, V.

Abiquiu

㉓ 24 mi northwest of Española via U.S. 84.

This tiny, very traditional Hispanic village was home to *genizaros*, people of mixed tribal backgrounds with Spanish surnames that came from Spanish families who used Native Americans as servants. Many descendants of original families still live in the area, although since the late 1980s

Abiquiu and its surrounding countryside have become a nesting ground for those fleeing big-city lifestyles, among them actresses Marsha Mason and Shirley MacLaine. Abiquiu—along with parts of the nearby Española Valley—is also a hotbed of organic farming, with many of the operations here selling their goods at the Santa Fe Farmers Market and to restaurants throughout the Rio Grande Valley. A number of artists have moved to Abiquiu in recent years, with several studios open regularly to the public and many others open each year over Columbus Day weekend for the **Annual Abiquiu Studio Tour** (☎ 505/685–4454 ⊕ www. abiquiustudiotour.org). A feeling of insider versus outsider and old-timer versus newcomer still prevails. Newcomers or visitors may find themselves resented; it's best to observe one very important local custom: no photography is allowed in and around the village.

You can visit **Georgia O'Keeffe's home** through advance reservation (four months recommended) with the **Georgia O'Keeffe Foundation** (☎ 505/ 685–4539 ⊕ www.abiquiuinn.com), which conducts one-hour tours Tuesday, Thursday, and Friday, mid-March–November, for $25. In 1945 Georgia O'Keeffe bought a large, dilapidated late-18th-century Spanish-colonial adobe compound just off the Plaza. Upon the 1946 death of her husband, photographer Alfred Stieglitz, she left New York City and began dividing her time permanently between this home, which figured prominently in many of her works, and the one in nearby Ghost Ranch. She wrote about the house, "When I first saw the Abiquiú house it was a ruin . . . As I climbed and walked about in the ruin I found a patio with a very pretty well house and a bucket to draw up water. It was a good-sized patio with a long wall with a door on one side. That wall with a door in it was something I had to have. It took me 10 years to get it— three more years to fix the house up so I could live in it—and after that the wall with the door was painted many times." The patio is featured in *Black Patio Door* (1955) and *Patio with Cloud* (1956). O'Keeffe died in 1986 at the age of 98 and left provisions in her will to ensure that the property's houses would never be public monuments.

Bode's (✉ U.S. 84 ☎ 505/685–4422 ⊕ www.bodes.com), across from the Abiquiu post office, is much more than a gas station. It's a popular stop for newspapers, quirky gifts, cold drinks, supplies, and hearty green chile stew, sandwiches, and other short-order fare. The station serves as general store and exchange post for news and gossip.

The **Dar al Islam** (✉ CR 155 at sign 42 ☎ 505/685–4515 ⊕ www. daralislam.org) adobe mosque was built by Egyptian architect Hassan Fathy, and visitors are welcome. The annual North American Muslim Powwow is held here each June. To reach the mosque from Bode's, drive ¼ mi north, turn right onto unpaved County Road 155, and proceed 3 mi, and make a left at the main entrance sign.

WHERE TO
STAY & EAT
$–$$

✕🖳 **Abiquiu Inn and Cafe Abiquiu.** Deep in the Chama Valley, the inn has a secluded, exotic feel—almost like an oasis—with brightly decorated rooms, including several four-person casitas, with woodstoves or fireplaces and tiled baths; some units have verandas with hammocks and open views of O'Keeffe Country. The café (¢–$$) serves commendable

Studio Tours

CLOSE UP

NORTH-CENTRAL NEW MEXICO IS A REGION of artists' colonies, and from the last weekend of September through the first weekend of December artisans in the villages of Galisteo, the Pecos Valley, El Rito, Abiquiu, Dixon, Jémez Springs, and Madrid take turns hosting studio-tour weekends. Homes and studios are open for browsing, shopping, and conversing; maps are provided to guide you to the open houses, where you can find reasonably priced arts and crafts. Wares include everything from pottery and paintings to wreaths, ristras, and dried-flower arrangements; homemade jellies, pestos, and chile sauces; and other food items; and wood carvings, religious paintings, clothing, and handmade furniture.

The quality varies, but bargains are abundant. Of course for many the real fun is the opportunity to experience village life and to get inside those charming old adobes that you can

only pass by at other times of the year. Many of the villagers provide refreshments, and you're encouraged to wander at a leisurely pace.

Because studio-tour planning passes from one chairperson to another each year, there's no central number to call for information. But if you're in the Santa Fe area during the fall season, check "Pasatiempo," the Friday supplement of the *Santa Fe New Mexican*, for a report about which village is open for touring and what items are for sale. There are also a few tours held annually, such as the High Road Arts Tour, which runs from Chimayo to Peñasco in mid-September; and the Dixon tour, which takes place every year on the first weekend in November. About a half hour south of Taos, Dixon was the first village to host a studio tour, and its version still has the largest number of participating artists and the greatest variety of merchandise.

New Mexican, Italian, and American fare, from blue-corn tacos stuffed with grilled trout to lamb–and–poblao chile stew; it's also known for its seasonal fresh-fruit cobblers. The inn is owned and operated by the Dar al Islam mosque and is the departure point for O'Keeffe-home tours. It has an exceptional art gallery, crafts shop, and gardens. ⊠ *U.S. 84* ⌖ *Box 120, Abiquiu 87510* ☎ *505/685–4378 or 888/735–2902* 🖷 *505/685–4931* ⊕ *www.abiquiuinn.com* ➱ *14 rooms, 5 casitas* ⌂ *Restaurant, some kitchens, cable TV, Wi-Fi, shops, meeting room* ▭ *AE, D, DC, MC, V.*

Ghost Ranch
㉔ *10 mi northwest of Abiquiu on U.S. 84.*

For art historians, the name Ghost Ranch brings to mind Georgia O'-Keeffe, who lived on but a small parcel of this 20,000-acre dude and cattle ranch. The ranch's owner in the 1930s—conservationist and publisher of *Nature Magazine*, Arthur Pack—first invited O'Keeffe here to visit in 1934; Pack soon sold the artist the 7-acre plot on which she lived summer through fall for most of the rest of her life.

In 1955 Pack donated the rest of the ranch to the Presbyterian Church, which continues to use Pack's original structures and about 55 acres of land as a conference center.

The **Ghost Ranch Education and Retreat Center** (✉ U.S. 84 ☎ 505/685–4333 or 877/804–4678 ⊕ www.ghostranch.org), open year-round, is busiest in summer, when the majority of workshops take place. Subjects range from poetry and literary arts to photography, horseback riding, and every conceivable traditional craft of northern New Mexico. These courses are open to the public, and guests camp or stay in semirustic cottages or casitas. After registering at the main office, you may come in and hike high among the wind-hewn rocks so beloved by O'Keeffe. Ghost Ranch offers guided tours of the ranch's landscape, which show the vistas that O'Keeffe painted during the five decades that she summered here. Her original house is not part of the tour and is closed to the public. These one-hour tours, which have nothing to do with the O'Keeffe studio tours offered in Abiquiu, are available mid-March through mid-November, on Tuesday, Thursday, Friday, and Saturday at 1:30; the cost is $25, and you must call first to make a reservation.

The **Ghost Ranch Piedra Lumbre Education and Visitor Center** has a gallery with rotating art presentations, exhibits on New Mexico's natural history, a gift shop, and two museums. The **Florence Hawley Ellis Museum of Anthropology** contains Native American tools, pottery, and other artifacts excavated from the Ghost Ranch Gallina digs. Pioneer anthropologist Florence Hawley Ellis conducted excavations at Chaco Canyon and at other sites in New Mexico. Adjacent to the Ellis Museum, the **Ruth Hall Museum of Paleontology** exhibits the New Mexico state fossil, the coelophysis, also known as "the littlest dinosaur," originally excavated near Ghost Ranch. ✉ *U.S. 84, just north of main Ghost Ranch entrance* ☎ *505/685–4312* ⊕ *www.ghostranch.org* 🎫 *Donation $3* ⊙ *Visitor Center: Mar.–Oct., daily 9–5. Hawley and Hall museums: Late May–early Sept., Tues.–Sat. 9–5, Sun. and Mon. 1–5; early Sept.–late May, Tues.–Sat. 9–5.*

OFF THE BEATEN PATH

MONASTERY OF CHRIST IN THE DESERT – Designed by renowned Japanese-American architect and wood-carver George Nakashima, this remote rock-and-adobe church—with one of the state's most spectacular natural settings—can be visited for daily prayer or silent overnight retreats (if requested in advance by mail or e-mail); there are basic accommodations for up to 16 guests (10 single and 3 double rooms), and there's a two-night minimum, with most visitors staying for several days. A suggested per-night donation of $50 to $125 is requested, depending on the room, and none have electricity. Day visitors can come anytime and stroll the grounds, visit the gift shop, and participate in different prayer services throughout the day. The road is rutted in places and becomes impassable during rainy weather—you can definitely get stuck here for a day, or even a few days, during particularly wet periods, such as summer monsoon season. Check weather forecasts carefully if you're only intending to visit for the day. ✉ *Guestmaster, Christ in the Desert; pass Ghost Ranch Visitor's Center and turn left on Forest Service Rd. 151;*

follow dirt road 13 mi to monastery ⬛ *Box 270, Abiquiu 87510* ☎ *No phone* ⊕ *www.christdesert.org.*

EN
ROUTE
The best and most interesting way to reach Ojo Caliente from Ghost Ranch is to return down U.S. 84 just past Abiquiu and then make a left turn (north) onto NM 554 toward El Rito, 12 mi away. This small, rural community known for its crafts making (especially weaving) has a

★ funky general store and the **El Farolito** (⬛ 1212 Main St. ☎ 505/581–9509), a minuscule dinner restaurant on the town's tree-shaded Main Street that serves State Fair blue-ribbon green chile and other New Mexican specialties, including a terrific posole. This place has a cult following, so expect a wait some evenings. The ride here offers a stunning view back east toward the Sangre de Cristos.

4

Chama

❷❺ *30 mi east of Jicarilla Apache Reservation and 95 mi west of Taos on U.S. 64, 59 mi north of Abiquiu on U.S. 84.*

A railroad town nestled at the base of 10,000-foot Cumbre Pass, lush and densely wooded Chama offers year-round outdoor activities, as well as a scenic railroad. From there, U.S. 84 hugs the Rio Chama and leads southward through monumental red rocks and golden sandstone spires that inspired Georgia O'Keeffe's vivid paintings of creased mountains, stark crosses, bleached animal skulls, and adobe architecture.

The booms and busts of Chama have largely coincided with the popularity of train transportation. The town's earliest boom, which precipitated its founding, occurred in the 1880s when workers piled into town to construct the Denver & Rio Grande Railroad. In those days, narrow-gauge trains chugged over the high mountain tracks carrying gold and silver out from the mines of the San Juan Mountains, which straddle the nearby Colorado–New Mexico border. Gambling halls, moonshine stills, speakeasies, and brothels were a fixture along the main drag, Terrace Avenue. The lumber industry also thrived during the early years, and the town still has quite a few houses and buildings fashioned out of spare hand-hewn railroad ties.

Chama's outdoor recreation opportunities are hard to beat. Vast meadows of wildflowers and aspen and ponderosa pines blanket the entire region. Hunters are drawn here by the abundant wildlife. There's cross-country skiing and snowmobiling in winter; camping, rafting, hiking, and fishing in summer, all in a pristine, green, high-mountain setting that feels like the top of the world. The temperate mountain air means that most lodgings in the area neither have nor need air-conditioning.

All directions are given in terms of "the Y," the town's only major intersection (of U.S. 64/84 and NM 17).

★ The big attraction in Chama is the historic **Cumbres & Toltec Scenic Railroad,** the narrow-gauge coal-driven steam engine that runs through the San Juan Mountains and over the Cumbres Pass. You chug over ancient trestles, around breathtaking bends, and high above the Los Pinos River—if the terrain looks at all familiar, you may have seen this railroad's "performance" in *Indiana Jones and the Last Crusade*. Midway through the trip you break for lunch and can switch to a waiting Colorado-based train to complete the 64 mi to Antonito, Colorado (from which you'll be shuttled back by bus), or return from this point on the same train. Train trip packages including stays at area lodgings are also available. ⊠ *15 Terrace Ave.* ☎ *505/756–2151 or 888/286–2737* ⊕ *www.cumbresandtoltec.com* ☒ *$59–$115* ☉ *Late May–mid.-Oct., daily departures at 10 AM.*

WHERE TO
STAY & EAT
¢–$

✗ **Elkhorn Cafe.** Here is the place for a plate of true-blue, stacked New Mexican enchiladas with posole (a New Mexican specialty of hominy slow-cooked in an herbed broth, often with chunks of pork), and beans nestled happily under tasty red chile. The *carne adovado* (pork marinated in red chile and slow-cooked until tender) is songworthy. The salad bar is simply stocked with fresh ingredients. Locals fill the place for breakfast, which starts at 6 AM, as well as lunch and dinner. ⊠ *2663 U.S. 64/84, on south end of town* ☎ *505/756–2229* ⬟ *Reservations not accepted* ▭ *DC, MC, V.*

$$$$

🏨 **The Lodge and Ranch at Chama Land & Cattle Company.** If you're looking for an outdoor-oriented vacation that's also luxurious, this is the place for you. The lodge and working ranch, owned by the Jicarilla Apache tribe, is on 32,000 idyllic acres on the Colorado border, at an elevation between 9,000 and 11,000 feet, with 10 lakes. Horseback riding, trophy fishing and hunting, touring the ranch, and sitting by the huge stone fireplace ought to relax the most stressed-out executive. The luxe 27,000-square-foot lodge is lavishly furnished. Gourmet meals and drinks from the bar are included in your room rate, and packages are available that include all ranch activities. The lodge also offers day-packages for fly-fishing (which include a guide and lunch), and fly-fishing school. ⊠ *16253 U.S. 84, Box 127, 87520* ☎ *505/756–2133* ☐ *505/756–2519* ⊕ *www.lodgeatchama.com* ⌨ *9 rooms, 2 suites* ⬠ *Dining room, cable TV, hot tub, sauna, gym, fishing, horseback riding, bar, meeting rooms; no TV in some rooms* ▭ *D, MC, V* ⎥⊙⎥ *AI.*

★ $–$$

🏨 **Gandy Dancer B&B Inn.** A five-minute walk from the rail depot in the center of town, this handsomely furnished pale-yellow Victorian inn offers the most charming accommodations in town, plus a well-prepared full breakfast. From the tree-shaded deck in back, watch hummingbirds feast at feeders all summer long, and enjoy the sight of countless other birds throughout the year. Rooms have railroad-related names (Cinders & Smoke, Caboose, Golden Spike) and contain a mix of Victorian and early-20th-century antiques, original artwork, and plush quilts and linens. ⊠ *299 Maple Ave., Box 810, 87520* ☎ *505/756–2191 or 800/424–6702* ⌨ *7 rooms* ⬠ *Cable TV, in-room VCRs, Wi-Fi, hot tub* ▭ *MC, V* ⎥⊙⎥ *BP.*

$

🏨 **Branding Iron Motel.** A spotless, old-time motel with rooms that have been attractively updated over the years, the Branding Iron lies a mile south of the railroad depot, along the main highway through town. There's nothing special about the decor, but the rooms do have all the basics, including coffeemakers and alarm clocks. Pine trees dot the peaceful grounds. ⊠ *1511 NM 17, 87520* ☎ *505/756–2162 or 800/446–2650* ⌨ *39 rooms* ⬠ *Restaurant, cable TV, Wi-Fi, some pets allowed* ▭ *AE, D, MC, V.*

$ ▦ **River Bend Lodge.** This comfortable, basic lodge has one of the few hot tubs in town. It's right on the Chama River, so you can walk out your door and cast a fly (just keep an eye out for black bears; you might see one meandering by). Management here is especially solicitous and accommodating, particularly for groups or family reunions. It also offers train packages. Cabins have kitchenettes and fireplaces. ⊠ *U.S. 84, Box 593, 87520* ☏ *505/756–2264 or 800/288–1371* 🖷 *505/756–2664* ⊕ *www.chamariverbendlodge.com* ⇥ *14 rooms, 7 cabins* ♨ *Cable TV, hot tub, meeting room* ☰ *AE, D, DC, MC, V.*

SPORTS &   Plenty of outfitters are here to help out with equipment and tours.
THE OUTDOORS   **Nordic Adventures** (☏ 888/660–9878 ⊕ www.yurtsogood.com) provides snowmobiles and yurts for rent and offers backcountry snowmobile and ski tours.

Looking to get on the water? You've got a few options for rafting and guided fishing trips. **Far Flung Adventures** (☏ 800/359–2627 ⊕ www.farflung.com) runs half-day, one-day, and multiday trips along the Rio Grande. **Los Rios** (☏ 800/544–1181 ⊕ www.losriosriverrunners.com) offers Rio Grande day trips and also overnight trips in Rio Chama. If you have your own boat, the folks at **Canyon REO** (☏ 800/637–4604 ⊕ www.canyonreo.com) will pick you and your equipment up in a shuttle, and even pack food for you to take along.

SHOPPING   **Local Color Gallery** (⊠ 567 Terrace Ave. ☏ 505/756–2604) carries photography and jewelry of local artisans. The sales of many goods at **Trackside Emporium** (⊠ 611 Terrace Ave. ☏ 505/756–1848) support the preservation of the railroad; here you can find books, signs, and other memorabilia pertaining to the trains. **Chama Valley Supermarket** (⊠ 2451 U.S. 84 ☏ 505/756–2545) at the "Y" intersection sells groceries and fishing supplies.

Los Ojos

❷❻ *13 mi south of Chama on U.S. 64/84.*

Los Ojos, midway between Tierra Amarilla and Chama, could well serve as a model for rural economic development worldwide. The little town has experienced an economic revival of sorts by returning to its ancient roots—the raising of churro sheep (the original breed brought over by the Spanish, prized for its wool) and weaving. Ganados del Valle, the community-based, nonprofit economic development corporation headquartered here, has created jobs and increased prosperity by returning to the old ways, with improved marketing. You can also find a smattering of artists' studios, most of them in rustic buildings with corrugated metal roofs.

★   The cooperative **Tierra Wools** produces some of the finest original weavings in the Southwest. Designs are based on the old Rio Grande styles, and weavers make rugs and capes of superb craftsmanship entirely by hand, using old-style looms. Weaving workshops are offered. ⊠ *91 Main St.* ☏ *505/588–7231 or 888/709–0979* ⊕ *www.handweavers.com* ⊗ *June–Oct., Mon.–Sat. 9–6, Sun. 11–4; Nov.–May, Mon.–Sat. 10–5.*

WHERE TO STAY
$ 　 🛏 **Cooper's El Vado Ranch.** This old-time hunting camp with simple, wood-paneled, gas-heated cabins on the river is a launch site for rafters and a favorite haunt of fishermen. They're still bragging over here about the state-record brown trout they caught in 1946. ☒ *3150 NM 112* 🖂 *Box 129, Tierra Amarilla 87575* ☏ *505/588–7354* ⊕ *www.elvado.com* 📟 *9 cabins* ⬙ *Kitchenettes, some pets allowed; no room TVs* 🗐 *AE, D, MC, V* ☾ *Closed mid-Dec.–mid-Mar.*

EN
ROUTE 　 Heading south on U.S. 84 from Los Ojos, you can reach the small town of **Tierra Amarilla,** from which you can access two state parks. Both parks have developed campsites. Eleven miles west of town, **Heron Lake State Park** (☒ NM 95 and U.S. 64 ☏ 505/588–7470 ⊕ www.emnrd.state.nm.us) is a designated "quiet lake" (powerboats may not exceed no-wake speed) ideal for sailing and trout fishing. Seventeen miles southwest of Tierra Amarilla is **El Vado Lake State Park** (☒ NM 112 ☏ 505/588–7247 ⊕ www.emnrd.state.nm.us), where you can water-ski, fish, and watch for bald eagles, osprey, and other birds in winter. From Heron Lake, the 5½-mi **Rio Chama Trail** crosses the Rio Chama, winds along the south slope of the canyon, goes up to a mesa top, and descends to the shore of El Vado Lake.

Ojo Caliente

❷❼ *28 mi northeast of Abiquiu by way of El Rito via NM 554 to NM 111 to U.S. 285, 50 mi north of Santa Fe on U.S. 285.*

Ojo Caliente is the only place in North America where five different types of hot springs—iron, lithia, arsenic, salt, and soda—are found side by side. The town was named by Spanish explorer Cabeza de Vaca, who visited in 1535 and believed he had stumbled upon the Fountain of Youth. Modern-day visitors draw a similar conclusion about the restorative powers of the springs. The spa itself, built in the 1920s, is a no-frills establishment that has seen better days but has received some much needed renovations in the past couple of years; it comprises a hotel and cottages, a restaurant, a gift shop, massage rooms, men's and women's bathhouses, a chlorine-free swimming pool, and indoor and outdoor mineral-water tubs. The hotel, one of the original bathhouses, and the springs are all on the National Register of Historic Places, as is the adjacent and recently restored Round Barn (the only adobe one in the nation), from which visitors can take horseback tours and guided hikes to ancient Pueblo dwellings and petroglyph-etched rocks. Spa services include wraps, massage, facials, and acupuncture. The setting at the foot of sandstone cliffs topped by the ruins of ancient Indian pueblos is nothing short of inspiring.

WHERE TO STAY
$–$$ 　 🛏 **Ojo Caliente Mineral Springs Spa and Resort.** Accommodations here run the gamut from spartan in the unfussy 1916 hotel (no TVs, simple furnishings) to rather upscale in the elegant suites, which were added in summer 2006. Rooms in the hotel have bathrooms but no showers or tubs—bathing takes place in the mineral springs (it's an arrangement that pleases most longtime devotees but doesn't sit well with others). The cottages are quite comfy, with refrigerators and TVs; some have kitchenettes, and as of this writing tile showers had been added to some and

were planned for the rest by 2007. In summer 2006, Ojo opened 12 spacious suites, which have such luxury touches as kiva fireplaces and patios; half of these have private double soaking tubs outside, which are filled with Ojo mineral waters. All lodgers have complimentary access to the mineral pools and *milagro* (miracle) wraps, and the bathhouse has showers. Horseback tours can be prearranged. The Artesian Restaurant serves world-beat fare in a charming dining room. Four-day and overnight packages are available, from $700 per person. There's also camping on-site, beside the cottonwood-shaded Rio Ojo Caliente—double-occupancy camping rates are $20 for tents, $40 for RVs. ✉ *50 Los Baños Dr., off U.S. 285, 30 mi north of Española* ☐ *Box 68, 87549* ☎ *505/583–2233 or 800/222–9162* 🖷 *505/583–2464* ⊕ *www. ojocalientespa.com* ⤴ *19 rooms, 19 cottages, 12 suites, 3 3-bedroom houses* ♿ *Restaurant, some kitchenettes, some refrigerators, spa, horseback riding, meeting rooms; no a/c, no room phones, no TV in some rooms* 🖃 *AE, D, DC, MC, V.*

Low Road to Taos

Widely considered to be the less scenic route to Taos, the Low Road actually offers plenty of dazzling scenery once you get through traffic-clogged Española and down into the Rio Grande Gorge. As you emerge from the gorge roughly 25 minutes later, NM 68 cuts up over a plateau that affords stupendous views of Taos and the surrounding mountains. Note that whether you take the Low Road or the High Road (described below), you first follow U.S. 285/84 north from Santa Fe for about 20 mi—this somewhat dull stretch of road was vastly improved in 2004 with a major road widening project. Whereas you exit the highway just north of Pojoaque in order to travel the High Road, you remain on U.S. 285/84 all the way to Española to follow the Low Road; once there, you pick up NM 68 north. Just before you descend into the Rio Grande Gorge, where you parallel the river for several scenic miles, you pass through tiny Velarde, which has a number of fruit and vegetable stands worth checking out. Without stops, it takes 80 to 90 minutes to make it from Santa Fe to Taos via the Low Road, whereas the High Road takes 2 to 2½ hours.

Dixon

28 *45 mi north of Santa Fe via U.S. 285/84 and NM 68, 20 mi south of Taos via NM 68.*

The small village of Dixon and its surrounding country lanes are home to a surprising number of artists. Artistic sensitivity, as well as generations of dedicated farmers, accounts for the community's well-tended fields, pretty gardens, and fruit trees—a source of produce for restaurants and farmers' markets such as the one in Santa Fe. It's simple to find your way around; there's only one main road.

The Dixon Arts Association has some four dozen members, many represented in a cooperative gallery attached to **Métier Weaving & Gallery** (✉ NM 75 ☎ 505/579–4111), which also has a showroom that sells the textiles and weavings of artists and owners Irene Smith and Lezlie

King. Dixon also hosts a popular studio tour (🌐 www.dixonarts.org) the first weekend in November, when area artists open up their home studios to the public.

WHERE TO STAY & EAT

¢–$$ ✕ **Embudo Station.** Set inside an 1880s railroad station, historic Embudo Station comprises a casual restaurant with a riverside patio; a smokehouse that cures delicious ham, turkey, pheasant, and rainbow trout; a winery open for tastings; and a cabin available for nightly or weekly rentals. The restaurant serves traditional New Mexican fare and barbecue; many dishes incorporate the house-smoked meats. Limited sandwich fare, beers, and wine are available on weekends during the off-season, but it's always best to call first. ✉ *NM 68, Embudo* ☎ *505/852–4707 or 800/852–4707* 🌐 *www.embudostation.com* 💳 *AE, MC, V* ⏲ *Closed Nov.–Mar. and Mon.*

$ 🏨 **Rock Pool Gardens.** A private guesthouse with two warmly furnished two-bedroom suites, Rock Pool is one of the few accommodations between Española and Taos, and it's also a good value. One suite has a kitchenette and a bathroom connecting the bedrooms, each of which has its own access and patio. The other has a full kitchen. The rustic walls, Mexican tile work, and willow twig furniture lend a country air to these otherwise contemporary suites, and lush gardens surround the building. There's a Jacuzzi under the trees and a heated pool set in natural rock. Each unit comes stocked with breakfast items. ✉ *NM 75, 87527* ☎ *505/579–4602* *2 suites* *BBQ, kitchens, refrigerator, cable TV, in-room VCRs, indoor pool, hot tub, some pets allowed* 💳 *No credit cards* *CP.*

The High Road to Taos

Fodor's Choice ★

The main highway (NM 68) to Taos along the Rio Grande Gorge provides dramatic close-ups of the river and rocky mountain faces, but if you have an extra hour or two, the High Road to Taos is worth choosing for its views of sweeping woodlands and traditional Hispanic villages. The High Road follows U.S. 285/84 north to NM 503 (a right turn just past Pojoaque), to County Road 98 (a left toward Chimayó), to NM 76 northeast to NM 75 east, to NM 518 north. The drive through the rolling foothills and tiny valleys of the Sangre de Cristos, dotted with orchards, pueblos, and picturesque villages, is stunning. And although most of these insular, largely Hispanic communities offer little in the way of shopping and dining, the region has steadily become more of a haven for artists. From Chimayó to Peñasco, you can find mostly low-key but often high-quality art galleries, many of them run out of the owners' homes. And during the final two weekends in September, more than 100 artists in these parts show their wares during the **High Road Art Tour** (☎ 866/343–5381 🌐 www.highroadnewmexico.com); call or visit the Web site for a studio map.

Depending on when you make this drive, you're in for some of the state's most radiant scenery. In mid-April the orchards are in blossom; summer turns the valleys into lush green oases; and in fall the smell of piñon adds to the sensual overload of golden leaves and red-chile ristras hanging from the houses. In winter the fields are covered with quilts of snow, and the lines of homes, fences, and trees stand out like bold pen-and-ink drawings against the sky. But the roads can be icy and treacherous—if in doubt, stick with the Low Road to Taos. If you decide to take the High Road just one way between Santa Fe and Taos, you might want to save it for the return journey—the scenery is best enjoyed when traveling north to south.

Chimayó

🐵 *28 mi north of Santa Fe, 10 mi east of Española on NM 76.*

From U.S. 285/84 north of Pojoaque, scenic NM 503 winds past horse paddocks and orchards in the narrow Nambé Valley, then ascends into the red-sandstone canyons with a view of Truchas Peaks to the northeast before dropping into the bucolic village of Chimayó. Nestled into hillsides where gnarled piñons seem to grow from bare bedrock, Chimayó is famed for its weaving, its red chiles, and its two chapels.

FodorsChoice **El Santuario de Chimayó,** a small frontier adobe church, has a fantasti-
★ cally carved and painted wood altar and is built on the site where, believers say, a mysterious light came from the ground on Good Friday in 1810 and where a large wooden crucifix was found beneath the earth. The chapel sits above a sacred *pozito* (a small hole), the dirt from which is believed to have miraculous healing properties. Dozens of abandoned crutches and braces placed in the anteroom—along with many notes, letters, and photos—testify to this. The Santuario draws a steady stream of worshippers year-round—Chimayó is considered the Lourdes of the Southwest. During Holy Week as many as 50,000 pilgrims come here. The shrine is a National Historic Landmark, and its altar and artwork underwent an ambitious and much needed restoration in 2004. It's surrounded by commercialism in the way of small adobe shops selling every kind of religious curio imaginable. ⊠ *Signed lane off CR 98* ☎ *505/ 351–4889* ⊕ *www.archdiocesesantafe.org/AboutASF/Chimayo.html* ☞ *Free* ☉ *June–Sept., daily 9–5; Oct.–May, daily 9–4.*

A smaller chapel 200 yards from El Santuario was built in 1857 and dedicated to **Santo Niño de Atocha.** As at the more famous Santuario, the dirt at Santo Niño de Atocha's chapel is said to have healing properties in the place where the *Santo Niño* was first placed. The little boy saint was brought here from Mexico by Severiano Medina, who claimed Santo Niño de Atocha had healed him of rheumatism. San Ildefonso pottery master Maria Martinez came here for healing as a child. Tales of the boy saint's losing one of his shoes as he wandered through the countryside helping those in trouble endeared him to the people of northern New Mexico. It became a tradition to place shoes at the foot of the statue as an offering. ☞ *Free* ☉ *Daily 9–5.*

WHERE TO ✕ **Rancho de Chimayó.** In a century-old adobe hacienda tucked into the
STAY & EAT mountains, with whitewashed walls, hand-stripped vigas, and cozy din-
$–$$ ing rooms, the Rancho de Chimayó is still owned and operated by the family that first occupied the house. There's a fireplace in winter and, in summer, a terraced patio shaded by catalpa trees. Good, if predictable New Mexican fare is served, but the ambience is the real draw here. You can take an after-dinner stroll on the grounds' paths. Reservations are

essential in summer. The owners also operate the seven-room **Hacienda de Chimayó B&B** (☎ 505/351–2222) just across the road. ⊠ CR 98 ☎ 505/351–4444 ⊕ www.ranchodechimayo.com ☰ AE, D, DC, MC, V ☉ Closed Mon. Nov.–May.

★ ¢ ✕ **Léona's Restaurante.** This fast-food-style burrito and chili stand under a massive catalpa tree at one end of the Santuario de Chimayó parking lot has only a few tables, and in summer it's crowded. The specialty is flavored tortillas—everything from jalapeño to butterscotch. Other treats include homemade posole stew, carne adovada, and green-chile cheese tamales. The tortillas have become so legendary that owner Léona Medina-Tiede opened a tortilla factory in Chimayó's Manzana Center and now does a thriving mail-order business. ⊠ Off CR 98, behind Santuario de Chimayó ☎ 505/351–4569 or 888/561–5569 ⊕ www. leonasrestaurante.com ☰ AE, D, DC, MC, V ☉ Closed Tues. and Wed. No dinner.

$–$$ ▦ **Casa Escondida.** Intimate and peaceful, this adobe inn has sweeping views of the Sangre de Cristo range. The setting makes it a great base for mountain bikers. The scent of fresh-baked strudel wafts through the rooms, which are decorated with antiques and Native American and other regional arts and crafts. Ask for the Sun Room, in the main house, which has a private patio, viga ceilings, and a brick floor. The separate one-bedroom Casita Escondida has a kiva-style fireplace, tile floors, kitchenette, and a sitting area. A large hot tub is hidden in a grove behind wild berry bushes. ⊠ CR 0100, off NM 76 ⧉ Box 142, 85722 ☎ 505/ 351–4805 or 800/643–7201 ⧉ 505/351–2575 ⊕ www.casaescondida. com ⧉ Some kitchenettes, Wi-Fi, outdoor hot tub, some pets allowed; no room phones, no room TVs, no smoking ⧉ 7 rooms, 1 suite ☰ MC, V ⧉ BP.

SHOPPING **Centinela Traditional Arts-Weaving** (⊠ NM 76, 1 mi east of junction with CR 98 ☎ 505/351–2180 or 877/351–2180 ⊕ www.chimayoweavers. com) continues the Trujillo family weaving tradition, which started in northern New Mexico more than seven generations ago. Irvin Trujillo and his wife, Lisa, are both award-winning master weavers, creating Rio Grande–style tapestry blankets and rugs, many of them with natural dyes that authentically replicate early weavings. Most designs are historically based, but the Trujillos contribute their own designs as well. The shop and gallery carries these heirloom-quality textiles, with a knowledgeable staff on hand to demonstrate or answer questions about the weaving technique.

Ortega's Weaving Shop (⊠ NM 76 at CR 98 ☎ 505/351–2288 or 877/ 351–4215 ⊕ www.ortegasdechimayo.com) sells Rio Grande- and Chimayó-style textiles made by the family whose Spanish ancestors brought the craft to New Mexico in the 1600s. The Galeria Ortega, next door, sells traditional New Mexican and Hispanic and contemporary Native American arts and crafts. In winter the shop is closed on Sunday.

In the plaza just outside the Santuario, **Highroad Marketplace** (⊠ Off CR 98 ☎ 505/351–1078 or 866/343–5381) stocks a variety of arts and crafts created all along the High Road, from Chimayó to Peñasco.

Cordova

30 *4 mi east of Chimayó via NM 76.*

A minuscule mountain village with a small central plaza, a school, a post office, and a church, Cordova is the center of the regional wood-carving industry. The town supports more than 30 full-time and part-time carvers. Many of them are descendants of José Dolores López, who in the 1920s created the village's signature unpainted "Cordova style" of carving. Most of the *santeros* (makers of religious images) have signs outside their homes indicating that santos are for sale. The pieces are fairly expensive, a reflection of the hard work and fine craftsmanship involved—prices range from several hundred dollars for small ones to several thousand for larger figures. There are also affordable and delightful small carvings of animals and birds. The St. Anthony of Padua Chapel, which is filled with handcrafted retablos and other religious art, is worth a visit.

Truchas

31 *4 mi northeast of Cordova via NM 76.*

Truchas (Spanish for "trout") is where Robert Redford shot the movie *The Milagro Beanfield War* (based on the novel written by Taos author John Nichols). This village is perched dramatically on the rim of a deep canyon beneath the towering Truchas Peaks, mountains high enough to be almost perpetually capped with snow. The tallest of the Truchas Peaks is 13,102 feet, the second-highest point in New Mexico. This is an insular town, and locals don't always take a shine to visitors, so be discreet and try not to wave your camera around, snapping photos of residents or their property. Truchas has been developing increased cachet with artsy, independent-minded folks from Santa Fe and Taos, who have been lured here in part because of the cheaper real estate and also the breathtaking setting. There are several galleries throughout town, most open by chance, as well as a small general store that sells a variety of snacks and even a few gifts. Continue 7 mi north on NM 76, toward Peñasco, and you come to the marvelous San José de Gracia Church in the village of Trampas. It dates from at least 1760.

SHOPPING In the heart of Truchas, **Cordovas Handweaving Workshop** (✉ Village center ☎ 505/689–2437) produces vibrant and colorful contemporary rugs.

Peñasco

32 *15 mi north of Truchas on NM 76.*

Although still a modest-size community, Peñasco is one of the larger towns along the High Road and a good bet if you need to fill your tank with gas or pick up a snack at a convenience store.

WHERE TO EAT ✕**Sugar Nymphs Bistro.** It's taken a little time for folks to learn about,
★ ¢–$ let alone find, this delightful little place set inside a vintage theater in sleepy Peñasco. In fact, it's right along the tourist-trodden High Road, and it's the best restaurant along this route. Chef-owner Kai Harper earned her stripes at San Francisco's famed vegetarian restaurant, Greens, and presents an eclectic menu of reasonably priced, inspired food: creatively

topped pizzas, bountiful salads, juicy bacon cheeseburgers, butternut-squash ravioli. Desserts are also memorable—consider the chocolate pecan pie. You can dine on the patio in warm weather. The Sunday brunch is excellent. ⊠ *15046 NM 75* ☎ *505/587–0311* ▤ *MC, V* ⊘ *Closed Mon.*

SPORTS & THE OUTDOORS   About 10 mi east of Peñasco, **Sipapu Lodge and Ski Area** (⊠ NM 518, Vadito ☎ 505/587–2240 or 800/587–2240) is a low-key, family-friendly compound with skiing and snowboarding in winter, and fishing, rafting, disc golf, hiking, mountain biking, and camping the rest of the year. There's a modest lodge with inexpensive rooms, camping, and a restaurant.

SIDE TRIPS FROM TAOS

Surrounded by thousands of acres of pristine Carson National Forest and undeveloped high desert, Taos makes an ideal base for road-tripping. Most of the nearby adventures involve the outdoors, from skiing to hiking to mountain biking, and there are several noteworthy campgrounds in this part of the state. Although these side trips can be done in a day, several of the ski-resort communities mentioned in this section have extensive overnight accommodations.

The Enchanted Circle

Fodor'sChoice ★   The Enchanted Circle, an 84-mi loop north from Taos and back, rings Wheeler Peak, New Mexico's highest mountain, and takes you through glorious panoramas of alpine valleys and the towering mountains of the lush Carson National Forest. You can see all the major sights in one day, or take a more leisurely tour and stay overnight.

From Taos, head north about 15 mi via U.S. 64 to NM 522, keeping your eye out—after about 15 mi—for the sign on the right that points to the D. H. Lawrence Ranch and Memorial. You can visit the memorial, but the other buildings on the ranch are closed to the public. Continue north a short ways to reach Red River Hatchery, and then go another 5 mi to the village of Questa. Here you have the option of continuing north on NM 522 and detouring for some hiking at Wild Rivers Recreation Area, or turning east from Questa on NM 38 and driving for about 12 mi to the rollicking ski town of Red River. From here, continue 16 mi east along NM 38 and head over dramatic Bobcat Pass, which rises to a tad under 10,000 feet. You'll come to the sleepy old-fashioned village of Eagle Nest, comprising a few shops and down-home restaurants and motels. From here, U.S. 64 joins with NM 38 and runs southeast about 15 mi to one of the state's fastest-growing communities, Angel Fire, an upscale ski resort that's popular for hiking, golfing, and mountain biking in summer. It's about a 25-mi drive west over 9,000-foot Palo Flechado Pass and down through winding Taos Canyon to return to Taos.

Leave early in the morning and plan to spend the entire day on this trip. During ski season, which runs from late November to early April, you may want to make it an overnight trip and get in a day of skiing. In spring, summer, and fall your drive should be free of snow and ice. A sunny winter day can yield some lovely scenery (but if it's snowy, don't forget your sunglasses).

Carson National Forest surrounds Taos and spans almost 200 mi across northern New Mexico, encompassing mountains, lakes, streams, villages, and much of the Enchanted Circle. Hiking, cross-country skiing, horseback riding, mountain biking, backpacking, trout fishing, boating, and wildflower viewing are among the popular activities here. The forest is home to big-game animals and many species of smaller animals and songbirds. For canyon climbing, head into the rocky Rio Grande Gorge. The best entry point into the gorge is at the Wild Rivers Recreation Area, north of Questa. You can drive into the forest land via NM 522, NM 150, NM 38, and NM 578. Carson National Forest also has some of the best trout fishing in New Mexico. Its streams and lakes are home to rainbow, brown, and native Rio Grande cutthroat trout.

The forest provides a wealth of camping opportunities, from organized campgrounds with restrooms and limited facilities to informal roadside campsites and sites that require backpacking in. If mountains, pines, and streams are your goal, stake out sites in Carson National Forest along the Rio Hondo or Red River; if you prefer high-desert country along the banks of the Rio Grande, consider Orilla Verde or Wild Rivers Recreation Area. Backcountry sites are free; others cost up to $7 per night.

If you're coming from a lower altitude, you should take time to acclimatize, and all hikers should follow basic safety procedures. Wind, cold, and wetness can occur any time of year, and the mountain climate produces sudden storms. Dress in layers and wear sturdy footwear; carry water, food, sunscreen, hat, sunglasses, and a first-aid kit. Contact the Carson National Forest's visitor center for maps, safety guidelines, camping information, and conditions (it's open weekdays 8–4:30). ✉ *Forest Service Bldg., 208 Cruz Alta Rd., Taos 87571* ☎ *505/758–6200* ⊕ *www.fs.fed.us/r3/carson.*

The Enchanted Circle Bike Tour takes place in mid-September. The rally loops through the entire 84-mi Enchanted Circle, revealing a brilliant blaze of fall color. In summer you can head up the mountainside via ski lift in Red River and Angel Fire.

Questa

㉝ *25 mi north of Taos via U.S. 64 to NM 522.*

Literally "hill," in the heart of the Sangre de Cristo Mountains, Questa is a quiet village nestled against the Red River itself and amid some of New Mexico's most striking mountain country. **St. Anthony's Church,** built of adobe with 5-foot-thick walls and viga ceilings, is on the main street. Questa's **Cabresto Lake,** in Carson National Forest, is about 8 mi from town. Follow NM 563 northeast to Forest Route 134, then 2 mi of a primitive road (134A)—you'll need a four-wheel-drive vehicle. You can trout fish and boat here from about June to October.

Although it's only a few miles west of Questa as the crow flies, you have to drive about 15 mi north of Questa via NM 522 to NM 378 to reach **Wild Rivers Recreation Area,** which offers hiking access to the dramatic confluence of two national wild and scenic rivers, the Rio Grande and

Red River. There are some fairly easy and flat trails along the gorge's rim, including a ½ mi interpretive loop from the visitor center out to La Junta Point, which offers a nice view of the river. But the compelling reason to visit is a chance to hike down into the gorge and study the rivers up close, which entails hiking one of a couple of well-marked but steep trails down into the gorge, a descent of about 650 feet. It's not an especially strenuous trek, but many visitors come without sufficient water and stamina, have an easy time descending into the gorge, and then find it difficult to make it back up. There are also 10 basic campsites, some along the rim and others along the river. ⊠ *NM 522, follow signed dirt road from highway, Cerro* ☎ *505/770–1600, 505/758–8851 camping information* 🖼 *$3 per vehicle; camping $7 per vehicle* ⊙ *Daily 6 AM–10 PM; visitor center late May–early Sept., daily 10–4.*

NEED A BREAK? Hip coffeehouses are something of a rarity in rural New Mexico, but funky **Paloma Blanca** (⊠ 2255 S. NM 522 ☎ 505/586-2261) is a hit, not only because of its excellent coffee drinks but owing to the excellent sandwiches, salads, pastries, and Taos Cow ice cream. It's the perfect place to stock up on food before hiking at Wild Rivers Recreation Area.

At the **Red River Hatchery**, freshwater trout are raised to stock waters in Questa, Red River, Taos, Raton, and Las Vegas. You can feed them and learn how they're hatched, reared, stocked, and controlled. The visitor center has displays and exhibits, a fishing pond, and a machine that dispenses fish food. The self-guided tour can last anywhere from 20 minutes to more than an hour, depending on how enraptured you become. There's a picnic area and camping on the grounds. ⊠ *NM 522, 5 mi south of Questa* ☎ *505/586–0222* 🖼 *Free* ⊙ *Daily 8–5.*

The influential and controversial English writer David Herbert Lawrence and his wife, Frieda, arrived in Taos at the invitation of Mabel Dodge Luhan, who collected famous writers and artists the way some people collect butterflies. Luhan provided them a place to live, Kiowa Ranch, on 160 acres in the mountains. Rustic and remote, it's now known as the **D. H. Lawrence Ranch and Memorial,** though Lawrence never actually owned it. Lawrence lived in Taos on and off for about 22 months during a three-year period between 1922 and 1925. He wrote his novel *The Plumed Serpent* (1926), as well as some of his finest short stories and poetry, while in Taos and on excursions to Mexico. The houses here, owned by the University of New Mexico, are not open to the public, but you can enter the small cabin where Dorothy Brett, the Lawrences' traveling companion, stayed. You can also visit the D. H. Lawrence Memorial, a short walk up Lobo Mountain. A white shedlike structure, it's simple and unimposing. The writer fell ill while in France and died in a sanatorium there in 1930. Five years later Frieda had Lawrence's body disinterred and cremated and brought his ashes back to Taos. Frieda Lawrence is buried, as was her wish, in front of the memorial. ⊠ *NM 522, follow signed dirt road from highway, San Cristobal* ☎ *505/776–2245* 🖼 *Free* ⊙ *Daily dawn–dusk.*

Red River

 12 mi east of Questa via NM 38.

Home of a major ski resort that has a particularly strong following with folks from Oklahoma and the Texas panhandle, Red River (elevation 8,750 feet) came into being as a miners' boomtown during the 19th century, taking its name from the river whose mineral content gives it a rosy color. When the gold petered out, Red River died, only to be rediscovered in the 1920s by migrants escaping the dust storms in the Great Plains. An Old West flavor remains: Main Street shoot-outs, an authentic melodrama, and square dancing and two-stepping are among the diversions. Because of its many country dances and festivals, Red River is affectionately called "The New Mexico Home of the Texas Two-Step." The bustling little downtown area contains souvenir shops and sportswear boutiques, casual steak and barbecue joints, and a number of motels, lodges, and condos. There's good fishing to be had in the Red River itself, and excellent alpine and Nordic skiing in the surrounding forest.

NEED A BREAK? In Red River stop by the **Sundance** (⊠ 401 High St. ☎ 505/754–2971) for Mexican food or a fresh-fruit sangria. The stuffed sopapillas here are particularly good. **Texas Red's Steakhouse** (⊠ 111 E. Main St. ☎ 505/754–2964) has charbroiled steaks, chops, buffalo burgers, and chicken. There's also a branch down in Eagle Nest, in the heart of downtown.

About 16 mi southeast of Red River, NM 38 leads to the small village of Eagle Nest, the home of New Mexico's most recently designated state park, **Eagle Nest Lake State Park** (⊠ NM 38/U.S. 64, just south of town ☎ 505/377–1594 ⊕ www.emnrd.state.nm.us ☑ $5), which became part of the park system in 2004. This 2,400-acre lake is one of the state's top spots for kokanee salmon and rainbow trout fishing as well as a favorite venue for boating; there are two boat ramps on the lake's northwest side. You may also have the chance to spy elk, bears, mule deer, and even reclusive mountain lions around this rippling body of water, which in winter is popular for snowmobiling and ice-fishing. The park is open 6 AM–9 PM, and camping is not permitted.

Thousands of acres of national forest surround rustic Eagle Nest, population 189, elevation 8,090 feet. The shops and other buildings here evoke New Mexico's mining heritage, while a 1950s-style diner, Kaw-Lija's, serves up a memorable burger; you can also grab some take-out food in town and bring it to Eagle Nest Lake for a picnic.

WHERE TO STAY 🏕 **Roadrunner Campground.** The Red River runs right through this woodsy mountain campground set on 25 rugged acres. There are two tennis courts and a video-game room. ⊠ *1371 E. Main St., Box 588, Red River 87558* ☎*505/754–2286 or 800/243–2286* ⊕*www.redrivernm. com/roadrunnerrv* ⚒ *Laundry facilities, flush toilets, full hookups, drinking water, showers, picnic tables, electricity, public telephone, general store, play area, swimming (river)* ⮡ *155 RV sites, 6 cabins* ☑ *$33 sites, $94 cabins* ⊘ *Closed mid-Sept.–Apr.*

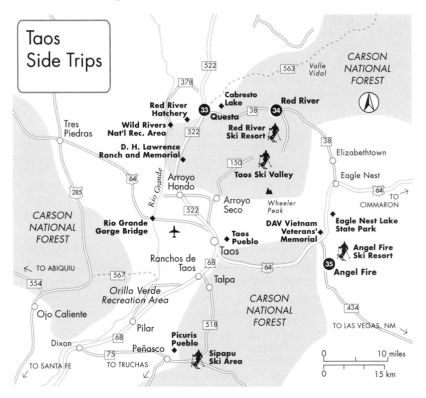

Taos
Side Trips

SPORTS & THE OUTDOORS

★

At the **Enchanted Forest Cross-Country Ski Area,** 24 mi of groomed trails loop from the two warming huts, stocked with snacks and hot cocoa, through 600 acres of meadows and pines in Carson National Forest, 3 mi east of Red River. ⊠ 417 W. Main St. ☎ 505/754–2374 or 800/966–9381 ⊕ www.enchantedforestxc.com ☎ $12 ⊙ Late Nov.–Easter, weather permitting.

The **Red River Ski Area** is in the middle of the historic gold-mining town of Red River, with lifts within walking distance of restaurants and hotels. Slopes for all levels of skiers make the area popular with families, and there's a snowboarding park. There are 58 trails served by seven lifts, and the vertical drop is about 1,600 feet. Red River has plenty of rental shops and accommodations. ⊠ 400 Pioneer Rd., off NM 38 ☎ 505/754–2223, 505/754–2220 snow conditions ⊕ www.redriverskiarea.com ☎ Lift tickets $50 ⊙ Late Nov.–late Mar.

Angel Fire
⑤ 30 mi south of Red River and 13 mi south of Eagle Nest via NM 38 and U.S. 64.

Named for its blazing sunrise and sunset colors by the Ute Indians who gathered here each autumn, Angel Fire is known these days primarily as a ski resort, generally rated the second-best in the state after Taos.

In summer there are arts and music events as well as hiking, river rafting, and ballooning. A prominent landmark along U.S. 64, just northeast of town, is the **DAV Vietnam Veterans Memorial,** a 50-foot-high wing-shaped monument built in 1971 by D. Victor Westphall, whose son David was killed in Vietnam.

WHERE TO STAY
$$–$$$

Angel Fire Resort. The centerpiece of New Mexico's fastest-growing and most highly acclaimed four-season sports resort, this upscale hotel is set at the mountain's base, a stone's throw from the chairlift. Indeed, winter is the busiest season here, but during the warmer months it's a popular retreat with hikers, golfers, and other outdoorsy types who appreciate retiring each evening to cushy and spacious digs. Even the standard rooms are a whopping 500 square feet, and the larger deluxe units have feather pillows, ski-boot warmers, and fireplaces. The resort also manages a variety of privately owned condo units, from studios to three-bedrooms, which are available nightly or long-term. ⊠ *10 Miller La., Box Drawer B, 87710* ☎ *505/377–4282 or 800/633–7463* 🖷 *505/ 377–4200* ⊕ *www.angelfireresort.com* 🖙 *139 rooms* ⚅ *4 restaurants, refrigerators, cable TV, 18-hole golf course, 6 tennis courts, fishing, mountain bikes, basketball, hiking, horseback riding, cross-country skiing, downhill skiing, ski shop, sleigh rides, snowmobiling, 2 bars, playground, business services, meeting rooms* 🖃 *AE, D, MC, V.*

Enchanted Moon Campground. In Valle Escondido, off U.S. 64 near Angel Fire, this wooded area with a trout pond has views of the Sangre de Cristos. Features include horse stalls, a chuckwagon, and an indoor recreation area with video games. ⊠ *7 Valle Escondido Rd., Valle Escondido 87571* ☎ *505/758–3338* ⊕ *www.emooncampground.com* ⚅ *Grills, flush toilets, full hookups, drinking water, showers, picnic tables, electricity, public telephone, play area* 🖙 *44 RV sites, 25 tent sites* 🖃 *RV sites $22, tent sites $15* ⊗ *Closed mid-Oct.–Apr.*

NIGHTLIFE &
THE ARTS

Music from Angel Fire (☎ 505/377–3233 or 888/377–3300 ⊕ www. musicfromangelfire.org) is a nightly series of classical (and occasional jazz) concerts presented at venues around Angel Fire and Taos for about three weeks from late August to early September. Tickets cost $18–$25 per concert, and the festival—begun in 1983—continues to grow in popularity and esteem each year.

SPORTS &
THE OUTDOORS

The 18-hole golf course at the **Angel Fire Country Club** (⊠ Country Club Dr. off NM 434 ☎ 505/377–3055), one of the highest in the nation, is open May to mid-October, weather permitting. The challenging front 9 runs a bit longer than the back and takes in great views of aspen- and pine-shaded canyons; the shorter back 9 has more water play and somewhat tighter fairways. Greens fees are $41–$58.

★ The fast-growing and beautifully maintained **Angel Fire Resort** is a busy ski destination, with 70 runs for all levels of skiers, five lifts, 19 mi of cross-country trails, and four terrain parks; the vertical drop is about 2,100 feet. Other amenities include a 1,000-foot snow-tubing hill, a well-respected ski and snowboard school, snowbiking (also taught at the school), ice fishing, a children's ski-and-snowboard center, and superb snowmaking capacity. ⊠ *N. Angel Fire Rd. off NM 434* ☎ *505/377–*

6401 or 800/633–7463, 505/377–4222 snow conditions ⊕ www. angelfireresort.com ✉ *Lift tickets $50* ⊙ *Mid-Dec.–early Apr.*

SIDE TRIPS ESSENTIALS

See the Essentials sections of the Albuquerque, Santa Fe, and Taos chapters for additional information on regional transportation, guided tours, visitor information, and other helpful travel resources in north-central New Mexico.

CAR TRAVEL

As there's virtually no public transportation that covers the towns and recreation areas covered in this chapter, a car is absolutely indispensable. Most of the major regions covered are accessed via well-paved and clearly marked two-lane state and U.S. highways, but a few off-the-beaten path attractions and recreation areas are along rutted dirt roads that can become impassable during rainy or snowy weather. If you're planning extensive side trips and forays into forests and outdoorsy areas, it's advisable to use a four-wheel-drive vehicle. Detailed maps showing most of the routes covered in this chapter can be obtained from the relevant visitor information centers listed below.

TOURS

Begun in New Mexico in 2004, **Audio CD Road Trips** (☎ 505/988–7016 ⊕ www.gallopinggalleries.com) produces extremely informative and engaging audio CDs that cover different unusual roads throughout north-central New Mexico. The three CDs cover the Turquoise Trail, Camino Real (I–25 from Albuquerque to Santa Fe), and the High Road to Taos. Each CD costs $19.50 and contains about an hour of stories and tour highlights, along with music by local New Mexico artists.

VISITOR INFORMATION

🖪 **Albuquerque Convention and Visitors Bureau** ✉ 20 1st Plaza NW, Suite 601, 87102 ☎ 505/842–9918 or 800/284–2282 ⊕ www.itsatrip.org. **Angel Fire Chamber of Commerce** ✍ Box 547, 87110 ☎ 505/377–6900 or 800/446–8117 ⊕ www.angelfirenm.com. **Chama Valley Chamber of Commerce** ✉ 499 S. Terrace Ave., 87520 ☎ 505/756–2306 or 800/477–0149 ⊕ www.chamavalley.com. **Española Valley Chamber of Commerce** ✉ 710 Paseo de Oñate ✍ Box 190, Española 87532 ☎ 505/753–2831 ⊕ www.espanolanmchamber. com. **Los Alamos Chamber of Commerce** ✉ 109 Central Park Sq., 87544 ☎ 505/661–4844 or 800/444–0707 ⊕ www.visit.losalamos.com. **Red River Chamber of Commerce** ✉ Off NM 38 ✍ Box 870, 87558 ☎ 505/774–2366 or 800/348–6444 ⊕ www. redrivernewmex.com. **Santa Fe Convention and Visitors Bureau** ✉ 201 W. Marcy St. ✍ Box 909, Santa Fe 87501 ☎ 505/955–6200 or 800/777–2489 ⊕ www.santafe.org. **Taos County Chamber of Commerce** ✉ 1139 Paseo del Pueblo Sur ✍ Drawer I, Taos 87571 ☎ 505/758–3873 or 800/732–8267 ⊕ www.taoschamber.com.

New Mexico Essentials

PLANNING TOOLS, EXPERT INSIGHT, GREAT CONTACTS

There are planners, and there are those who fly by the seat of their pants. We happily place ourselves among the planners. Our writers and editors try to anticipate all the issues you may face before and during any journey, and then they do their research. This section is the product of their efforts. Use it to get excited about your trip to New Mexico, to inform your travel planning, or to guide you on the road should the seat of your pants start to feel threadbare.

GETTING STARTED

We're really proud of our Web site: Fodors. com is a great place to begin any journey. Scan Travel Wire for suggested itineraries, travel deals, restaurant and hotel openings, and other up-to-the-minute info. Check out Booking to research prices and book plane tickets, hotel rooms, rental cars, and vacation packages. Head to Talk for on-the-ground pointers from travelers who frequent our message boards. You can also link to loads of other travel-related resources.

▌RESOURCES

ONLINE TRAVEL TOOLS

Check out the New Mexico Home page (⊕ www.state.nm.us) for information on state government, and for links to state agencies on doing business, working, learning, living, and visiting in the Land of Enchantment. A terrific general resource for just about every kind of recreational activity is ⊕ www.gorp.com; just click on the New Mexico link under "Destinations," and you'll be flooded with links to myriad topics, from wildlife refuges to ski trips to backpacking advice. Check the site of the New Mexico Film Office (⊕ www.nmfilm.com) for a list of movies shot in New Mexico as well as links to downloadable clips of upcoming made–in–New Mexico movies. A wide range of reviews and links to dining, culture, and services in Albuquerque and Santa Fe is available at ⊕ www.citysearch. com and ⊕ http://cityguide.aol.com, and ⊕ www.999dine.com is a site that sells steeply discounted meal certificates to dozens of top restaurants in Albuquerque, Santa Fe, and Taos. Visit ⊕ www. farmersmarketsnm.org for information on the dozens of great farmers' markets around the state, and see ⊕ www.nmwine. com for tours and details related to the region's burgeoning wine-making industry.

ALL ABOUT NEW MEXICO

Safety Transportation Security Administration (TSA) ⊕ www.tsa.gov

Time Zones Timeanddate.com ⊕ www. timeanddate.com/worldclock can help you figure out the correct time anywhere.
Weather Accuweather.com ⊕ www. accuweather.com is an independent weather-forecasting service with good coverage of hurricanes. **Weather.com** ⊕ www.weather.com is the Web site for the Weather Channel.
Other Resources CIA World Factbook ⊕ www.odci.gov/cia/publications/factbook/index.html has profiles of every country in the world. It's a good source if you need some quick facts and figures.

VISITOR INFORMATION

The New Mexico Department of Tourism can provide general information on the state, but you'll find more specific and useful information by consulting the local chambers of commerce, tourism offices, and convention and visitors bureaus in individual communities throughout the state (⇨ individual chapter *Essentials*).

CONTACTS

Statewide Information New Mexico Department of Tourism ☎ 505/827-7400, 800/733-6396 Ext. 0643 ⊕ www.newmexico.org. **Indian Pueblo Cultural Center** ☎ 505/843-7270, 800/766-4405 outside New Mexico ⊕ www.indianpueblo.org.
National Forests USDA Forest Service, Southwestern Region ☎ 505/842-3292, 877/864-6985 for fire restrictions and closures ⊕ www.fs.fed.us/r3.

▌THINGS TO CONSIDER

GEAR

Typical of the Southwest and southern Rockies, temperatures can vary considerably in North-Central New Mexico from sunup to sundown. Generally, you should **pack for warm days and chilly nights** from late spring through early fall, and for genuinely nippy days and freezing nights in winter if you're headed to Taos and Santa Fe (Albuquerque runs about 10 to 15 degrees warmer). Because temperatures vary greatly even within this relatively compact area, it's important to check local weather conditions before you leave home and pack accordingly. In April for instance, you may need to pack for nighttime lows in the 20s and daytime highs in the 60s in Taos, but daytime highs in the low 80s and nighttime lows in the 40s in Albuquerque. Any time of year pack at least a few warm outfits and a jacket; in winter pack very warm clothes—coats, parkas, and whatever else your body's thermostat and your ultimate destination dictate. Sweaters and jackets are also needed in summer at higher elevations, because though days are warm, nights can dip well below 50°F. And **bring comfortable shoes;** you're likely to be doing a lot of walking.

New Mexico is one of the most informal and laid-back areas of the country, which for many is part of its appeal. Probably no more than three or four restaurants in the entire state enforce a dress code, even for dinner, though men are likely to feel more comfortable wearing a jacket in the major hotel dining rooms, and anyone wearing tennis shoes may feel out of place.

The Western look has, of course, never lost its hold on the West, though Western-style clothes now get mixed with tweed jackets, for example, for a more conservative, sophisticated image. You can wear your boots and big belt buckles in even the best places in Santa Fe, Taos, or Albuquerque, but if you come strolling through the lobby of the Eldorado Hotel looking like Hopalong Cassidy, you'll get some funny looks.

Bring skin moisturizer; even people who rarely need this elsewhere in the country can suffer from dry and itchy skin in New Mexico. And **bring sunglasses** to protect your eyes from the glare of lakes or ski slopes. High altitude can cause headaches and dizziness, so check with your doctor about medication to alleviate symptoms. Sunscreen is a necessity. When planning even a short day trip, especially if there's hiking or exercise involved, always pack a bottle or two of water—it's very easy to become dehydrated in New Mexico.

> **WORD OF MOUTH**
>
> After your trip, be sure to rate the places you visited and share your experiences and travel tips with us and other Fodorites in Travel Ratings and Talk on www.fodors.com.

SHIPPING LUGGAGE AHEAD

Imagine globetrotting with only a carry-on in tow. Shipping your luggage in advance via an air-freight service is a great way to cut down on backaches, hassles, and stress—especially if your packing list includes strollers, car-seats, etc. There are some things to be aware of, though.

First, research carry-on restrictions; if you absolutely need something that's isn't practical to ship and isn't allowed in carry-ons, this strategy isn't for you. Second, plan to send your bags several days in advance to U.S. destinations and as much as two weeks in advance to some international destinations. Third, plan to spend some money: it will cost at least $100 to send a small piece of luggage, a golf bag, or a pair of skis to a domestic destination, much more to places overseas. Some people use Federal Express to ship their bags, but this can cost even more than air-freight services. All these services insure your bag (for most, the limit is $1,000, but you should verify that amount); you can, however, purchase additional insurance for about $1 per $100 of value. Resources **Luggage Concierge** ☎ 800/288-9818 ⊕ www.luggageconcierge.com. **Luggage Express** ☎ 866/744-7224 ⊕ www.usxpluggageexpress.com. **Luggage Free** ☎ 800/361-6871 ⊕ www.luggagefree.com. **Sports Express** ☎ 800/357-4174 ⊕ www.sportsexpress.com specializes in shipping golf clubs and other sports equipment. **Virtual Bellhop** ☎ 877/235-5467 ⊕ www.virtualbellhop.com.

TRIP INSURANCE

What kind of coverage do you honestly need? Do you even need trip insurance at all? Take a deep breath and read on.

We believe that comprehensive trip insurance is especially valuable if you're

Trip Insurance Resources

INSURANCE COMPARISON SITES		
Insure My Trip.com		www.insuremytrip.com.
Square Mouth.com		www.quotetravelinsurance.com.
COMPREHENSIVE TRAVEL INSURERS		
Access America	866/807-3982	www.accessamerica.com.
CSA Travel Protection	800/873-9855	www.csatravelprotection.com.
HTH Worldwide	610/254-8700 or 888/243-2358	www.hthworldwide.com.
Travelex Insurance	888/457-4602	www.travelex-insurance.com.
Travel Guard International	715/345-0505 or 800/826-4919	www.travelguard.com.
Travel Insured International	800/243-3174	www.travelinsured.com.
MEDICAL-ONLY INSURERS		
International Medical Group	800/628-4664	www.imglobal.com.
International SOS	215/942-8000 or 713/521-7611	www.internationalsos.com.
Wallach & Company	800/237-6615 or 504/687-3166	www.wallach.com.

booking a very expensive or complicated trip (particularly to an isolated region) or if you're booking far in advance. Who knows what could happen six months down the road? But whether or not you get insurance has more to do with how comfortable you are assuming all that risk yourself.

Comprehensive travel policies typically cover trip-cancellation and interruption, letting you cancel or cut your trip short because of a personal emergency, illness, or, in some cases, acts of terrorism in your destination. Such policies also cover evacuation and medical care. Some also cover you for trip delays because of bad weather or mechanical problems as well as for lost or delayed baggage. Another type of coverage to look for is financial default—that is, when your trip is disrupted because a tour operator, airline, or cruise line goes out of business. Generally you must buy this when you book your trip or shortly thereafter, and it's only available to you if your operator isn't on a list of excluded companies.

If you're going abroad, consider buying medical-only coverage at the very least. Neither Medicare nor some private insurers cover medical expenses anywhere outside of the United States besides Mexico and Canada (including time aboard a cruise ship, even if it leaves from a U.S. port). Medical-only policies typically reimburse you for medical care (excluding that related to pre-existing conditions) and hospitalization abroad, and provide for evacuation. You still have to pay the bills and await reimbursement from the insurer, though.

Expect comprehensive travel insurance policies to cost about 4% to 7% of the total price of your trip (it's more like 12% if you're over age 70). A medical-only policy may or may not be cheaper than a comprehensive policy. Always read the fine print of your policy to make sure that you are covered for the risks that are of most concern to you. Compare several policies to make sure you're getting the best price and range of coverage available.

■ TIP→ OK. You know you can save a bundle on trips to warm-weather destinations by traveling in rainy season. But there's also a chance that a severe storm will disrupt your plans. The solution? Look for hotels and resorts that offer storm/hurricane guarantees. Although they rarely allow refunds, most guarantees do let you rebook later if a storm strikes.

BOOKING YOUR TRIP

Unless your cousin is a travel agent, you're probably among the millions of people who make most of their travel arrangements online. But have you ever wondered just what the differences are between an online travel agent (a Web site through which you make reservations instead of going directly to the airline, hotel, or car-rental company), a discounter (a firm that does a high volume of business with a hotel chain or airline and accordingly gets good prices), a wholesaler (one that makes cheap reservations in bulk and then re-sells them to people like you), and an aggregator (one that compares all the offerings so you don't have to)? Is it truly better to book directly on an airline or hotel Web site? And when does a real live travel agent come in handy?

▌ ONLINE

You really have to shop around. A travel wholesaler such as Hotels.com or Hotel-Club.net can be a source of good rates, as can discounters such as Hotwire or Priceline, particularly if you can bid for your hotel room or airfare. Indeed, such sites sometimes have deals that are unavailable elsewhere. They do, however, tend to work only with hotel chains (which makes them just plain useless for getting hotel reservations outside of major cities) or big airlines (so that often leaves out upstarts like jetBlue and some foreign carriers like Air India). Also, with discounters and wholesalers you must generally prepay, and everything is nonrefundable. And before you fork over the dough, be sure to check the terms and conditions, so you know what a given company will do for you if there's a problem and what you'll have to deal with on your own.

▌ **TIP→** To be absolutely sure everything was processed correctly, confirm reservations made through online travel agents, discounters, and wholesalers directly with your hotel before leaving home.

Booking engines like Expedia, Travelocity, and Orbitz are actually travel agents, albeit high-volume, online ones. And airline travel packagers like American Airlines Vacations and Virgin Vacations—well, they're travel agents, too. But they may still not work with all the world's hotels.

An aggregator site will search many sites and pull the best prices for airfares, hotels, and rental cars from them. Most aggregators compare the major travel-booking sites such as Expedia, Travelocity, and Orbitz; some also look at airline Web sites, though rarely the sites of smaller budget airlines. Some aggregators also compare other travel products, including complex packages—a good thing, as you can sometimes get the best overall deal by booking an air-and-hotel package.

WITH A TRAVEL AGENT

If you use an agent—brick-and-mortar or virtual—you'll pay a fee for the service. And know that the service you get from some online agents isn't comprehensive. For example Expedia and Travelocity don't search for prices on budget airlines like jetBlue, Southwest, or small foreign carriers. That said, some agents (online or not) *do* have access to fares that are difficult to find otherwise, and the savings can more than make up for any surcharge.

A knowledgeable brick-and-mortar travel agent can be a godsend if you're booking a cruise, a package trip that's not available to you directly, an air pass, or a complicated itinerary including several overseas flights. What's more, travel agents that specialize in a destination may have exclusive access to certain deals and insider information on things such as charter flights. Agents who specialize in types of travelers (senior citizens, gays and lesbians, naturists) or types of trips (cruises, luxury travel, safaris) can also be invaluable.

A top-notch agent planning your trip to Russia will make sure you get the correct visa application and complete it on time; the one booking your cruise may get you a cabin upgrade or arrange to have a bottle of champagne chilling in your cabin when you embark. And complain about the surcharges all you like, but when things don't work out the way you'd hoped, it's nice to have an agent to put things right.

■ TIP➔ Remember that Expedia, Travelocity, and Orbitz are travel agents, not just booking engines. To resolve any problems with a reservation made through these companies, contact them first.

There isn't a great advantage to using a travel agent to book a trip to New Mexico, as this is a region that's most often visited by independent travelers, and relatively few companies offer package deals and major tours. You'll generally have as much luck using online travel sites, such as Expedia.com and Orbitz.com, to book airfare, car rentals, and hotels as you would using a travel agent.

Agent Resources **American Society of Travel Agents** ☎ 703/739-2782 ⊕ www.travelsense. org.

■ ACCOMMODATIONS

With the exceptions of Santa Fe and Taos, two rather upscale tourist-driven destinations with some of the higher lodging rates in the Southwest, New Mexico has fairly low hotel prices. Albuquerque is loaded with chain hotels, and four or five new ones seem to open each year, further saturating the market and driving down prices. During busy times or certain festivals (the Balloon Fiesta in Albuquerque, some of the art markets and events in Taos and Santa Fe), it can be extremely difficult to find a hotel room, and prices can be steep. Check to make sure there's not a major event planned for the time you're headed to New Mexico, and book well ahead if so. New Mexico Central Reservations offers good deals at a number of properties throughout the state, but you'll find an even bigger selection (and often better deals) by checking the usual major

travel sites, such as ⊕ www.expedia.com. You'll be charged a hotel tax, which varies among towns and counties, throughout New Mexico.

Most hotels and other lodgings require you to give your credit-card details before they will confirm your reservation. If you don't feel comfortable e-mailing this information, ask if you can fax it (some places even prefer faxes). However you book, get confirmation in writing and have a copy of it handy when you check in.

If you book through an online travel agent, discounter, or wholesaler, you might even want to confirm your reservation with the hotel before leaving home—just to be sure everything was processed correctly.

Be sure you understand the hotel's cancellation policy. Some places allow you to cancel without any kind of penalty—even if you prepaid to secure a discounted rate—if you cancel at least 24 hours in advance. Others require you to cancel a week in advance or penalize you the cost of one night. Small inns and B&Bs are most likely to require you to cancel far in advance. Most hotels allow children under a certain age to stay in their parents' room at no extra charge, but others charge for them as extra adults; find out the cutoff age for discounts.

■ TIP➔ Assume that hotels operate on the European Plan (EP, no meals) unless we specify that they use the Breakfast Plan (BP, with full breakfast), Continental Plan (CP, continental breakfast), Full American Plan (FAP, all meals), Modified American Plan (MAP, breakfast and dinner) or are all-inclusive (AI, all meals and most activities).

Reservations **New Mexico Central Reservations** ☎ 800/466-7829 ⊕ www.nmtravel. com.

APARTMENT & HOUSE RENTALS
Some parts of New Mexico are popular for short- and long-term vacation rentals, such as Santa Fe, Taos, and Ruidoso. See the book's individual regional chapters for rental listings in these locations.

BED & BREAKFASTS

B&Bs in New Mexico run the gamut from rooms in locals' homes to grandly restored adobe or Victorian homes. Rates in Santa Fe and Taos tend to be high; they're a little lower in Albuquerque and rival those of chain motels in the outlying areas. See the book's individual chapters for names of local reservation agencies.

Reservation Services Bed & Breakfast.com ☎ 512/322–2710 or 800/462–2632 ⊕ www. bedandbreakfast.com also sends out an online newsletter. **Bed & Breakfast Inns Online** ☎ 615/868–1946 or 800/215–7365 ⊕ www. bbonline.com. **BnB Finder.com** ☎ 212/432–7693 or 888/547–8226 ⊕ www.bnbfinder.com. **New Mexico Bed and Breakfast Association** ☎ 800/661–6649 ⊕ www.nmbba.org.

HOME EXCHANGES

With a direct home exchange you stay in someone else's home while they stay in yours. Some outfits also deal with vacation homes, so you're not actually staying in someone's full-time residence, just their vacant weekend place.

Exchange Clubs Home Exchange.com ☎ 800/877–8723 ⊕ www.homeexchange. com; $59.95 for a 1-year online listing. **Home-Link International** ☎ 800/638–3841 ⊕ www. homelink.org; $80 yearly for Web-only membership; $125 includes Web access and 2 catalogs. **Intervac U.S.** ☎ 800/756–4663 ⊕ www.intervacus.com; $78.88 for Web-only membership; $126 includes Web access and a catalog.

HOSTELS

Hostels offer bare-bones lodging at low, low prices—often in shared dorm rooms with shared baths—to people of all ages, though the primary market is young travelers, especially students. Most hostels serve breakfast; dinner and/or shared cooking facilities may also be available. In some hostels you aren't allowed to be in your room during the day, and there may be a curfew at night. Nevertheless, hostels provide a sense of community, with public rooms where travelers often gather to

WORD OF MOUTH

Did the resort look as good in real life as it did in the photos? Did you sleep like a baby, or were the walls paper thin? Did you get your money's worth? Rate hotels and write your own reviews in Travel Ratings or start a discussion about your favorite places in Travel Talk on www.fodors.com. Your comments might even appear in our books. Yes, you, too, can be a correspondent!

share stories. Many hostels are affiliated with Hostelling International (HI), an umbrella group of hostel associations with some 4,500 member properties in more than 70 countries. Other hostels are completely independent and may be nothing more than a really cheap hotel.

Membership in any HI association, open to travelers of all ages, allows you to stay in HI-affiliated hostels at member rates. One-year membership is about $28 for adults; hostels charge about $10–$30 per night. Members have priority if the hostel is full; they're also eligible for discounts around the world, even on rail and bus travel in some countries.

Several New Mexico communities have hostels, including Albuquerque, Cedar Crest (on the Turquoise Trail, near Albuquerque), Santa Fe, and Taos.
Hostelling International–USA ☎ 301/495–1240 ⊕ www.hiusa.org.

❚ AIRLINE TICKETS

Most domestic airline tickets are electronic; international tickets may be either electronic or paper. With an e-ticket the only thing you receive is an e-mailed receipt citing your itinerary and reservation and ticket numbers. The greatest advantage of an e-ticket is that if you lose your receipt, you can simply print out another copy or ask the airline to do it for you at check-in. You usually pay a surcharge (up to $50) to get a paper ticket, if you can get one at all. The sole advantage of a paper ticket is that it may be easier to endorse over to another airline if your flight is canceled and the airline with which you booked can't accommodate you on another flight.

■ TIP→ Discount air passes that let you travel economically in a country or region must often be purchased before you leave home. In some cases you can only get them through a travel agent.

The least expensive airfares to New Mexico are priced for round-trip travel and must usually be purchased in advance. Because the discount airline Southwest serves Albuquerque, fares from here to airports served by Southwest are often 20% to 40% less than to other airports (whether or not you actually fly Southwest, as competing airlines often match Southwest's fares). For instance, it's almost always cheaper to fly from Hartford, Providence, or Baltimore (all served by Southwest) to Albuquerque than from Boston, New York, or Washington. Airlines generally allow you to change your return date for a fee; Southwest Airlines is, again, the exception—they allow you to change your return date or cancel your flight for no fee, although you'll have to pay any higher fare if the flight you rebook costs more than your original one.

■ RENTAL CARS

When you reserve a car, ask about cancellation penalties, taxes, drop-off charges (if you're planning to pick up the car in one city and leave it in another), and surcharges (for being under or over a certain age, for additional drivers, or for driving across state or country borders or beyond a specific distance from your point of rental). All these things can add substantially to your costs. Request car seats and extras such as GPS when you book.

Rates are sometimes—but not always—better if you book in advance or reserve through a rental agency's Web site. There are other reasons to book ahead, though: for popular destinations, during busy times of the year, or to ensure that you get certain types of cars (vans, SUVs, exotic sports cars).

■ TIP→ Make sure that a confirmed reservation guarantees you a car. Agencies sometimes overbook, particularly for busy weekends and holiday periods.

You really need a car to explore most of New Mexico—even in cities like Albuquerque and Santa Fe, it's easiest to get around with a car. All the major car-rental agencies are represented at Albuquerque's airport, and you can also find a limited number of car-rental agencies in other communities throughout the state.

Rates at Albuquerque's airport begin at around $23 a day and $140 a week for an economy car with air-conditioning, automatic transmission, and unlimited mileage; although you should expect to pay more during busier times. If you want to explore the backcountry, consider renting an SUV, which will cost you about $40 to $60 per day and $200 to $400 per week, depending on the size of the SUV and the time of year. Dollar in Albuquerque has a fleet of smaller SUVs, still good on dirt roads and with much better mileage than larger ones, and they often run extremely reasonable deals, as low as $175 a week. You can save money by renting at a nonairport location, as you then are able to avoid the hefty (roughly) 10% in extra taxes charged at airports.

CAR-RENTAL INSURANCE

Everyone who rents a car wonders whether the insurance that the rental companies offer is worth the expense. No one—including us—has a simple answer. It all depends on how much regular insurance you have, how comfortable you are with risk, and whether money is an issue.

If you own a car and carry comprehensive car insurance for both collision and liability, your personal auto insurance will probably cover a rental, but read your policy's fine print to be sure. If you don't have auto insurance, then you should probably buy the collision- or loss-damage waiver (CDW or LDW) from the rental company. This eliminates your liability for damage to the car. Some credit cards offer CDW coverage, but it's usually supplemental to your own insurance and rarely covers SUVs, minivans, luxury models, and the like. If your coverage is secondary, you may still be liable for loss-of-use costs from the car-rental company (again, read the fine print). But no credit-card insurance is valid unless you use that card for *all* transactions, from reserving to paying the final bill.

■ TIP➡ Diners Club offers primary CDW coverage on all rentals reserved and paid for with the card. This means that Diners Club's company—not your own car insurance—pays in case of an accident. It *doesn't* mean that your car-insurance company won't raise your rates once it discovers you had an accident.

You may also be offered supplemental liability coverage; the car-rental company is required to carry a minimal level of liability coverage insuring all renters, but it's rarely enough to cover claims in a really serious accident if you're at fault. Your own auto-insurance policy will protect you if you own a car; if you don't, you have to decide whether you are willing to take the risk.

U.S. rental companies sell CDWs and LDWs for about $15 to $25 a day; supplemental liability is usually more than $10 a day. The car-rental company may offer you all sorts of other policies, but they're rarely worth the cost. Personal accident insurance, which is basic hospitalization coverage, is an especially egregious rip-off if you already have health insurance.

■ TIP➡ You can decline the insurance from the rental company and purchase it through a third-party provider such as Travel Guard (⊕ www.travelguard.com)—$9 per day for $35,000 of coverage. That's sometimes just under half the price of the CDW offered by some car-rental companies.

■ VACATION PACKAGES

Packages *are not* guided excursions. Packages combine airfare, accommodations, and perhaps a rental car or other extras (theater tickets, guided excursions, boat trips, reserved entry to popular museums, transit passes), but they let you do your own thing. During busy periods packages may be your only option, as flights and rooms may be sold out otherwise. Pack-

Car Rental Resources

AUTOMOBILE ASSOCIATIONS		
U.S.: American Automobile Association (AAA)	315/797-5000	www.aaa.com; most contact with the organization is through state and regional members.
National Automobile Club	650/294-7000	www.thenac.com; membership is open to California residents only.
LOCAL AGENCIES		
Enterprise	800/325-8007	www.enterprise.com.
Sears	800/527-0770	www.sears.com.
Thrifty	800/367-2277	www.thrifty.com.
MAJOR AGENCIES		
Alamo	800/462-5266	www.alamo.com.
Avis	800/230-4898	www.avis.com.
Budget	800/527-0700	www.budget.com.
Hertz	800/654-3131	www.hertz.com.
National Car Rental	800/227-7368	www.nationalcar.com.

ages will definitely save you time. They can also save you money, particularly in peak seasons, but—and this is a really big "but"—you should price each part of the package separately to be sure. And be aware that prices advertised on Web sites and in newspapers rarely include service charges or taxes, which can up your costs by hundreds of dollars.

■ TIP➜ Some packages and cruises are sold only through travel agents. Don't always assume that you can get the best deal by booking everything yourself.

Each year consumers are stranded or lose their money when packagers—even large ones with excellent reputations—go out of business. How can you protect yourself? First, always pay with a credit card; if you have a problem, your credit-card company may help you resolve it. Second, buy trip insurance that covers default. Third, choose a company that belongs to the United States Tour Operators Association, whose members must set aside funds to cover defaults. Finally, choose a company that also participates in the Tour Operator Program of the American Society of Travel Agents (ASTA), which will act as mediator in any disputes. You can also check on the tour operator's reputation among travelers by posting an inquiry on one of the Fodors.com forums.

Organizations American Society of Travel Agents (ASTA) ☎ 703/739-2782 or 800/965-2782 ⊕ www.astanet.com. **United States Tour Operators Association** (USTOA) ☎ 212/599-6599 ⊕ www.ustoa.com.

■ TIP➜ Local tourism boards can provide information about lesser-known and small-niche operators that sell packages to only a few destinations.

▌GUIDED TOURS

Guided tours are a good option when you don't want to do it all yourself. You travel along with a group (sometimes large, sometimes small), stay in prebooked hotels, eat with your fellow travelers (the

cost of meals sometimes included in the price of your tour, sometimes not), and follow a schedule. But not all guided tours are an if-it's-Tuesday-this-must-be-Belgium experience. A knowledgeable guide can take you places that you might never discover on your own, and you may be pushed to see more than you would have otherwise. Tours aren't for everyone, but they can be just the thing for trips to places where making travel arrangements is difficult or time-consuming (particularly when you don't speak the language). Whenever you book a guided tour, find out what's included and what isn't. A "land-only" tour includes all your travel (by bus, in most cases) in the destination, but not necessarily your flights to and from or even within it. Also, in most cases prices in tour brochures don't include fees and taxes. And remember that you'll be expected to tip your guide (in cash) at the end of the tour.

Recommended Companies New Mexico Guides Association ☎ 505/988-8022 ⊕ www.nmguides.com.

TRANSPORTATION

A tour bus or car is the best way to take in the entire state. Public transportation options do exist in some metropolitan areas, but they are not very convenient for visitors. City buses and taxi service are available only in a few larger communities such as Albuquerque and Santa Fe. Don't expect to find easy transportation for rural excursions.

■ TIP➜ Ask the local tourist board about hotel and local transportation packages that include tickets to major museum exhibits or other special events.

■ BY AIR

To reach north-central New Mexico by air, it's best to fly into Albuquerque. Visitors to Taos may also want to consider flying into Denver, which is an hour or two farther than Albuquerque but receives a high number of direct domestic and international flights. Santa Fe also receives very limited commercial flights from Denver. From Albuquerque airport, ground transportation is available to both Santa Fe and Taos. Although Albuquerque has a small, clean, and user-friendly airport, it also has relatively few direct flights compared with larger cities around the country. With a few exceptions, travelers coming from the East Coast and to a certain extent the West Coast have to connect through other airports to fly here.

Flying time between Albuquerque and Los Angeles is 2 hours for direct flights (available only on Southwest Airlines) and 3½ to 4 when connecting through another airport; Chicago, 2 hours and 45 minutes; New York, 4½ hours for direct flights (available only on Continental Airlines) and 5½ to 6½ when connecting through another airport; Dallas, 1 hour and 45 minutes.

Airlines & Airports Airline and Airport Links.com ⊕ www.airlineandairportlinks.com has links to many of the world's airlines and airports.
Airline Security Issues Transportation Security Administration ⊕ www.tsa.gov has answers for almost every question that might come up.

AIRPORTS

The major gateway to New Mexico is Albuquerque International Sunport (ABQ), which is 65 mi southwest of Santa Fe, 130 mi south of Taos, and 180 mi southeast of Farmington. Some travelers to Chama, Raton, and Taos prefer to fly into Denver (four to five hours' drive), which has far more direct flights to the rest of the country than Albuquerque—it's a scenic drive, too.

The major gateway to North-Central New Mexico is Albuquerque International Sunport (ABQ), which is 65 mi southwest of Santa Fe and 130 mi south of Taos.

■ TIP➜ Long layovers don't have to be only about sitting around or shopping. These days they can be about burning off vacation calories. Check out ⊕ www.airportgyms.com for lists of health clubs that are in or near many U.S. and Canadian airports.
Airport Information Albuquerque International Sunport ☎ 505/244-7700 ⊕ www.cabq.gov/airport. **Denver International Airport** ☎ 303/342-2000 ⊕ www.flydenver.com. **El Paso International Airport** ☎ 915/780-4749 ⊕ www.elpasointernationalairport.com.
Municipal Airports Cavern City Air Terminal (CNM), Carlsbad ☎ 505/887-6858. **Four Corners Regional Airport (FMN), Farmington** ☎ 505/599-1285. **Grant County Airport (SVC), Silver City area** ☎ 505/388-4554. **Roswell Municipal Airport (ROW)** ☎ 505/624-6700. **Santa Fe Municipal Airport (SAF)**

☎ 505/955-2908. **Sierra Blanca Regional Airport (SRR), Ruidoso area** ☎ 505/336-8111.

GROUND TRANSPORTATION

From the terminal at Albuquerque Airport, it's 5 to 20 minutes by car to get anywhere in town. Taxis, available at clearly marked stands, charge about $10 to $25 for most trips from the airport to around Albuquerque. Sun Tran Buses stop at the sunburst signs every 30 minutes; the fare is $1. Some hotels provide shuttle service to and from the airport. Airport Shuttle and Sunport Shuttle both cost less than $10 to most downtown locations.

Shuttle buses between the Albuquerque International Sunport and Santa Fe take about 1 hour and 20 minutes and cost about $20 to $25 each way. Shuttle service runs from Albuquerque to Taos and nearby ski areas; the ride takes 2¾ to 3 hours and costs $40–$50. There's also Greyhound bus service between Albuquerque International Sunport and many New Mexico towns and cities; fares are considerably less than those charged by the shuttle services listed here.

TRANSFERS BETWEEN AIRPORTS

Around Albuquerque Airport Shuttle ☎ 505/765-1234. **Sun Tran Bus** ☎ 505/843-9200 ⊕ www.cabq.gov/transit. **Sunport Shuttle** ☎ 505/883-4966 or 866/505-4966 ⊕ www.sunportshuttle.com **Between Albuquerque & Santa Fe Sandia Shuttle Express** ☎ 505/474-5696 or 888/775-5696 ⊕ www.sandiashuttle.com. **Santa Fe Shuttle** ☎ 505/243-2300 or 888/833-2300. **Between Albuquerque & Taos Faust's Transportation** ☎ 505/758-3410 or 888/830-3410 ⊕ www.newmexiconet.com/trans/faust/faust.html. **Between El Paso & Southern New Mexico Destinations Las Cruces Shuttle Service** ☎ 505/525-1784 or 800/288-1784 ⊕ www.lascrucesshuttle.com.

FLIGHTS

Most major domestic airlines provide service to Albuquerque. Mesa Airlines offers shuttle flights between Albuquerque and Farmington, Colorado Springs, Roswell, Hobbs, and Carlsbad. Great Lakes Airlines flies from Denver to Santa Fe and from Albuquerque to Silver City and Clovis (and then from Clovis on to Amarillo, Texas). Frontier Airlines flies daily from Denver to Albuquerque. Skywest Airlines, a subsidiary of Delta, flies between Albuquerque and Salt Lake City. **Airline Contacts Alaska Airlines** ☎ 800/252-7522 or 206/433-3100 ⊕ www.alaskaair.com. **American Airlines** ☎ 800/433-7300 ⊕ www.aa.com. **ATA** ☎ 800/435-9282 or 317/282-8308 ⊕ www.ata.com. **Continental Airlines** ☎ 800/523-3273 for U.S. and Mexico reservations, 800/231-0856 for international reservations ⊕ www.continental.com. **Delta Airlines** ☎ 800/221-1212 for U.S. reservations, 800/241-4141 for international reservations ⊕ www.delta.com. **jetBlue** ☎ 800/538-2583 ⊕ www.jetblue.com. **Northwest Airlines** ☎ 800/225-2525 ⊕ www.nwa.com. **Southwest Airlines** ☎ 800/435-9792 ⊕ www.southwest.com. **Spirit Airlines** ☎ 800/772-7117 or 586/791-7300 ⊕ www.spiritair.com. **United Airlines** ☎ 800/864-8331 for U.S. reservations, 800/538-2929 for international reservations ⊕ www.united.com. **US Airways** ☎ 800/428-4322 for U.S. and Canada reservations, 800/622-1015 for international reservations ⊕ www.usairways.com.

Smaller Airlines Frontier ☎ 800/432-1359 ⊕ www.frontierairlines.com. **Great Lakes Airlines** ☎ 800/554-5111 ⊕ www.greatlakesav.com. **Mesa Airlines** ☎ 800/637-2247 ⊕ www.mesa-air.com. **Skywest Airlines** ☎ 435/634-3000 ⊕ www.skywest.com.

▌ BY BUS

Bus service on Texas, New Mexico & Oklahoma Coaches, affiliated with Greyhound Lines, connects Albuquerque, Santa Fe, and Taos with many towns and cities elsewhere in the state and throughout the Southwest and Rocky Mountain regions.

Greyhound offers the **North America Discovery Pass,** which allows unlimited travel in the United States (and certain parts of Canada and Mexico) within any 7-, 15-, 30-, or 60-day period ($283–$645, depending on length of the pass). You can also buy similar passes covering different areas (America and Canada, the West Coast of North America, the East Coast of North America, Canada exclusively), and international travelers can purchase international versions of these same passes, which offer a greater variety of travel periods and cost considerably less. Greyhound also has senior-citizen, military, children's, and student discounts, which apply to individual fares and to the Discovery Pass.

Approximate standard sample one-way fares (based on 7-day advance purchase—prices can be 10% to 50% higher otherwise), times, and routes (note that times vary greatly depending on the number of stops) on major carriers: Albuquerque to Santa Fe, 70 minutes, $15; Albuquerque to Taos, 3 hours, $30; Albuquerque to Las Cruces, 4–5 hours, $25; Denver to Santa Fe, 9–10 hours; $50; Oklahoma City to Albuquerque, 11–12 hours, $70; and Phoenix to Albuquerque, 9–10 hours, $60.

Bus Information Greyhound/Texas, New Mexico & Oklahoma Coaches ☎ 800/231-2222 ⊕ www.tnmo.com.

▌ BY CAR

A car is a basic necessity in New Mexico, as even the few cities are challenging to get around strictly using public transportation. Distances are considerable, but you can make excellent time on long stretches of interstate and other four-lane highways with speed limits of up to 75 mph. If you wander off major thoroughfares, slow down. Speed limits here generally are only 55 mph, and for good reason. Many such roadways have no shoulders; on many twisting and turning mountain roads speed limits dip to 25 mph. For the most part, the scenery you'll take in while driving

makes the drive a form of sightseeing in itself.

Interstate 40 runs east–west across the middle of the state. Interstate 25 runs north from the state line at El Paso through Albuquerque and Santa Fe, then angles northeast to the Colorado line through Raton.

U.S. highways connect all major cities and towns in the state with a good network of paved roads—many of the state's U.S. highways, including large stretches of U.S. 285 and U.S. 550, have four lanes and high speed limits. You can make nearly as good time on these roads as you can on interstates. State roads are mostly paved two-lane thoroughfares, but some are well-graded gravel. Roads on Native American lands are designated by wooden, arrow-shape signs and you'd best adhere to the speed limit; some roads on reservation or forest land aren't paved. Even in cities, quite a few surface streets are unpaved and often bumpy and narrow—Santa Fe, for instance, has a higher percentage of dirt roads than any other state capital in the nation.

Morning and evening rush-hour traffic is light in most of New Mexico, although it can get a bit heavy in Albuquerque. Keep in mind also that from most cities in New Mexico, there are only one or two main routes to Albuquerque, so if you encounter an accident or some other delay on a major thoroughfare into Albuquerque (or even Santa Fe), you can expect significant delays. It's a big reason to leave early and give yourself extra time when attempting to drive to Albuquerque to catch a plane.

Parking is plentiful and either free or inexpensive in most New Mexico towns, even Albuquerque and Santa Fe. During busy times, however, such as summer weekends, parking in Santa Fe, Taos, and parts of Albuquerque can be tougher to find.

Here are some common distances and approximate travel times between Albuquerque and several popular destinations, assuming no lengthy stops and averaging the 65 to 75 mph speed limits: Santa Fe is 65 mi and about an hour; Taos is 135 mi and about 2½ hours; Farmington is 185 mi and 3 hours; Gallup is 140 mi and 2 hours; Amarillo is 290 mi and 4 hours; Denver is 450 mi and 6–7 hours; Oklahoma City is 550 mi and 8–9 hours; Moab is 290 mi and 6–7 hours; Flagstaff is 320 mi and 4½ hours; Phoenix is 465 mi and 6½ to 7½ hours; Silver City is 230 mi and 3½–4 hours; Las Cruces is 225 mi and 3½ hours; Ruidoso is 190 mi and 3 hours; Carlsbad is 280 mi and 4½–5 hours; El Paso is 270 mi and 4 hours; Dallas is 650 mi and 10–11 hours; and San Antonio is 730 mi and 11–12 hours.

GASOLINE

There's a lot of high, dry, lonesome country in New Mexico—it's possible to go 50 or 60 mi in some of the less-populated areas between gas stations. For a safe trip **keep your gas tank full.** Self-service gas stations are the norm in New Mexico, though in some of the less-populated regions you can find stations with full service. The cost of unleaded gas at self-service stations in New Mexico is close to the U.S. average, but it's usually 10¢ to 20¢ more per gallon in Santa Fe, Taos, and certain spots off the beaten path.

ROAD CONDITIONS

Arroyos (dry washes or gullies) are bridged on major roads, but lesser roads often dip down through them. These can be a hazard during the rainy season, late June–early September. Even if it looks shallow, **don't try to cross an arroyo filled with water**—it may have an axle-breaking hole in the middle. Wait a little while, and it will drain off almost as quickly as it filled. If you stall in a flooded arroyo, get out of the car and onto high ground if possible. In the backcountry, never drive (or walk) in a dry arroyo bed if the sky is dark anywhere upstream. A sudden thunderstorm 15 mi away could send a raging flash flood down a wash in a matter of minutes.

Unless they are well graded and graveled, **avoid unpaved roads in New Mexico when they are wet.** The soil contains a lot of caliche, or clay, which gets slick when mixed with water. During winter storms roads may be shut down entirely; call the State Highway Department for road conditions.

At certain times in fall or spring, New Mexico winds can be vicious for large vehicles like RVs. Driving conditions can be particularly treacherous in passages through foothills or mountains where wind gusts are concentrated.

New Mexico has a high incidence of drunk driving and uninsured motorists. Factor in the state's high speed limits, many winding and steep roads, and eye-popping scenery, and you can see how important it is to drive as alertly and defensively as possible. On the plus side, major traffic jams are a rarity even in cities—and recent improvements to the state's busiest intersection, the I-40/I-25 interchange in Albuquerque, has helped to reduce rush-hour backups there. Additionally, a major highway widening and improvement along U.S. 285/84, north of Santa Fe, has also greatly smoothed the flow and speed of traffic up toward Taos.

Road Conditions **State Highway Department**
☎ 800/432–4269 ⊕ www.nmshtd.state.nm.us.

ROADSIDE EMERGENCIES

In the event of a roadside emergency, call 911. Depending on the location, either the New Mexico State Police or the county sheriff's department will respond. Call the city or village police department if you encounter trouble within the limits of a municipality. Indian reservations have tribal police headquarters, and rangers assist travelers within U.S. Forest Service boundaries.

▌ BY TRAIN

Amtrak's *Southwest Chief,* from Chicago to Los Angeles via Kansas City, stops in

Raton, Las Vegas, Lamy (near Santa Fe), Albuquerque, and Gallup daily.

In summer 2006 the City of Albuquerque launched the state's first-ever commuter train line, the *New Mexico Rail Runner Express*. As of this writing, service is from Bernalillo south through the city of Albuquerque, continuing south through Los Lunas to the suburb of Belén, covering a distance of about 50 mi. The second and final phase of the project, expected to be completed by late 2008, will extend the service north to Santa Fe.

Amtrak offers a **North America rail pass** that gives you unlimited travel within the United States and Canada within any 30-day period ($999 peak, $709 off-peak), and several kinds of **USA Rail passes** (for non-U.S. residents only) offering unlimited travel for 15 to 30 days. Amtrak also has senior-citizen, children's, disability, and student discounts, as well as occasional deals that allow a second or third accompanying passenger to travel for half price or even free. The **Amtrak Vacations** program customizes entire vacations, including hotels, car rentals, and tours.

Sample one-way fares on the *Southwest Chief* are $140 from Chicago to Lamy; $40 Denver to Las Vegas; and $60 Albuquerque to Los Angeles.

The *New Mexico Rail Runner Express* was running only on weekdays as of this writing, but it's expected to add weekend service by 2007. Tickets cost $2 for any one-way ride on the system.

Amtrak ☎ 800/872-7245 ⊕ www.amtrak. com. *New Mexico Rail Runner Express* ☎ 505/245-7245 ⊕ www.nmrailrunner.com.

▌COMMUNICATIONS

INTERNET
Since the early 2000s, the number of accommodations throughout the state offering Wi-Fi or wired high-speed Internet, if not in room then at least in common areas or business centers, has increased dramatically. In most of New Mexico, it's

the exception rather than the rule to find a hotel or inn that doesn't offer this service. However, in smaller communities, you're more likely to encounter properties that have only dial-up Internet capacity. If it's important to you, check ahead. In the larger cities and primary tourist destinations in the region, you can find at least one or two coffeehouses or cafés with computer terminals that have Internet access as well as a library. Restaurants, coffeehouses, and bars with Wi-Fi have also become quite common throughout the state.

Cybercafes ⊕ www.cybercafes.com lists over 4,000 Internet cafés worldwide.

▌EATING OUT

New Mexico is justly famous for its distinctive cuisine, which utilizes ingredients and recipes common to Mexico, the Rockies, the Southwest, and the West's Native American communities. Most longtime residents like their chile sauces and salsas with some fire—throughout North-Central New Mexico, chile is sometimes celebrated for its ability to set off smoke alarms. Most restaurants offer a choice of red or green chile with one type typically being milder than the other. If you want both kinds with your meal, when your server asks you if you'd like "red or green," reply "Christmas." If you're not used to spicy foods, you may find even the average chile served with chips to be quite a lot hotter than back home—so proceed with caution. Excellent barbecue and steaks also can be found throughout New Mexico, with other specialties being local game (especially elk) and trout. The restaurants we list are the cream of the crop in each price category. Properties indicated by a ✕▦ are lodging establishments whose restaurant warrants a special trip.

MEALS & MEALTIMES
Statewide, many kitchens stop serving around 8 PM, so **don't arrive too late** if you're looking forward to a leisurely dinner. Unless otherwise noted, the restaurants

listed in this guide are open daily for lunch and dinner.

PAYING

Credit cards are widely accepted at restaurants in major towns and cities and even most smaller communities, but in the latter places, you may occasionally encounter smaller, independent restaurants that are cash only. For guidelines on tipping *see* Tipping *below.*

RESERVATIONS & DRESS

Regardless of where you are, it's a good idea to make a reservation if you can. In some places (Hong Kong, for example), it's expected. We only mention them specifically when reservations are essential (there's no other way you'll ever get a table) or when they are not accepted. For popular restaurants, book as far ahead as you can (often 30 days), and reconfirm as soon as you arrive. (Large parties should always call ahead to check the reservations policy.) We mention dress only when men are required to wear a jacket or a jacket and tie.

Online reservation services make it easy to book a table before you even leave home. OpenTable covers most states, including 20 major cities, and has limited listings in Canada, Mexico, the United Kingdom, and elsewhere. DinnerBroker has restaurants throughout the United States as well as a few in Canada.

WORD OF MOUTH

Was the service stellar or not up to snuff? Did the food give you shivers of delight or leave you cold? Did the prices and portions make you happy or sad? Rate restaurants and write your own reviews in Travel Ratings or start a discussion about your favorite places in Travel Talk on ⊕ www. fodors.com. Your comments might even appear in our books. Yes, you, too, can be a correspondent!

OpenTable ⊕ www.opentable.com. **Dinner-Broker** ⊕ www.dinnerbroker.com.

WINES, BEER & SPIRITS

Like many other states, New Mexico has some fine microbreweries, with the most prominent producer, Sierra Blanca Brewing Co., found in the unlikely and highly remote location of Carrizozo, in south-central New Mexico—Sierra Blanca's excellent beers are served throughout the state. New Mexico also has a growing number of wineries, some of them producing first-rate vintages. Franciscan monks first planted their vines here before moving more successfully to northern California, and the state's winemaking industry has really taken off since the late '90s. The New Mexico Wine Growers Association provides extensive information on the many fine wineries around the state as well as details on several prominent wine festivals. **New Mexico Wine Growers Association** ☎ 866/494-6366 ⊕ www.nmwine.com.

▌ELECTRICITY

Consider making a small investment in a universal adapter, which has several types of plugs in one lightweight, compact unit. Most laptops and mobile phone chargers are dual voltage (i.e., they operate equally well on 110 and 220 volts), so require only an adapter. These days the same is true of small appliances such as hair dryers. Always check labels and manufacturer instructions to be sure. Don't use 110-volt outlets marked FOR SHAVERS ONLY for high-wattage appliances such as hair dryers. **Steve Kropla's Help for World Travelers** ⊕ www.kropla.com has information on electrical and telephone plugs around the world. **Walkabout Travel Gear** ⊕ www. walkabouttravelgear.com has good coverage of electricity under "adapters."

▌HOURS OF OPERATION

Although hours differ little in New Mexico from other parts of the United States, some businesses do keep shorter hours here than in more densely populated parts of the country. In particular, outside of the larger towns in New Mexico, it can be hard to find shops and restaurants open past 8 or 9 in the evening. Within the state, businesses tend to keep later hours in Albuquerque and Santa Fe than in rural areas.

Most major museums and attractions are open daily or six days a week (with Monday or Tuesday being the most likely day of closing). Hours are often shorter on Saturday and especially Sunday, and a handful of museums in larger cities stay open late one or two nights a week, usually Tuesday, Thursday, or Friday. New Mexico's less populous areas also have quite a few smaller museums—historical societies, small art galleries, highly specialized collections—that open only a few days a week, and sometimes only by appointment during slow times. It's always a good idea to call ahead if you're planning to go out of your way to visit a smaller museum.

Banks are usually open weekdays from 9 to 3 or a bit later and some Saturday mornings, the post office from 8 to 5 or 6 weekdays and often on Saturday mornings. Shops in urban and touristy areas, particularly in indoor and strip malls, typically open at 9 or 10 daily and stay open until anywhere from 6 PM to 10 PM on weekdays and Saturday, and until 5 or 6 on Sunday. Hours vary greatly, so call ahead when in doubt.

On major highways and in densely populated areas you can usually find at least one or two supermarkets, drugstores, and gas stations open 24 hours, and in Albuquerque, you can find a smattering of all-night fast-food restaurants, diners, and coffeehouses. Bars and discos stay open until 1 or 2 AM.

▌ MONEY

In North-Central New Mexico, Santa Fe is by far the priciest city: meals, gasoline, and motel rates are all significantly higher in the state's capital. Overall travel costs

in Santa Fe, including dining and lodging, typically run 30% to 50% higher than in Albuquerque and other communities in the state. Taos, too, can be a little expensive because it's such a popular tourist destination, but you have more choices for economizing there than in Santa Fe. As the state's largest metropolitan area, Albuquerque has a full range of price choices.

CREDIT CARDS

Throughout this guide, the following abbreviations are used: **AE**, American Express; **D**, Discover; **DC**, Diners Club; **MC**, MasterCard; and **V**, Visa.

It's a good idea to inform your credit-card company before you travel, especially if you're going abroad and don't travel internationally very often. Otherwise, the credit-card company might put a hold on your card owing to unusual activity—not a good thing halfway through your trip. Record all your credit-card numbers—as well as the phone numbers to call if your cards are lost or stolen—in a safe place, so you're prepared should something go wrong. Both MasterCard and Visa have general numbers you can call (collect if you're abroad) if your card is lost, but you're better off calling the number of your issuing bank, since MasterCard and Visa usually just transfer you to your bank; your bank's number is usually printed on your card.

Reporting Lost Cards American Express ☎ 800/992-3404 in U.S., 336/393-1111 collect from abroad ⊕ www.americanexpress.com. **Diners Club** ☎ 800/234-6377 in U.S., 303/799-1504 collect from abroad ⊕ www.dinersclub.com. **Discover** ☎ 800/347-2683 in U.S., 801/902-3100 collect from abroad ⊕ www.discovercard.com. **MasterCard** ☎ 800/622-7747 in U.S., 636/722-7111 collect from abroad ⊕ www.mastercard.com. **Visa** ☎ 800/847-2911 in U.S., 410/581-9994 collect from abroad ⊕ www.visa.com.

TRAVELER'S CHECKS & CARDS

Some consider this the currency of the cave man, and it's true that fewer estab-

WORST-CASE SCENARIO

All your money and credit cards have just been stolen. In these days of real-time transactions, this isn't a predicament that should destroy your vacation. First, report the theft of the credit cards. Then get any traveler's checks you were carrying replaced. This can usually be done almost immediately, provided that you kept a record of the serial numbers separate from the checks themselves. If you bank at a large international bank like Citibank or HSBC, go to the closest branch; if you know your account number, chances are you can get a new ATM card and withdraw money right away. **Western Union** (☎ 800/325-6000 ⊕ www.westernunion. com) sends money almost anywhere. Have someone back home order a transfer online, over the phone, or at one of the company's offices, which is the cheapest option.

lishments accept traveler's checks these days. Nevertheless, they're a cheap and secure way to carry extra money, particularly on trips to urban areas. Both Citibank (under the Visa brand) and American Express issue traveler's checks in the United States, but Amex is better known and more widely accepted; you can also avoid hefty surcharges by cashing Amex checks at Amex offices. Whatever you do, keep track of all the serial numbers in case the checks are lost or stolen.

American Express now offers a stored-value card called a Travelers Cheque Card, which you can use wherever American Express credit cards are accepted, including ATMs. The card can carry a minimum of $300 and a maximum of $2,700, and it's a very safe way to carry your funds. Although you can get replacement funds in 24 hours if your card is lost or stolen, it doesn't really strike us as a very good deal. In addition to a high initial cost ($14.95 to set up the card, plus $5 each time you "reload"), you still have to

pay a 2% fee for each purchase in a foreign currency (similar to that of any credit card). Further, each time you use the card in an ATM you pay a transaction fee of $2.50 on top of the 2% transaction fee for the conversion—add it all up and it can be considerably more than you would pay when simply using your own ATM card. Regular traveler's checks are just as secure and cost less.

American Express ☎ 888/412-6945 in U.S., 801/945-9450 collect outside U.S. to add value or speak to customer service ⊕ www. americanexpress.com.

∎ TAXES

The standard state gross receipts tax rate is 5%, but municipalities and counties enact additional charges at varying rates. Even with additional charges, you will encounter no sales tax higher than 7%.

∎ TIME

New Mexico and a small portion of west Texas (including El Paso) observe mountain standard time, switching over with most of the rest of the country to daylight saving time in the spring through fall. In New Mexico, you'll be two hours behind New York and one hour ahead of Arizona (except during daylight saving time, which Arizona does not observe) and California.

∎ TIPPING

The customary tipping rate for taxi drivers is 15%–20%, with a minimum of $2; bellhops are usually given $2 per bag in luxury hotels, $1 per bag elsewhere. Hotel maids should be tipped $2 per day of your stay. A doorman who hails or helps you into a cab can be tipped $1–$2. You should also tip your hotel concierge for services rendered; the size of the tip depends on the difficulty of your request, as well as the quality of the concierge's work. For an ordinary dinner reservation or tour arrangements, $3–$5 should do; if the concierge scores seats at a popular restaurant or show or performs unusual services (getting your laptop repaired, finding a good pet-sitter, etc.), $10 or more is appropriate.

Waiters should be tipped 15%–20%, though at higher-end restaurants, a solid 20% is more the norm. Many restaurants add a gratuity to the bill for parties of six or more. Ask what the percentage is if the menu or bill doesn't state it. Tip $1 per drink you order at the bar, though if at an upscale establishment, those $15 martinis might warrant a $2 tip.

TIPPING GUIDELINES FOR NEW MEXICO	
Bartender	$1 to $5 per round of drinks, depending on the number of drinks
Bellhop	$1 to $5 per bag, depending on the level of the hotel
Hotel Concierge	$5 or more, if he or she performs a service for you
Hotel Doorman	$1–$2 if he helps you get a cab
Hotel Maid	1$–$3 a day (either daily or at the end of your stay, in cash)
Hotel Room-Service Waiter	$1 to $2 per delivery, even if a service charge has been added
Porter at Airport or Train Station	$1 per bag
Skycap at Airport	$1 to $3 per bag checked
Taxi Driver	15%–20%, but round up the fare to the next dollar amount
Tour Guide	10% of the cost of the tour
Valet Parking Attendant	$1–$2, but only when you get your car
Waiter	15%–20%, with 20% being the norm at high-end restaurants; nothing additional if a service charge is added to the bill

EFFECTIVE COMPLAINING

Things don't always go right when you're traveling, and when you encounter a problem or service that isn't up to snuff, you should complain. But there are good and bad ways to do so.

TAKE A DEEP BREATH. This is always a good strategy, especially when you are aggravated about something. Just inhale, and exhale, and remember that you're on vacation. We know it's hard for Type A people to leave it all behind, but for your own peace of mind, it's worth a try.

COMPLAIN IN PERSON WHEN IT'S SERIOUS. In a hotel, serious problems are usually better dealt with in person, at the front desk; if it's something quick, you can phone.

COMPLAIN EARLY RATHER THAN LATE. Whenever you don't get what you paid for (the type of hotel room you booked or the airline seat you pre-reserved) or when it's something timely (the people next door are making too much noise), try to resolve the problem sooner rather than later. It's always going to be harder to deal with a problem or get something taken off your bill after the fact.

BE WILLING TO ESCALATE, BUT DON'T BE HASTY. Try to deal with the person at the front desk of your hotel or with your waiter in a restaurant before asking to speak to a supervisor or manager. Not only is this polite, but when the person directly serving you can fix the problem, you'll more likely get what you want quicker.

SAY WHAT YOU WANT, AND BE REASONABLE. When things fall apart, be clear about what kind of compensation you expect. Don't leave it to the hotel or restaurant or airline to suggest what they're willing to do for you. That said, the compensation you request must be in line with the problem. You're unlikely to get a free meal because your steak was

undercooked or a free hotel stay if your bathroom was dirty.

CHOOSE YOUR BATTLES. You're more likely to get what you want if you limit your complaints to one or two specific things that really matter rather than a litany of wrongs.

DON'T BE OBNOXIOUS. There's nothing that will stop your progress dead in its tracks as readily as an insistent "Don't you know who I am?" or "So what are you going to do about it?" Raising your voice will rarely get a better result.

NICE COUNTS. This doesn't mean you shouldn't be clear that you are displeased. Passive isn't good, either. When it comes right down to it, though, you'll attract more flies with sugar than with vinegar.

DO IT IN WRITING. If you discover a billing error or some other problem after the fact, write a concise letter to the appropriate customer-service representative. Keep it to one page, and as with any complaint, state clearly and reasonably what you want them to do about the problem. Don't give a detailed trip report or list a litany of problems.

INDEX

PHOTO CREDITS

Cover Photo: ThinkStock/SuperStock. 5, *New Mexico Tourism Department*. 7, *Joe Viesti/viestiphoto. com*. 10, *Sylvain Grandadam/age fotostock*. 11, *Walter Bibikow/age fotostock*. 13, *Mark Nohl/New Mexico Tourism Department*. 14, *Joe Viesti/viestiphoto.com*.